To See a Promised Land

To See a Promised Land

Americans and the Holy Land in the Nineteenth Century

Lester I. Vogel

The Pennsylvania State University Press
University Park, Pennsylvania

Library of Congress Cataloging-in-Publication Data

Vogel, Lester Irwin.
　To see a promised land : Americans and the Holy Land in the
nineteenth century / Lester I. Vogel.

　　p.　　cm.
　Includes bibliographical references and index.
　ISBN 0-271-00884-9
　1. Palestine—Description and travel.　2. Christian pilgrims and
pilgrimages—Palestine—History—19th century.　3. Palestine—
Foreign public opinion, Americans—History—19th century.
4. Americans—Palestine—History—19th century.　5. Public opinion—
United States—History—19th century.　I. Title.
DS107.V635　　　1993
956.94'03—dc20　　　　　　　　　　　　　　　　92–32742
　　　　　　　　　　　　　　　　　　　　　　　　　　CIP

Published by The Pennsylvania State University Press,
Suite C, Barbara Building, University Park, PA 16802-1003

It is the policy of The Pennsylvania State University Press to use acid-free
paper for the first printing of all clothbound books. Publications on uncoa-
ted stock satisfy the minimum requirements of American National Standard
for Information Sciences—Permanence of Paper for Printed Library Materials, ANSI Z39.48–1984.

And the generation to come . . .

the foreigner that shall come from

a far land . . . even all the nations

shall say: "Wherefore hath the

Lord done thus unto this land?"

—Deut. 29:21–23

Contents

List of Illustrations

Preface

All people of the Jewish, Christian, and Islamic faiths share a cultural legacy: the concept of "Holy Land." Whether the designation "holy" is due to the presence of God, of his prophets, or of his people, "Holy Land" represents a fusion of geography, histories, cultures, religious practices, and beliefs. The net effect is that a special regard for a certain place is transmitted from one generation to the next. And for those who do experience the place, the weighty combination of factors is likely to make people's perceptions of it different from their perceptions of other, mundane locales.

This book examines one aspect of the Holy Land legacy: the relationship between Americans and their culture, on the one hand, and the territory Western thought calls "Holy Land," on the other hand. It surveys pre-1918 American historical experience in, and cultural relationship with, the specific geographical area in Western Asia known variously as Canaan, Zion, Palestine, or Israel. The concept of an acknowledged "sacred" land altogether removed from the North American continent has been a persistent theme in American civilization ever since the arrival of the first European settlers in the seventeenth century. The ensuing relationship between Americans and the Holy Land is seen in the ever-increasing number of Americans who made the voyage to Middle Eastern soil, and it is still evident in the enduring preoccupation with Holy Land imagery among Americans. This "Holy Land" concept has implications that are wide-ranging and not confined to any particular region of the United States, segment of the American people, or period in American history.

Most historical analyses of Americans' relationship with the Holy Land confine their attention to the political disposition of the land and the national aspirations of those fighting for its possession. In favor of investigating the origins of the later political situation, they often overlook the intrinsic appeal of the Holy Land for the American public. Instead, aspects of Arab nationalism, the gradual emergence of a Jewish state and receptivity to that emergence, reactions to Zionism and its program for Jewish restoration, and Arab-Palestinian aspirations are focuses of such studies. The deeper, more generalized provenance of American interest—aside from the obvious fascination of American evangelicals with the land of the Bible—has largely been left unexplored. This is unfortunate because a fuller picture of American attachment is so vital to an understanding of present realities.

I have therefore chosen to look at the period before 1918 and the breakup of the Ottoman Empire—the quiet years before the Holy Land became the focus of a political maelstrom—and to examine what Americans knew and thought about the Holy Land during that earlier time, before the land became politicized and embroiled in conflict between Arab and Jewish national interests. The chief focus in this book is the nature of American Christian, and mostly Protestant, attachments to the Holy Land. Before all else, in the minds of Americans, the Holy Land has been a classic geographical image, a far-off place of both real and imagined features peopled by groups about whom Americans already had well-formed preconceived notions. Perceptions of the Holy Land were affected by cultural factors, and interaction with it was shaped by those perceptions. Because interaction between Americans and the Holy Land was particularly rich during the years between 1865 and 1918, coming as it did at the close of a major phase of Holy Land history and during a dynamic period in U.S. history, I have chosen to focus especially on that watershed era.

I am reluctant to categorize the historical relationship between America and the Holy Land according to a specific disciplinary subfield. To do so would rob this interesting association of its prodigious scope. For example, to confine the relationship between America and the Holy Land solely to religious or church history or to ethnic or minority affairs would exclude many other pertinent fields: diplomacy, literature, scientific investigation, commerce, and even naval matters. I have therefore chosen an interdisciplinary approach, which offers the greatest flexibility for dealing with facts culled from a variety of sources. David Potter's classic *People of Plenty* served as an inspiration in this regard, and I have tried to emulate Professor Potter's charming integration of interdisciplinary elements. Although I employ social science terminology to construct a framework for understanding, I am fond of describing what follows as simply an "interpretive history," and I shall leave the labeling—social, intellectual, religious, or geographical—to others. The foundation of this work is historical experience, and the historical record is that which is elucidated.

My theme is built around several basic premises. The first premise is that, before 1918, Protestant Christianity, more than any other faith, was in a position to exert great influence on American culture. Second, in American culture the idea of a Holy Land, as a religiously based concept, was largely influenced by that Protestant perspective, though certain other cultural traditions with regard to the Holy Land were also inherited as part of the general Western cultural heritage to which America was heir. And finally, in American culture the idea of a Holy Land assumed the dimensions of a geographical myth that, like the myth of the West in Henry Nash Smith's *Virgin Land,* played a motivating role, influencing and directing much of the practical American experience with regard to the actual, real place. As a framework to define this perhaps unique relationship between Americans and a particular foreign land, I chose the term *geopiety,* coined by the American geographer John Kirtland Wright, although I have used it here in an explicitly Holy Land context for the first time.

To explore this phenomenon of cultural attachment to a special place, I use five recurrent points of American contact with the Holy Land during the appointed time period: American tourists/pilgrims, American missionaries, American settlers/colonists, American explorers/archaeologists/biblical scholars, and American diplomats. The last category includes commercial interests monitored by consular officials of the U.S. government. As the primary producers of written accounts of the Holy Land meant for American audiences of the time, these five groups played a major role in both shaping American perceptions and affecting the extent of American experience in the Holy Land. But American attachment to the Holy Land was not limited to these points of contact, and I mention a few other sources of interest, such as popular education and entertainment.

In the opening chapters, I look at the concept of "Holy Land" as a cultural heritage in American life and thought, beginning with the Chautauqua movement as an exemplary setting for the interplay between image and myth-shaping reality. Then, stepping back, I summarize the reality of the Holy Land as a geographical place under Ottoman Turkish rule. From there I move to the religious and cultural idea of a "holy" land, characteristics of its imagery, and the role of religion and the Bible in America. I also touch on the earliest Holy Land associations with America, from the heritage of Eliza-

bethan travelers and the Puritan concept of Zion, to the biblical imagery of the early Republic.

The main body of this book concentrates on the five key points of
contact, beginning with American travel experiences. In the final
chapter I look at the ramifications of the Holy Land as an American
cultural myth and show how the myth, as a mixture of place, past,
and faith, correlates with "geopiety." I conclude with a description of
the end of Turkish rule and implications for later developments.

This book brings together in narrative survey form the diverse
elements of the earliest connections between Americans and the
Holy Land. During several years of research, materials from collections in various libraries and archives in the United States and Israel
were examined, but most of the materials on which this study is
based—usually public written records of the American encounter
with the Holy Land—are in the general collections of the Library of
Congress, that huge repository of Americana. This was done pur-
posely.

The book originated as a study by the author entitled "Zion as
Place and Past" prepared in part to shed light on the richness of the
Library of Congress collections as a resource for the study of American themes and of relations between America and the Holy Land in
particular. It was also a self-declared adjunct to the fine biblio-
graphic and archival work of the America–Holy Land Project. This
Project, jointly sponsored by the Institute of Contemporary Jewry of
the Hebrew University of Jerusalem and the American Jewish Historical Society, had produced a four-volume *Guide to America–Holy
Land Studies, 1620–1948* (edited by Nathan Kaganoff et al. and published in 1980–84 by Arno Press and Praeger Publishers), which
highlighted resource material at various repositories in the United
States, Great Britain, Turkey, and Israel. Although the *Guide* covered Washington's National Archives in great detail, it largely
avoided the Library of Congress.

In addition to making available many primary sources that reveal
American "public thought" about and interaction with the Holy
Land, the Library of Congress provides an unparalleled single location for studying the entire spectrum of relations between America
and the Holy Land because it has the widest array of materials on
ancillary topics, such as the history and influence of religion in
American life; the role of the Bible in America; public opinion and
the formation of foreign policy; the social, commercial, and political
history of the Middle East; and geographical imagery, perception,
and myth—to name a few of the directions. And also, illustrative

matter in the various collections offer ample visual supplements to narrative. This book keeps faith with the intent of the original study by serving as an invitation to others to mine the resources of America's Library of Congress, especially in the America–Holy Land field.

An extensive bibliography reflecting materials held at the Library of Congress is provided here as both aid and inducement to those who accept the invitation, as well as to those who want to further explore this fascinating field. The bibliography, entitled "America's Holy Land, 1610–1918: A Selective Bibliography," is selective in that it includes only the sources consulted during the preparation of this book. It is organized into units that parallel the topical arrangement of the text: American Backgrounds; Holy Land Realities; Travel, Tourism, and Pilgrimage; Missionaries; Settlers and Colonists; Consuls, Diplomacy, and Commercial Interests; Archaeologists, Explorers, and Scholars; and Past Places and Sacred Spaces.

This work has been a great passion for me, and my family and friends have borne an unfair burden through my absences and distractions while I tended to it. I am grateful for their loving goodwill and tolerance and want them to know that I have missed them too, especially Elana and Dodi, all the while.

I would like to thank Howard Sachar for his guidance and ready advice during the formative stages of my thinking and for his encouragement that my work be seen through to publication. Thanks are also due to Robert Walker, Bernard Mergen, and the late Marcus Cunliffe for their earlier comments, as well as to my many colleagues at the Library of Congress. Among the latter have been my associates within the Collections Services department at the Library, as well as Marvin Kranz, specialist in American history. Particular thanks are due to Moshe Davis and Robert Handy, whom I revere as "men of renown" and "giants on the earth" in nothing less than a biblical sense; their friendship and encouragement has been a continuous source of inspiration. I thank the staff at the Hebrew University of Jerusalem, in the Department of Historical Geography and at the Institute of Contemporary Jewry, for their hospitality and stimulation during the year my family and I came to study among them. I am especially grateful to Yehoshua Ben-Arieh and Ruth Kark for their always warm interest. Indeed, I thank all of the tight-knit "family" in historical geography and the extended clan of America–Holy Land Studies for their suggestions and contributions over the many years of our enjoyable association. Thanks are due to the Trustees of the Boston Public Library and the Trustees of the

New York Public Library for permission to use and quote from manuscript sources within their collections. A special thanks is due a very able assistant, Dodi Vogel, for her careful help with the Bibliography. I am grateful to all for their intellectual reinforcement, but I alone bear the burden of any errors that may appear.

Thanks are due as well for financial support that made the foreign-study aspects of this work possible: to the Council for International Exchange of Scholars and the United States–Israel Educational Foundation for providing an impetus to work in Israel as well as opportunities to travel to Cairo and Berlin as a Fulbright recipient; to the Educational Department of the World Zionist Organization, whose undemanding goodwill asked only that their support be acknowledged; to the Institute of Contemporary Jewry for critical support toward the end of my period abroad; and to Louis Kaplan and the Meyerhoff Foundation for their willingness to assist me in a follow-up visit to the Middle East. I am grateful for the congenial and professional guidance from Peter Potter at Penn State Press.

Finally, although my sincerest thanks and good wishes go out to all of the above for their helpfulness, this work is dedicated solely to one, my life partner, Sandy: "Changeable as the aspects of a summer cloud, but beautiful in all their changes, for the light they reflected was borrowed from Heaven."

How Easy It Is to See a Promised Land

In western New York State, near the junction of Lake Erie and the Pennsylvania border, there is a romantic lake whose cool summertime surroundings were a popular attraction to heat-wearied Americans in the nineteenth century. A young New Jersey minister, John Heyl Vincent, decided to use the quiet hamlet of Fair Point, on the shores of the lake, to hold a summer school for Sunday school teachers in 1874. The idea blossomed into an educational, cultural, and social phenomenon whose impact swept the United States in a movement named for the little lake—Chautauqua.

The Chautauqua idea grew into a multifaceted attempt to offer American adults an opportunity for moral and intellectual improvement similar to the lyceum movement in the United States earlier in the nineteenth century. Always meant to entertain as well as to enlighten, the Chautauqua movement functioned through a literary circle and magazine, summer study programs, lectures, and eventually a network of loosely affiliated traveling tent shows. In its way, Chautauqua was indicative of a peculiarly American-democratic approach to popular adult education, and it flourished until other instructional devices, such as film and radio, made it quaint but outmoded after the 1920s.

During its prime, Chautauqua was a proud monument to American civility. "Chautauqua is the most American thing about America," Theodore Roosevelt once pronounced during a visit to the movement's home in 1905.[1] Others echoed those sentiments, including Aleck Hill, host of Rudyard Kipling during Kipling's first visit to the United States. Despite Hill's promotion of Chautauqua as a typically American institution, it took some doing to convince the twenty-four-year-old journalist to visit the resort in the summer of 1889.

Palestine Park

While quietly strolling around the grounds, "lost in admiration of scores of pretty girls," Kipling suddenly found himself in the midst of an "elaborately arranged mass of artificial hillocks surrounding a mud puddle and a wormy streak of slime connecting it with another mud puddle. Little boulders topped with square pieces of putty were strewn over the hillocks—evidently with intention."[2] The confused and ungenerous Kipling had stumbled on one of Chautauqua's proudest monuments, its "Park of Palestine." Laid out in the Sunday school instruction area, Palestine Park was an extensive topographic model that bordered Lake Chautauqua and used the shoreline as its "Mediterranean coast."

The park was the work of a Dr. Wythe of Meadville, Pennsylvania, who had obsessively constructed the salient features of the land of the Bible in an area about 75 feet wide by 120 feet long. Working despite discouragements and not a little ridicule, Wythe produced the model, complete with miniature plaster cities, in 1874, during Chautauqua's first summer. The idea for the model originated with Vincent, who meant to use it to enhance one of his "visual education" aids. In fact, an earlier prototype had been attempted in a grove adjacent to Vincent's New Jersey congregation. There, on level ground, a map of Palestine was staked out to help orient the Sunday school staff.[3]

Elaborate despite its size, the Wythe model was a labor of devotion that made a lasting impression on many of Chautauqua's visitors. In 1880 presidential candidate James Garfield remarked, "It has been the struggle of the world to get more leisure, but it was left for Chautauqua to show how to use it," reportedly referring to the model as his example of leisure time put to good use.[4] On a more prosaic level, Kipling observed two young people flirting on a peak overlooking "Jerusalem" and a small boy sitting on "Safad" casting a fishing line into Chautauqua Lake. Author Ida Tarbell delightedly recalled playing tag on the model as a youth, straddling Jerusalem for safety and stealing Damascus or Nazareth and carrying it away with mischievous intent.[5]

Although it inspired praise and merriment, the model had a single, serious purpose: it was intended for instruction, careful study, and contemplation. The land it depicted was dearly familiar to Chautauqua's members, and indeed to many other Americans. Most had never actually been to the Holy Land, but they knew it intimately through study of the Bible, geography, history, and the accounts of contemporary travelers. The Chautauqua model was designed to make the already familiar more "real," to turn the image of the Holy Land—already in the mind's eye—into a tangible though miniaturized landscape. The leaders of Chautauqua were confident of the degree to which people already held such an image, and they were so confident that their model was consistent with reality that they even claimed examination of the model in conjunction with a proper text would be "almost equivalent to an actual tour of the Holy Land."[6] The model allowed viewers to process their assorted perceptions and form them into a distinct image that was consistent with popular understanding.

The bumptious Kipling was right when he characterized the unabashedly Protestant Christian Chautauqua as the "apotheosis of popular information,"[7] and, in its way, Chautauqua's Palestine Park typified what Americans in that earlier age knew about the place called the Holy Land. Americans had preconceived notions about the shape and flavor of the cities, sites, topography, coloration, and inhabitants there. Such notions were pieces of a general image that many Americans found credible, whether those notions corresponded to reality or not.

Imagery is simply the composite of perceptions. Though there may be differences in the ways peoples of diverse cultures perceive the same object,[8] they all formulate an image based on their perceptions. The characteristics of that image of a given object are seen, observed, and accumulated inevitably from a "near infinitude of potential percepts"—that is, people are most likely to focus on certain features associated with the object of their interest. Such perceptual selection, during the process of image formation, depends both on which features capture one's attention first and on the interests, needs, and values of the individual.[9] The perceptive process in individuals is naturally influenced by education, both formal and informal, as well. All this is true on the societal level too: interests, needs, values, and education affect which characteristics associated with an object are selected from among any number of features.

One notion consistently transmitted in American culture that has deep roots in Western Christian civilization is the idea of a discrete "Holy Land." Because the Holy Land concept corresponded to a defined, physically identifiable geographical area, and because it remained an item of interest with wide appeal to a people of hegemonic faith, it had the strong potential for being translated into a trenchant image in the collective consciousness, or cultural "mind," of Americans. "That vast and amorphous subject embraced in the phrase 'American mind'"[10] includes the turnings elsewhere of the American spirit—specifically, in this context, to the land of the germination of Western religious history, the Holy Land. The premise to be explored here, to paraphrase Henry Steele Commager, is the distinctly American way of thought, character, and conduct as revealed in patterns of contact and published thought, in this case about the Holy Land. That such thought existed is not surprising. What is remarkable is the volume of materials related to the Holy Land produced by and for Americans. For example, during the late-nineteenth-century period roughly contemporaneous with Chautauqua's prime, hundreds of popular monographs and periodical articles about the Holy Land were available to American readers, amounting to a huge storehouse of thoughts and descriptions that testified to America's deep-seated interest in the Holy Land.[11] "Around it [the Holy Land] still linger the memories, the pride, and the affection of the Jews," wrote American tourist Charles Elliott in 1867. "Upon it the eyes of Christians are turned with love and adoration, as the spot on earth where the beauty and majesty of God have been revealed to man."[12] And Frank DeHass, a former American consul at Jerusalem, observed, "No other land is so fruitful a theme for meditation or so hallowed in its association; and what is remarkable, it never loses its interest. . . . The more we know about Palestine the more interest it awakens."[13]

Throughout history, images of the Holy Land have motivated many peoples and nations to various activities and reflections. For Americans, the popular image of the Holy Land has had significant and long-lasting consequences. In the years before 1918 (that is, before the image was overcome by political considerations), actions rooted in the popular image shaped how Americans interacted with the Holy Land, and the resulting relationship was the foundation for many of the interests and attitudes of today's Americans. Our focus is the popular American image of the Holy Land and the actual relationship between Americans and the Holy Land that came about as a result of that image during this "pre-political" age.

But why concentrate on the more remote past? Understanding the image of the Holy Land in its earlier and fairly pristine form contributes to a more lucid interpretation of today's transactions. From the perspective of the late twentieth century, the words "Holy Land," "Zion," "Palestine," and "Israel" have too often become identified with strife and bloodshed caused by religious, ethnic, and national passions wrestling over a place considered sacred by the faithful of three monotheistic religions. With the land also a keystone in a region of great strategic importance, this impression of struggle invokes for many people inevitable fears for the very safety of humankind, fears of being drawn into apocalyptic cataclysm.[14] This is not an area that contemporary history or current world affairs can ignore. It is a place whose image has become one of partisan consequence: The image one has of the Holy Land indicates where one stands with regard to quite emotional issues.[15]

Before 1918 the Holy Land was primarily a cultural icon to most Americans, an idea that faded in and out of focus, an image rooted in holiness as the Bible's land and Jesus' spatial milieu. At the same time, it was seen as a far-off place and therefore, like much of the rest of the world, not especially relevant to the plowing of the "back forty" or the secular doings in town. The Holy Land was as much a legacy of folklore as anything else: a land said to have been blessed once and then cursed for unpardonable sin; a land abandoned but still desired by Jews, peopled with Muhammadans, neither too pretty nor too advanced; a land of faded or perhaps some future promise; a land controlled by neglectful Turks as heirs of the Saracen victory over the Christian Crusaders centuries before.

Perhaps more than anything during that earlier inceptive period, the Holy Land to most Americans (when they thought about it at all) was a concept infused with emotional and sentimental associations.[16] As an emotional idea, it was powerfully bound with other idealisms held quite close to many hearts: the Bible, one's church, and even one's home, for frequently the emotions that arose within many were of the sweetest associations of youth and hearth, of Bible stories and fireside readings.[17] Consequently, the Holy Land occupied a distinctive niche in the American popular imagination, and to a degree it still does.

Although the American image of the Holy Land has since 1918 accrued such diversionary themes as concession to or rejection of Jewish restoration, Palestinian aspirations, or Christian fundamentalist eschatology, elements of the earlier image are still very much at hand. For example, the slogan "Land of the Bible, the Patriarchs, Jesus, and history" remains prominent in tourist promotional lures, as travel sections of many Sunday newspapers in the United States will testify.[18] On quite another level, a number of American presidents (Harry Truman and Jimmy Carter are obvious examples) have reflected openly on the hallowed history and import of the land when faced with practical questions of policy.[19] The image of the Holy Land as "sacred space" is still powerful, despite professed secular or geopolitical considerations.

The original notion that the Holy Land is special, unique, or different can even be detected in the quest for conflict resolution and establishment of a lasting peace in the Middle East. Many people reason that because it is sacred it is entitled to an atmosphere of contemplative serenity. That it had not achieved such tranquillity is a source for poignant comment. Illustrating this is the penetrating irony of Bethlehem at Christmas peopled by the faithful and Israeli security forces in full combat gear—an image that has become a staple of American print and electronic media since 1967, when Bethlehem came under Israeli military administration. Because the land lacked the peace it deserved, some also believed an injustice had been done by the very process of politicization itself. This attitude is indeed a throwback to that earlier time when the image Americans had of the Holy Land was not complicated by claims of "It's *my* land!"

Throughout American history, then, "Holy Land" has been a familiar term associated with religion and culture and with the history and geography of a specific locale. The label has stirred people to illogical quests, moved others to sublime contemplations of faith and God on earth, and, in the twentieth century, become enmeshed in a Gordian knot of conflicting national aspirations and international political struggle. Regard for this part of the world is so nearly universal that an understanding of its appeal to any given group or nation will increase understanding of the interplay between people, places, the past, and, even more important, the present.

"Image/Reality" and "Geopiety"

The path toward understanding the appeal a given place has for a particular culture has already been blazed. The popular image of the Holy Land held by the majority of Americans before 1918 is as discernible as the image of the American West so creatively diagnosed by Henry Nash Smith in his classic work *Virgin Land*.[20] Smith's approach was a watershed in American cultural historiography. He called such terms as "myth" and "symbol" intellectual constructions that "fuse concept and emotion into an image." Rather than being the creation of a single intellect, said Smith, such myths and symbols are the collective representations of a culture. In *Virgin Land*, Smith identified three myths associated with Americans' conceptions of the West and then demonstrated how important these conceptions were as motivating factors in American history, politics, economics, and letters.

The image of the Holy Land materialized in the practical affairs of Americans just as the image of the West discussed by Smith eventually manifested itself. As conditions of travel improved during the nineteenth century, the land more frequently became a goal on the itineraries of Americans abroad, primarily because it was the site of the Bible drama, not for any remarkable contemporary attractions. Because of its historical connection to the nascent spread of Christianity, the land acquired unique prestige as a starting point and symbolic target for Christian missions. It also held an attraction as a setting for anticipated millennial and apocalyptic scenarios and for study aimed at better understanding, interpreting, and analyzing the Bible. Such manifestations in the practical affairs of Americans reveal something about the concept and emotion, myth and symbol, associated with the image of the Holy Land in American culture.

The perceptual process whereby the collective view of the Holy Land was formed in the minds of Americans, and through which it exerted its influence on everyday affairs, might be termed "image/reality," a hybrid descriptor of a state of awareness based on perceived imagery. In American culture, the collective view of the Holy Land was one of reality seen through the tapestry of image—a way of viewing the present through the veil of the past and enabling the individual to "be there" without actually having to be there. The collective view was "myth" in a lofty sense, not as fantasy but as digested reality. If this myth was such a potent factor in the American Holy Land experience, is there a more specific construct that explains the interplay between imagery, reality, geography, and sacred space?

The term that comes closest to describing this is "geopiety," which American geographer John Kirtland Wright first used.[21] Wright looked like a scholarly Gary Cooper. The drawn, almost gaunt patrician with an open and approachable look served as a researcher, editor, librarian, and director of the American Geographical Society for more than thirty years before his death in 1969. Because he worked outside academia, with its strict protocols and constant search for relevance, he was able to explore many untraditional geographical concepts and invent new hybrid terms to describe them— for example, georeligion, geotheology, geoteleology, geoeschatology, geodiluviology, seismotheology, and geodemonology.

Geopiety was a fencepost along one of the border zones in the Wright region of geosophy—the nature of geographical ideas among different peoples. To Wright, geopiety expressed the emotional or thoughtful piety aroused by awareness of terrestrial diversity, which was especially prevalent in American writings down through the Civil War. The authors of the pieces Wright analyzed wrote about mountains, rivers, deserts, and other geographical features with terms of awe and pious wonder. Wright used "piety" in an orthodox, narrow sense, and it was not until geographer Yi-fu Tuan, a friend of Wright's, wrote an essay in 1976 that the geopiety construct was expanded. Tuan wrote about classical Roman and Chinese examples of worship of local divinities, defining geopiety as a special complex of relationships between humans and nature, with "geo" representing earth, planet, surface, soil, land, country, and nation, and "piety" representing reverence and attachment to one's family and homeland and the gods who protect them.[22]

Tuan's definition of piety can be augmented further with terminology from the *Oxford English Dictionary*, where "piety" also means dutifulness and devotion, and from *Webster's Third New International Dictionary*, where piety is habitual reverence—with all that "habitual" implies about unintentional lack of sincerity or that which grows out of the routine. Geopiety, then, in the sense being used here, is the expression of dutiful devotion and habitual reverence for a territory, land, or space. In this broader form, the term seems tailor-made to describe the range of national attachments to the Holy Land, a place that has evoked devotion and habitual reverence among peoples and cultures in various ages. We will, of course, be looking at exclusively American expressions of geopious behavior toward the Holy Land.

In his use of the term "geopiety," Tuan emphasizes that he saw it exposing "the roots of certain modern concepts . . . [that] lie in profound human experiences that were given other (largely religious) expressions in the past." He continues: "It leads us to see how human territoriality, in the sense of attachment to place, differs in important ways from the territoriality of animals unburdened by symbolic thought."[23] Geopiety does provide a way of examining the largely religious concept of "Holy Land" in a secular context while gauging the weight and extent of its symbolic import. However, in his discussion of geopiety as a narrower expression of relations between human beings and nature, Tuan asserts that Christianity "denuded" the natural world of spirits and mysteries. "No place in Christendom was holy above all others," Tuan states. In this, the record of Christian—even American Protestant—attachment to the Holy Land indicates only that the "spirits and mysteries" existed on a different cultural plane.

In medieval Christianity, the church cultivated a high regard for certain places by promoting pilgrimages to shrines. Unfortunately, however, this was part of a system of indulgences and pardons through which grace was automatically conferred on sinners by the very process of physically journeying to a specified, approved place. At its birth, Protestantism sought freedom from the hold of the church of Rome, and with it the promotion of pilgrimage as a devotional act. Some early English Protestants, such as Samuel Purchas, exemplified this independent-minded spirit when he voiced the opinion that "the best pilgrimage is the peaceable way of a good conscience to that Jerusalem which is above."[24] To Purchas, ascribing sanctity to a place was nothing more than "Jewish," meaning that it had no place in progressive Christianity. But it is difficult to determine how much of this disapproval was due to revulsion at the crass exploitation for profit that pilgrimage had become under the church and how much was due to genuine spiritual objection. The growth in pilgrimage activity among Protestants (not to local shrines but to the Holy Land) seems to be evidence that pilgrimage itself was not the problem. Even to Protestants, then, there was a place that was holy in a way other places were not.

Americans, according to Tuan, developed the characteristic of having no strong bond to place, as evidenced by the national saga of Western migration.[25] This feature was observed as far back as Lord Dunmore, the royal governor of Virginia in 1774, who wrote to the Earl of Dartmouth, secretary of state for the colonies, that Americans "acquire no attachment to place: but wandering about seems engrafted to their Nature." This seeming lack of rootedness had its consequences, Tuan said, as evidenced by the strain of "exile from home, as when in a foreign country or on a journey."[26] What is obvious, however, is that again Tuan's discussion of geopiety concentrates on the sentimental one-to-one relationship between person and place—specifically, attachment to the land or locale of one's birth.

As devised by Wright and Tuan, geopiety would be too narrow to encompass the phenomenon of image and reality associated here with national attachment to a sacred geographical region. But in terms of the Holy Land, geopiety is a label of prescient applicability. In the context of this study, the attachment of Christians to the Holy Land is an attachment to the land of the birth of what is held to be the incarnation of the religion's deity and, by extension, the land where the society's acknowledged culture of the sacred was born. This is certainly the expression of pious regard for a unique place. It remains to be shown how this regard translated into everyday activity.

The Stereoscope

Tracking the cultural image of the Holy Land is not difficult; it is apparent through many writings and period artifacts. One of the most delightful and revealing of these is a curious device found in most parlors in America from the mid-nineteenth to the early twentieth centuries: a mechanical viewer that allowed a person to gaze simultaneously at two distinct though largely identical photographic prints, producing an illusion. The viewing device was called a stereoscope, and the dual images mounted on cards were called stereographs.

Stereographs were created by a special dual-lens camera, the distance between each lens being the same as between two human eyes. The dual images produced by the camera were two-dimensional illustrations that differed ever so slightly in terms of perspective, yet when seen through the stereoscope the dual images blend and the illusion of space and depth is created. The result is a new "reality" in the user's mind that simulates three-dimensionality.

Among the host of subjects that lent themselves to the "stereo" process in the years following the Civil War were views of foreign countries, which were extremely popular. Views of the Holy Land were the most desired and prevalent of this type of subject.[27] One example of the marketing ingenuity in meeting the demand for Holy Land stereo views was the series of Holy Land stereograph views produced by the American firm of Underwood & Underwood in 1914 and accompanied by maps and a small volume of commentary written as if to lead the user on actual tour to the sites depicted.[28] The "tour" was conducted by two popular and respected authorities on biblical geography and religious education: Jesse Lyman Hurlbut of the Methodist Episcopal Church, and Charles Foster Kent of Yale University.

Hurlbut, in the spirit of John Heyl Vincent, was a well-known "teacher-preacher" and a Chautauqua stalwart intensely involved in religious education. Kent, with a Puritan background, received his training in Semitic languages and held the post of Woolsey Professor of Biblical Literature. Kent produced so many readable books in his area of expertise that he earned approbation for doing "more than any other scholar of his day to make accessible to the public the significant results of modern biblical study."[29] Both Hurlbut and Kent had actually toured the Holy Land too, so a collaborative work on the subject would seem to be eminently reliable.

Hurlbut and Kent introduced their stereograph commentary by praising the medium's uniqueness. They claimed that through the slides the user could experience "actual parts of Palestine itself in their power to teach and affect us." Palestine, they noted, had been called the "Fifth Gospel," and experiencing the land through the accompanying stereographs would make the Bible, its setting, and its personalities "more real." But they cautioned that one must "go back in imagination from the ignoble present of this land into its mighty past" to ensure the kind of experience an American visitor to the Holy Land would want.

For example, on first sighting the land at Jaffa—"the Joppa of the Bible!" they noted breathlessly—Hurlbut and Kent ecstatically recalled tales of cedar trees floating down the coast from Lebanon (intended for building Solomon's Temple) and the story of Jonah, who reportedly sailed from Jaffa's harbor before being swallowed by the whale. Meanwhile, the stereoscope user saw only a lump of a town risen from the water behind a tumbledown breakwater, and nothing more than a Turkish customs officer's boat approaching in the foreground. Ashore and in Jaffa's open-air market, the "guides" asked the viewer to ignore "the few people in semi-European dress—combining Paris with Baghdad fashions" and "easily imagine that we have been transported back a couple of thousand years and that we are looking on a Joppa throng as the Apostle Peter saw it. . . . We are in a Bible landscape, among people clad in biblical garments."[30]

Apparent reality notwithstanding, Hurlbut and Kent were urging users to see a dimension in the slides that was not quite present in the factual picture. The guides were catering to an image in the user's mind that merged certain visual and conceptual perceptions, simultaneously objective and subjective: one of the present, the other of the past; one of the senses, the other of the heart.

Thus, Hurlbut and Kent's stereograph commentary is an example of another acceptable way, in addition to Chautauqua's Palestine Park, for Americans of the period to understand the contemporary reality of the Holy Land within the context of its popular imagery: through two levels of consciousness, simultaneously, as a fusion of temporal reality and sacred association. Thus, they can discuss a staged view of scrawny sheep shepherded by an Arab fellah dressed in near rags and couple it with an ideal of biblical pastoralism to transform the scene into an inspirational diorama that is acceptably true-to-life in the mind of the viewer.

The commentary of Hurlbut and Kent provides a larger window on the process of image formation as a cultural phenomenon than Chautauqua's Palestine model presented. Where the model lacked detail and the capacity to bring the viewer to ground level, the stereo views succeeded in making the landscape perceivable. As a result, for us, the perceptual process Hurlbut and Kent promoted amounts to a metaphor about the formation and composition of the Holy Land's image during that earlier time. Like the stereoscope's illusion of three-dimensionality, formed by the convergence of two perspectives, the image of the Holy Land in the minds of many Americans over many years was a fusion of reality and cultural-religious sentiment rooted somewhere in the historical past. This "image/reality" process was extensive in American life and pervasive in the practical Holy Land–related affairs of Americans in specific realms of activity.

The stereoscope as instrument and metaphor demonstrates the characteristic perceptual process in the formation of the Holy Land's image as we will approach it. This mode of perception, this insistence on a reference point in the past when viewing a current Holy Land scene, should not be construed as limited solely to pictorial or three-dimensional representations as seen through the stereographs or the Chautauqua Palestine model. It was widely present also in the writings of many Christian Americans, especially those who had traveled to or lived in the Holy Land and knew it firsthand, who viewed and assimilated facts about the Holy Land in conjunction with preexistent, culturally induced sentiment. As the "elite" class producing information about the Holy Land for popular American consumption, they shaped the nature of the American popular image significantly—that is, they nurtured the "image/reality" process of Holy Land image formation for fellow Americans. Examples of this perceptual approach, and the ways in which the geopiety label encompasses the relationship between Americans and the Holy

Land, will be presented at length, but first we must touch on the dimensions and characteristics of the Holy Land's image, the sympathetic aspects within American culture that incubated this image, and the reality of the Holy Land during the period before 1918 that the image was supposed to mirror.

Holy Land
Reality and Image

The idea of a "Holy Land" was among the concepts that traversed the ocean from the Old World to the New, carried by most European settlers within the pages of their Bibles. At its simplest, this "Holy Land" was the "name commonly given to Palestine on account of the many places sanctified by the presence of Jesus, and identified on the grounds of scriptural documents, history, or legend."[1] On a more complex level, interest in a "Holy Land" could be attributed to the unique human drama that had been played out in that particular place over the course of human history. As the setting for events that were historically and culturally significant, or at least distinguishable, the land supplied the backdrop and occasionally the impetus for the story of human progress from prehistory to the present.

That Land Apart, at the Center

Basic to the land's importance has been its geographical position in the Middle East region. Although the borders of the Holy Land have been subject to timeless debate,[2] it is usually agreed that the multinamed wedge of territory lying between the Mediterranean in the west and the Jordan River and Rift Valley in the east, and between the Bay of Acre and Mount Hermon in the north and Gaza and the Red Sea at Akaba-Eilat in the south, is included in the designation "Holy Land." This territory, situated at the central junction of the Eurasian and African continental masses, is unlike either of the two adjacent areas on those continents from which the earliest civilizations, Egypt and Mesopotamia, emerged. In a region where water has always been a fundamental consideration, the two larger locales were regularly irrigated and fertilized by central river systems. The Holy Land instead depended on a less-sure source of water: rainfall. Whereas the populated regions of Egypt and Mesopotamia are generally flat and monotonous river valleys formed by the gradual buildup of mud and silt deposits, the Holy Land is geologically and geographically diverse for such a small area.

The land itself was formed by enormous geological upheavals, the most prominent evidence of which is the rift down the Jordan River valley—a rift that includes the lowest point on the earth's surface, the Dead Sea. Also within the area lies a fertile belt of land that bridges Africa and Asia and that historically served as a habitable causeway between a sea of water and an ocean of sand. The ancient culture that arose in this unique environment was imbued with elements derived from the two larger, adjacent civilizations, and yet the stark reality of its geographical position provided an unstable element. "Palestine was dependent on Heaven for its life," George Barton, an American orientalist and biblical scholar, wrote in 1916.[3] The Holy Land, he implied, was thus a more suitable incubator for lofty spirituality than either of its ancient neighbors—which conveniently explains the Holy Land's significance as the birthplace of abstract monotheistic thought. In turn, the religions that stemmed from that thought ascribe to the land a single, durable quality: holiness.

"Holiness" is a quality that can be bestowed on a variety of things: times, places, literature, food, and clothing, for example, all divinely hallowed or ascribed as such by believers.[4] But holiness is not a perceivable quality, at least not in a sensory way. Whereas other sensorially perceptible qualities—such as color, odor, sound, and taste—are linked to specific organic parts of the human body and are scientifically explainable, holiness as a quality is not. It is an intellectually/emotionally discerned quality built on the foundations of other intellectually and emotionally discernible qualities, such as fearfulness, powerfulness, goodness, and separateness.[5]

Fearfulness is neither ordinary fear of obvious danger nor pathological fear. It is emotional fear, a unique combination of awe, dread, and fascination.[6] Powerfulness is likewise qualifiable: powerfulness that is holy is termed "mighty, unknown, mysterious, and divine."[7] Goodness is that which is obviously moral or ethical. Separateness is linked to the concept of wholeness or completeness, so that specific objects called "holy" are made complete and form part of a greater, divine whole.

The quality of separateness has special import for the "holiness" ascribed to the Holy Land. In the Bible, the very source of the Holy Land's notability, the land was separate from other places in that it was singled out in explicit covenantal promises to patriarchal figures. Even more so, the declaimed presence of the divine within the country's boundaries enhanced the land and made it special for three faiths. The land was the dwelling place of the "Holy People" and the site of the "Holy Temple" of Judaism. It was the home ground of a form of divinity made human (Christianity) and the earthly access point to heaven (Islam). The presence of the divine elevated the land in the minds of the faithful, making it "separate" from the surrounding lands. Historically, this separateness has also been responsible for placing the Holy Land at the nucleus of the known world, as medieval maps make graphically clear.

The idea that the Holy Land occupied a central geographical location on earth is correlated with the explanation of sacred and profane spaces offered by historian of religions Mircea Eliade. According to Eliade, the sacred space is that locale which has witnessed an "irruption of the divine," an irruption that has breached the sameness of the profane[8] and at the same time has caused the place to become the focal point of the faith. It is therefore readily apparent how the Holy Land became identified with the physical hub of the world. The concept that this particular land was at the center of the earth was inferred from the importance that biblical narrative and poetics assigned to the land. The concept was reinforced and constantly reasserted in Bible commentaries and rabbinic literature.[9] It was also an idea Christianity flirted with for centuries.

There is an interesting difference in the way Christian and Jewish attachments to the Holy Land are theologically grounded. In traditional Judaism, the land plays a primary, covenantal role[10] and is central to many elements of the faith. An array of religious obligations and observances are tied to the land, bearing witness to the compact between people, place, and deity. Of course, some circumstances and schools of thought devalued this attachment at certain times and within certain strains of Jewish thought, the most recent example being in the Reform movement of the nineteenth and early twentieth centuries as Jews began to cope with modernity opened by liberalism, on the one hand, and a desire for social (and political) acceptability, on the other hand. Nevertheless, the land remains today an integral part of the triad of faith, people, and land (or *Torat Yisra'el*, *'Am Yisra'el*, and *Erets Yisra'el*) in Judaism. This doctrinal structure is quite different from that of Christianity, in which the role of the land is fundamentally relegated to secondary importance.[11] Both the reduction and retention of the concept of "Holy Land" are due to the primacy of the figure of Jesus in Christianity.

According to theologian and early-twentieth-century biblical archaeologist George Robinson, the doctrine of holiness in Christian scriptures is predicated on a design of symmetry and perfection.[12] The practical application of this doctrine demands foremost devotion to the deity, a consecration that is complete and ideal and that consigns the land to only associate status. It was logical, then, that early Christianity was too preoccupied with Jesus' spiritual message to attach immediate significance to his physical setting. In the fourth century, for example, Jerome saw no particular advantage to visiting the Holy Land other than for enhancing personal knowledge of scripture and attaining a better understanding of the spiritual message. Gradually, however, the notions that Jesus' person had sanctified[13] his physical environment and that it was possible to move closer to God by experiencing those same temporal surroundings arose in Christianity to the point where people were motivated to pilgrimage. Eventually the church itself incorporated the pilgrimage effort into its spiritual panoply.[14]

Another interesting aspect of the Christian connection to the Holy Land was that in Christianity the figure of Jesus was more closely associated with the landscape of the countryside than with the recognized holy places extant during his lifetime. Like most Jews of the era, Jesus was aware of the Jerusalem Temple's spiritual role in the life of the nation. However, he appears to have had greater personal spiritual attachment to the desolate places, the deserts and mountains, and the spiritual privacy they supplied.[15] Historically Jesus was known as an outdoors person, a circumstance the popular American traveler Henry Van Dyke emphasized in *Out-of-Doors in the Holy Land*.[16]

Christianity and Judaism viewed the Holy Land from different perspectives. Christianity deemphasized the land's centrality for Christian doctrine but underscored the land's importance because of its role as witness. However, Judaism and at least some segments of Christianity tend to converge over the Holy Land of the future.

Fig. 1. AN AMERICAN TOURIST ENCAMPMENT IN THE HOLY
LAND. The experience of tenting out in the Holy Land was a necessary part of a Palestine tour because there was no reliable system of
hotel lodging. However, tenting out was reminiscent of lifestyles depicted in the Bible, thereby enriching the tourist experience.

Both faiths assign important and occasionally similar roles to the
land in their respective eschatologies: The land will be reborn and
will regain its stature through a recommitment of the deity at some
eventual time.

The idea of a discrete "Holy Land" identified with a specific locale
endured in the New World setting as it had in Europe, but the idea
was also subject to the same forces that altered European Christianity, forces that ensured that American and European religious
expression would be distinct from each other. The one element of
the equation that remained consistent between 1517 and 1917 was
the reality of the place itself.

The Reality of Ottoman Palestine

In the spring of 1516 a doting and gullible Mamluk sultan of Egypt
was enticed by a ruse to send his forces into Syria to attack the army

of Selim I, sultan of the emerging empire of Ottoman Turks. Selim's troops were massed, supposedly, for a second campaign against the Persians when he impugned that the Persians had allied themselves with the Mamluks. Drawn north far beyond their bases of supply, the Egyptians were beaten by the vigorous Turks in late August of the same year, clearing the way for Ottoman sovereignty over the Holy Land.[17]

The Turks occupied Palestine for virtually four hundred years, between 1517 and 1917, during most of which time Palestine was relegated to near-inconsequential status within the Turkish realm. It lacked a unified political identity (though it retained its spiritual one), and it was governed by means of a disjunctive mélange of bureaucracies. But it was part of an enormous domain whose single focus was the sultan in Constantinople, and the condition of the country echoed the tone of the faraway sultanate.

When the Ottomans supplanted the withered rule of the Mamluk beys, the Holy Land saw an improvement in its overall circumstances. Sultan Suleiman I ("the Magnificent"), Selim's successor, imposed order and security where it had been lacking, inaugurating a golden age when Ottoman rule in the Holy Land brought about a flourishing of agriculture, trade, and population growth. But by the end of the seventeenth century the empire began to disintegrate. Sultans frequently ruled under precarious circumstances: imperiled by a supercilious imperial guard of Janisarries, a corrupt administrative organization, an economy that tottered from crisis to crisis, the depletion of its tax revenues along with the loss of some of its domains, and the eroding pressures exerted by ascendant European nations. In the Holy Land, conditions reflected this degenerative state during the last centuries of Ottoman rule.

From the start of the eighteenth century it became apparent that the empire was declining, that it was a "sick man"[18] whose terminal illness would leave a void in the increasingly strategic lands of the Middle East. The prospect of such a void motivated Europeans to imperialist struggle throughout the nineteenth century. For Americans, the prospect of Ottoman dissolution, though hardly vital to American interests, was also a source of concern, particularly in the areas of commerce and religion.[19] American impressions of the condition of Ottoman Palestine (which incorporated both the American idea of the Holy Land and the story of the American presence in the land) were part of the larger prefiguration of American impressions of the empire itself.

The Turkish Empire was an absolutism governed by the sultan

from Constantinople, who was the temporal sovereign of Turkey and its provinces and theoretically imbued with unrestricted administrative power. In fact, however, the power of the sultan was limited by custom, by the influence of his advisers, and by whatever fears he might entertain about popular or ecclesiastical responses to his policies. In order to administer the affairs of state, the sultan usually appointed a "grand vizier," who in turn would select various subordinates. Taken as a whole, this administrative hierarchy was known as the Sublime Porte.[20]

Until the end of the eighteenth century, Ottoman sway was mostly feudal in character. The sultan posed as the acknowledged overlord of indigenous vassals who gathered the empire's revenues and turned them over to the Porte's representatives.[21] Later, the lands of the empire were divided for administrative purposes into provinces, called *vilayets*, which were governed by Constantinople-appointed officials called *valis*, and those provinces were subdivided into *sanjaks*, or districts, over which were appointed *mutasiarrifs*. The area that included the Holy Land was divided into several *sanjaks*, most of which were part of the *vilayet* of Damascus until 1841, when they became part of the *vilayet* of Beirut. The *sanjak* of Jerusalem, which ranged variously from Gaza and Jaffa on the coast to Nablus in the Samarian hills, formed a separate administrative unit that was, from time to time and steadily after 1873, accountable directly to the Sublime Porte.[22] Yet no matter how the realm was divided, the lack of dynamic economic growth in the Holy Land contributed to the seeming retention of primitive, biblically posed conditions when observed by Americans.

The economy of the Holy Land during the years of Ottoman rule was stagnant and constrained by government policy. Palestine was heavily agricultural, with the largest segment of the population, the peasantry, confined to a state of near subsistence-level. There were areas, though, where specific crops provided the basis for a more sophisticated economic order. Wheat and olive oil were the staple foods of most areas, though other grains and produce were grown; along the coastal plain, various citrus crops were cultivated; elsewhere, grapes, figs, tobacco, and sesame were farmed. At one time, substantial quantities of cotton were produced, making cotton a staple crop of the country's economy, primarily during the late eighteenth century.[23] But the competition from cotton cultivation in Egypt undermined the demand for the crop, except for a brief period during the American Civil War.[24] In the rural areas, livestock such as cattle, sheep, and camels were husbanded. In the villages and cities, trade revolved mostly around this agricultural base but was not restricted to it. Being near major commercial and pilgrimage routes, the Holy Land's small artisan and commercial classes endured and occasionally prospered. However, prosperity in the Ottoman world was a relative condition. With an agriculturally centered economy, the periodic inundations of locusts and outbreaks of plague frequently worsened economic conditions and diminished overall progress. The economy of the Holy Land therefore ranged from dormant to depressed, much the same as elsewhere within the empire.

Lack of economic development in the Holy Land caused it to produce little that could bolster the Turkish treasuries or Ottoman military strength. Its chief value was the country's religious attraction for three major faiths, and normally that was unimportant and nonstrategic to the Sublime Porte. But by the mid-nineteenth century the drawing power of the pilgrimage sites and the disposition of control over the holy places,[25] along with the drama of European power-plays for strategic advantage over passage to the Far East,[26] made the central Turkish government more aware of the land's potential.

The roots of this realization can be traced to Napoleon's incursion into the Holy Land during his Egyptian campaign. In 1798 a confident and emboldened Napoleon attempted to wreak strategic havoc on Britain's growing colonial ties to India and the Far East by straddling the vital land bridge at Suez through establishment of a French revolutionary enclave in Ottoman Egypt. Egypt had been a perpetual problem for the Turks, and full Ottoman control had never really been gained over its Mamluk beys. To Napoleon, this weak Ottoman outpost was the perfect device for a surrogate attack on his main adversary, the British.

Britain fully realized the geopolitical and military advantage of such a move. By August 1798, Admiral Nelson, in charge of the British Mediterranean squadron, was able to engage and destroy at Abukir the naval fleet that had carried the French invasion force to Egypt.[27] Meanwhile, the Turks massed their own forces in Syria for a conclusive drive to expel the French and reclaim Egypt. But Napoleon was not about to wait passively for a final showdown with a combined British and Ottoman host.

In January 1799 the French mounted a response of their own. Striking northward into Palestine, Napoleon hoped to seize the country and destroy its Turkish garrison before it could be reinforced. Then, with Palestine as an added buffer, Napoleon thought he could return to Egypt in time to repel any future British-Ottoman ventures. The French troops, the first European army to do battle in the Holy Land since the Crusades, moved up the coast but were slowed by an outbreak of plague. Heavy casualties, lingering disease, insufficient equipment, and British offshore support of the Turks were ruinous to Napoleon's plans. The French drive was halted at the ancient fortress city of Acre, headquarters of the local Turkish regent Ahmed Pasha, infamously known as "al-Jazzar"—the Butcher. Napoleon withdrew his troops in May 1799, returning to Egypt after tasting in the Holy Land the unfamiliar fruit of military defeat for the first time in his career.[28] What he left behind, however, was a new awareness among nations of the Holy Land's strategic importance in the Levant.

Palestine's population in the years following Napoleon's invasion was probably around 300,000,[29] and it presented a mosaic of ethnic groups and religious communities of various sizes. The indigenous population consisted of Muslims, Christians, and Jews, which were in turn divided into ethnic subgroups and ecclesiastical denominations. In addition, by the 1840s there were growing communities of foreigners, whom the Turks sometimes referred to as "Franks," a historically rich term directly related to the Muslim recollection of Crusader times.

The largest single element of the Holy Land's population were Muslim Arabs, generally called *fellahin*, most of whom lived settled, agrarian lives in the country's towns and villages. A smaller number of Muslim Arabs were nomadic or semi-nomadic bedouins. Other Muslim groups, of sizable significance, were Turks and Circassians. The vast majority of Muslims were Sunni—orthodox followers of the tradition that gained canonical authority through the first caliphs. An early dissenting sect from this orthodoxy, the Shiites, rejected this body of tradition and the authority of the caliphs, choosing instead to follow Ali, the son-in-law of Muhammad and the line of imams associated with Ali. The Shiites, however, lived primarily in Persia and were almost nonexistent in Palestine, although an interesting heresy from this group, the Druze, inhabited areas in the northern parts of the Holy Land as well as Lebanon and Syria.[30]

Non-Muslim groups, in particular, composed a living history of religious schisms and diversity, each group bearing witness to the Holy Land's role in the development of sectarian thought. There were, for example, remnants of very early Jewish schisms in the presence of small numbers of Samaritans[31] and Karaites. The Christian population itself, though relatively small compared with the Muslim population, consisted of a myriad of denominations and sects. Most of the native Christians were members of the "Eastern churches," which were relics of the early primitive Christian church of the eastern Roman and Byzantine empires. The largest number of these were members of the Greek Orthodox church, and a much smaller number could be counted as adherents of various other Eastern rites: Jacobite, Gregorian (Armenian), Coptic, Abyssinian, and Nestorian. Some of these smaller sects were often present only as colonies of religious functionaries posted to the Holy Land, not as appreciable elements within the population. Most Eastern Christians lived clustered around the towns and cities important to Christianity—Jerusalem, Bethlehem, and Nazareth—and it was only in the north, toward Lebanon and Syria, that there were significant numbers relative to the general population.

Aside from the Eastern Christians, there were Christians associated with the Roman Catholic church (either as direct members or by association with a Latin-affiliated sect, such as the Maronites) or, after the mid-nineteenth century, with a Protestant-sponsored mission or foreign colony. The presence of these various Christian minorities within the overwhelmingly Muslim empire gave the European powers a growing pretext during the nineteenth century to intercede with the Turks—ideally on behalf of a self-assumed client group but more often as an extension of national interest in gaining a claim to the "Sick Man's" legacy. Russia, for example, was active at different times and to varying degrees in "protecting" the Eastern Orthodox Christians. France carved out a claim based on the interests of the Latin Christians. Germany and Britain laid claim to the minuscule Protestant groups, while the British and the Americans also played a role with regard to Jewish interests.[32]

The Jewish community in the Holy Land during the nineteenth century was in an even greater state of incontrovertible expansion than either the Muslim or the Christian population. The Palestinian Jewish community, called the *Yishuv*, numbered a scant 25,000 at the start of the nineteenth century,[33] the majority of which were Sephardim, having "Oriental," Spanish, Asian, or North African ancestry. The remainder of the Jewish community were Ashkenazim, Jews of Central and Eastern European backgrounds. By 1840 the Jewish population of Palestine had doubled, while the country's Muslim and Christian populations remained nearly at the same levels. The most significant increase was in the number of European Jews who were settling in Palestine. These were not, however, the "pioneers" associated with the movement later in the century to revive Jewish nationalism (eventually known as Zionism). They were for the most part pious Jews who were settling largely in the four cities holy to Judaism: Jerusalem, Hebron, Safed, and Tiberias. Essentially a community of faith and study, the Jews of this original community were supported by charity funds, called *halukah*, collected from abroad and distributed through a system that created and maintained flimsy but pretentious centers of power within the community.[34]

As an Islamic state, the empire officially relegated Jews and Christians to the status of *dhimmi*, non-Muslims of a recognized religious tradition who were permitted religious freedom in return for payment of certain taxes.[35] Ottoman relations with the spectrum of religious and ethnic groups under the empire's control were aided through the millet system of administration. The millet system functioned in addition to the elaborate system of geographical subdivisions through which the sovereignty of the sultan and the policies of the Sublime Porte were universally exercised. All non-Muslim religious groups constituted their own millets, headed by their own leaders. The Porte dealt with members of the millets through these recognized leaders just as it would deal with the citizens of a particular geographical area through its appointed *valis* and *pashas*. Through the millets, each religious group was empowered to exercise a degree of judicial responsibility over its members, hearing and ruling on cases involving such matters as inheritance, marriage, and contracts that were generally regarded as the domain of ecclesiastical policy. When such matters involved Muslims and non-Muslims, of course, the cases fell under the jurisdiction of the Muslim courts.

The millet system had a curious effect on the degree of Ottoman authority over individual subjects. In a sense, it decentralized Ottoman rule in that the imperial government's role was diminished, replaced by the millet. Yet the millet's functioning as an intermediary in the affairs of the minority also gave the minority a means of expressing its concerns to the central government.

A further complication in the intricate structure of Ottoman rule became more conspicuous during the nineteenth century as a result of capitulations granted by the sultan to foreign powers. Under the capitulations, which were originally extended by the Turks to friendly nations as a logical outgrowth of the millet system and to encourage trade,[36] the growing numbers of Western nationals resident in the empire were granted a type of extraterritorial status, a privilege that entitled them to the protection and jurisdiction of their particular national consular agents as well as the right to be tried only within their respective consular courts. In the Holy Land, this arrangement gave unusual dominion to the consuls of the West, who found themselves acting as proxies in their respective nations' battles for power and influence in the eroding empire.[37]

Because of the complexity of Ottoman rule, the rights of individuals frequently became subsumed to the arbitrary or capricious whims of local officials. Although Muslims in the Holy Land generally were free from religious persecution, they suffered from the burden of overtaxation and a complex system of levies and imposts, as well as from a corrupt and foreign government structure. Christians and Jews were subject to religious persecution in addition to the temporal conditions shared by their fellow subjects. The various millets collected the important land and poll taxes levied on non-Muslim subjects. These funds were turned in to the local officials, who were also responsible for collecting the land taxes levied on Muslims as well as customs duties.[38] If these usual sources of revenue failed to raise sufficient funds, in any single administrative area, other taxes on agricultural products were levied on all elements of the population.

With local Ottoman officialdom empowered to collect the empire's revenues, corruption at the local level was inevitable. Conditions throughout the empire in matters of civil security were spotty, reflecting the degree of corruption and independence of the local authorities. Although the Porte was occasionally sensitive to prominent citizens' protests about the quality of the local Turkish administration, which sometimes even led to replacement of local Ottoman officials,[39] the Porte was generally content to allow its agents the freedom to exercise their imperium, constrained only by the expectation that they conform to the legal dictates of the Muslim faith. This situation frequently led to an overall decline in civil order, especially when local authorities were weak.

A succession of strong pashas ruling the northern portions of the Holy Land from Acre between 1775 and 1831 brought about a restoration of some civil control throughout the area.[40] However, those regents remained defiant toward the authority of the central government and were occasionally excessively cruel and oppressive—witness the reputation of "al-Jazzar." But the height of defiance against the sultan by one of his pashas was yet to come.

Mehemet Ali, the maverick governor of Egypt, used the pretext of a dispute with the Turkish commander of Acre in 1831 to send his Egyptian forces under the leadership of his adopted son Ibrahim Pasha on an invasion of Palestine and Syria. The powerful Mehemet Ali had come to the sultan's aid years before, during the Greek War of Independence, by supplying the sultan with an Egyptian fleet with which to quell the rebellion. But in 1827 a combined alliance of European powers interfered on behalf of the Christian Greeks, and in response to the sultan's rejection of their demand for a grant of independence for Greece, they engaged and destroyed the Turkish forces at the battle of Navarino. Mehemet Ali believed his sacrifice was ignored by his suzerain, so he decided to exert his power and defy the authority of the Porte. The victorious Egyptians were so successful in challenging Constantinople that the sultanate was nearly wrested from the Ottomans. The reintervention of the Europeans again, albeit this time on behalf of the sultan in 1840, forced an eventual withdrawal of Egyptian troops and the restoration of Turkish control over the Holy Land.[41]

The years of Egyptian occupation of the Holy Land, from 1831 to 1840, were marked by the rarity of a strong, centralized government that was tolerant of minorities and intolerant of local corruption and that enforced a superior degree of security within its borders.[42] Under the administration of Ibrahim Pasha, who established himself in Damascus, the Levant region was administratively reorganized and the Holy Land was included within a single district for the first time in centuries. Although Ibrahim Pasha asserted a heavy and severe measure of authority over the populace, the result was an improved and modernized government and a freer, less discriminatory atmosphere for non-Muslims,[43] to which the Europeans were quick to respond. Economic, cultural, and missionary activity expanded as the Holy Land reopened to Western consciousness.

When Turkish control was restored in 1840, the progress of the Egyptian years was not dismantled. The empire was caught up in its own reform movement called the *Tanzimat*, under which the Turks reorganized their former administrative structure and made its officials more accountable through a hierarchy answerable to the central government. While the new arrangement did not eliminate corruption and local abuses, the independence of local officials was cut back. Most lands of the realm, including Palestine, became relatively safe, and their people enjoyed an easing of peremptory subjugation. In fact, efforts to raise the status of religious minorities continued. Meanwhile, Western missionary groups were allowed to establish educational programs, and permanent Western consulates were opened. The Ottoman Empire was gradually incorporated into the community of modern nineteenth-century nations. In the 1830s, regular steamship service between Europe and Jaffa began, and by 1865 Jerusalem and other cities in the Holy Land were connected to the empire's new telegraphic system.[44] Ottoman Palestine was emerging from obscurity into the modern world.[45] For Americans, that relatively new people, the idea of the Holy Land was a separate matter. It was a concept firmly rooted in their faith, and it had been taking shape from the very beginnings of American culture.

A Christian and Bible-Reading People

Writing in 1835, Alexis de Tocqueville observed the strong influence of religion on American life: "There is no other country in the world where the Christian religion retains a greater influence over the souls of men than in America."[46] While this may have been an unusual phenomenon in Tocqueville's post-Enlightenment times, the foundation of this influence was set deep in the American experience. American Christianity had always identified closely with the radical wing of the Protestant Reformation. One of the dominant reformist themes involved salvation through personal faith, as opposed to salvation through the church and through "works," and an extension of this doctrine included the right and duty of individuals to exercise judgment in matters of religion and morality. With individual believers dealing directly with God, the respective roles of church and state were altered. In the New World, particularly on the frontier, these tendencies nourished new levels of democracy within religion that complemented the growth of American secular democracy.

During America's colonial period, the spread of Christianity had been a fundamental goal of the settlers, and certain denominations even enjoyed the advantage of a carryover from Europe, the established church. Although American independence was inspired and won in an age of enlightened and frequently anticlerical thought, the new nation retained its commitment to Christianity, and indeed religion flourished through a series of "awakenings," despite the ordeal of disestablishment.

The formalized political doctrine of religious liberty and voluntary choice benefited Protestant churches, just as individualism and enterprise were characteristics that were thoroughly amenable to Protestant theology. The influence of Protestantism extended well beyond the bona fide church members because large numbers of Americans accepted Protestant social polity. Evidence of this wider influence in nonchurch affairs during America's pre–Civil War era is the moral outrage of the antislavery movement, the acceptance of a universal public (really Protestant-dominated) school system, and the growth of higher education, which in the United States was frequently tied to religious purposes.[47] Also during the pre–Civil War period, Protestantism's sway in religious life could be seen in the maturation of the American missionary movement, in the forging of new sects as a result of heightened millennialist expectation, and in the frequent great revivals that rhythmically swept up the hearts of the marginally committed.

Protestantism emerged as the regnant religious force in American life during the nineteenth century. Church historian Winthrop Hudson observed that American Protestantism has been fertile, multiform, and versatile. Noting that it had already taken shape by 1787, Hudson wrote that, down through 1914, "America was shaped in an essentially Protestant mold; it was the era of 'Protestant America.'"[48] In another sense, by the mid-nineteenth century Protestantism "had established undisputed sway over almost all aspects of national life."[49] During this preeminence, Protestantism shaped the nature of the relationship between America and the Holy Land to a greater degree than either Catholicism or Judaism.[50] Hudson termed the post–World War I age "post-Protestant" because Protestantism had lost its exclusive position in American life, owing to such developments as increased immigration, "theological erosion," and rural reconcentration and urban growth.

At the height of its influence in American life, Protestantism was fractured into countless subgroups. However, it still consisted of several major, key denominations[51] that shared certain common points of origin and patterns of faith.[52] For example, the Reformation heritage of Protestantism as distilled through these major denominations bequeathed several significant Holy Land–oriented traditions to American culture, among which were a commitment to the figure of Jesus, an interest in his life and times, and, perhaps more important, devotion to the concept of individual Bible study.[53]

American attachment to the Bible is a good example of the influence of Protestantism in America prior to World War I. The American, a bemused Tocqueville observed in the 1830s, does not turn to his business ledgers on returning home after a day's work; he opens his treasured volume of Holy Scripture instead.[54] Familiarity with biblical events, personages, and locales was widespread among the American people simply because of the near-universal popularity of Bible reading.[55] The early American preference for biblically derived personal names, which perusal of census lists or cemetery tombstones will reveal, is one obvious result. So too a hard look at the map of the United States will reveal "almost a thousand names of biblical derivation"[56] scattered across the nation. Names like Ezra, Jeremiah, and Rachel, and places like Bethlehem, Bethany, and Bethel, are evidence today of the influence of the Bible in American life and across the American landscape, a direct result of the pervasiveness of Protestantism in American culture.

The Bible was responsible for the initial exposure of the American mind to the Holy Land as a physical setting. The English translation of the Bible into what was known as the King James Version was undeniably a part of America's cultural heritage; it was produced in the same period as the early English settlement of North America and could almost be deemed a subliminal connection between the Anglo-Saxon people and the Holy Land.[57] In the nineteenth century, the American initiator of modern scientific study of the Holy Land, Edward Robinson, said that Holy Land exploration was so appealing to Americans as a people because of the Bible's popularity. For him and for most of his compatriots, especially those in pious New England, the scenes of the Bible made a deep impression from earliest childhood:

> Indeed in no country in the world, perhaps, is such feeling more widely diffused than in New England, in no country are the scriptures better known, or more highly prized. From his earliest years the child there is accustomed not only to read the Bible for himself, but he reads or listens to it in the morning or evening devotions of the family, and in the daily village school, in the Sunday school and Bible class, and in the weekly ministrations of the sanctuary.[58]

Another aspect of American preoccupation with the Bible was the tendency to locate the American nation within the Bible's prophecies. During the Civil War, for example, the Rev. George S. Phillips of the Tiffin (Ohio) Methodist Episcopal Church delivered a series of lectures that purported to show how the divinely graced American Republic had been foreshadowed in Scriptures.[59] Phillips compared the Hebrew theocratic commonwealth of old with the United States and declared that America was the successor to the joint missions of freeing humankind from the yoke of human tyrants andspreading the gospel of liberty, republican democracy, and Christianity.[60]

A third aspect is the frequent association of the land of the Bible with the concept of utopia, which is well established in many aspects of Christian thought, from theological tracts to worshipful hymns.

The Bible itself initiated this concept by repeatedly describing the land the Israelites would occupy in glowing, sensual terms, such as "flowing with milk and honey." To Americans, the connection between a utopia and the Holy Land was there from the earliest settlers in the New World. To them, America was not only the new Eden but also the new land of Canaan. The New England commonwealth of the Puritans was to be a utopia ruled by biblical precept. As laid out in John Eliot's *Christian Commonwealth* (1659), the new Zion would be founded on a recognition of Jesus' kingship and an acknowledgment that all laws must be mandated in the Bible.[61] These elements would make it possible to carve the New Jerusalem out of the primal North American wilderness.

One development that was unthinkable to the Puritan mind but that had a significant effect on the triangular relationship between Americans, the Holy Land, and the Bible was the challenge of biblical criticism. Maturing during the latter half of the nineteenth century, the movement to subject the Bible to textual analysis and criticism was a crucial challenge for American Protestantism as well. The Bible had been a central part of the American scene, and its imagery and words, especially as taken from the King James Version, were integral parts of American speech and culture. Biblical criticism was a threat to this state of affairs.

Literal interpretation of the Bible was a heritage of the Reformation. During the Middle Ages, the Bible was subject to several layers of interpretation—literal, ethical, allegorical—depending on the needs of the Bible's chief users, the clergy.[62] But the Reformation (assisted by the continued development and spread of printing technology) made the Bible nearly universally accessible, and there was less need for interpretations that were other than literal. In the early days of the American nation, especially in the afterglow of the succeeding "Great Awakenings," "personal and literal readings of Scripture seemed to form part of the democratic framework of the Republic, wherein all people were responsible for their own salvation."[63] Placed in the domestic context, reading and understanding the Bible according to the literal meaning of the text became a foundation of American Protestantism that was severely shaken by the introduction of biblical criticism.

The revolution in thought implied by the acceptance of higher criticism was slow in starting. It grew first in the theological schools, where the atmosphere of liberal exchange made it palatable. Slowly it spread through a trained clergy and reached the churches, where its full implication caused organized reaction. Some of the reaction was modernist in tone, accepting the premise of higher criticism and adapting the theological frame of reference to it. Other reaction was conservative in nature, arguing for the literalist approach to the Bible. Although basic contextual pictures of the Holy Land described in the Bible remained unchallenged, the view of the Bible as sole authoritative source was severely battered.

Nonetheless, the Bible's role in American culture and its impact on the formation of America's Holy Land imagery are of paramount importance. But the Bible was not the only means by which Americans learned about biblical scenes and locales. Other forms of literature bolstered their image of the Holy Land as well. For instance, classical works, such as those of the Roman-Jewish historian Flavius Josephus, contributed to the American conception of a past-oriented Holy Land, and then there was the popular literature written by nineteenth-century contemporaries—travel accounts, explorers' accounts, reports in newspapers and periodicals, and belles lettres, such as General Lew Wallace's enormously popular *Ben Hur*. Added to this were the meetings of Chautauqua groups, missionary societies, and graphic images in photographic or print media. Protestantism provided the milieu for nurturing the American idea of the Holy Land, but that idea existed in the American psyche in quasi-utopian and sentimental form—distorted, removed, and elevated above the reality of the actual place. This was, however, certainly not because of a lack of contact with the Holy Land.

Earliest American Links with the Bible's Land

To most Americans, the Holy Land was an abstraction closely identified with some ideal. To the Puritans, the consummate polity was theocratic in form and symbolically associated with Zion. The New World was the Canaan where Puritans had come to build the true biblical commonwealth. This theme of a fresh start in a special place recurred periodically as various religious groups sought refuge from European and, later, American religious intolerance. And this theme was not limited to religious accommodation. The enlightened framers of the Declaration of Independence—Adams, Jefferson, and Franklin—proposed for the obverse of the new nation's seal the image of the Children of Israel on the safe shore of a divided sea, watching tyranny sink beneath the tide before marching forth to the wilderness toward the Promised Land.[64] Even in American literature

down through at least the mid-nineteenth century, the idea of Holy
Land or Zion was usually presented in either metaphysical, meta-
phorical, or millenarian terms.[65]

It has been popular to say that trade and spreading the Gospel
were the prime motivators of Europeans attracted to the New
World. Both elements were certainly present in New England, and
both involved a connection between New Englanders and the Holy
Land. The Puritan settlers were especially enamored with the idea of
Zion in the New World, but in addition there were from time to time
sporadic commercial contacts between the American colonies and
the Levant region. As early as 1676, one Boston merchant, Edward
Randolph, observed that fellow merchants paid little heed to British
laws that strictly regulated trade by the colonies. He pointed out that
American merchants were being sent as far as Scanderoon, another
name for Alexandretta, Syria.[66] The contacts that were made were
probably conducted under the protection of the English Levant
Company, which for a financial consideration made the contact secure from governmental interference.[67]

If the East was a market objective of colonial America, it was also
seen as a contributory source to the stream of Anglo-Saxon civilization. Literary and legendary links between the Holy Land and the
British people were carried to the New Land.[68] Yet actual contact
with the Holy Land was limited to very few Americans during the
colonial period. Most colonists had to be content with printed reports and occasional graphic representations. Only infrequently did
they hear about the Holy Land from firsthand experience. But such
reports did reach the colonists, and perhaps the earliest came remarkably soon after the beginning of the British colonial effort in
North America.

In the year 1610, George Sandys, a son of the Archbishop of
York, was thirty-two years old, "restless and eager to escape for a
time from his surroundings." Sandys had suffered through a disastrous marriage and saw the wealth his father had accumulated dissi-
pate in a flurry of litigation. Sobered by the ways of the world, he
was a "true son of the Renaissance," and "with his cynicism he combined an immense curiosity to see the world, a willingness to aid his
country to an empire, and romantic love of the past in architecture
and in literature."[69] Elizabethan adventurer, poet, and scholar,
Sandys departed for a trip to the East. On August 20, 1610, three
years after the founding of the Jamestown settlement by the London
Company, he left Venice to journey through Greece, Turkey, Egypt,
and the Holy Land. What makes Sandys so significant is not that he

was a well-to-do gentleman "who, following the routes opened up by
the Levant Company, voyaged out of curiosity to the classic lands of
Greece and the Aegean, the biblical lands of Palestine and Egypt,
and the fabled wonders of Constantinople, ancient seat of the Eastern Empire,"[70] or that he told of his travels in an immensely popular
work, *A Relation of a Journey begun An:Dom: 1610*.[71] Other Eliza-
bethans accomplished the same feat during this period of "merchant
adventurers." George Sandys is notable because he was the earliest
firsthand connection between the Holy Land and America.

Ten years after visiting the Holy Land, Sandys succeeded his brother
Edwin as treasurer of the Virginia Company and accompanied his
niece's husband, Sir Francis Wyatt, to Virginia. Wyatt, about the
same age as Sandys, was appointed the new governor of the Virginia
colony in 1621. George Sandys lived in Virginia through 1631 and
played an active official role in the affairs of the colony. At the same
time, be completed the first translation of a classical work (Ovid's
Metamorphoses) ever done in America.

Even though a number of years separated Sandys's Holy Land
experience from his telling of the journey to his Virginia neighbors,
his published account of the Holy Land trip reveals Sandys's impressions of the Holy Land, which he most likely described for the new
Americans. Detailed and dispassionate, his view of the Holy Land
presaged the peculiar way Americans in later years would envision
and reflect on the state of the Holy Land. To Sandys, the Holy Land
was

> where God himself did plant his own Commonwealth, gave
> laws and oracles, inspired his Prophets, sent Angels to con-
> verse with men; above all where the Son of God descended to
> become man; where he honored the earth with his beautiful
> steps, wrought the work of our redemption, triumphed over
> death, and ascended to glory . . . but which has become the
> most deplored spectacle of extreme misery . . . which calam-
> ities of them so great and deserved, are to the rest of the
> world as threatening instructions.[72]

He noted gloomily that Jerusalem's older buildings seemed "all ruined" and that the newer ones were "contemptible." He wrote that
the city was inhabited by Christians out of devotion and by Turks
"for the benefit received by Christians; otherwise perhaps it would
generally be abandoned."[73]

The reflections of Sandys may be incorporated into an observation made by historian Barbara Tuchman: "Up to 1600 Palestine had been to the English a land of purely Christian associations, though lost to the Christian world through the unfortunate intrusion of Islam. Now [during the period of Puritan ascendancy] it came to be remembered as the homeland of the Jews, the land carrying the scriptural promise of Israel's return."[74] Indeed, Sandys described the Holy Land as "now inhabited by Moores and Arabians." He continued: "Turks there be few; but many Greeks, with other Christians, of all sects and nations, such as impute to the place an adherent holiness. Here also be some Jews, yet inherit they no part of the land, but in their own country doe live as aliens."[75] Sandys may have been better attuned to the reality of the Holy Land than some of the Americans who would follow him in the nineteenth century. Yet there is still the element of the past in his views of contemporary sights. Sandys was a tangible link between his Virginia neighbors and the Holy Land during a time when most Americans looked to the West rather than the East.

Early Americans also formed connections and perceptions about the Holy Land, in a contrived but popular fashion, through exhibits of dioramas, models, and panoramas. In the June 4, 1764, *New York Mercury*, notice was given that "Jerusalem, a view of that famous city, after the work of 7 years [was] to be seen at the House of Tho. Evans, Clock & Watch Maker—an artful piece of Statuary." Perhaps the same model was later featured in newspapers in 1790 and 1802: "Panorama of Jerusalem at Lawrence Hyer's tavern, Chatham St. 62—the sight is most brilliant by candlelight."[76] Perhaps it was best that the model of the Holy City be seen by candlelight; the reality of Jerusalem—indeed, of all the Holy Land—then under Ottoman control was quite another matter. Even so, such displays had vital roles as entertainment and educational tools,[77] and their existence underscores the compelling nature of the appeal of the Holy Land.

The Challenge of the Nineteenth Century

Because interest in the Holy Land was a feature of American Protestantism that disregarded the sectarian chasms dividing Protestant denominations, the Holy Land at the beginning of the nineteenth century was a factor common to most if not all Protestant groups. Thus, American opinion and perceptions of the Holy Land were conditioned by other important factors—for example, the influential pulpits, the leading seminaries and colleges,[78] the religious press, and the forces of change working within Protestantism or prevalent in nineteenth-century American life. The turn toward the new mercantilism of the Gilded Age in reaction to the Civil War; the reaction to industrialization and urbanization; the increased absorption of new immigrants from different cultures; the gradual incorporation of Darwinism into the cultural outlook of America—all these factors were part of the groping of liberal, progressive America in coming to terms with modern life. Protestantism's reaction to such forces fomented the split between liberal and conservative that would become known in the twentieth century as the "modernist-fundamentalist controversy."

In addition to these influences on American Protestantism, which in turn affected the formation of the Holy Land's image in American culture generally, there was a blurring of distinctions among Americans who experienced the Holy Land firsthand. This relatively small number of Protestants was powerfully influential in forming the Holy Land's image for most Americans. An understandably large number of Americans who visited the Holy Land were clergy or people with strong ties to the clergy, but some of these were also archaeologists and biblical scholars, or archaeologists and explorers who were also diplomatic consuls or missionaries, or some missionaries who were popular travel writers, and so on. The result was a clearly identifiable core of individuals who significantly molded American opinion about the Holy Land.

Several key groups exposed Americans to the Holy Land during the closing fifty years of Ottoman rule: American tourists, missionaries, colonists, archaeologists, biblical scholars, and consular personnel. Because of their importance as clergy, laypeople, or political or cultural leaders, and because they can be overwhelmingly identified as adherents of Protestantism, they can be said to have been the "policy-forming elite" of American Protestantism, at least as far as the American connection with the Holy Land was concerned.[79] The products of the collective "mind" of this elite fellowship, at a time when Protestantism dominated American culture, probably approximate the significant formulations of the "American mind" on the subject of the Holy Land.[80] Although these groups appear to be diverse, from a twentieth-century perspective, they actually shared similar motivations and interests that took each to the Holy Land and allowed each one to experience it firsthand. They also shared their experiences in and reactions to the Holy Land afterward with the literate American public.

Fig. 2. RETRACING THE EXODUS FROM EGYPT ON CAMELBACK.
The lure of a trip through the Holy Land in the nineteenth century
frequently included the adventure of retracing journeys described in
the Bible. These two Holy Land tourists (center and right) were photographed as they were about to embark on a camelback trip retracing
the journey of the Israelites out of Egypt and into Canaan.

The years from the end of the Civil War through the end of
World War I witnessed momentous geopolitical, demographic, and
social changes both in the Holy Land and in America—and those
changes are at the foundation of today's realities. In the Holy Land,
the Jewish community slowly overcame years of inertia and became
infused with a new sense of dynamism; old economic, cultural, and
demographic patterns were replaced by a new, secular impetus. The
Palestinian Jewish community contributed toward the animation and
growth of a vigorous political movement, Zionism, which advocated
reestablishment of Jewish sovereignty in the Land of Israel. By comparison, the indigenous Muslim and Christian populations continued to appear relatively static to many Westerners. In truth, the various changes taking place within Arab culture and the Levant were
much more subtle and obscure, especially to American observers.
The gradual influence of Western education, the growth of secret
Arab societies, and a heightened cultural awareness were all factors
that eventually induced Arab reassertion of political nationalism
during World War I.[81] The period also saw the long-anticipated dissolution of established Ottoman rule, which was replaced by British
administration over the Holy Land.

In the United States, the same period saw an ever more expansive,

confident, and assertive American Protestantism reach its zenith as a
potent factor in American life before gradually giving ground to the
forces of secularization in an increasingly "post-Protestant" age.
Within Protestantism, conservative and liberal impulses conflicted
with each other more and more, exposing a rift in the long-standing
American tradition of devotion to the Bible. Critical and naturalist
dissection of Scripture, as well as the general decline in the hold of
religion on America's increasingly urbanized and industrialized population, affected American thought about the Holy Land.[82] But the
dilution of Protestant hegemony was a process that occurred over an
extended period of time. Meanwhile, the growing number of reports
from Americans in Palestine gave Americans at home popular exposure to the idea of the Holy Land as geographical reality.

American missionary activity was increasing during the time, and
the missionary establishment was gathering strength enough to become an effective force in the formation of American Middle East
foreign policy. Heightened millennialist expectations occasionally
brought unusual colonies of Americans to the Holy Land for the
purposes of settlement. The level of scholarly interest in the land of
the Bible was surging too, intensified by refinements in archaeological techniques, undertones of nationalistic pride and imperialistic
scheming among Western nations, spiritual conflict, and the sheer
romance of excavation for Bible-proofs and treasure. And with
more Americans than ever visiting the Holy Land, American consular personnel in Palestine were caught up in the swell of a growing
American presence, mostly in reaction to the other activities drawing
Americans to the Holy Land in record numbers, not as an assertive,
diplomatic initiative. Commerce, though meager, was also a function
of consular officials.

To return to the metaphor of the stereoscope, America's Holy Land
image had two parts: a vision that existed as a result of certain cultural associations, and a reality offered by the condition of Ottoman
Palestine. American Protestantism provided the logical context for
the subjective influences within American culture and American
Protestantism that nurtured the idea of the Holy Land. Despite the
stresses of growth, division, and adaptation that the period between
the Civil War and World War I brought to American Protestantism,
the Protestant faith was a strong enough force in American life to
pave the way toward the formation of a collective Holy Land image
in the American mind. It was also effective enough to perpetuate a
past-oriented view of the Holy Land as a frame of reference for

American activities and thought. Eventually, some trends in American Protestantism—notably the evolution of liberal and conservative camps—figured into aspects of American awareness of specific developments in the Holy Land, such as the emergence of Zionism. But the role of the past and its influence in American Holy Land imagery was unyielding throughout.

CHAPTER 2

Pilgrimage, Tourism, and Exodus
Americans Go East

On a blustery spring afternoon, with the executive business concluded for the day, President and Mrs. Lincoln rode out of the White House grounds in an open carriage on a brief outing to the Washington Navy Yard. The burdens of war finally lifted from his shoulders, the president was in a cheerful, almost playful, mood. Only days before, news of the Confederacy's capitulation had reached Washington, and now, with a free moment alone with his wife on a bright afternoon, the president could relish the occasion with buoyant conjectures about his personal future. During the ride, he spoke about travel—about a possible journey to California and even one abroad at the conclusion of his second term. But of all the places to see, the president appeared to relish most a tour of the Holy Land.[1] The idea of a pilgrimage to Jerusalem was appropriate that afternoon. It was Good Friday, April 14, 1865. Later that evening, Mr. and Mrs. Lincoln attended the fateful performance of "Our American Cousin" at Ford's Theater, and the dreams of pilgrimage came to an abrupt and tragic end.

Heading for the Promised Land

Although Lincoln was assassinated before fulfilling his ambition to visit the Holy Land, his talk of such a trip was by no means idle fancy. The Holy Land was a travel destination on the lips of many Americans. It already existed as a concept in the collective mind of Americans, a peculiar fusion of geographical place with historical past. Furthermore, because it was an actual place, it was rarely considered unreachable by Americans. Indeed, beginning with George Sandys and continuing down through the mid-nineteenth century, Americans learned of the Holy Land—and heard Americans' impressions of it—either by word of mouth from the few who were lucky enough to have visited it, or through written reports and graphic representations. Until Mehemet Ali's invasion of the Holy Land in 1831, however, such reports from American sources were rare. In order to satisfy their curiosity about the romantic "fabled East," Americans depended mostly on the contemporary works of British travel writers and older classics.[2]

The easing of civil conditions in the Holy Land during and after the Egyptian invasion correlated with an increase in the American presence in the Holy Land. This period saw a confident, expanding America sustain its first earnest attempt to penetrate the eastern Mediterranean. Such American authors as John Lloyd Stephens, George William Curtis, Bayard Taylor, John W. De Forest, William Cullen Bryant, John Ross Browne, and Herman Melville ranged over a more secure though still perilous Holy Land.[3] So too did Americans like Edward Robinson and William Francis Lynch push methodical study of the Holy Land into new realms of science as a result of their journeys. American naval vessels, such as the USS *Delaware* in 1833 and 1834, occasionally called along the coast of the Holy Land. While American missionaries abandoned Jerusalem in favor of Beirut as their center of operation toward the end of the period, the same time saw the federal government sluggishly open a consulate in Jerusalem.[4] This activity came to a halt, however, as a result of the tension tearing across American society as the United States lapsed into civil war.

After the war's conclusion the interest was rekindled on an unprecedented scale. More Americans than ever before began rushing overseas to see the land of the Bible. A new wave of American experience in the Holy Land was about to begin. But in April 1865 many of those who would play roles in shaping that experience were otherwise engaged:

The man who clinched victory for the Union, Lieutenant General Ulysses S. Grant, was supposed to be sitting with the Lincolns in the presidential box that sorry night, but a change in plans made him leave Washington for Burlington, New Jersey, earlier in the day. Secretary of State William Seward, though, was in Washington. Recuperating from a carriage injury at his home across from the White House, Seward was attacked and knifed in his bed as part of the plot against Lincoln. He survived the attack and, like Grant, went on to live Lincoln's dream of pilgrimage. Grant and Seward were two of many prominent Americans who traveled to the Holy Land in the years after the Civil War.[5]

Congregational minister Selah Merrill was serving as a chaplain to the 49th U.S. Infantry, a black regiment, in April 1865. The clergyman saw action at Vicksburg and now faced the uncertainties of resuming an interrupted career when he left the Army. The next few years were spent in pulpits in New York, San Francisco, and New Hampshire, after which Merrill studied in Berlin to make up for his shortened education. Ultimately Merrill assumed the responsibility of representing official American interests in Jerusalem during a career that would last into the twentieth century.

Up along the Maine coast in April 1865, a fiery preacher worked to establish his Church of the Messiah. The Rev. George Jones Adams, a distant relation of the illustrious Boston Adams family, had a grand design for his new congregation and converts. His life and theirs were sorrowfully linked with the Holy Land over the next two years in an episode of scandal and shame.

Chicago lawyer Horatio Spafford was building a reputation as one of Chicago's most upstanding citizens in April 1865, serving on boards of medical schools, seminaries, and churches. It took nearly sixteen years for events to lead him and his family to the Holy Land.

In April 1865 the Holy Land was an insignificant backwater of the decaying Ottoman Empire ruled by a hulking, half-mad Sultan Abdülaziz who had inherited the throne from his brother in 1861. By this time the sultans were drowning in their wild extravagance and unable to keep their empire financially sound. As a neglected subdivision of the Ottoman realm in April 1865, the Holy Land's true potential to draw American visitors remained to be realized. It took an event of unusual and celebrated proportions to open the way: the first organized excursion by an American group to the Holy Land.

The voyage launched an era of unprecedented travel for Americans newly at peace and with cash to spend. It also launched a singularly American literary career, that of "Mark Twain," a creation of one of the travelers.

The volume of material on American travels to the Holy Land during this period makes it necessary to divide discussion of tourists/ pilgrims into two separate chapters. The remainder of the present chapter introduces a selection of some American travelers who experienced and reported on the Holy Land. The backgrounds of these tourists, the circumstances of their travels to the Holy Land, and their literary legacies with regard to the Holy Land are recounted here. The next chapter examines the experiences and observations of these travelers.

A Grand Pleasure Excursion of Brooklynites

On December 15, 1866, Samuel Clemens departed from San Francisco, sailing to New York by way of the Isthmus of Nicaragua. Clemens, a young reporter who apparently loved ocean travel,[6] had been engaged by the newspaper *Alta California* to write a series of letters about a trip, possibly to Peking on an invitation from Anson Burlingame, the U.S. minister to China.[7] Clemens was on his way through New York to St. Louis,[8] where he would spend some time with his mother before leaving for the Orient. While in New York he became aware that "prominent Brooklynites are getting up a great European pleasure excursion for the coming summer, which promises a vast amount of enjoyment for a very reasonable outlay."[9]

The forthcoming trip to Europe and the Holy Land was being planned primarily by members of Henry Ward Beecher's Plymouth Church. Beecher, a prominent churchman, was scheduled to lead the tour, and it was rumored that he intended to use the trip to Palestine as preparation for a book on the life of Jesus.[10] Clemens found himself drawn into the affair both on its merits and by the attendant hoopla that had much of New York aroused. Rumors circulated that celebrities would abound as part of the excursion: Union war hero William Tecumseh Sherman himself would lead the party in capturing the sights, and the entire affair would receive publicity in the nation's press because several well-known New York newspaper publishers would be present. P. T. Barnum had report-

edly secured an agent to accompany the excursion and help participants collect "antiquities, relics, and curiosities from the different
places visited"[11]—all to be displayed, properly labeled and with a
photograph of the donor next to his or her contribution, in a special
department of Barnum's famous Manhattan museum. With such inducements, the tour naturally became one of the most discussed
events of the year.

Clemens convinced the *Alta* people to send him to cover the great
event, and he arranged for the *Alta* to publish his letters from along
the route. The *Quaker City* cruise, with the thirty-one-year-old
Clemens on board, would not only inaugurate organized American
tourist travel to the Holy Land but also boost Clemens's career in
American letters, for the dispatches, rewritten, would become his
first commercially successful book, *The Innocents Abroad; or, The New
Pilgrims Progress* (1869).

Mary Mason Fairbanks, another *Quaker City* cruise participant, observed that Clemens was "not inflated with expectations" upon traveling outbound, though she recalled he did demonstrate a "youthful
cynicism." She also recalled that he "lolled about the ship as one
committed to utter indolence" and that he was conspicuous among
the passengers for his sense of humor, which nightly produced
"peals of contagious laughter" at his table.[12] Aside from recalling
Clemens's presence, Fairbanks explained that "for an American ship
to go cruising in foreign seas simply for pleasure was in those days a
new departure, and although the witty author did not glorify the
American traveler, his book was the event of the year." Clemens had
published one other book before *Innocents Abroad*, but his new book
would place him among an exclusive number of authentic American
literati. Fairbanks summed up the impact the cruise had on Clemens
quite well: "The *Quaker City* sailed out of New York Harbor with no
celebrities on board. She brought back the Great American Humor-
ist."

Innocents Abroad struck a chord in a receptive readership. People
appreciated the humor of this "New American Vandal" who called
himself "Mark Twain"; they liked his irreverent trashing of what
others revered. And Clemens's work has remained accessible despite
the passage of time. In its posture as a seemingly fresh and realistic
glimpse of the East through an unfettered American gaze, it serves
well in a study of American travel experiences in the Holy Land and
how those experiences were affected by, or themselves implicated,
the image of the Holy Land in the American mind.[13]

Literary critic Alfred Kazin prefaced a 1964 edition of *Innocents Abroad* with the observation that the work's narrator was a relatively new creation called "Mark Twain." This new character emerged as a "self-declared and self-describing" type of literary figure: "the American," an image "more consciously a disturbance than a hero," a character who "made a game of opposing himself to settled patterns of tradition and culture. Forever on the move, the character insisted that his unrest be taken for freshness and innovation."[14] Kazin said Clemens's use of "the American" was what made *Innocents Abroad* "such a distinct and comic creation." The book was a portrait of this new character as Clemens set about contrasting New World

RETURN IN WAR-PAINT.

Fig. 3. "MARK TWAIN" AS THE "AMERICAN VANDAL." The comic creation "Mark Twain" as the "American Vandal," an obviously New World figure in buckskin, capable of a fresh view of the Old World. Illustration from *Innocents Abroad*.

attitudes against the culture of the Old World. Clemens's work thereby became the initiator of a new age of Holy Land awareness; having spied out the Promised Land, this "American Vandal" saw neither milk, honey, giant inhabitants, nor overripe fruit. What he did see was the myth of a land encumbered with preexistent imagery.

Americans have usually measured themselves against their images of others. Historian Daniel Boorstin pointed out that, as a people, Americans are "dominated by the spectre of known foreign ancestors . . . obsessed by a parental image" derived from a knowledge of their point of departure from the Old World and a "point of arrival" in the New.[15] One result of this obsession, in the nineteenth century, was the idea of an antithesis between European and American. The European represented the corrupt and accumulated vices of the past. The American was the "New Man" with a fresh outlook facing virgin possibilities—an idea that resonated with the Puritan view of America as utopia or Eden. This was the attitude Clemens carried with him to the Holy Land. Yet for all his ridicule, Clemens occasionally displayed a certain reverence for the authentically aged, a reverence that momentarily suspended his narrator's sardonic manner and allowed him to express a sense of "awe and appreciation," such as when (apparently in earnest) he exclaimed over the sight of the biblical Bethel: "What a history this place has! How strange to stand here on the camping-ground of the Patriarchs."[16] This mix of fresh spirit, skepticism, and innocence made the Gilded Age the great watershed period for reflections of American travelers to the Holy Land.

Kazin noted too that much of the cockiness associated with Americans in *Innocents Abroad* related to a time when Americans still thought they were the only democrats and levelers in the world and when they were mostly Anglo-Saxon and Protestant. "This historic confidence of the Anglo-Saxon-cum-Protestant is very important to the *Innocents Abroad*."[17] Charles Nieder, editor of a compilation of Clemens's travel writings, even questioned how accurate the "innocents" of the title was, in light of the just-concluded Civil War. Nieder suggested that "many members of the group were going to seek innocence, not in Europe, but in the Holy Land."[18] By contrast, Kazin suggested, the title implied only "innocent of tradition but nothing else."[19]

Regardless of the title's implications, *Innocents Abroad* demands attention—not solely for the quality of its prose or the extent to which it underwent revision and change, but also because it summarized several American experiences and reactions to the Holy Land. As literary historian Franklin Walker noted, "It does not seem arbitrary to assert that Browne's *Yusef*, Melville's *Clarel*, and Mark Twain's *The Innocents Abroad* are the three most important literary works to result from American visits to the Holy Land during the nineteenth century or, for that matter, up to the present time."[20] Clemens's account of the *Quaker City* trip became a classic in American literature because of its unique sarcasm and sense of humor, but it was not the only telling of the *Quaker City* story. Moses Beach, owner of the *New York Sun*, wrote a series of thirty letters to his paper published under "Editorial Correspondence." And the journal letters of Emily Severance, another *Quaker City* passenger who traveled to Palestine in the company of Mary Fairbanks, were published by her family in 1938. Written to the "folks back home," the Severance letters provided another perspective on the "grand excursion." The thoughts of both Fairbanks and Severance are included in next chapter's analysis.

Fellow American Vandals

An array of other Americans, in parties of various sizes, traveled to the Holy Land between 1865 and 1882. Among them was Henry Whitney Bellows, a Unitarian clergyman born in Boston in 1814 to an old New England family. As a young minister, he assumed the prestigious pulpit of New York City's First Unitarian Church. Bellows was known as a brilliant conversationalist and was a popular club member as well. "In his preaching he was always springing some surprises on the community, sometimes a bold theological heresy, sometimes the advocacy of an unpopular reform, and sometimes the championship of a misunderstood class."[21] Bellows was a true liberal in the best Unitarian tradition. He was a man of "wide reading, quick insight, and great power of interpretation. . . . Conservative in feeling, he was often radical in thought."[22] His book *The Old World in Its New Face* gave his impressions of his foreign travels, and the five reprintings attest to its popularity.[23]

John Franklin Swift—merchant, lawyer, politician, and diplomat—was born in Missouri to poor parents in 1829. He was a self-made man in the finest American tradition. Migrating west with a mule train in 1852 after learning the tinsmithing trade in St. Louis, Swift ended up in San Francisco, where he studied law in his spare time while earning money as a successful produce merchant and was later admitted to the bar. In 1865 he was appointed registrar of the U.S. Land Office of San Francisco by President Lincoln, but he soon resigned to tour Europe and the Middle East. After his return to California in 1868, he became involved in politics and eventually ran unsuccessfully for governor in 1880. He concluded his long career by serving as U.S. minister to China and Japan.

Swift had a reputation as an "exceptionally popular after-dinner speaker," and in this vein he wrote *Going to Jericho*, a narrative of his 1867 trip through Palestine. In the opening pages Swift declared that he "endeavored to be truthful and to represent what I saw of the world as I saw it, and to comment on what I saw from my own standpoint." He continued:

> If I did not look with absolute veneration upon all ancient things simply because they were ancient, and did sometimes question the verity of well-authenticated traditions, it is rather the fault of an education that has been practical to the fullest extent of the American idea, and an education that demands proofs to sustain arguments.[24]

The parallels between Swift's and Clemens's books are tidy: both were written from retranscribed and adapted letters first published in San Francisco daily newspapers, and both were the products of minds that had matured in the American West. The story of the genesis of Swift's trip to the Holy Land is as amusing as Mark Twain's, only more frivolous. Swift related that the circumstances of his trip eastward were haphazard, the result of an incidental remark a fellow Californian made while the two of them were in Paris. During some light conversation, the Californian had remarked to Swift that Paris was getting cold and dull. "Very well, where shall we go?" Swift asked his friend, who responded, "I am indifferent. I will go to Spain, to Italy, to Jericho, if you please." "Suppose we go to all of them in that order, beginning with Spain," Swift offered. "That is better; we will do it and start tomorrow," was the reply. And so they did, going to Spain first, then Italy, and then by boat to Alexandria and on to Jaffa.

One traveler who experienced the Holy Land with a little more planning than Swift was Charles Wyllys Elliott. Elliott, born in Guilford, Connecticut, on May 27, 1817, was a lineal descendant of John Eliot, the famed "Apostle to the Indians" of early New England. Elliott's background was not theological in any other sense; he had studied landscape gardening and horticulture and was successful in the iron business. Active in various literary, philanthropic, and civic pursuits, Elliott was the author of *Remarkable Characters and*

Places of the Holy Land, which first appeared in 1867 and was reprinted in 1868, 1869, and 1874; an expanded, revised version came out in 1885 under a new title: *Heroes of the Bible and Bible Lands*. The work served to supplement the scriptures, examining the "human side" of the Bible in order to bring out "human nature and the real life of the wonderful characters which have lived in the Holy Land."[25] Even though Elliott did not have a theological education, his book had a tone of authoritative sanctity.

By contrast, the work of another traveler, Nathaniel Clark Burt, approached a level of scholarly detachment. A Princeton-trained Presbyterian minister, Burt was born in New Jersey in 1825 and died in Rome, Italy, in 1874. Traveling to Europe and the Levant for his health in 1866–67, he tried to apply his theological and biblical knowledge to investigations of localities and sites of the Bible. He published two works on the Holy Land: *The Far East: A Collection of Letters from Egypt, Palestine, and "Other Lands of the Orient,"* which appeared in 1868, and his more substantial *The Land and Its Story*, which appeared in 1869; the latter was primarily concerned with the historical geography of the Holy Land.

Burt intended to place the geography of the Holy Land in the context of its "sacred history,"[26] so *The Land and Its Story* is therefore largely a geographical work that describes the sites and localities of the Bible as they existed in 1867 and in the land's distant past. Burt visited Palestine equipped with what he believed was "a good knowledge of its historical geography, having not only given attention to the subject for many years, but having also gone over it, systematically and repeatedly, with the young people of my pastoral charge."[27] Yet when he visited the scenes of sacred story he found his previous views lamentably defective and erroneous. As a result of his trip, Scripture history assumed a new, vivid distinctness and reality for Burt.

William Leonard Gage was a Congregational minister from Hartford, Connecticut. He too, like Nathaniel Burt, had a passion for geography and exploration. In 1869 Gage's *Studies in Bible Lands* appeared, developed from a course of twelve lectures Gage delivered in the spring of 1867 at the Lowell Institute in Boston. The volume was received unenthusiastically at first, so it was republished in a more enticing format under the more direct title *The Land of Sacred Mystery*.

Gage's purpose in writing a work on biblical geography was entirely pragmatic. He sought to show the visible growth of the ancient Israelites from the times of the Patriarchs by tracing the intermingling of Bible history with physical locality. But he was defensive about the depth of his study, arguing that much of the detailed and debatable portions of other works were "utterly unattractive to most Americans at least." He added:

> The antiquarian instinct is not strong with us as a nation: wherever it exists, it is unexceptional; and it would be folly to presume on interesting an American public in problems which invoke no enthusiasm beyond a circle comprising a few hundred Englishmen, Frenchmen, and Germans. . . . It will best answer our purposes to take the results of scholarly inquiry and endeavor to apply them to our single and simple end, the making of our Bible reading and study more intelligible and therefore more interesting.[28]

Jacob Freese was a physician who also served as a U.S. commissioner to the Paris Exposition of 1867, a target destination of the *Quaker City* cruise. Freese had the reputation of learning as much as possible about the subject matter of his books, and he wrote a number of volumes on a wide variety of subjects—medical, civic, and religious. His work on Palestine first appeared in 1869 under the title *The Old World*, but by the time it was published in its fourth edition its title had changed to the more appropriate *Travels in the Holy Land*.

Freese's goal was to write a faithful firsthand account of the country, and he believed that "in faithfulness of description the following pages will bear comparison with others heretofore written by travelers." Essentially, the book reproduced Freese's journal for his trip to the Holy Land and through Asia Minor in March and April of 1867, a technique that was almost endemic to the genre of travel literature. In the preface, Freese wrote that Palestine must be seen and felt to know it well, suggesting that merely knowing the sources of its literary importance was insufficient because one must "suffer more or less of personal discomfort while traveling day after day and week after week over paths the most rugged, mountains the most desolate, and plains the most sterile of all the world beside."[29]

Joseph Inskeep Taylor's travel account, *A Gyre Thro' the Orient*, was not, according to the author, written to fall among other travel books, sitting unsold, "buried in the tomb of oblivion." Taylor, "acting upon the trite old adage, that a bird in the hand is worth two in the bush," caught his "gulls" before starting to write; he sold his work by subscription prior to "adventuring in the enterprise" and made it known to subscribers that if any of them felt they did not get what they bargained for, "let the matter be a quarrel between them and myself; let those who are not subscribers stand aloof; it's not their funeral; let them understand that the *Gyre* was not written for them; that they are eaves-droppers, poachers, climbers-over-the-wall, for reading it at all."[30] The book was produced simply to perpetuate the author's experiences in his own mind and to instruct and amuse his personal friends.

In 1867 Taylor traveled from Switzerland, Bavaria, and Austria, through the Balkans, Turkey, and on to the Levant. Although he also traveled in Italy and Egypt, he did not write about his experiences in those countries. He claimed to be glad to concentrate on "that most interesting of all countries of earth—Palestine." In a delightfully provincial style, he also apologized for any excesses of description: "That we have put the varnish on a little thick in places is probable, we modestly suggest, that justice might ascribe this to the zeal and enthusiasm of an ardent nature, rather than a willingness to exaggerate or misstate the facts."[31] Taylor wrote that he would not be surprised if "a few (so-called) orthodox Christian readers may be found, who will see some things on the pages of the *Gyre*, that will not be entirely dished up to suit their palates" and pledged

Fig. 4. JOSEPH TAYLOR, HOLY LAND TOURIST. Midwesterner Joseph Taylor was typical of many American Holy Land tourists in the nineteenth century. After his 1867 tour of Palestine, he returned to the United States and felt compelled to share his travel experiences with other Americans. Taylor wrote about them in a delightful, no-nonsense manner.

that he had tried to treat the subject "as a neutral man, and not as a lawyer [Taylor was a lawyer by profession] or sectarian devotee." Actually, he wrote, "I am happy . . . in the faith that the Christian believer will find much to approve in what I have said about Palestine; if I had not been able to fill the measure of his approbation, I can't help it; it is better to come a little short of this, than be a hypocrite."[32]

There were also a number of prominent (or yet-to-be prominent) Americans who toured the Holy Land during the Gilded Age and wrote about (or had others write about) their experiences. The Roosevelt family, including young Theodore Jr., left New York for a tour of Europe and the Levant in the autumn of 1872. The previous summer the asthmatic fourteen-year-old had been given his first rifle, prompting the discovery that the boy needed spectacles.[33] The glasses opened up new vistas to the already nature-observant Theodore (he was just beginning to learn taxidermy), and his diary entries during his tour displayed a talent for keen observation. According to the journal, the future president very nearly shot up the Holy Land, felling all manner of fowl on almost every day of the family's sojourn. At one point, traveling between Jaffa and Jerusalem, the overeager shootist even mistook an unfortunate cat for a rabbit.[34]

A prominent churchman who traveled to the Holy Land around that time was Edwards Amasa Park, the last of the Protestant theologians of the old, orthodox Calvinist school. Park was a teacher at Andover Theological Seminary, and among his pupils was the future U.S. consul to Jerusalem, Selah Merrill, who believed Park was one of the "highest ranks of leaders."[35] Park toured the Holy Land in 1869 and took up a brief residence in Jerusalem, "the city of his love," where he was said to wander alone, absorbed in religious meditation. He investigated the city's topography and explored the geography and history of such Holy Land sites as the Dead Sea, the Jordan, and the Sea of Galilee. Park worked to gather "a rich harvest of biblical learning and Christian sentiment from the places which have been consecrated by the feet of the prophets and apostles and of the great Teacher of the World."[36]

Church historian Philip Schaff was moved to travel to the East in 1876 by the tragedy of the death of a daughter, to "gain relief and fresh inspiration for Bible studies." He wrote letters to his friends at home out of a sense of obligation to share his experiences and privilege in being able to travel. "Bible lands, like the Bible itself," Schaff postulated, "are of such universal and perennial interest that they continually demand new books and new comments."[37] He therefore decided to give his letters a wider circulation, and published them in book form in 1878.

Acclaimed Presbyterian clergyman Thomas DeWitt Talmage made his trip to the Holy Land in December 1889. Worried that he might be shown false or spurious locations and antiquities—seeing the wrong sites, he feared, might shake his faith—he was reassured when he realized he only needed to be prepared first. For example, Talmage arranged to baptize a Christian in the Jordan River, to ensure that he would enjoy a proper experience at that particular site.[38]

Henry Van Dyke, a versatile author and clergyman, had reservations about confronting the reality of Palestine firsthand, so he put off a trip to the Holy Land until he was in the right frame of mind and the right circumstances. Van Dyke had entertained a boyhood dream to go to Palestine, but lack of money and time made him postpone the trip. Then, in early manhood, "I was afraid to go to Palestine, lest the journey should prove a disenchantment, and some of my religious beliefs be rudely shaken, perhaps destroyed. But that fear was removed by a little voyage to the gates of death, where it was made clear to me that no belief is worth keeping unless it can bear the touch of reality."[39]

Former President Ulysses S. Grant's journey around the world between 1877 and 1879 was heralded as "one of the most important events in modern history":[40]

> The distinguished American ex-president, though traveling as a simple citizen of the United States, has made the most remarkable journey in all recorded history, seeing more, and being more honored and admitted to closer confidence, by the rulers of mankind, than any individual who ever undertook to seek instruction or recreation by extensive travels through foreign lands. The whole journey was like a romance.[41]

The trip seized the imagination of the American public and held it. On May 17, 1877, former President and Mrs. Grant left Philadelphia for England. Their trip lasted two years and was proclaimed "perhaps the grandest tour an American couple had ever had." As William McFeely observed in his recent biography of Grant,

> The two tourists were themselves on display. The unpretentious man in the dark suit was his country's greatest warrior-hero, and the world wanted to have a look at him. The gen-

Fig. 5.   PRESIDENT AND MRS. GRANT ON TOUR IN THE MIDDLE EAST.   The unflappable general and former U.S. president, with his wife Julia and a retinue of reporters, toured the Middle East during a two-year world tour that began in 1877. The Grants were among a number of prominent citizens whose tours of the Holy Land were of keen interest to Americans at home.

eral and his lady were ambassadors of both American simplicity and American power. They exemplified their strange democracy, which had uneasily made itself into a nation-state and was about to become a great power.[42]

The Grant trip started as a personal getaway after eight trying years in the White House that concluded with a growing catcall over the corruption of Grant's administration. The former president and his wife decided to vacation in Europe to escape the public row of politics. With a daughter already living in England, the British Isles were a natural destination, but the trip would not remain a quiet family visit. It began to accrue an entourage as the European clamor to see America's champion rose and more social commitments were made. John Russell Young, reporter for the *New York Herald* and a future Librarian of Congress, reported on the trip to a curious nation.

After a tumultuous tour through Britain, during which they were embraced by working people and entertained by the queen, the Grants went on to Paris in October 1877, where their party assumed more of the guise of a grand tour rather than a pseudo-political trip that brought out crowds in England. By winter, the party boarded the U.S. Navy's *Vandalia* for a Mediterranean cruise that included Italy and Egypt before reaching the Holy Land.

Correspondent Young reported that, aboard the *Vandalia*, the Grant party was anxious about the weather, since foul weather would prevent a landing at Jaffa and imperil the tour of Palestine. "The idea of a visit to the East without setting our feet on the Holy Land was not to be endured," Young wrote. The party was therefore thankful when they found they could land at Jaffa in calm seas.

All these travelers to the Holy Land do not by any means form a comprehensive group, but they are representative of American tourists and pilgrims of the time who responded to the powerful allure of the Holy Land by actually journeying to see the place. As American Protestants in the Gilded Age, they descended on the Holy Land in record numbers, ready to scrutinize the land and pass along their impressions.

Doing Canaan

One of the most intriguing aspects of the *Quaker City* cruise was its designation as a "pleasure excursion," a voyage devoted entirely to the pleasures of its passengers—in a typically nineteenth-century Victorian sense, spiritual, intellectual, and educational. Indeed, if the jargon of the nineteenth century shows something of what its people were thinking, then the description that American travelers "did" the sites during their tours (moving about with impatience and at a generally accelerated pace) implies for us that the "doing" of nineteenth-century touring was quite rigorous.[43] This was especially true for the Holy Land tourist, who until late in the nineteenth century was subject to a number of perils when traveling through Palestine. As late as 1882, one American consul-general, J. Augustus Johnson, offered a discouraging assessment of the Holy Land's tourist environment. The climate, Johnson wrote, "is unfavorable for the foreigner, and is often fatal to the tourist. The graves of modern travelers and explorers may be seen from Dan to Beer Sheba, and from Jerusalem to Damascus."[44]

Johnson might have been given to some exaggeration, but one American tourist struck a note of macabre pride at the discovery of

Fig. 6. THE *QUAKER CITY* AT SEA.   Despite being touted as a "plea-sure excursion," the first organized tour of Europe and the Holy Land had its perils, as did most Holy Land travel during the nineteenth cen-tury. Here the ship *Quaker City* is depicted as riding out a violent storm at sea. Illustration from *Innocents Abroad*.

an American cemetery on Mount Zion, next to the Armenian, Greek, and English cemeteries. Tourist Joseph Taylor described the cemetery as

> fitted up with far more elegance and extravagance than any or either of the others; it comprises an area of nearly half an acre of ground, enclosed with a substantial stone wall about fourteen feet high, smoothly plastered with clean, white stucco; and is entered through a ponderous iron door from the east side. It contains the graves of eight or ten Americans.

He also informed his readers with peculiar pleasure and sarcastic reassurance that should any of them contemplate making a pil-grimage and be unfortunate enough to "fall a victim to pestilence or lose his scalp among the Bedouins . . . his remains will repose secure from the raids of the hungry vulture and jackal that hold their carnivorous feasts daily and nightly upon the shallow-buried dead in the neighboring graveyards."[45] In spite of such glum assessments of the survivability of visitors to the Holy Land, Americans flocked eastward in record numbers after the Civil War.

At Jaffa in 1867, Californian John Franklin Swift observed that of the twenty-five passengers disembarking from his steamer all were Americans and all but one were Protestants.[46] Henry Bellows, also traveling in 1867, found that Americans were common during the season of his visit.[47] And Jacob Freese recorded that aboard his boat traveling to Alexandria, Egypt, and Jaffa were sixteen Americans bound for the Holy Land and Europe. Freese took special pleasure in meeting compatriots so far from home and expressed delight in sharing experiences "where everything is new, and strange, and untried; and it gives us pleasure to add that now, more than ever before, that [an] American, traveling in foreign lands, is proud to own himself a citizen of the Great Republic."[48] Freese's comments bespoke that great, collective sigh that the Civil War was over. It was a time for travel, to spend as well as to accumulate wealth. Freese noted further:

> The number of American travelers now in Jerusalem, and traveling through Syria, is far greater than ever was known before, and far exceeds in numbers those of any other nation, and who, so far as we have found their acquaintanceship, are generally such as represent American thrift, enterprise, and intelligence.[49]

Perhaps thrift and enterprise were better represented among the Americans than intelligence, at least in the eyes of other, non-American travelers in the Holy Land. Certainly, the cost of a trip to the Levant made travel there prohibitive to most Americans, but the Americans who were rushing overseas and visiting the Holy Land during the Gilded Age were an educated lot, newly sobered by a bloody, four-year war and capable of astutely observing the reality of what they viewed. They were neither overtly sanctimonious nor unrepentantly blasphemous. Nonetheless, it should be clear that their impressions and experiences were not derived entirely from what they saw, but also from what they anticipated seeing: a land that existed in the remote past, locked in a time Americans were aware of only through their most sacred traditions and literature.

As American tourist travel to the Levant increased after the Civil War, so did the potential for an alteration in America's image of the Holy Land. The very fact that the land was exposed to greater scrutiny by a larger number of Americans is sufficient cause to suppose that the Holy Land would come into sharper focus as a reality. A heightened awareness was one of the generic effects of touring as a social process, according to sociologist Willis Sutton: "Touring may often make for genuine communication and an increase in realistic understanding. . . . The newness and specialness of the situation for the visitor may leave him open to new ideas."[50] Such was not quite the case, however. Americans' views of the Holy Land were steeped in the myth of the past, and America's bi-form perspective—the image/reality process whereby the Holy Land was perceived as place and past—steadfastly shaped travelers' views of Palestine's landscape and peoples.

During the Gilded Age, for example, Americans arrived in the Holy Land with a variety of expectations derived from certain preconceived notions. Some expected to see the Bible's setting and its cast of characters, and some even expected to see scriptural dramas enacted before their eyes. Some Americans expected the Holy Land's landscape to be larger, more mountainous, or greener, its rivers longer and broader, its cities more familiar. Some arrived expecting to see remnants of the primitive and evidence of the past in everyday Holy Land life: survivals from the pagan Canaanites, defeated or renewed Jews, infidel Muslims, and backward, ignorant Eastern Christians. These expectations surfaced in the observations of Americans and in some ways molded the tourist experience. There were prescribed conventions, routes to follow, adventures to be sampled, and also certain rewards to be gained in terms of personal growth. For some, a trip to the Holy Land was believed necessary for a better homiletical understanding of the Bible:[51] The landscape of Palestine would provide inspiration and elucidation, and the peoples of Palestine and their condition would provide living illustrations of biblical customs and the results of biblical prophecies. Some Americans believed that seeing the land associated with the life of Jesus could provide his followers with a better picture of his ministry, or that the land itself would make it clear how it came to be so important to three faiths. Besides such expectations, Americans had many experiences in common once they arrived in the Holy Land—modes of travel, accommodations and food, and also visits to sacred sites, the countryside, the cities, and contacts with the native populace.[52] Travelers' recollections of these experiences usually reflected an orientation to the past. It was inevitable as well that specific mannerisms became associated with the behavior of American Holy Land travelers. These mannerisms were usually shared and identified as being characteristically "American" traits, such as informality, independence, and impatience. While in themselves interesting as expressions of the "American spirit," these traits had a dual effect: they both highlighted the extent and nature of America's Holy Land imagery and served as evidence of American expressions of geopiety.

Themes in the accounts of the American tourist experience in the Holy Land, and in the reactions to the reality of Ottoman Palestine, fall into several categories: conditions of touring, perceptions of the landscape, perceptions of the native populace and their situation, the credibility of sacred sites, and mannerisms of traveling Americans. The travelers' reports reviewed in the next chapter provide a sampling of the American tourist experience and reveal these patterns.

CHAPTER 3

Sojourns in Dreamland
Understanding on Holy Ground

Travel through the Holy Land during the late Ottoman period was an increasingly pleasant experience. Before 1914, modern technological and civil improvements were slow in coming to Palestine, but when they finally came, such improvements as better roads were the direct result of tourism, not of native requests. Walls were breached and telegraphs were installed to accommodate visiting dignitaries, and in 1892 a railway opened between Jaffa and Jerusalem to facilitate travel of Western Christians to Jerusalem. Curiously, improvement of Jaffa's harbor, an obviously related necessity, was not undertaken.

Tenting Under Sacred Skies

The period that saw the visits of Samuel Clemens, Theodore Roosevelt, and President Grant was perhaps the golden age of tent-travel life in the Holy Land. Lacking a developed network of reliable hotels, tourists contracted the services of "dragomen," who coordinated all travel arrangements, including field accommodations, provisions, and surface transportation (most often horses and donkeys).

The adventure of securing dragomen and their services, however, was one of the pitfalls of touring. Even before arriving in the Holy Land, the excursionists aboard the *Quaker City* were anxious about the state of Palestine's transportation services. "We knew very well," wrote Clemens, "that Palestine was a country which did do a large passenger business, and every man we came across who knew anything about it gave us to understand that not half our party would be able to get dragomen and animals."[1] Consequently, the *Quaker City* tourists began frantically wiring the American consuls in Alexandria and Beirut "to give notice that we wanted dragomen and transportation." Clemens went on:

> We were desperate, would take horses, jackasses, camelopards, kangaroos—anything. . . . As might have been expected, a notion got abroad in Syria and Egypt that the whole population of the province of America (the Turks consider us a trifling little province in some unvisited corner of the world) were coming to the Holy Land—and so, when we got to Beirut yesterday, we found the place full of dragomen and their outfits.

The tumult created by the needs of so large a party as the one on the *Quaker City* can well be imagined. Clemens reported that the preparations for overland travel were a fearful nuisance to the U.S. consul at Beirut. "I cannot help admiring his patience, his industry, and his accommodating spirit," Clemens wrote, especially in light of what seemed to Clemens a lack of proper appreciation by others in the ship's company.

The *Quaker City* excursionists were treated to the option of choosing the way they would prefer entering the Holy Land. At Beirut, all passengers toured the adjacent areas of Lebanon and Syria, primarily Baalbek and Damascus. After several days, the ship sailed down the coast to Haifa harbor, at the foot of Mount Carmel. One group of passengers, however, elected to travel into Palestine over land instead of returning to the ship. Clemens joined that party.

The group was outfitted for its overland ride—a trip that lasted three weeks, until they rejoined the ship at Jaffa—by a delegated "business committee," which secured a competent dragoman and reported to the others that "we would live as well as at a hotel." Clemens was not to be duped, however. He prepared for the trip by gathering the barest necessities, anticipating what would be lacking in the field. He packed a blanket and a shawl to sleep in, pipes and tobacco, two or three woolen shirts, a portfolio, a guidebook, and a Bible, as well as "a towel and a cake of soap, to inspire respect" among the natives "who would take me for a king in disguise."[2] Clemens left Beirut for Jerusalem in a party of eight excursionists, six dragomen, fourteen serving men, and twenty-four mules and horses.[3]

The first night, after unsaddling and washing his horse, Clemens was surprised to find "five stately circus tents were up—tents that were brilliant within with blue and gold and crimson and all manner of splendid adornment. I was speechless." He also described the camping accoutrements with a sense of wonder, implying that the arrangements rivaled those aboard the *Quaker City*. Clemens was taken in by the luxury of the experience, the "soft mattresses and pillows and good blankets and two snow white sheets, . . . the pewter pitchers, basins, soap, and white towels," the carpets on the floor, the dining saloon tent—"a gem of a place"—and a sumptuous feast of a meal. "They call this camping out," he wrote. "At this rate it is a glorious privilege to be a pilgrim to the Holy Land."[4] Clemens later

Fig. 7. UNEXPECTED COMFORTS WHEN TENTING OUT. Unanticipated luxury frequently made the out-of-doors tour through the Holy Land surprisingly comfortable for Americans. Here members of the *Quaker City* party dine elegantly under canvas. Illustration from *Innocents Abroad*.

expressed bewilderment about the way the pack animals did not reveal any of their cargoes, including the camp bathtub. He conjectured that the dragomen actually concealed an Aladdin's lamp for these purposes and said he wouldn't be surprised if the dragomen had brought along a piano as well.[5]

Another *Quaker City* traveler, Emily Severance, took the ship from Beirut to the foot of Mount Carmel, where she sampled the camp life and wrote, "We live like princes."[6] For San Franciscan John Franklin Swift, tent life was almost as pleasant as it was for Clemens, but in retrospect he said the experience could be summed up in this way: "The first night of tent life is the best night of tent life." He was not unhappy with the experience, however.

> When we returned to bed it was evidently the settled opinion of every one of the party that of all modes of life that had ever been thought of, tent life was the one that was best calculated to produce perfect happiness. And further, that of the different circumstances under which tent life could be followed, that of tent life in the Holy Land came nearest absolute perfection. The dinner was good, the beds were soft, the air balmy, and all nature seemed to join in a general design to make us comfortable and happy.[7]

Tenting was not always a pleasant experience for the tourists, especially those caught in the occasionally heavy wind and rain storms of the late winter season. For example, in March 1874 a spate of unusually foul weather throughout the Levant caused several tourist bands to huddle in overcrowded convents or to brave the outdoors, where they might find their shoes, pants, and baggage floating next to them in tents that were rapidly becoming unpinned.[8]

The availability of shelter in convents was a long-standing feature of Holy Land travel, and the hospitality of some convents was apparently highly regarded. Clemens was impressed by the service offered: "Without these hospitable retreats, travel in Palestine would be a pleasure which none but the strongest men could dare undertake. Our party, pilgrims and all, will always be ready and always willing to touch glasses and drink health, prosperity, and long life to the convent Fathers of Palestine."[9] Like Clemens, Swift was quite impressed with the selfless hospitality of the Catholic Franciscans, and he felt he should caution those who would procure the services of a dragoman to make sure the dragoman did not cheat the kindly clerics in the freewill offerings after enjoying a convent's hospitality.[10]

Although competent dragomen tended to the food needs of American tourists, Joseph Taylor noticed one particularly bothersome aspect of Holy Land cuisine: there were no hogs or milk cows to be seen in Palestine, so there was no lard or butter or "other kinds of shortening used in Christian countries. As a result, everything that one eats in the form of food is seasoned with everlasting sheep's tail." This peculiarity of Eastern cooking made all food "taste sheepy —the very kitchens of the country smell like sheep folds. From all of which I deduced the conclusion, that the land, instead of flowing with milk and honey as it used to do, now flows with sheeptallow."[11]

Travel conditions during the Gilded Age were considerably safer for Westerners than earlier in the nineteenth century. However, there were some reminders of the perils of the former days. In leaving the town of Tiberias, the local sheikh imposed on Clemens's party "a wretched-looking scallywag . . . as a guard" to protect the group from marauding nomads, but in fact, Clemens wrote, his party never once saw a bedouin. This led Clemens to scorn the supposed danger of bedouin marauders. The "protection" supplied by the mangy, ill-armed guard out of Tiberias was a splendid target for his barbs. His annoyance was not concealed during the journey either, when, stumbling around in the dark, his party could not find the Jordan River. Clemens and a companion fell asleep on the ground, incensing the guard the next morning, for it demonstrated scorn for the guard's protection in what was reputed to be the most dangerous area of the country.[12]

Emily Severance said her party was also warned about the treachery of bedouins. Occasionally, she fearfully noted "their black tents in several places, and in the distance, five mounted horsemen, all quite in advance of us." When her party turned to water their mounts at a fountain, the bedouins did likewise, but no trouble ensued because, she reasoned, her party outnumbered them and several of the men in her group were well armed.[13] As for the mandatory native guards attached to their group, Severance noted that they "were not very war-like in appearance."[14]

Clemens's group traveled down the Lebanon Valley, visited Baalbek and Damascus as planned, and continued on into the Holy Land. With any clear demarcation lacking, Clemens was not quite awed by his entrance into the country. He observed that his party "had hardly begun to appreciate yet that we were standing upon any different sort of earth than we had always been used to,"[15] yet he noted reverently, while touring Caesarea Philippi, that he was at "the first place we have seen whose pavements were trodden by Christ."[16]

Fig. 8. FIRST VIEW OF THE HOLY LAND. Unlike tourists who arrived by sea and landed at Jaffa, Mark Twain had his first view of the
Holy Land as he looked westward from Mount Hermon toward Nim-
rod's Castle, called Subeibah today. This view of the Holy Land,
nestled in the valley below with the mountains of Lebanon rising beyond, moved Twain to observe how a cannonball could easily traverse
the holy ground and reach profane land beyond.

    Differentiating between Palestine and Syria was difficult for an-
other American traveler too. Clara Erskine Waters visited the Holy
Land in the 1860s in the company of four other Americans, and
when she returned she printed a small pamphlet-like souvenir of her
recollections, in which she wrote: "It is difficult to separate Syria
from Palestine in our minds, they are so connected in history; and as
we pass through them, it is quite impossible for us to do so."[17] The
color and confusion that was the reality of the East was somewhat
different from Waters's notions of the land of the Bible. The nodding palms, fruit trees, empty deserts, trains of camels, and "swarthy
Turks in fez or turbans, with their flowing garments and broad
sashes, and scimitars" were aspects she had not associated with the
land of the Bible, the Patriarchs, Joshua, David, and Jesus. And yet
the sites formed a palpable whole to her:

What other land holds out such varied inducements, or makes so many promises to travelers of every class? . . . We are all of us, to a greater or less extent, wide awake dreamers; that is to say, that, in our most wakeful and thoughtful hours we picture ourselves things apparently as strange and unlikely to be experienced as any of the weird, disjointed pictures of the real dream-land.[18]

Unitarian minister Henry Bellows's first glimpse of the Holy Land came in the late afternoon on a bright day as he was coming down off the Mount Hermon range toward Acre. From a distance, he thought, some of the stone villages in the midst of spring-green fruit trees and lemon groves gave the immediate impression of New England. Yet as he approached these villages he found them

gloomy, filthy, and repulsive. The farming is all shiftless and primitive in its tools and methods; the people are inconceivably wretched. But with the evening light upon these hills and athwart this broad level, with the Mediterranean breaking upon the western shore, I am willing to accept this first view of Palestine as not unworthy the Holy Land. Everything seems gentler and more fertile.[19]

In sharp contrast, Clemens described the area approaching the Lake of Galilee as "a horrible, rocky, barren desert (like Nevada)."[20]

Joseph Taylor was quick to describe the land as abounding with the "overwhelming evidences of the truth of scriptural prophecy." Despite its delightful climate and fruitful soil, Taylor declared, the land stood as mute testimony of the Lord's "punishment" of a wayward people. The silent remains "stand thickly by the wayside of the tourist, as he journeys over the country, to testify that here once existed a great and powerful race: far advanced in the arts and sciences, and in wealth, and enterprise."[21] Continuing in the vein that what he was seeing was the result of divine damnation, Taylor remarked that the tight clustering of Palestine's dwellings—never more than one hundred yards separated neighbors—was attributable to the marauding attacks of bedouins who

have infested this country for centuries past; successfully defying all the authorities and powers of the wretched government that claims dominions over the land. These things wonderfully fulfill the prophecy of Ezekiel, offered when the Jews ruled the country with laws that gave some protection to life

and property: I will give it [Palestine] into the hands of the
strangers for a prey, and to the wicked of the earth for a
spoil. . . . Robbers shall enter in and defile it. . . . The land is
full of bloody crimes, and the city is full of violence.[22]

Because Clara Waters had come by way of Egypt, she landed at
Jaffa instead of traveling down from Syria as Clemens had done.
Waters observed that Jaffa was an inconvenient port at which to land
because it had no natural harbor—all passengers had to be off-
loaded into smaller boats, which would then slip through the narrow
opening of a breakwater many yards offshore—an unmajestic and
unfitting way, perhaps, to enter the Holy Land. Before leaving Jaffa,
the Waters party gathered on the roof of the town's hotel, "the very
worst hotel it has been my fortune to see," from which they could
view

> luxuriant orange groves and green fields. . . . Distant moun-
> tains, lifting their heads to kissing clouds, seemed to beckon
> us on to scenes hallowed by our Savior's lowly life of love and
> sacrifice: and my heart went out in earnest prayer that an
> enlarged faith should be given men, and spiritual good, as
> well as increased knowledge, be the result of the pilgrimage in
> the Holy Land.[23]

Young Theodore Roosevelt arrived at Jaffa on February 24, 1873,
and was immediately dismayed at the house of Simon the Tanner,
which "looked modern and unreal." As for Jaffa itself, the teenage
boy called it "thoroughly oriental with very pretty women and children."[24] And in his journey to Jerusalem from Jaffa, Swift observed:
"the progressive character of the nineteenth century has stamped
itself even upon this ancient pathway. The road of Solomon and of
Samson, of Judas Maccabeus and Simon Peter, had been marked by
the investive genius of America. The poles and wires of the magnetic
telegraph mark and bound the slender trail."[25]

Although modern technologies were, for some, a source of pride
in their American origins,[26] the intrusiveness of modernity and technology was a lamentable element for many travelers. They spoiled
the pastoral ideal the travelers carried to the Holy Land, and represented a further retreat from the Holy Land's primitive abandoned
and decayed state, a condition that had been prophesied in the Bible.

After landing at Jaffa, the Roosevelt family departed for Jerusalem, stopping overnight at Ramleh. The journey on horseback gave young "Teddie" the chance to observe the quality of the group's mounts. Roosevelt thought his horse was the best of a good lot, with some Arab blood in him, swift, pretty, and spirited; the lad nicknamed him "Grant."[27] By contrast, Clemens was forced to select a mount from among the "hardest lot I ever did come across."[28] Travel in the Holy Land on an array of sickening, sore-infested horses punctured Clemens's romantic fantasy of the "Arab's idolatry of his horse." The love Arabs were rumored to have for their horses was a fraud, he concluded. As for his steady mount, the sarcastic Clemens called him "Baalbek" because the horse was "such a magnificent ruin."[29]

The horses reserved for the party of former President Grant were considerably better. Leaving Jaffa, the Grants rode off for Jerusalem, where, American Consul Joseph G. Wilson reported, the former president received many official attentions both from the foreign consular corps and from the native authorities at Jerusalem. They were "met at Kalourah, five miles from Jerusalem, by the dragomen and guards of the several consulates, of the Greek Patriarch, and of the Pasha of Palestine, and by a company of cavalry." At Jerusalem itself, the general was welcomed into the city with military honors. In fact, during the stay at Jerusalem "the Pasha's military band . . . was in attendance upon him daily."[30] Not all Americans received that kind of welcome to Jerusalem, of course. Yet Jerusalem, from the time it first came into view, was the centerpiece of tourist experiences and impressions.

Mighty Images Tumbled

Fabled Jerusalem's size was the first aspect of the city to strike Samuel Clemens. To a person of his experience, both in the American West and in America's burgeoning eastern cities, the sight of Holy Jerusalem was disenchanting:

> Perched on its eternal hills, white and domed and solid, massed together and hooped with gray walls, the venerable city gleamed in the sun. So small! Why it is no larger than an American village of forty thousand inhabitants, and no larger than an ordinary Syrian city of thirty thousand. Jerusalem numbers only fourteen thousand people.[31]

The size of Palestine in general had made an earlier, immediate impression on Clemens that foretold his reaction to Jerusalem. When approaching the Holy Land from the Lebanese hills, Clemens observed that from his vantage point "a cannon ball would carry beyond the confines of the Holy Land and light upon profane ground three miles away."[32] He also dismissed the Bashan Valley as merely a "respectable strip of fertile land. . . . There is enough of it to make a farm."[33]

Clemens and his fellow travelers dismounted and gazed at the Holy City "with very few words of conversation . . . and noted those prominent features of the city that pictures make familiar to all men from their school days till their death." This first sighting did not stir Clemens to tears, although "I think," he said, "there was no individual in the party whose brain was not teeming of thoughts and images and memories invoked by the grand history of this venerable city that lay before us. . . . I suppose it was the only detachment that ever entered Jerusalem without crying about it." Making a mockery of the reaction of crying at the sight of the Holy City, the young reporter continued, saying, "I have read all the books on Palestine, nearly that have been printed, and the authors all wept." William Prime, author of *Tent Life in the Holy Land*[34] and a favorite target of Clemens's sarcasm about Holy Land travel books, was singled out as having "got such a start that he never could shut himself off; and went through Palestine and irrigated it from one end to the other. . . . Whenever he found a holy place that was well authenticated, he cried; whenever he found one that was not well authenticated, he cried anyhow and took his chances; whenever he couldn't find any holy places at all, he just cried 'for a flier.'" With the prospect of the city directly before him, Clemens swore that he would never again believe the accounts of "these boastful Jerusalem weepers," because if his group—which would "go into sentimental convulsions at the merest shadow of provocation"—did not shed tears, then probably no one else really did either.[35]

On her first sight of Jerusalem, Emily Severance wrote: "All of us were too tired to feel enthusiastic or the least bit solemn" about the prospect of the Holy City. Clara Waters, on the other hand, recalled that her first sight of the "city which the prophet called the 'Joy of the whole Earth'" produced unrestrained tears.

Jacob Freese was disappointed at his first sight of Jerusalem, but he felt differently by the time he turned around for a lingering last look at the city. With all its faults "and though all our subsequent examinations have been accompanied with a feeling of sadness akin to disappointment, still we cannot turn our back upon it without a feeling of regret."[36] Henry Bellows was disappointed with his first view of Jerusalem, especially because it did not materialize satisfactorily until he was close to the low-slung walls. He regretted that none of the popular representations of the city was from the direction of his approach, and he found the intrusion of the Russian hospice and Prussian school disturbing enough that he urged his readers to avoid arriving at the city from that direction.

Once inside Jerusalem, Bellows saw a "fetid, squalid and mean in the extreme" sight. Wherever it was built up, the city was crowded, yet there also seemed to be a great number of vacant spaces, even within the narrow walls. The open spaces, Bellows said, were "as much a wilderness as if a hundred miles from habitation." He was also appalled by the Jewish quarter: "In the narrow and dark streets dwell, in their mud houses, hundreds of poor and wretched Jewish families, steeped in filth and terrible odors of the sewers that empty in their neighborhood."[37] Nonetheless, Bellows admitted, the dignity and grandeur of the city's main attractions were greater than what he had been prepared to find.

Joseph Taylor described his first view of Jerusalem in romantic terms:

> The sun was well down the western sky over the rocky brows of the mountains of Ephraim, his autumnal rays gilding a constellation of low, round hills ahead of us in the distant south, with rich, purple tints peculiar to the atmosphere of the Orient. One of these hills, in the midst of the group, seemed to wear a golden crown; domes, minarets, cupolas, and towers were seen there, promiscuously commingled together, the whole surrounded by towering walls notched with embrasures and embattlements. "Jerusalem, Jerusalem," we ran along our column, and then all were silent.[38]

Taylor could think only of the scene of Jesus' crucifixion and death, and of what he thought the great crusading armies from Europe must have felt when they saw the city for the first time. Theodore Roosevelt found the prospect of Jerusalem to be what he expected, except, like Clemens, he thought it "remarkably small."[39]

Another site central to the touring goal of Americans was the Jordan River. Like Jerusalem, the Jordan was often a disappointment to American travelers, whose image of such Holy Land sites did not necessarily correspond to reality. Clemens's image of the river was

shattered even though he never saw it in daylight. He and his group
had arrived on the river's banks after dark, and the former Mississippi pilot judged its width by wading through it. The experience
was sufficient for him to pronounce that it was narrower than a
good many streets in America.

> I always thought the river Jordan was four thousand miles
> long and thirty five miles wide, and so I have been miserably
> disappointed again. It is only ninety miles long and so crooked
> that a man doesn't know which side of it he is on half the
> time. . . . How is it that such a creek as this imposed itself
> upon me all my life as a mighty river? This is a country of
> disappointments. Nothing is as one expects it to be.[40]

Jacob Freese dismissed the river, saying, "Aside from its biblical
associations, it is not a stream that would excite any interest in any
country."[41] Likewise, Theodore Roosevelt discovered that the river
would be only "a rather small creek in America," and the Dead Sea,
nearby, "a singularly beautiful lake."[42]

The characteristic of size was important to Clemens as he assessed
the reality of the Holy Land against the imagery he carried from
America. For example, he used the size of the country's grapes to
show his disappointment, recalling childhood Bible picture books
representing two Israelite spies bearing a "monstrous bunch" of
grapes on a pole as "one of my most cherished juvenile traditions."
He came to realize, however, that "the Sunday school books stretched
it a little. The grapes are most excellent to this day, but the bunches
are not as large as those in the pictures. I was surprised and hurt
when I saw them."[43]

It is clear that Clemens arrived in the Holy Land with a full set of
expectations about the landscape and physical characteristics of the
country that were not met. Although couched in humorous, satirical
terms, the difference between expectation and reality was apparent.
For instance, Clemens thought that Palestine's scenery was dismal—
barren, dull hills of unpicturesque shapes, valleys that were little
more than deserts, and inland "seas" (the Galilee and the Dead Sea)
little more than lakes: "It is the most hopeless, dreary, heartbroken
piece of territory out of Arizona. I think the sun would skip it if he
could make schedule time by going around. What Palestine wants is
paint. It will never be a beautiful country while it is unpainted. Each
detachment of pilgrims ought to give it a coat."[44]

Fig. 9.   CHERISHED IMAGE OF THE HOLY LAND'S PRODUCE.   As was
the case with so many other images associated with the Holy Land,
Twain lamented that the reality did not live up to what was expected.
Illustration from *Innocents Abroad*.

Traveling northward from Jerusalem, Clara Waters was immersed
in biblical lore as she noticed that the country was "becoming more
fruitful and better cultivated." She continued: "We had left the land
of Judah, and passed through that of Benjamin. Now we were in
that of Ephraim and the luxuriance of the vines, the olives and the
figs, explained the meaning of Jacob, when he said, 'In thee shall
Israel bless, saying make thee as Ephraim.'"[45] But the improved
scenery was not enough for Waters to forget the preconceived notions of the country's beauty, so she was soon disappointed with the
view of Galilee:

> One who looks for beautiful scenery here, having in mind the
> lovely lakes of our own country or those of Switzerland, will
> be disappointed. . . . The whole spirit of the place is that of
> quiet and desertion. But as we read the accounts of the differ

ent events connected with Jesus and his disciples, that have
occurred here, our imagination paints vivid pictures.

Confronted with the reality of Ottoman Palestine, it was easy to
turn from the present to the past, as Waters had done. Likewise, it
was easier to explain the reality in sweeping, universal terms.
Nathaniel Burt saw Palestine's condition as epitomizing the geography of the world in its diversity, thereby affording the former peoples of the country a chance to be representative of humanity and to
produce "a revelation with wide, varied, universal adaptations."[46] To
Burt, the Holy Land was dreary and desolate, especially in the context of the biblical passage that advertised the land as luxuriantly
flowing with milk and honey. But Burt imagined that the land had
been good in ages past, that "it requires little observation and reflection, on the part of the traveler in Palestine, to perceive that the
country possesses great natural capabilities and must, at a former
period, have sustained an immense population."[47] When Burt recalled that the land's present condition fulfilled scriptural prediction
exactly, he showed more interest in the spectacle of the land's desolation than he did in evidences of prosperity. For two thousand
years, he reasoned, Palestine had been under the curse of tyrannical
misrule, of devastating wars, and of ceaseless strife between races
and religions. It would therefore have been a miracle of Providence
if the country were any better than "a land forsaken and desolate."
    Charles Elliott's perspectives as a horticulturist and landscape ar-
chitect were very much in evidence in his explanation of how the
Holy Land, described as a garden in Scripture, did not match up to
his own experience:

> Monotonous and uninviting as much of the Holy Land will
> appear . . . to English readers, accustomed to the constant
> verdure, the succession of flowers, lasting almost throughout
> the year, the ample streams as the varied surface of our coun-
> try—we must remember that its aspects to the Israelites after
> the weary march of forty years through the desert, and even
> by the side of the brightest recollections of Egypt that they
> could conjure up, must have been very different. After the
> "great and terrible wilderness" with its fiery serpents, its scor-
> pions, drought, and rocks of flint—the slow, sultry march all
> day in the dust of that enormous procession, . . . how grateful
> must have been the rest afforded by the Land of Promise.[48]

As for its present state, Elliott seemed to offer the Holy Land an extenuation for its connection to the non-occidental world when he described Palestine's geographical position as

> on the very outpost—on the extremest western edge of the East. On the shore of the Mediterranean it stands, as if it had advanced as far as possible towards the West. . . . Thus it was open to all the gradual influences of the rising communities of the West, while it was saved from the retrogression and decrepitude which have ultimately been the doom of all purely Eastern States whose connections were limited to the East only.[49]

Elliott seemed to be almost willing to excuse the present state of the hapless country because of its position at the edge of the East.

Henry Bellows was more direct. From his liberal Protestant viewpoint, he saw the condition of the Holy Land as a reflection of the condition of Islam. Bellows took as evidence "the remnants of the once feared Moslem faith," believing that "the monuments of its military and its religious pomp and power, now in ruins all over Egypt, Syria, and Turkey, fully attest" to Islam's immense vigor during the Middle Ages.[50] As for the present, the reality of the Holy Land seemed barely redeemable. Even though he was surprised, for instance, by the condition of the country's agriculture in the fertile Sharon Plain (Bellows thought it was "rude and wasteful"), such sights nevertheless made "the country smile at least a sad smile, and relieves the general melancholy that prevails in this desolated region."[51] And Jacob Freese also put the responsibility for the state of the Holy Land at the door of the Ottoman rulers. Contemplating the condition of Safed, Freese wrote:

> The present ruinous and desolate condition of this city and, indeed, of all others throughout Palestine, affords striking evidence of the weakness and vices of the Ottoman rulers, as their vast dimensions and solidity of structure do of the efficacy and magnificence of that of their founders. No element in the Mussulman character is more remarkable, or more unfavorable to national prosperity than the indifference to the progress of decay, the unwillingness to repair the ravages of time.[52]

On the whole, Americans were soberly disappointed with the Holy Land's landscape and physical features. The desolate conditions they found in Palestine did not correlate with the image carried into the sojourn. The tourists tried to reason out the dichotomy through faith-enhancing formulas or to arrive at a new level of consciousness, but this did not come easily. Some, like Samuel Clemens, were remorseful:

> I hope I am not unjust toward the natural scenery of Palestine. And yet, I have been so disappointed that such a thing is almost possible. . . . We had nothing much on board the ship to read but travels in Palestine, and very naturally we got Palestine drilled into us thoroughly. All these books of travel manage, somehow, to leave us with a sort of vague notion that Palestine was very beautiful—a notion that we were about to enter a modified form of fairy land. And so bitter disappointment awaited us. The fairy land was modified too much, it was a howling wilderness instead of a garden. This has incensed us against all our Holy Land authors and inclined us to say intemperate things about the land itself.[53]

Others were reassured. Emily Severance was initially set back by the way the sights on her tour manifested the reality of the Holy Land, but she took heart:

> Traveling here takes away the poetry and the romance with which we have invested the Scriptures, but I am glad to be able to tell you that it has increased our belief in their truthfulness. So many of these habits and customs of the people are the same that we cannot fail to recognize their force as illustrations, and at the same time must feel that the character of the people cannot change much.[54]

This was an interesting and typical rationale among Holy Land tourists. With the sites not living up to expectations, their actuality must surely confirm the truth of the Bible, if for no other reason than *because* of their utter realism. Once having experienced that shocking realism (and having come to the moment of commitment, when the traveler decides either to stay or to travel on),[55] Severance wrote, "We shall probably never regret having been to Palestine, nor do I think we shall be desirous of coming again."[56] This sentiment was echoed in a terse note Clemens penned when observing Jericho: "No Second Advent—Christ been once, will never come again."[57]

Spying the Peoples of Palestine

Closely allied with travelers' views of the landscape and physical features of the Holy Land were the travelers' perceptions of the peoples of Palestine. The Holy Land's populace was ethnically and religiously diverse. The largest groups were Muslim Arabs, Eastern Christians, and Jews. During that more innocent and less strife-filled time, American perceptions of Arabs and Jews offered intriguing insights into another facet of Americans' awareness of the Holy Land.

Samuel Clemens viewed the Arab peoples as akin to the Indians he had seen back in the United States, especially the women and children. He was clearly disturbed by the silent manner in which they sat patiently waiting for morsels of food dropped or left over by the tourists: "They sat in silence, and with tireless patience watched our every motion with that vile, uncomplaining impoliteness which is so truly Indian and which makes a white man so nervous and uncomfortable and savage that he wants to exterminate the whole tribe."[58] Some of the rancor many tourists expressed could be attributed to the occasional hostile reception by some of the local peoples. Harassment of "Franks" was frequent in certain areas, and when such prejudicial behavior was experienced by some Americans—perhaps for the first time in their lives—it tended to arouse anger. Clemens and his party had been pelted with stones during the night they were encamped at Mount Meron in Galilee; the local Arabs had even tried to stampede the party's horses. Traveling through Samaria, the party was again the target of rock-throwers, although this was to be expected in that region.

Equating Middle Eastern peoples with American Indians was not unique to Clemens. In the 1760s artist Benjamin West was one of the first Americans to study the antiquities of the Mediterranean and the East firsthand. When contemplating the newly discovered statue of the Apollo Belvedere in the Vatican Museum, West declared, "My God, how like it is to a young Mohawk warrior!" While in Rome, West was also intrigued by Egyptian antiquities: "Of all the monuments of ancient art in Rome, the obelisk brought from Egypt in the reign of Augustus, interested [West's] curiosity the most—the hieroglyphs appeared to resemble so exactly the figures on the Wampum belts of the Indians, that it occurred to him, if ever the mysteries of Egypt were to be interpreted it might be by the aborigines of America."[59] Like Clemens, Joseph Taylor compared the Arabs of Galilee to America's Indians. For example, Taylor saw the appearance of a poor Arab woman as "but slight improvement upon that of the Sioux or Pottawotomie squaw of America."[60] Apparently the correlation in the minds of some Americans between Arabs and Indians was based on the common denominator of poverty.

For a Miss M. R. Parkman, a young American who traveled to the Holy Land in 1871, the sight of the Holy Land's poor was wrenching. After encamping overnight at Ramleh, during the journey to Jerusalem from Jaffa, she and her companions "were besieged by the most wretched looking beggars, more dreadful looking creatures even than the beggars in Egypt, for besides looking more emaciated, generally, many of them held up to us mere stumps of hands, destroyed by leprosy, we learned later—they were almost naked, literally in tatters and clamorous to a degree even passing those of Egypt." The beggars were so aggressive and persistent that one man in the tourist party had to drive them back. To see such human beings was sobering, but for Miss Parkman, seeing them "here, in the Holy Land, was more depressing even than to see them in Egypt." Once in Jerusalem, Miss Parkman voiced similar disillusionment that such sad sights should exist—of all places—in the Holy Land: "To see all this wretchedness in this city, of all places in the world, 1800 years after Jesus lived and died here, is peculiarly painful."[61] Emily Severance too was besieged by natives imploring charity whom she described as being "such dirty, ragged people you never saw!"[62] By contrast, the experience of the Waters party with the local Arabs of Galilee was playful. Waters wrote that they seemed contented and happy and often played music and danced for the passersby in an effort to elicit gratuities, called "baksheesh."

Joseph Taylor was struck by the incidence of eye infirmities among the people of Galilee. He offered three possible explanations, none of which was his own: exposure filtered through turban and handkerchiefs; conflict in which the eye was gouged; or eyes punched out to avoid military service. Taylor was beguiled by Nazareth, finding its situation and its women to be the most beautiful in Palestine, but the strife-filled situation at Nazareth's Virgin's Well—perpetual squabbling among the Nazarene women—was disturbing. Other American travelers also witnessed it. Emily Severance, for example, observed that the Nazareth women always seemed to be quarreling over who would be the first to draw water and that the quarrelers would yield whenever a man with camels or donkeys came along and pushed the women aside.[63] Taylor believed "a little forethought and enterprise could easily solve the problem, but the solution is an enterprise not to be thought of; they are too

Fig. 10. A WOMAN CARRYING WATER NEAR NAZARETH. Another popular, biblically inspired image was that of a woman carrying water near Nazareth. As with many images, it succumbed quickly to the reality of everyday life in Ottoman Palestine viewed firsthand by Americans.

much like building a turnpike, a railroad, or boring an artesian well."[64]

Taylor was not put off by the activities in Nazareth. In fact, among the first things he marveled at in the East were the civility, gentility, and politeness people showed toward strangers, in contrast to "the spirit of every fellow to look out for himself" that he found in his own native land. Taylor believed that while Americans were busy sending missionaries to the East to teach the ways of salvation, there should be some exchange to have people from the East come "to teach our enlightened people how to be civil and polite towards the stranger."[65] In contrast to the treatment of strangers, at another time he decried the lack of civility demonstrated toward women in Palestine after he witnessed a barbaric incident near Bethlehem in which a woman who offered to draw water for the touring party without charge was nearly stoned to death by a man for making such an offer. Taylor asked, "Where are our Women's Rights men of

America? Let me invite them to come to the rescue—here is work for them."⁶⁶ Samuel Clemens expressed genuine sympathy for the native peoples, who endured Turkish rule and excessive taxation: "If ever an oppressed race existed, it is this one we see fettered around us under the inhuman tyranny of the Ottoman Empire."⁶⁷

John Franklin Swift's observations about the condition of the Jews in Jerusalem were discerning. He saw the Jews of the city as illustrating an interesting phenomenon: "The Jews of every country upon the globe into which, by tyranny of their fellow men, they have been driven, are wiser, better, more civilized, healthier, and happier than are the same people left in Jerusalem, their central city and capital."⁶⁸ Even though Jerusalem was "at the great fountain and reservoir of Jewish nationality," the Jews of perhaps anywhere else were better off than in Jerusalem. It was strange, Swift thought, that all the Jews he saw in the city seemed to be "foreigners," Jews of European origin. In other matters too, he believed Jerusalem's Jews opposed "the received notions" of what Jewish conduct and affairs should have been. Swift observed Jews who supported themselves in the city in either skilled or unskilled labor and not in the "capacity of his brain for supplying all his wants." Swift was also amazed to find out that most of Jerusalem's Jews were paupers supported by charity, and not the charity of Muslims or Christians but charity supplied by other Jews, even though "they are the poorest and most miserable, as a class, of all the inhabitants of the Holy City."⁶⁹

Swift's observations about the Jewish community in Jerusalem led him to a satirical judgment: "When a Jew is good for nothing else he is good to send to Jerusalem." Actually, Swift accurately understood a truism of the Jewish presence during this pre-Zionist period of the *Yishuv*: "Each of them understands himself to be a sort of employee of the rest of the Jewish brotherhood throughout the world, his duty being that of remaining at Jerusalem to hold possession of it, or perhaps to regenerate it in the Hebrew interests. They therefore consider themselves in light of paid missionaries."⁷⁰ Swift believed that the "system of pensioning paupers upon the country to hold a footing in it" (he was referring to the *halukah* system of charity distribution among the city's Jews) was of most doubtful propriety. "Nor is it charity," Swift claimed. He believed *halukah* furthered dependence and stifled initiative. "In striking contrast with this mistaken charity of the great body of European Israelites, is that of Sir Moses Montefiore, the well-known Englishman of that faith."⁷¹ Swift was impressed that Montefiore did not spend his money supporting idleness, but rather invested in the regeneration of the city's Jews. Swift described Montefiore's school on the hill opposite the Citadel and Jaffa Gate as "the only green and blooming twig that I have beheld upon the dead and almost decayed trunk of Jerusalem" and found it remarkable that the students of the Montefiore school were being educated according to Western notions, with many students able to speak English. "All were as bright, intelligent, and well-behaved as the youths of the same age in American schools." Montefiore should be quite proud of his school, according to Swift, "for nothing like it has adorned the desolate hills of Palestine for many a century."

Taylor's visit to the Western (or "Wailing") Wall on a Friday was at first only to occupy his time, because there wasn't much else to do in the city because of the Muslim Sabbath. He observed perhaps a hundred Jews occupying the open space before the Wall, many in "strange costumes," some old, some young, like one young man "in the hey-day of life, in the meridian of his manhood, well-dressed, tall and graceful, with the kinky, black hair, and dark eyes, and unmistakable Hebrew nose, just such as we may see at the doors or behind the counters of the clothing stores of America."[72] But Taylor found the anguished scene at the wall a "pitiable and touching spectacle." Captivated by the sight, he lingered, thinking that these "unmistakable lineal descendants of David and Solomon" were now "cast off, forbidden, persecuted, and driven abroad over the world, homeless, and without a nationality or country."[73] At the Western Wall, Clemens called the assembled Jews "Pharisees."[74]

Swift and his group made their way with a guide to the Western Wall, where the Jews were permitted "only as a great favor . . . to approach the walls which once enclosed the Temple." Through the dark, narrow lanes and alleys, Swift and his party knew they were getting closer to the wall by the sound of the crowd of Jews at the site.

> It was a most strange and indescribable sight that burst upon us as we entered the wailing place. The nearly one hundred men, women and children were either sitting and intoning in sad, monotonous voices scriptural references to the city's downfall and defilement, or clamorously lamenting their predicament by throwing themselves on the pavement or burying their faces deep within the joints and cavities of the wall while real tears stream down their cheeks. It is the most touching ceremony to be met with in all the strange and melancholy things to be seen in or about Jerusalem.[75]

Fig. 11. A CROWD AT THE WESTERN WALL. Jerusalem's Western (or
Wailing) Wall was often a tourist objective in the nineteenth century.
The assembled Jews usually evoked in American minds thoughts about
biblical prophecy and the Jewish condition. Meanwhile, American consuls frequently found themselves involved with aspects of local Jewish
affairs.

Miss Parkman, with a good deal of sensitivity, described her party's
visit to the Western Wall:

> This street was filled with men and women, a line of them
> standing with their faces to the wall, and many others sitting
> on the pavement or standing, their backs to the opposite wall.
> Some too, sat or stood in the middle of the street. Nearly all
> had books in their hands, their scriptures, which they were
> reading from in a wailing voice. We stood for a few minutes
> among the men, from whom a low murmur, from many voices,
> proceeded. I didn't notice any particular marks of emotion
> here, but I couldn't see most of their faces which were against
> the wall, which they kissed.

Some clusters of Jews showed little emotion, but Miss Parkman was
attracted by others:

They cried with loud wailing voices, some of them sobbing and were evidently working themselves up to considerable excitement. . . . I, after a few minutes, saw two turn away from the wall (to go home) and then I saw that the tears were running down their faces. I felt out of place, here, and was glad after some moments more, we came away. . . . It was a saddening sight, however, we all thought, these poor people shut out and crying outside of this high, massive wall—outcasts from the temple of their fathers. Perhaps too, they find it a relief in some of their private griefs, to go and cry there.[76]

To Nathaniel Burt, the dispersion of the Jews was evidence of "providential purpose yet to be accomplished," and he believed that by preventing the Jews from "obtaining a country anywhere else, they shall yet be brought home to that country once their own by divine promise and gift."[77] In comparison, the description of Jerusalem's Jewish Quarter in Charles Elliott's work harks back to the theme of the accursed plight of the Jews and their decline since the ancient days, in contrast to the progress of Western Christians. This was a theme related to the idea that the new dispensation of Christianity had supplanted Judaism:

On the same ridge of Zion, but lower down the slope, when it falls away into the Cheesemongers Valley, lies the Jewish Quarter, which a man may smell afar off; a quarter goodly in itself, once covered with palaces of priests and kings, but now the danger and opprobrium of the Holy Land. There lies, in the midst of alleys and courts unspeakably offensive to eye and nostril, the synagogues of the Ashkenazim and Sephardim; the Polish synagogue, a new and tawdry work, with a cupola built in the Saracenic style; the ancient synagogue, a vault half buried in the soil; a Jewish hospice for pilgrims; and a Jewish infirmary for the sick, of whom there is abundant supply. Around these edifices reek and starve about four thousand Israelites, many of these living in a state of filth as unlike the condition of their clean bright ancestors as the life of an English gentleman under Victoria is unlike that of a British serf under Boadicea.[78]

Elliott's prejudices were obvious in his discussions of the Holy Land. Describing the phenomenon of cities located on hilltops rather than in the valleys around, he wrote, "to people so exclusive as the Jews there must have been a constant satisfaction in the elevation and inaccessibility of these highland regions."[79]

Jacob Freese expressed himself frequently in terms typical of both an American democrat abroad and a Christian. He had pity and sympathy for the downtrodden Jews gathered at the Western Wall, for example, but he added that in time their sufferings would end when they were converted to Christianity. Freese found the scene at the wall "a very sad sight, and one that we should not care again to witness," and continued:

> To see the representatives of a people once so glorious, and once the possessors and rulers of this land, now so abject and downtrodden that only by permission dare they lift their eyes toward the outer walls of their once glorious temple; to see them weeping and wailing over their departed glory, and with agony of soul beseeching the God of their fathers to return them once more; to see them condemned and buffeted, and spit upon, even by the half-civilized Moslems, in their own city of David; to see them crouching along the street, and crawling as it were amidst the shadows of their rulers and oppressors; and to know that not only in Jerusalem and throughout Palestine, but everywhere throughout the civilized globe, this people, once the chosen of God, are now wanderers and sojourners on the earth, without a distinct nationality and without a Redeemer—oh! who can but pity and sympathize with them in their hard affliction?[80]

A stop at the Tomb of Rachel on the road near Bethlehem and an encounter with a party of Jews led Jacob Freese to observe: "There is no one trait of the Jewish character more strongly marked than love of ancestry, and the attachments they have for the country they once owned. All travelers in Palestine observe this, and several have written concerning it in terms at once truthful and beautiful."[81]

In a characteristically playful manner, Theodore Roosevelt found his party's tour of the Mosque of Omar strenuous—especially since his group was supplied at the site with slippers they kept losing and had to run around and hunt for. The next day, young Teddie hunted the Jerusalem countryside for fowl and then visited the Western Wall, where, he thought, many of the women were mourning in earnest but "most of the men were evidently shamming."[82]

Trying to equate the Arabs of the Holy Land with American Indians—even jocularly, as Clemens did—implied a perception of the

Arab populace as essentially primitive. This was not altogether im-
probable in light of the search by most travelers for the remote past.
They had come seeking the primitive and were prepared to apply
the label, however superficially, to any element in the population
that met their expectations. Certainly, the occasionally adversarial
relationship many travelers had with unnamed Arabs did not leave
room to correct preconceptions. Similarly, preconceptions about the
Holy Land's Jews, especially phrased in terms of a "dispossessed
people" or "living witness to biblical truth," left little room for altering the pivotal image of the Holy Land.

The American Spirit Confronts the East

Thus far, the tourist experiences and recollections of Americans
have been examined in terms of perceivable objects: the condition of
the landscape and the circumstances of the native peoples. However,
to most Americans, the chief features of the Holy Land were the
numerous sites with sacred associations, which were the primary attraction for the devout. Yet confronting the sites in their mundane
settings was risky.

Joseph Taylor astutely pointed out that at times a state of incredu-
lity steals over visitors to the holy sites. Taylor described it as "a
weakness in our reasons that leads us to expect, or want to see at
these places, more lingering traces, shadows, or footprints of the
mysterious scenes once enacted there,"[83] a sort of skepticism that
Taylor credited to an inclination to trace all results to natural and
legitimate causes and, lacking these, to see the site of miracles as not
associated with the site laid out before the traveler. It is interesting
that among Taylor's own party of clergymen, a doctor, a lawyer, and
an artist, Taylor recalled .that only the artist fully believed in the
validity of most of the historical sites. This was a revealing comment
on the romantic concept in some travelers' minds.

Absorbing the impact of the sights and making them fit preconceived notions of what they should look like was hard enough for
tourists, but when the commentaries of crass dragomen and guides
accompanied the tourist's perceptual experience, the difference between preconceptions and reality was enough to drive the tourist
into a shell. Miss Parkman, for example, was quite put off by her
tour guide, Zackariah, who "went on, with his heartless *valet de place*
manner, to point out the place where Jesus received the blow, the

tree to which he was tied and other places, such mockery, it seemed, became painful. Fortunately, one can keep at a little distance from him, and lose what he says, when one desires."[84]

With a Yankee appreciation for sparseness of detail, Jacob Freese declaimed the "gauze and tinsel of over-zealous religionists" that had destroyed much of the grandeur and interest inherent in the Holy Sepulchre: "As well might one attempt to 'gild refined gold or paint the lily' as to place marbles and lamps and pictures and tapestry, around the tomb of Jesus." As for the tomb's authenticity, Freese reflected on the work Captain Warren was doing for the British Palestine Exploration Fund. At that time, Warren was digging at the Damascus Gate in order to fix the position of the elusive Second Wall of the Second Temple period and determine whether the traditional sepulchre site was authentic. Said Freese:

> Until new facts are presented sufficient to destroy a well-defined tradition of only about three hundred years from the time of Jesus to the time of Empress Helena, and unquestionable historical records from that time until the present, we should be content, as before stated, to regard the Church of the Holy Sepulchre as containing within its walls the two great landmarks of Christianity—namely, the place of crucifixion and the place of resurrection.[85]

And within the Holy Sepulchre, Clemens thought, only the sword and spurs of Godfrey of Bouillon, the Crusader king of Jerusalem, were authentic.[86] Taylor's party was also disillusioned with the Holy Sepulchre, and they doubted its authenticity. Theodore Roosevelt's visit to the Church of the Holy Sepulchre caused him to write sarcastically that it was a wonderful sight and reminded him of "the bones of the saints (or turkeys) in Italy." The thought that the church stood on the site of the crucifixion did inspire some awe in the fourteen-year-old boy, as did the tomb of Crusader Godfrey.[87]

Clara Waters visited the Holy Sepulchre soon after entering the city. To her the Holy Sepulchre was "painful to Protestants to see . . . in the hands of the Greeks and Romish churches, and that it is impossible to believe the many things which are told you about it." But the place became "singularly sacred . . . from its human associations," having been hallowed by tears and prayers from the time of Helena. In other respects, the recollections of Waters's Jerusalem stay sound much like the words her guide or guidebook might have used to point out features.[88]

In his biography of General Grant, William McFeely wrote that the list of places the Grants saw in the Holy Land was "numbing." John Russell Young wrote, "Of course, to feel Jerusalem one must come with faith," which left the Grants somewhat unprepared.[89] Young acknowledged that some people in the party were guilty of "heathen questionings," but he wrote that seeing the past carried a person away from unbelief. As for Grant himself, "the general trudged, rode donkeys, and took it all in. Mark Twain helped"[90]—a comment that provides sufficient insight into the general's frame of mind when he was viewing the sacred sites.

Once abroad, especially in alien surroundings, Americans demonstrated certain characteristics that distinguished them from other foreigners. They also developed reputations, for better or worse, that other peoples were quick to invoke or exploit. While none of these characteristics was endemic to the American tourist experience in the Holy Land, they were nevertheless readily identifiable as uniquely American. Speed, impatience, a sense of curiosity (that was occasionally superficial), and frequently an amiable naiveté seemed characteristic of a good number of American tourists, and these qualities were probably just as evident in Rome and Paris as in the Holy Land. But the perceived condition of the Holy Land may have exacerbated and accentuated these American inclinations.

A "sporting gentleman from New York" made the shipboard acquaintance of Joseph Taylor before either of them reached the Holy Land. Taylor recounted that the man's sole aim in traveling to the Holy Land was to bathe in the Jordan River. Indeed, while Taylor's own party was leaving its steamer at Beirut, word came to him that the New Yorker had landed at Jaffa, had traveled directly to the Jordan after hiring a dragoman and horses, and had headed back to Jaffa, passing Jerusalem without stopping—making the round trip in thirty-six hours.[91]

More comprehensible was the American fascination with the realities of the biblical sites. In Samaria, for example, at the sites of Mount Ebal and Mount Gerizim, the clergymen in the party traveling with Joseph Taylor insisted on scattering the group around the basin between the two hills to see whether the blessings and curses read before the ancient congregation of Israelites by Joshua[92] could really have been heard over the distance by the multitude. To the group's amazement, the experiment worked.

The sense of curiosity extended, quite naturally, into the irrepressible urge to be reassured that the Holy Land had not changed but had stayed the same as in the past. The random observation of

Miss Parkman on the condition of the Mount of Olives demonstrates
this searching, quasi-scientific need to understand. Observing the
condition of the hill's soil, Miss Parkman remarked that it seemed
overly sandy and capable of supporting only a thin grass covering,
since anything richer would probably cause the hill to be overly cultivated, thereby changing its original condition.[93]

The amiable nature of many Americans did not always make for
predictable outcomes. After arrival in Jerusalem, John Franklin
Swift and a group of fellow Californians went to see the American
consul to obtain permission to visit the Temple Mount. After the
conducted tour of the Mount and its principal feature, the Dome of
the Rock, the large party of Christians (not limited to Swift's party
alone) granted access slowly broke down into smaller units around
various dragomen and guides to hear the marvelous stories associated with the site. Swift related that one American woman from New
York amazed a Muslim schoolmaster with whom she had been talking convivially. The woman pulled out all her upper front teeth and
showed them to the Muslim in a bunch. "God is great and Mohammed is the prophet of God," the astonished schoolmaster
blurted out. According to Swift, the man continued to gaze won-
deringly at the woman, no doubt expecting "to see her underjaw
come away next."[94]

In a decidedly derogatory sense, Eliza Bush, a British traveler
going to Jerusalem from Jaffa in 1865, wrote that she met "a large
party coming from the Holy City, Americans, some of whom
stopped me with characteristic questions, but amiable, in moving off,
gave us information in return, intended to be useful."[95] Although
the Americans were well intentioned, the Bush party thought they
knew better. The true nature of Bush's opinion of American Holy
Land travelers was demonstrated more acutely during her return
trip to Jaffa from Jerusalem: "These Americans were worthy people,
with few ideas between them all, except those of getting over the
ground as quickly as they could, and giving an occasional guess or
two as to the scenes they visited."[96] Similar thoughts were echoed by
John MacGregor, author of a series of travel books for which he
undertook canoe trips in a vessel named the *Rob Roy*. MacGregor
observed, "These cousins of ours do their sightseeing so uncommon
quick."[97]

The records of America's tourist encounter with the Holy Land
show other, less peculiarly American attributes of American travelers. One was an understandable irritability brought on by the con-

ditions of travel. For example, one American complained that sight-seeing in Jerusalem was overly wearisome, "as in any other part of the Old World. If you go on foot, you are constantly annoyed by the bad walking and filthy streets, and in danger of breaking your neck or being run over by the crowd; and if you go on horseback, the danger is scarcely less."[98] The need to get together with fellow Americans was occasionally demonstrated, as was the expected tinge of homesickness. When Clara Waters first visited Egypt, she came to realize just how far from New England's "frosts and snows" she was. She gradually "learned the ways of adjustment" to her new surroundings, but still, "we either received or made evening visits with other Americans, even when on our Nile boat or in tent. This was extremely agreeable and helped us to forget how far we had wandered from our homes."[99]

One potentially humorous characteristic was a penchant for garnering souvenirs and leaving remembrances behind. The impulse toward souvenir-hunting and treasure collecting was strong, for example, among the *Quaker City* pilgrims. Clemens noted, with some annoyance:

> The incorrigible pilgrims have come in with their pockets full of specimens broken from the ruins. I wish their vandalism could be stopped. They broke off fragments from Noah's Tomb: from the exquisite sculptures of the temples of Baalbek; from the houses of Judas and Ananias, in Damascus; from the tomb of Nimrod the mighty hunter in Jonesborough; from the worn Greek and Roman inscriptions set in the hoary walls of the castle of Baniyas; and now they have been hacking and chipping these old arches here that Jesus looked upon in the flesh. Heaven protect the Sepulchre when this tribe invades Jerusalem.[100]

Unlike those pilgrims who grabbed for souvenirs among the ruins of Baalbek, a young American in Joseph Taylor's party disgraced his companions by painting "a great American flag, in permanent and brilliant colors, on a prominent place upon one of the standing pillars of the great Temple of the Sun." Despite his companions' protests, the young man persisted, and even announced that he would paint under the flag the names and addresses of his compatriots and the date of their visit. "This announcement filled the cup of indignation, already full, to overflowing—and it was more than even a

preacher could be expected to bear, to stand quietly by and see himself thus conspicuously advertised to the whole world as a great ass."[101]
Only after the party, in a biblical mood, threatened to stone the man
did he desist.

British vicar Alexander Boddy shared a story a German dentist
who had recently commenced practice in Jerusalem told him. In
broken English the dentist related how an American woman rushed
into his office one morning, saying, "Doctor, I reckon I want a tooth
stopped." The dentist said he told the woman to have a seat and
open her mouth. Carefully looking in and examining the state of her
teeth, the dentist was forced after a while to ask which tooth was
bothering the woman because he could see no apparent problem.
"Oh, that makes no matter—any tooth," the woman replied. When
the dentist objected because he could not find a tooth that needed
work, the woman adamantly demanded, "I'm going to have a tooth
stopped in Jerusalem, anyhow, even if you put in so little gold, it will
do, but I must have a memento of this city, whatever I pay for it."[102]
To satisfy the enthusiastic souvenir-hunter, the dentist said he managed to make a hole and put in some gold, for which he was hand-
somely rewarded.

Two more attributes associated with nineteenth-century Americans were conspicuous in the Holy Land. One was a drive for progress, a willingness to be unshackled by convention in certain circumstances; the other was a spirit of bravado. Alexander Wallace, a
Scottish clergyman, told the story of an American victory of sorts
during his travel experience. After journeying from an important
site, it was apparently customary to make the first day's march
shorter than usual, so that if any baggage was inadvertently left behind it could be fetched.

> But this did not suit the views of our American friend, and he
> would teach the Arabs how they might go ahead. He got
> down from his camel, pulled up the tent pins, and ordered
> the dragoman to see that the camels were at once reloaded for
> a march of at least two hours more. The Arabs were rather
> surprised, and neither they nor the dragoman liked their
> mode of treatment. It was breaking through the custom of the
> ages, and it seemed for a time as if they would not comply.
> Our party all moved forward, and, at last, when we were
> about a mile in advance, we saw the encampment move. The
> American spirit of progress was triumphant in the desert and
> the slow motion of the East was compelled to yield to it.[103]

"I WEPT."

Fig. 12. WEEPING AT THE SIGHT OF JERUSALEM. Mark Twain ridiculed accounts of weeping at the sight of Jerusalem, though for many tourists the first view of the city was a memorable experience. In this sarcastic depiction of a "Jerusalem weeper" from *Innocents Abroad*, notice two tools of the American Holy Land tourist on the ground: an umbrella for the sun and a pistol for fostering respect. Illustration from *Innocents Abroad*.

Clemens frequently parodied the spirit of bravado, especially as recorded in the works of earlier travelers, such as William Prime. Even so, travel writers contemporary with Clemens continued to supply examples of American brashness or boastfulness. For example, Jacob Freese and his party tried to descend the stairway of Mount Zion that led to the reputed tomb of David, but they were deferred by the Muslim guard's "hullabaloo." After the offer of baksheesh failed to change the guard's mind, Freese was led off sulking, and thinking cavalierly to himself:

> Had a half-dozen other Americans been present, each with a revolver in hand, we should have liked to force our passage to the tomb, and laughed at the guards in their efforts to prevent us. That such miserable fellaheen, backed only by a government of the weakest and meanest on earth, should forbid the entrance of a Christian (only because he is such) to any place of biblical interest, is a disgrace to the civilization of the

age; and the Christian nations of the earth owe it to themselves to correct this state of things, either by diplomacy or the
sword, at the earliest possible moment.[104]

Sometime later, when Freese was touring Hebron, he was again enraged by the Muslim "bigotry" that prevented him from seeing the
Tomb of the Patriarchs closer than from within ten feet of the gate
of the mosque's outer court. According to Freese's calculations this
time, a dozen armed Americans were needed to clear the way. Fum-
ing, Freese added that he understood the "zealous and holy enthusiasm of the Crusaders, and had we lived in their day, we should have
liked to join them in ridding Palestine of these bigoted Mohammedans."[105]

Taylor took playful offense at the refusal of Jerusalem's pasha to
grant Taylor's group a firman (letter of permission) to use the fin-
ished sections of the road then under construction between Jaffa
and Jerusalem—on the grounds that the large number of Christians
in the party (there were nine) might "feloniously pick up the fin-

Fig. 13. JAFFA AND ITS ROCKY BREAKWATER. For many Americans, the sight of the town of Jaffa was their first (or last) encounter
with the reality of Ottoman Palestine.

ished portion of the road and carry it away with us." Taylor was bothered by the denial, not so much for himself as for the six clergymen of the party who suffered from "this most wanton and scandalous imputation by this heathen ruler." He said, "I now, and here, desire to hold him up to the indignant reprobation of all mankind in all christianized and civilized lands."[106]

Because tourism is an ongoing activity, it is not easily chronicled. This sampling of travelers and their thoughts during a single period—the Gilded Age—demonstrates how Americans' preconceived image of the Holy Land affected their tourist experience in Ottoman Palestine. The dutiful devotion to and habitual reverence for a place Americans were seeing for the first time shed light on the "image/ reality" process of perception and the character of American geopiety. Interposing itself between Americans and their perceptions of the Holy Land's landscape, peoples, and features, the myth of the past caused American tourists either to be disappointed with the reality of Ottoman Palestine or to have their previously held assumptions reinforced. It also shaped most travel itineraries in Palestine by promoting traditional sites over contemporary ones, and it directly or indirectly affected the routine activities of the tourists, for instance, by encouraging extensive souvenir-gathering. But tourism is only a transitory experience.[107] The more assiduous American experiences in Palestine examined in the next chapters provide a way of further gauging the effects of Americans' Holy Land imagery.

CHAPTER 4

Evangelizing the Motherland of Missions

The heavy scent of orange blossoms greeted Miss Parkman when she first made her way on deck in the early morning of Monday, April 3, 1871. The steamer she and her family had boarded in Port Said, Egypt, now lay off the breakwater at Jaffa. Although the ship was hundreds of yards from shore, the odor was so strong Miss Parkman could hardly believe it came from land. Later that day, after being ferried by a Turkish seaman through the breakwater's treacherous rocks and landing amid a "motley crowd of natives," the young American tourist found herself marveling happily that she was standing in the bright, beautiful sunshine of the Holy Land.

Jaffa offered a number of attractions for newly arrived tourists, but the minor chores and drudgeries of travel engaged Miss Parkman's first attentions. She and a few of her party sought out the home of the American consular agent in order to leave some baggage for safekeeping during her group's trek up to Jerusalem. The agent's house was away from the center of Jaffa, though it was easily found: it had an American eagle over the door. Oddly out of character with its surroundings, the house seemed like a small wooden New England home, only "more genial" because "instead of being darkened, the rooms were full of light and the windows offered a view unlike anything in New England." The home was occupied by two American sisters—"very New England looking women," Miss Parkman observed, "a little stiff at first, though kindly and thawing into cordiality as they talked, as Yankees do."

The two women explained that they were operating a missionary school in Jaffa and that the son of one of them, who was the consular agent, was abroad lecturing at a missionary training school. The sisters said they had met little opposition to their teaching activities among the Muslims. When asked about the house, they described for their visitors how it had originally been brought from America "by Yankee mechanics" who were part of an unfortunate colony of Second Adventists, which had been dissolved after being "swindled by the scamp at their head, their leader, a Mr. Adams." The last of those colonists had been sent home through the generosity of an American tourist only four years before. Miss Parkman later wrote in her diary that she found the little New England house with its "thoroughly New England women" a pleasant episode during her travels. "The ladies appeared so unchanged," she noted, "as if they had just stepped 'round from New Haven. . . . It was quite refreshing, we felt, as we passed out again into Eastern life."[1]

The two women in the little New England–style house on Jaffa's fragrant shores were Mary Briscoe Baldwin and Ann Maury Hay. Mrs. Hay's son, John Baldwin Hay, was the absent consular agent and soon to be appointed U.S. consul-general for Syria, working out of Beirut. Mrs. Hay was a widow; her sister Mary had never married. It is amusing how the flavor of the incongruous surroundings led young Miss Parkman to conclude that the sisters were New England Yankees. Actually, they were blue-blooded Virginians, born on their grandfather's estate in the Shenandoah Valley, two of the twelve children of a highly respected physician, and grandnieces, through their mother, of President James Madison.[2] The women's lengthy residence abroad—first in Greece and then in Jaffa—had eroded their Southern "charms" down to a Yankee-like severity, to a stranger like Miss Parkman.

The story of the two sisters and their encounter with a passing tourist introduces a further dimension of the story of American experiences in Ottoman Palestine and of the relationship of those experiences to the image of the Holy Land in American minds. Several groups of Americans—missionaries, colonists, and diplomatic consuls, that is, people who stayed overseas longer than tourists—represented various kinds of long-term commitments to an American presence in Palestine. The people in each of these groups had different motivations for being in the Holy Land, and their respective efforts differed in terms of continuity. Yet each group demonstrated, in their various ways, the powerful and pervasive legacy of Holy Land imagery in their respective affairs.

Miss Parkman's encounter with the Jaffa sisters also highlights the extent of interconnections among members of these long-resident groups. John Hay was a consular appointee living, and perhaps occasionally working, with his mother and aunt, who were missionaries; their shared residence was an abandoned property of the aborted Adams Colony. The colony and the American consular presence are taken up separately in later chapters. Here we consider the longest sustained American presence in the Holy Land: that of the missionaries.

The Missionary Imperative

The Jaffa sisters Miss Parkman met that spring 1871 represented the only significant effort of one of the major American Protestant churches to penetrate the Holy Land in the nineteenth century. Yet their work and that of other individuals and groups of American evangelical Protestants came to be eclipsed by the better-known efforts of the American Board of Commissioners for Foreign Missions, the interchurch New England body that nearly monopolized the Near East mission field throughout the nineteenth century. The American Board had the greatest impact on the most influential members of America's religious establishment, but as the presence of the two women at Jaffa indicates, American missionary work in the Holy Land was not confined to the American Board and its fieldworkers. Moreover, the work of American missionaries of all affiliations played a role in forming and sustaining certain Holy Land images and motifs.

Motivated by the desire to spread Christianity, a diverse assortment of American Protestants attempted to base their evangelistic activities in the Holy Land. Some of their efforts were desultory, truncated by a lack of resources, personnel, or desire to compete in an already crowded and unpromising field; the efforts of others showed some durability. All American missionary efforts, however, displayed two important features. First, their ventures in the Holy

Land were somewhat erratic, comprising incohesive, discontinuous episodes that lacked a sense of progression or growth. Second, the Holy Land as a mission field always had special meaning to Americans who were willing to stake a claim to it, simply because the Holy Land was the land where Christianity was born and from which it had spread centuries before. It was the land of Jesus, whose message Christianity bore, it was the land of the remnants of the earliest and most primitive churches, it was the land that Christians had won and lost during the Crusades, and, above all, it was both a land that was inextricably part of the Christian past and an opportune place for spreading the Christian future, as conceived in the nineteenth century. It was, in short, a land made special through the geopious regard of Americans.

Unusual inducements made the Holy Land an attractive and almost irresistible field for missionary work. But the Americans were just one of several national groups trying to gain a foothold there. British and European Protestant missionary efforts, in particular, served as a context into which the Americans fit. The "context" slowly became formalized in the development of the Protestant bishopric in Jerusalem, first centered at the city's Christ Church. In the first half of the nineteenth century, British missionary efforts were dominated by the London Society for Promoting Christianity Among the Jews (also called the London Jews Society) and the Church Missionary Society (for a time an arm of the Anglican church and the model for the American Board). The Protestant bishopric in Jerusalem was established in 1841 as a post jointly sponsored by Britain and Germany, to further Christianity and later to support their imperialist pretensions at protecting the Protestant citizenry of the Ottoman domains.[3]

The concept of spreading the faith and proselytizing nonbelievers dates back to the foundation of Christianity. That feature animated the faith and enabled it to survive the numerous schisms and dissensions that tore into the Church—not the least of which fomented the creation of numerous Protestant denominations from the 1500s onward. American Protestantism demonstrated a missionary impulse from the very genesis of the American church. One primary purpose in founding British colonies in North America had been to spread the gospel—that is, the message of Christianity. Both in Virginia and in Massachusetts (even though the ecclesiastical forms of religion were markedly dissimilar), the extension of the Christian faith to native "heathens" was a stated goal of those involved in the colonial venture.

From these beginnings, Christian missionary expression found its way into many facets of American life. It spread the gospel among the native populace, brought it to noncommitted, hereditarily Christian Americans, and delivered it to people imported as slaves. From this base of North American "home mission" work, Americans were ready to turn their attentions overseas by the early nineteenth century.

The missionary outlook of American Protestants was global in scope early in the history of the United States. The goal was to extend American Protestant influence "to the remotest corners of the ruined world."[4] This attitude correlated well with the spirit of mission engendered in the American democratic spirit. Missionaries promoted both Christianity and democracy in their uniquely American forms.[5] The most conspicuous institutional example of this fusion, the American Board of Commissioners for Foreign Missions, was born under legendary circumstances.

The American Board

In 1806 it was said that five Williams College undergraduates, led by Samuel Johnson Mills, took refuge under a haystack during a violent thunderstorm. While the heavens crashed over the huddled students' heads, the group pledged themselves to carry the gospel abroad. America's foreign mission movement was conceived. Two years later, taking his pledge seriously, Mills founded the Society of the Brethren, whose purpose was to "effect in the persons of its members a mission or missions to the heathen." Shortly thereafter, its main center relocated to Andover Theological Seminary, one of the nation's premier Protestant schools. By 1810 a more formal organization for foreign mission work arose in the Society's stead: the American Board of Commissioners for Foreign Missions. The first American Protestant missionaries to arrive in the Holy Land were members of the American Board, and between 1821 and 1844 Board personnel used Jerusalem as a central base in the Levant region, although there were periods when no Board people were working in the Holy Land itself.

American missionary thrusts into Palestine took place not long after similar British moves were made in the area, a fact that had ramifications later in the century. Joseph Wolff, an apostate German Jew, settled in England in 1819 and became a member of the

Church of England.[6] After two years of study at Cambridge, Wolff became a worker for the London Jews Society, then one of the largest British missionary associations. He toured the Middle East, including the Holy Land, at approximately the same time the American Board was getting ready to send its first workers to Palestine.

The American missionary approach to the various peoples of the Ottoman realm was shaped largely by the strategy developed by the American Board. By default, the strategy in spreading the Gospel was aimed at Eastern Christians. These "primitive" and "underdeveloped" Christians were to be readied to assume an evangelical role in spreading Christianity to Muslims and Jews. The reason for this circuitous attack on adherents of other faiths, historian Joseph Grabill has made clear, was simply that personal, voluntary choice in religious affiliation was illegal within the Turkish Empire. For Muslims, outright conversion to Christianity was not only a religious iniquity but also a capital crime against a theocratic state. Unfortunately, Board missionaries interpreted this Ottoman stance "all too often in terms of the righteousness of Protestantism and the sinfulness of Ottoman life—a view which hindered realistic analysis."[7]

Because a simple frontal approach to Muslims was not possible, when Americans began their missionary work in the area they steered clear of direct contact with the Muslim population and concentrated on the native Christian churches and their nominal adherents. Because the Americans viewed these churches as corrupt, impure forms of Christianity, the task of the missionary was to regenerate these churches and make them better examples of the rightness of Christianity to the Muslim majority, opening the way to wide-scale conversion of Muslims.

Initially, Jews in the Ottoman Empire also seemed an enticing and safe target for Protestant evangelical work. But the Jewish communities within the Turkish realm were quite cohesive in certain impenetrable respects. As an officially recognized minority, Jews usually displayed strong ethnic and religious loyalties. Furthermore, in the Holy Land, Jewish resistance to evangelical meanderings was buttressed by economics: the welfare of the individual and the family could be jeopardized if the *halukah* (charity fund) stipend used to sustain many Jewish residents was withheld.

With the Eastern Christians marked as the primary target of missionary work, the initial tactic of the Board was the distribution of Bibles, a method plainly indicative of the Protestant belief in the inherently regenerative qualities of the Bible and the power of individual interpretation in sparking reform. On the island of Malta, the

Board set up a printing press and a regional center for distributing Bibles.

The pioneering work of the Board in the Holy Land was performed by Levi Parsons and Pliny Fisk, two young idealists from Boston. Their departure addresses delivered in Boston on the last Sunday of October 1819 show that they were keenly aware of the import of their mission. Parsons spoke of the "dereliction and restoration of the Jews" in terms that linked the forthcoming enterprise, which would be centered at Jerusalem where "every eye is fixed," with a movement leading to the eventual conversion of all Jews.[8] Fisk soberly enumerated the factors that made them choose the Holy Land to start their mission: the attractions of the land, its sacred associations, and its peoples; the advantages of success in such a central location; the challenges posed by the many difficulties of the field; and the favorable indications of Providence for success. "But though we are cheered with animating hopes," Fisk said prophetically, "yet we go, not knowing the things that shall befall us. Whether we shall be buried in a watery tomb; whether disease shall bring us to an early grave."[9]

Parsons and Fisk traveled up and down the Mediterranean coast in 1821, preaching and distributing their Bibles in Egypt, Palestine, and Syria. But the rigors of this life proved too taxing for the New Englanders. By 1822 Parsons was dead at Alexandria, and his partner lasted only three years more, dying in Beirut in October 1825. Meanwhile, other American churchmen had been motivated by the call of the East. When news of Parsons's death reached Paris, Jonas King, an American student, offered his services to Fisk and the Board. In October 1823, King was joined by several missionaries who had come with their wives: William Goodell and Frank Bird.

But when King and Fisk told Goodell and Bird that conditions at Jerusalem were too tenuous for the Board's purposes, the newcomers headed for Beirut. The conditions that ensured the prosperity of that Lebanese city—a safe, accessible harbor with a large foreign national presence[10]—also ensured that the work of the American Board too would prosper in a more northern setting. The mission attracted visitors of diverse religious persuasions, and the able people of the mission were quick to engage in amiable discussions. It became clear that the character of American missionary activity functioned best through educational (rather than, for example, medical) practices. The educational approach was a logical extension of the American impulse to spread both Christianity and democracy. Free and open education was a concept that fit the American like a

Fig. 14. LEVI PARSONS, AMERICAN BOARD MISSIONARY. Parsons, together with Pliny Fisk, was the first American missionary sent to the Holy Land by the American Board of Commissioners for Foreign Missions. Conditions unanticipated at the time of their departure in 1819 were responsible for Parsons's death by 1822.

Fig. 15. PLINY FISK, AMERICAN BOARD MISSIONARY. Fisk was only slightly more hardy than his partner, Levi Parsons. Fisk worked in the mission field until his death in 1825, but he had the pleasure of knowing that others were following his lead.

Fig. 16. JONAS KING OF
THE AMERICAN BOARD
IN NATIVE COSTUME.
Parsons and Fisk were followed by other Americans
deeply committed to evan-
gelization in the Holy
Land. Jonas King, depicted
here in native dress, interrupted his studies in Paris
to join in the work of the
American Board.

glove, especially in an area where formal schooling was not universal. The Americans established several schools around the city and
even ventured into the innovative area of female education. Eventually, they established such respected institutions as Roberts College
in Constantinople and the American University in Beirut.

At first, the Americans were courteously received by the Eastern
Christian leadership, but relations soon deteriorated. They met bitter resistance from some leaders, especially those affiliated with the
Roman Catholic church, such as the Maronites and Melchites. In
1824 these anti-Protestant forces induced Sultan Mahmud II to for-
bid Bible distribution within the empire. In Jerusalem certain missionaries had been arrested for hawking their Bibles, but the inter-
vention of the British consul and the subsequent removal of the
governor made other Turkish authorities reluctant to enforce the
order. That reluctance, however, did not mean the Americans were
on the verge of being accepted.

The Maronite patriarch pronounced a peremptory curse on all

who would carry on commerce with the Americans, and by 1839 the Protestants even claimed a martyr for their cause when one of the native members succumbed to tortures inspired by the Patriarch's wrath. The resistance had the effect of altering the Americans' strategy: they would raise up an independent, native Protestant church, instead of working with the established Eastern churches. This strategy produced an assertive independence on the part of native peoples, which came to be identified as a uniquely American contribution.

The turbulent internal affairs of the empire also affected the work of American Board personnel. The Greek revolt, for example, spilled into the eastern Mediterranean between 1828 and 1830 and forced relocation of mainland missionaries to the island base at Malta. And the revolt of Mehemet Ali and the subsequent reconquest of the region by the Turks, with European aid, caused severe dislocations. Strife between Druze and Maronite minorities also tore through the area and damaged the interests of the Americans. These developments reinforced the desirability of Beirut, with its quick access to the sea, as the center for American Board work rather than Jerusalem.[11] If the Board's decision-makers had not been so convinced by their image of the Holy Land as the appropriate motherland of missions, they might have foreseen or better analyzed the conditions that mandated the relocation and never have bothered starting at Jerusalem.

One early triumph of the Americans was their recognition of the importance of a superior Arabic language body of tract literature produced in an acceptable typescript. This work proceeded under the able direction of physician Eli Smith, a remarkable figure. Born in 1801 in Connecticut and a graduate of Yale and Andover Theological Seminary, Smith arrived in the Levant in 1824 to run the Board's printing operations. With a keen scholarly eye Smith reviewed and corrected nearly everything that passed through the press. As an orientalist, he was diligent and open to new challenges. One such challenge came in 1830 and 1831 when Smith and fellow missionary William Goodell explored the eastern reaches of Asia Minor in search of a better understanding of Armenia's ancient Christian community. In 1837, 1838, and again in 1852, Smith explored the Holy Land as guide for the pioneer biblical archaeologist Edward Robinson, but perhaps his greatest contribution was his extensive translations of the Bible into Arabic.

Other American Board missionaries were closely linked with the Holy Land during their service in Lebanon. Such names as Bird,

Jessup, Van Lennep, and Bliss were widely recognized by Americans as embodying connections between the American Board and the Holy Land, even after the initial labors of Fisk, Parsons, and King came to end and the center of Board operations was focused in Beirut. But of all the American Board workers to be associated with the Holy Land, one in particular stands out for having made the broadest contribution to American Holy Land consciousness: Dr. William M. Thomson.

It was widely believed that Thomson visited and traveled through the Holy Land more often than any other nineteenth-century Western figure. Working in the region over a forty-year period, Thomson came to know Palestine intimately. From his extensive knowledge, he wrote *The Land and the Book* (1859), one of the most widely read and used works about the Holy Land ever written by an American. Thomson's volume was used as a Sunday school prize for generations of Americans,[12] and in England it outsold any previous American book except *Uncle Tom's Cabin*. In a polished literary style, as a way of illuminating the Bible, Thomson described the topography, sites, and beauty of the Holy Land in their biblical context, as well as the manners and customs of the land's populace.

The work of the American Board was undeniably part of America's missionary experience in the Holy Land. The efforts of the Board to establish a foothold in the Holy Land, though thwarted, illustrate how seriously the Board took the charge of the apostle Luke to preach "among all nations, beginning at Jerusalem." While it is true that the Board's activities eventually shifted into Lebanon and Syria, its missionaries continued to be associated with the Holy Land in the minds of the American people.

Meanwhile, in practical terms, the British continued to make inroads in Palestine, and a tacit arrangement evolved between British and American missionary institutions to honor each other's sphere of influence. Thus, Henry Bellows observed during his visit to Jerusalem in 1867 that there appeared to be no American missionaries in the city because of the agreement to leave the field to the British, "who seem to work it faithfully."[13] Traveler Joseph Taylor reflected from a different perspective. He saw the missionaries

> as one of the hopeful signs of the times, as one of the first rays of light, shooting through the gloom of the long black night that has shrouded this God-forsaken land in darkness, for so many centuries; and would seem to give augury of the coming day to Palestine. It is a beautiful thought that this land

of the far East, from whose sacred shores the light of the Gospel was shed abroad, until the great western world became illuminated with it, and then went out from here into darkness; that now, the first glimmer of the return of this glorious light from the far west, as seen faintly, but surely, resting upon the hills of Judea and of Galilee. We believe . . . [there are] many Providences at work here, that will eventuate in the radiation of this once goodly land with Christian light; that this once goodly land will again flow with milk and honey as of yore, and that peace, and comfort, and joy, and good will, and all the other blessed concomitants of Christianity will again gladden the land.[14]

Despite the relocation of American Board work to Lebanon and Syria, Palestine was never quite abandoned by American Protestants as a mission field. Other Americans engaged in evangelical work in the Holy Land, and those missionaries were equally important parts of the entire American experience in Ottoman Palestine. Their stories too illustrate the persistence of the American image of the Holy Land. Most of these other missionaries were affiliated with recognized organizations, such as the Society of Friends and the Christian and Missionary Alliance. Others were singularly motivated, perhaps preaching in the streets during a Holy Land sojourn, such as the ranting American "missionary" that Charles "Chinese" Gordon saw in Jerusalem in 1883.[15] Of the recognized groups, the efforts of two are especially representative of the missionary experience: the Disciples (the Christian Church) and the Society of Friends.

Disciples and Friends

With the words "Here am I, send me," the Rev. James Turner Barclay volunteered his services to the Mission Board of the Christian Church (the Disciples) in 1848. Barclay, a resident of Virginia,[16] convinced the Board to send him and his family to Jerusalem to establish a missionary presence, and they arrived in the Holy City on February 8, 1851.[17] Barclay represented the efforts of the Christian Church, an indigenous American denomination that sought the reunification of Christianity through a restoration of fundamental, "primitive Christianity." The call for this church to send a missionary to Jerusalem was sounded by the denomination's leader, Alexander Campbell, when he wrote:

> We strongly incline to the opinion that, of all the foreign fields that claim our attention, to which energies can be directed, and our means employed, Jerusalem, that great center of attraction, that great rendezvous—visited by men of all climes and of all foreign tongues—demands our first efforts and our earliest attention.[18]

Barclay's early enthusiasm for the new post soon fell victim to frustration over the state of affairs in Jerusalem. "There is no worse missionary ground in all the earth than this city,"[19] he finally reported back in exasperation. Barclay soon began expending his energies in nonmissionary directions as compensation for failure as a missionary. In 1853 he was commissioned by Sultan Abdülmecid to advise the Turkish architect carrying out repairs to the Dome of the Rock.[20] Since access to the Temple Mount had officially been denied to Franks for years, Barclay's opportunity gave him several weeks of unique viewing and enough material to compose an interesting look at the Haram (the Temple Mount enclosure and platform) and contemporary Jerusalem in a book, *City of the Great King*. To this day, Barclay's name remains archaeologically associated with Jerusalem, for it was he who first drew attention to a walled-up portal of the Second Temple period in the southwestern section of the great retaining wall, only yards away from the famous Robinson's Arch; it is still known as "Barclay's Gate."

In addition to service as a missionary and his contribution to the public's knowledge of contemporary Jerusalem and its sights, Barclay's impact extended indirectly into the diplomatic area of relations between America and the Holy Land, though not to the degree that American Board missionaries would affect them later in the early twentieth century.[21] Barclay's only daughter, Sarah, became the wife of J. Augustus Johnson, U.S. consul at Beirut. Sarah Barclay Johnson personified the connection between missionaries and diplomats. In her own right, she also contributed to the Holy Land consciousness of Americans as the author of a popular work, *Hadji in Syria*. Titus Tobler, the nineteenth-century Swiss scientist and explorer, lauded *Hadji* somewhat backhandedly, describing it as "the best book about the Holy Land written by a woman."[22]

Another American denomination that attempted to establish a missionary presence in the Holy Land was the Society of Friends, the

Quakers. The height of the evangelical movement within the Friends corresponded to establishment of a mission station and school at Ramallah in 1869 by a husband-and-wife team acting independently of any specific Friends group. Eli and Sybil Jones had journeyed from Boston on April 10, 1867, having been sent off by a prestigious company of well-wishers, among whom were a general and the governor of Massachusetts. The couple traveled extensively in Egypt before reaching Lebanon in October 1867. At Beirut, they observed the work of the American Board and were given a chance to "winter over" before setting off to establish themselves. Their first effort was in Syria, but it faltered due to Sybil's ill health. The couple was forced to retreat to England during 1868.

By May 1869 the Joneses received a sustaining sum of money for their proposed work in the East, and they returned to the region with renewed vigor. While passing through Ramallah, then a mostly Muslim village located north of Jerusalem, a young girl approached their party and pointed out that the town had a school for boys but none for girls. The candid and winning child admitted that she herself had been educated in a German school in Jerusalem, and she volunteered to conduct the Ramallah school herself if she could get assistance. The Joneses were touched by her enthusiasm and were inspired to open their mission in the town, along with a girls' school.

Sybil Jones died in December 1873. Eli carried on and eventually had a role in establishing a school at Brumanna, near Beirut. With British and American Friends working together closely, the two stations functioned under a sort of bi-national control until 1887, after which the Ramallah school was placed under the exclusive care of American Friends. Because Timothy and Anna Hussey were assigned to the Ramallah post after the death of Eli Jones,[23] the efforts of the Joneses in the Holy Land were significantly more enduring than those of the American Board or the Disciples, for the school still functions in Ramallah, albeit in an altered and expanded form.

In addition to these church-associated groups and individuals, there were other Americans doing missionary work in the Holy Land throughout the nineteenth century. Frequently, these were people who lacked the backing of formal missionary bodies. For example, an American woman, a Miss Ford, was said to have worked from a base in the Galilee city of Safed during the 1870s, extending her mission to the Druze of the Golan region. Achieving some reputed success, she later asked the American Presbyterian Mission in Syria, a successor organization to the American Board, to adopt her efforts and sustain them. Eventually, two small Protestant congregations were said to have arisen from her work.[24]

Two Jaffa Sisters

The disorganized nature of some missionary enterprises has caused many historians of missions to overlook them. Unfortunately, the work of the American sisters at Jaffa fell into this category. As noted previously, the work of one of them, Mary Baldwin, represented the only serious attempt of a major American church to missionize in the Holy Land. In 1871, when Miss Parkman met the women, Mary Baldwin had worked overseas for thirty-six years, with only a few months leave spent in the United States during all that time. She was the first unmarried woman sent out by the Foreign Committee of the Protestant Episcopal church's Mission Board, which made her also one of America's first single female missionaries.[25]

Fig. 17. JAFFA MISSIONARY MARY BRISCOE BALDWIN. Protestant Episcopal missionary Mary Briscoe Baldwin was founder of a boys' school at Jaffa in 1869. With the severe look of a New England Yankee, she served a special function as a missionary link between Americans and the Holy Land.

Mrs. Hay, unlike her sister, was not a missionary in a formal sense. She resided with her sister and aided in the former's work, but she received no stipend from a mission board. In fact, the Episcopal church worked in the Holy Land only through Mary Baldwin, for after Mary's death in 1877 the church board terminated its financial support of the mission school Mary had started in Jaffa, even though it continued to operate under Mrs. Hay's direction. Mary Baldwin's life story is studded with several well-known nineteenth-century personalities. She was a protégé of William Meade, the Protestant Episcopal bishop of Virginia; she was a personal friend of Florence Nightingale; and support for her desire to work at Jaffa was an adopted cause of Virginia Farragut, the American admiral's wife.

Born in 1811, Mary grew up an intelligent and independent though impressionable youth. As a young woman, she had been delivered to the missionary cause by a chance remark during a sewing meeting. A friend would later recall, "We had been reading the life of some devoted servant of God, and all felt aglow with admiration of his sacrifice"[26] when someone asked Mary if she would like to serve. Despite an affirmative desire, Mary was initially constrained. "Being (much to my sorrow) a female, I could not possibly enter the ministry," she later confided in an autobiographical sketch. "Next to this, my thoughts turned to missionary life, and this too seemed to me to be a sphere quite out of my reach."[27] However, Mary was soon moved enough to renounce "a very unprofitable life, that of pleasure seeking only," in order to pursue a career as a teacher. Before long, she volunteered to assist a Mr. and Mrs. Hill, who had opened an Episcopal mission school in Athens. Off she went to Greece, salaried by the Foreign Committee at $250 per year.

The Episcopal church first sent missionaries to Greece shortly after the Greeks won independence from the Turks in 1829. The Greek missions were the Episcopal church's first overseas efforts and were motivated as much by sympathy for the suffering the revolt caused as by the desire to claim souls. The Greek people were seen as nominal Christians who "needed a pure, practical, sound form of doctrine and an open Bible" instead of their professedly Christian, but "corrupt church." Mary Briscoe Baldwin was sent to Greece in 1835. She worked under the committee's direction at Athens through 1864, at which time a change in her health required her to give up some duties. Although she continued to work, Mary retired at last from the Athens post in June 1869, when she left to join her sister at Jaffa.[28]

John Baldwin Hay received his appointment to the Jaffa post in 1867, the same year the ill-fated Adams Colony from Maine disbanded. Joined by his mother, who had been living with Mary, the two Hays then offered classes for destitute boys as a counterpart to a girls' school founded in 1863 and run by a Miss Walker Arnott of the Scottish Presbyterian church's Tabitha Mission.[29] Once Mary arrived, the Jaffa boys' school began to assume more formal proportions.

During its first years, the school was supported by travelers' donations and a few overseas patrons. Then Mary returned to the United States in 1872, partly to visit her native land and kindred, and partly to ask the Foreign Committee to support and "take charge of my work."[30] The committee approved of the school and Mary's efforts, but it did not formally adopt the school as an extension of its interests until 1874.[31] So Mary felt compelled to turn to a public appeal. While in the United States, Mary Baldwin lectured about her school and, no doubt, also about the Holy Land. As a result, she was able to raise some funds, chiefly in the South. Three days after arriving in New York, however, she suffered a fall coming out of a church and was confined for three months.

Because her movements were restricted and it was necessary for her to return to Jaffa, Mary Baldwin turned to written communications about the school. Although most of the letters she wrote were directed to individuals, Mary frequently addressed them to the recipients' Sunday school class or mission society. In response to a contribution, she would assign one of her pupils to the donor, describing the student's circumstances, talents, and potential for conversion while getting the student—if capable—to write a letter as well. Many of these letters were also reprinted in *The Spirit of Missions*, a widely circulated missionary journal that also provided "timely and interesting" descriptions of Jaffa and conditions in the Holy Land generally. In Mary's words, she used *The Spirit of Missions* "for the comfort of my numerous friends, to whom I cannot write now."[32]

Mary Baldwin died at Jaffa on June 20, 1877. With her death, the Foreign Committee reconsidered its backing of the school, and though the school itself remained open under the direction of Ann Hay, the committee decided to let its commitment stand only through the end of 1877, notifying Mrs. Hay that the school's appropriation would then be terminated. Mrs. Hay, however, steadfastly continued to operate the school (during Mary's lifetime the "Joppa Mission School" and after her death the "Mary Baldwin Memorial School") as a private enterprise.[33] The school's apex came in 1876 with an enrollment of fifty-two, including Muslims, Jews, and Christians. However, attendance did not guarantee that the student would become a Protestant Christian. There is no way to gauge the mission's success as an evangelical institution. The mission came to a

Fig. 18. MISSIONARIES HAY AND DAVIDSON. Mary Baldwin's sister, Ann Hay, and assistant, Miss Davidson, tried to sustain the mission school at Jaffa after Baldwin's death but could not secure continued funding from their church's Foreign Committee.

close as an American venture when it was absorbed into the educational work being done at Jaffa under the direction of the Anglican Church Missionary Society.[34] Meanwhile, the Episcopal School in Athens, at which Mary Baldwin had once worked, was funded by the Episcopal church through 1899, "when it was continued as a private venture of interested church people."[35] The commitment to run and fund missionary ventures was not always unwavering.

The "Y," Students, and an Alliance

Regardless of the status of missions in individual Protestant churches, the missionary impulse present in American Protestantism during the early and mid-nineteenth century did not wane as time wore on. Instead, the pace of evangelical outreach accelerated into what has become known as a great age of Christian expansion. During this new age, "the leadership and initiative in Protestant foreign missionary enterprise" passed from European control to American control.[36] The goal of the American leadership was to help Christianity "become the first and only religion with a widely dispersed, intercontinental constituency."[37] Kenneth Scott Latourette, historian of Christianity's expansion, has noted that through missionary purpose and vision Americans helped to create a "world embracing fellowship" among Protestant Christians,[38] a fellowship that was built around self-governing, self-supporting, and self-propagating churches, associations, and movements united through a common purpose.[39]

One result of evangelical ferment was the World Missionary Conference held in Edinburgh, Scotland, in 1910, "an ecumenical gathering of twelve hundred Protestant missionaries from every part of the earth."[40] Although it was an unprecedented event, it emerged as a result of several trends, not the least of which was the evolution of the aforementioned stronger, better organized, multidenominational missionary associations and movements. Three examples of such movements and groups are notable in terms of the American experience in the Holy Land.

The first example is the YMCA (Young Men's Christian Association) movement. Luther Wishard was the first American YMCA official to have contact with the Holy Land as a potential field for expansion, but his initial impressions of the field were quite negative. "The Promised Land is the most unpromising land for successful association work I have yet visited," Wishard wrote during a world tour of YMCA foreign missions in 1891.[41] An early advocate of Christian associations for young men on American college and university campuses, Wishard was also chiefly responsible for turning these student YMCAs into an intercollegiate movement with a definite evangelical purpose. At Jerusalem, Wishard discovered a small British YMCA that had been founded in 1890 by W. Hind Smith of the English National Council of the YMCA. There had been even earlier attempts to found similar ventures at Jerusalem, as far back as 1876 and 1878. Having been there first, the British were chiefly responsible for the success of the association at Jerusalem before World War I. Only after the war did Americans assume a larger role in the Jerusalem "Y," especially under the guidance of John R. Mott.

For most of his ninety years of life, John Mott was at the epicenter of the American missionary enterprise. As a product of evangelist

Dwight Moody's summer program for college men, Mott turned his zeal into a creative force that gave birth to the Student Volunteer Movement, an offshoot of the YMCA program. Mott's call to "evangelize the world" during his generation eventually led to his chairing the Edinburgh conference. It also led to the creation of the World Student Christian Federation, the International Missionary Council, and the World Council of Churches. Mott became a force in world affairs and received the Nobel Peace Prize in 1946.[42] In terms of the pre-1918 Holy Land, however, Mott was important for his contribution to the Student Volunteer Movement.

The Student Volunteer Movement served as a clearinghouse for student volunteer missionaries,[43] who were sent to corners of the globe where evangelical work was under way. Because it was removed from the bureaucratic and practical necessities of fielding a missionary operation, the movement served as a goad to further expansion. For example, when S. M. Zwemer addressed the Fifth International Convention of the Student Volunteer Movement in Nashville, Tennessee, in 1905, on "The Evangelization of the Mohammedan World in This Generation," he called the audience's attention to the (justifiable) reluctance of established missionary boards to inaugurate Muslim missions. Zwemer was not concerned with practicalities. He appealed to the students "to concentrate their lives and lay them down, if need be, in this great work."[44]

The Student Volunteer Movement did append young missionaries to some posts in the Holy Land and the Levant during its heyday, but records of these activities are spotty. As a missionary enterprise, the movement missed the mark in a crucial, fateful sense. Before World War I, most volunteers came from large university campuses, but after the war only denominational schools and colleges could be relied on to produce enough potential new missionaries. In a changing America, secular higher education could no longer be depended on to supply the number of recruits for the missionary cause it once had. Religious indifference and secular influences were beginning to take their toll, and only the denominational schools seemed immune.[45] By the 1930s, the movement had expended itself for lack of available personnel.

A third example of a refocused, latter-nineteenth-century missionary group displayed considerably more success. This group was the Christian and Missionary Alliance, an organization that began operating a mission station in Jerusalem and several other locales in the Holy Land in the 1890s. The Christian and Missionary Alliance grew out of the vision of Albert B. Simpson,[46] a Canadian-born Presbyterian minister and natural orator, who believed that the duty to spread the gospel rested on the shoulders of all believers, not just on the shoulders of the specialized mission societies of the various churches. From a pulpit in New York City, Simpson carried forth this message of his ministry.

Inspired by Simpson, a Mr. H. Conly of Pittsburgh, Pennsylvania, was moved to donate $5,000 toward establishment of a Christian and Missionary Alliance station at Jerusalem in 1889. One year later, in 1890, the first missionary activity associated with the Alliance was performed at Bethany (just outside of Jerusalem) by a Miss Lucy Dunn, along with an English woman. In the fall of that year, a Miss Eliza J. Robertson joined the effort. The field was given its first real boost through the visit of Simpson himself, who in 1893 took a world tour of the mission field. "His brief visit to the Holy Land was one of the sweetest memories of his life," a biographer wrote in 1920.

> "Sweet Olivet, sweet Bethany, my heart shall oft remember thee" is a couplet from one of several beautiful hymns and poems which he composed during the visit. He was kindly received by the missionaries of other societies in Jerusalem and assisted in the opening services of the Mildmay Mission Hospital at Hebron, then under the charge of Mrs. Bowie of England. The Alliance had no mission in Palestine at that time, but Miss Lucy Dunn and Miss E. J. Robertson had been in Jerusalem for three years supported by friends of the Alliance. On Mr. Simpson's return to New York, the board decided to take up work in the Land of our Lord.[47]

The Simpson visit presaged the arrival of more missionaries at Jerusalem. A day school for boys was soon established in the Holy City, and a second Christian girls' school was set up at Jaffa as a result of the momentum Simpson generated. In 1899, under the direction of the Rev. F. H. Senft, the girls' school was moved to Jerusalem, and the American Free Church at Jerusalem was organized under the direction of Albert E. Thompson. Although efforts at Jerusalem took precedence, the Alliance was strong enough to establish stations at Hebron, Ein Karem, and Beersheba. Its most meaningful achievements during this period were the creation of a training school and the establishment in Jerusalem of a strong, centralized authority for mission work. The key to this authority was the Alliance's American Free Church.

Fig. 19. THE CHRISTIAN AND MISSIONARY ALLIANCE CHURCH IN
JERUSALEM. The church is on Prophets Street in downtown Jerusalem today. Its pulpit was made available to visiting American ministers
touring the Holy Land with their congregations.

The Alliance church at Jerusalem attracted a broad spectrum of
worshipers. With a pulpit open to traveling ministers and evangelists, it provided a touch of the exotic together with a taste of home
for traveling Americans. The church building itself, constructed of
native stone, took six years to complete. Construction began in 1908,
but contradictory government regulations and a lack of money plagued
the project. Many donations came from the offerings of tourists,
gifts that helped sustain the church and the mission even after its
dedication in 1914.[48]

By about the same time, 1914, there were eight American missionary societies represented in the Holy Land and Syria, fielding an
overseas staff of more than 120 people: 28 ordained and 23 short-
term workers, 42 wives, and 30 unmarried women and widows.
These American missionaries were spread out at 13 residential stations, though not necessarily in 13 different cities. The work of these
missionaries was augmented by 316 native Christians, an auxiliary
force that included 14 ordained men, 206 unordained men, and 96
women. The Levant boasted 46 American-organized Protestant
churches and 37 other worship sites. In all, the 8 American societies

compared with a total of 20 British and 6 European Protestant societies operating in the same area.[49] It is interesting to note, however, that while the Europeans allowed Americans to take the lead in evangelical work worldwide, they apparently retained their predominance in the Near East field, perhaps on account of imperialistic designs over the fate of the crumbling Ottoman realm.

Missionary Impact

During the late nineteenth and early twentieth centuries, conditions in the Ottoman Empire had become increasingly favorable to the work of Protestant missionaries. Obstructionist policies were occasionally thrown at missionaries by the Ottoman authorities, but these authorities also provided missionaries with an advantageous economic and administrative setting. Toleration of religious and ethnic minorities was the official policy of the state, and the state was in turn subject to diplomatic pressures from foreign powers. As for the state's authority over foreign nationals within its borders, the Turks were constrained by the "capitulations," the system of rights that essentially gave Ottoman authorities no control at all over Western nationals. All these conditions made the lack of any imperial sense of authority a sore point for the Turks but a boon to the infiltration of Western ideas through the Protestant evangelical program.[50]

No other activity of Americans in the Near East had a greater residual effect than the activities of the missionaries.[51] American missionary work flourished in the region, in part because of the size and influence of the support constituency at home. After all, these foreign ventures were not the result of the attitudes of a few leaders and devout followers, but part of a broad consensus of religious interest on the part of most church people,[52] expressed in the solid terms of financial backing.

In addition to the size of the supporting community back home for the missionaries, the Americans (as Englishman Charles Starbuck claimed) brought with them to the field their "peculiar adaptedness . . . to effective work among the levantine races."

> Their carelessness of etiquette tends to make the Orientals ashamed of their excessive ceremoniousness, their carelessness of dress, of their excessive ostentatiousness, and in short, life, animated even to excess, will not . . . destroy the dignity

of the East, but will enable it to disengage dignity from dilatoriness. And in religion, American Puritanism in its doubly intensified contempt for tradition, as Puritan, and as American, has been exactly what was needed to shock Eastern Christianity out of that long nightmare of tradition. . . . To Americans, at least, it seems the most natural thing in the world that a sensible man should be pious, and that a pious man should be sensible.[53]

The sensibility of many missionary workers did not, however, preclude a sometimes foolish willingness to confront residents of the Levant in a spirit of avid combativeness. American Board personnel, for example, have been described as a liberal force in the Ottoman domain, but they had "as much potential for disruption as for renewal," being led by their puritanical commitment to a "City on a Hill" into conflict with competing ideas, contrary to the advice of leaders to avoid offending behavior.[54] Competition occasionally led to the betterment of local affairs. For example, the competition for souls among various missionary groups motivated the indigenous religious bodies, and the Ottoman authorities themselves, to provide social services never before so widely available. Even though provision of these services was meant to offset the lure of foreign theologies, the effect was that new institutions for the public welfare were emerging throughout the realm at unprecedented rates. Schools, hospitals, orphanages, and other institutions arose from the struggle for salvageable souls. The miserable lives of those in need of such services were of only secondary import to this soul-centered competition.[55] But whatever the motives of the missionaries in this competition, they acted as a leavening agent in the region.

They had an important effect in America too. Foreign missionary work had a penetrating influence on the American consciousness. The high profile of missionary work, and the interest it subsequently sparked at home, caused the American missionary experience to offer its own enhancement to the image of the Holy Land in the minds of Americans. This is a somewhat different departure from the pattern observed up to now, where the influence of the image of the Holy Land appeared in the record of American experience. Here we see that the experience exerted an influence on the formation and nature of the image.

Historian Kenneth Scott Latourette wrote in 1949 that the Christian missionary enterprise subtly molded Americans' outlook on the world.[56] His colleague, Clifton Jackson Phillips, observed that missionaries were "readier with pen and voice" than other groups of Americans who had gone abroad, and were therefore able to capture a weightier share of the popular American imagination. "Their reports from the field," Phillips wrote, "which were regularly publicized through ecclesiastical channels, probably did more to form the American image of the outside world than any other source."[57] John K. Fairbank, another historian interested in reclaiming the missionary contribution from obscurity, cited the missionary's "influence at home, his reports and circular letters, his visits on furlough, and his symbolic value for his home constituency" as factors in the missionary's historic role.[58] So one way in which missionaries exerted their influence was by letting the American public know about their work and circumstances. This was a benign, inspirational type of contribution, one that helped Americans form their impressions of the rest of the world.

Foreign missions were supported by millions of Americans through individual contributions and church activities. Domestic clergy and laity involved in an endless campaign of education that had to reach the broadest popular levels stimulated the financial support. The missionaries themselves (either while abroad or on furlough), the officers of the various mission boards, and even informed advocates of foreign missions were all involved in a ceaseless effort that used the media of public address, the periodical press, and specially designed monographs to motivate believers to support the overseas work.[59]

> Publications and talks by missionaries expanded understanding in the United States of foreigners. American churches gave benevolent and technical assistance overseas, forming unconsciously an advance guard for possible direct action by Washington. Included in the missionary baggage, along with Bibles and tracts, were sewing machines and books on free government. . . . Also, the Social Gospel was breaking down some resistance among Protestants to plans for improvement of communities and governments in foreign lands. And after the Spanish-American War, ideas of manifest destiny and Social Darwinism about the natural superiority of Anglo-Saxon institutions were widespread.[60]

American missionaries were "leavening the Levant" by introducing elements of Western culture. At the same time, these missionaries enlightened the American people about the world. Mary Bald-

Fig. 20. FACULTY AND STUDENTS OF THE JAFFA MISSION SCHOOL,
1870s. American missions frequently served the dual role of introducing elements of Western culture to Middle Eastern peoples while enlightening Americans back home about conditions in the Holy Land.

win's work in Jaffa, along with her efforts to raise funds for her
school, promote its activities, and keep in touch with the people who
supported it by means of her accounts in *The Spirit of Missions*, exem-
plifies this interplay. There are other examples as well, such as the
conscious efforts of the Alliance church in Jerusalem to provide visiting clergymen with an American backdrop for their preaching
while on tour—a primitive though effective public relations gesture
on the part of the church that probably yielded donations from the
pastors' traveling church members, if present, as well as from the
home parishioners who sat listening to the ministers' travelogue-
homilies on Sundays.

    There was another dimension to missionary influence on Ameri-
cans' consciousness of the Holy Land, a dimension that was greater
in magnitude even than the scope of the missionary enterprise itself.
This was the effect the missionary presence had on other aspects of
the America–Holy Land connection. The missionaries of the Holy
Land were an interconnected part of a larger American presence.
Eli Smith and William Thomson, we have seen, became closely identified with the exploration and study of the Holy Land; the Jaffa
sisters occupied an Adams Colony house; James Barclay's son-in-law

was Beirut Consul J. Augustus Johnson. But aside from these natural interconnections (being compatriots abroad, they had much in common in the Holy Land's foreign environment), there were other ramifications to the missionary presence.

The link between the missionary enterprise and the development of an American scholarly corps that was intimately knowledgeable about other lands is well known. With regard to China, for example, "most of the prominent American sinologists have been missionaries or the children of missionaries."[61] The impact of this "scholarly corps" and the dependence on it by America's foreign-policy-makers have been fascinating components of the history of America's Near East policy.

That American foreign policy should have been so closely linked to the cadre of missionary-related scholars was natural. In the United States, as historian Alan Geyer observed, religion, politics, and international affairs are intertwined. "This is not a matter of choice; it is a fact of history."[62] In the area of foreign affairs, this relationship between religion and government took on new meaning as the missionary establishment articulated, with increasing aggressiveness, its vision for the practical direction of American foreign policy, especially with regard to areas where missionary and U.S. involvements coincided. Joseph Grabill explored this other, assertive aspect of the missionary role in his *Protestant Diplomacy and the Near East*. In reference to the Middle East, he found that "missionary influence on United States policy during the breakdown of the Ottoman Empire in the 1910's and 1920's was more concrete than in any other time or place in American history." Missionary figures contributed to the movement of American diplomacy "away from venerated isolationism."

> Probably having more effect than public officials upon American relations with the Near East during the collapse of the Turkish Empire, these administrators, in cooperation with philanthropists, sought mandates by the United States over part or all of Turkey. They desired America thereby to facilitate autonomy or independence among subject peoples—the Armenians and Syrian Arabs—to whom they had tethered their careers.[63]

Thus it developed that American missionary leadership took a position that was essentially hostile to emergent Zionist aspirations for the Land of Israel. The missionary establishment was afraid that the penetration of Palestine by a Jewish state would introduce into the Near East an element to compete with their own cultural concepts; they were vigorous antagonists to Zionism. When they unfolded before the policy makers the vision of an Arab world under American tutelage, their interest was assuming forms akin to cultural imperialism, but it could not fail to be an attractive prospect to any nation.[64]

The missionary establishment did not have a monopoly on the formation of American policy, nor did it have a thorough and disinterested knowledge of Middle East culture and folkways. Its knowledge of the area was keyed to the accomplishment of the goal of evangelization. The missionary establishment did, however, have a disproportionate voice because of the sophistication of its organization, its membership, and its long history.

The American missionary effort in the Holy Land also illustrates some of the practical consequences of geopious regard for the land. The missionary presence did not necessarily mean that the Holy Land was of primary importance to the American missionary program. In truth, Americans often neglected Palestine as a mission field, either because missionary efforts were being expended elsewhere in the Levant or because the land had been deemed the domain of British Protestants, or because it was simply a difficult field in which to work. But when American missionaries were motivated to attend to the Holy Land, it was invariably because of their image of the land. The Holy Land appeared attractive because it was the paramount "holy" land. Winning it for Christianity was seen as striking a disproportionately severe blow to Islam and Judaism. Furthermore, winning a Christian-believing Holy Land would enhance Christianity by bringing it closer both to its roots and to the elusive goal of Christian unity. After all, implicit in the missionary movement was a spirit of ecumenism that was lacking in other interchurch affairs. The missionaries were in a sense practical dreamers, willing to labor to achieve a goal—Christian unity—that many suspected would not be achieved in their lifetimes. It was at least partially on account of their geopious regard for the Holy Land that they pursued such a vision. Having been primarily motivated to a spirit of self-sacrifice by a driving evangelical commitment to spread the Gospel, the missionary impulse toward Palestine was glossed by a reverence and regard for the land in which souls were being sought. Even when the missionary efforts of some Americans shifted to nearby lands, the geopious regard for the Holy Land remained steadfast, bolstered by the land's proximity and the easy access missionaries had to its holy places.

Although there were certain similarities between the two, the missionaries contrasted sharply with another category of American Holy Land residents, a group that, through romantic impatience and compelling millennial credos, was anxious to see Christian affairs reach an apocalyptic climax. It is to this group—American settlers and colonists in the Holy Land—that we now turn.

CHAPTER 5

Colonies of the Faithful

The history of plans for settling Western Christians in the Holy Land during the nineteenth century is full of delusion, romance, humor, and tragedy. A number of settlement efforts involved Americans and, like American missionary work, the tale of American colonial schemes was episodic and disjointed. But also like the missionary work, there was a common theme. For American colonists, this theme was the advent of the End of Days.

The End of Days as the Beginning

Millennial expectation had increased during the final years of the eighteenth century all over the world. In Europe, the rule of the mob, the downfall of the ancien régime, and the growth of secular thought seemed to correspond to the prophetic visions of Christianity's apocalypse. In the United States, a second wave of religious enthusiasm swept the people into a movement called the Second Great Awakening. It was a tempting time to offer precise calculations of the world's final day. In New Jersey, for example, a Reverend David Austin predicted that the end of the world would occur on May 15, 1796.

But when the sun rose the next day without incident, his efforts turned instead to preparing embarkation facilities in New Haven, Connecticut, for sending America's small Jewish population off to the Holy Land as part of the anticipated redemption. Needless to say, Austin's work was futile.[1]

Most efforts involving Holy Land settlement were derived either from the missionary imperative of evangelical Protestantism or from the millennialist dreams of fragmentary sects. Despite the inspiration behind them, the practical programs always seemed to founder on the reality of nineteenth-century Palestine. And yet people continued to come and try their luck. For many of the Americans involved in such schemes, the image/reality dichotomy of the Holy Land as place and as past was more than a benign vision; it was an obsession.

After leaving the consular post at Beirut, J. Augustus Johnson expressed the opinion that "colonization eastward, like all efforts to turn back the hands of time, is likely to meet with little success."[2] Johnson had been personally involved with the demise of one American effort to colonize the Holy Land; he spoke from a worldly perspective. All the necessary elements for successful establishment of American Christians in the Holy Land were lacking. American colonists, who relied largely on agriculture, could not be assured of successful harvests, commercial opportunities were not attractive, the country's ports were inaccessible and unprotected, and the climate was unfriendly. Despite these handicaps, Johnson lamented, the country had always exerted "a mysterious, indefinable attraction" for new settlement schemes.

The "indefinable attraction" was the image of the Holy Land, the geopious regard for the distant place. Unfortunately, however, when zealous expectations combined with unrealistic assessments of conditions in Ottoman Palestine, a volatile situation was created. The remote, romantic image of the Holy Land in the American mind was maliciously destructive to practical American colonial settlement in Palestine. And yet, as sad testimony to the overt power of American imagery of the Holy Land, the history of settlement schemes by American Christians in the Holy Land is substantial.

A Romantic Heritage

Before 1832 the only resident communities of Western Christians in the Holy Land were orders of Catholics, such as the Franciscans and Carmelites. These small, cloistered groups of European Christians served the needs of visiting pilgrims and were frequently subject to persecution by the local authorities and the Muslim populace. Their simple purpose in residing in Palestine was that they wanted to be in the land of Jesus and the Bible. But other Europeans settled in the land for different reasons. The most legendary of these Western residents came from an unlikely background and was a source of wildly romantic fascination for many Americans.

Lady Hester Stanhope, niece of British Prime Minister William Pitt (the Younger), was perhaps a feminist out of her time. The single-mindedly independent Stanhope was moved to escape from the repressiveness of British aristocratic society by the death of a brother who had died during the Napoleonic wars. She sought out the solace of the East after hearing of a Bedlam asylum inmate's vision that Stanhope would lead world Jewry back to the Promised Land. Upon arriving in the Levant, she adopted male dress so that she would get respectful treatment, and she was successful. Her adventures in the region were storied. She visited Palmyra, at the time thought to be inaccessible because of fierce bedouin marauders—but those marauders chose instead to entertain their outlandish visitor. Later she led a treasure-hunting expedition to Ashqelon, south of Jaffa, as a result of a map monks gave her while she recovered from an illness. Stanhope invested much faith in the outcome of the search, thinking that her find could solidify British-Turkish relations. The expedition yielded only a giant, headless statue of a Roman, which Stanhope rashly destroyed; she had been seeking gold instead. Crushed in spirit, she established herself on a Lebanese mountaintop on the Mediterranean coast near Sidon and did not stir abroad again. She died in 1839, leaving behind only a reputation as a recluse and an eccentric.[3]

After 1840, a new era in Western residence in the Holy Land began. New institutions, frequently linked to European ecclesiastical authorities, appeared in the country. A Protestant bishopric was established at Jerusalem as a joint venture of Great Britain and Prussia, at least during its early years. With European interest in the Holy Land taking on an assertive character, and the number of diplomatic missions and missionary outposts growing, pilgrim traffic from the West increased during mid-century. And largely as a means of furthering their influence within the crumbling Ottoman realm, European states became involved with the building of hospitals, churches, schools, and hospices for the growing number of Westerners passing through or residing in the Holy Land. The native populace also benefited from these institutions, but the positive results masked the European scramble for client groups among the native peoples.

Because the Holy Land was traditionally regarded as an agrarian country, many Westerners placed their hopes for the land's progress in agricultural programs. Agriculture and religion had a long history of symbiosis in the Holy Land, under many cultures. The first modern Christian effort involving the reclamation of the land through agriculture—called the "Brüderhaus"—was begun by a Swiss cleric named Spittler, who tried to establish a circuit of missionary outposts radiating into Asia and Africa from a hub at Jerusalem. The first group was to be a chain of twelve stations, called collectively the "Apostelstrasse," extending into Egypt, down along the Nile Valley, and on into Central Africa. Between 1846 and 1848, four European men, all pledged to celibacy for the duration of the project, were dispatched to Jerusalem to carry out the plan.

> The general idea was that living together unmarried, and teaching native youths mechanical arts and trades in connection with religious instruction, they might gain the confidence of the people and exert an influence as Christians, both by precept and example. Their hopes, however, were not fulfilled, and they eventually left and went into other employments where they might labor more effectively and without the restraint of celibacy.[4]

After its failure, one Brüderhaus member went on to serve the Anglican Church Missionary Society as a teacher under the direction of Samuel Gobat, the second Protestant bishop in Jerusalem, who was himself of Swiss origin. Another independently founded a mission station under German auspices at Bethlehem. The third member, Conrad Schick, became an agent for the London Jews Society at Jerusalem while pursuing an interest in archaeology. Schick was a frequent contributor to the *Quarterly Statement of the Palestine Exploration Fund* and was regarded as an authority on underground Jerusalem. The fourth Brüderhaus member, a man named Henry Baldensperger, established a partnership with a Hebrew-Christian Jerusalem hotel owner, which eventually led to establishment of the first American agricultural colony in the Holy Land.

Mrs. Minor's Colony at Artas

A Sephardic Jew from England who converted to Anglicanism, John Meshullam, settled in the Holy Land in 1842, opening a hotel in Jerusalem and acquiring some fertile property in a pleasant little valley named Artas, near Bethlehem. Henry Baldensperger, the fourth Brüderhaus survivor, moved to the site in 1849 and lived there with his dog inside a tent, despite frequent trouble from harassing bedouins. In February 1850 the lonely Baldensperger was briefly joined by several German families, but conditions soon caused their dispersal. Baldensperger remained at the site and saw it further utilized as a settlement by a group of American millennialists known as "Millerites."[5]

The Millerite movement was begun by a New York farmer named William Miller, who became obsessed with what he took to be a clue in the biblical book of Daniel that revealed the precise time of the End of Days. Daniel 8:13–14 relates how the prophet overheard a saintly conversation about how long the sanctuary would lay desolate. The obscure answer was "Unto two thousand and three hundred days," from which Miller calculated that the prophesied time would elapse shortly after March 1843. Miller's preaching caused a great deal of excitement, and he had attracted numerous followers, especially among Methodists and Baptists. Many of these devout people trusted Miller so much that they began to withdraw from everyday life: taking children from school, leaving their farms and crops unworked, selling their property before the predicted apocalypse. Clorinda Minor, a former Congregationalist and wife of a respected Philadelphia merchant who had never personally committed himself to Miller's timetable, was caught up in the Millerite frenzy and soon became one of the movement's leaders. She opened her home to Miller's followers and zealously carried his message to the public through addresses, song, and print.

When March 1843 passed and nothing happened, the faithful were concerned. At one point, Miller prophesied that October 25, 1843, would be the exact day of doom, but that too passed quietly. Not to be put off, the movement's leaders recalculated the date based on what they decided was a simple error: use of the Christian, rather than Jewish calendar, which the prophet Daniel likely had in mind. The new date was reckoned to be October 25, 1844. Because of the certainty of the new date, many of Miller's followers set up a camp outside Philadelphia as the day approached. On its eve, people were heard declaring their farewells to unconvinced neighbors. The gathered throng waited throughout the appointed hours, but nothing happened. By late evening of the twenty-fifth, many of the faithful had fallen asleep after a rigorous day of prayer and supplication. Inconveniently, a howling wind and rainstorm arose, knocking down most of the encampment and sending the faithful in a panic back to their abandoned homes and the ridicule of their neighbors.

Unshaken in her belief in the fundamental correctness of the Millerite doctrine, Mrs. Minor spent the next two years trying to understand where the group had miscalculated. In time, she believed that
she herself had become God's instrument, and that therefore she
should depart for the Holy Land in order to prepare it for the Second Coming. Mrs. Minor was joined by another Adventist who believed he had the same mission. With the approval of their respective spouses, the two departed for the Middle East, accompanied by
Mrs. Minor's teenage son to ensure propriety. At Marseilles, however, the boy was sent home on account of his "frailty."

Mrs. Minor and her companion reached Jerusalem on September
5, 1849. They stayed at John Meshullam's hotel and were quickly
introduced to the idea of a Christian agricultural settlement at Artas.
Mrs. Minor saw the opportunity as her chief calling, a way to prepare the Holy Land for assuming its position as the center of the
earth in the End of Days. Reinvigorated with a new sense of mission,
Mrs. Minor returned to the United States to raise funds and sup-
porters for the settlement. In America, the disappointed followers of
Miller now had new hope and an apparent explanation of why their
calculations had not materialized as expected: There was work to be
done in the Holy Land! The response to Mrs. Minor's call was
strong, especially among Adventists, Seventh-Day Baptists, and even
Presbyterians.

When Mrs. Minor set sail again for the Holy Land on November
3, 1851, she was accompanied by a small, select group of enthusiastic
Americans, which included a mechanic and a farmer. Because her
husband had died in the intervening years, her son came with her,
and she intended to stay until the job was done. The group brought
along many provisions for establishing a working colony: tents, fur-
niture, tools, clothing, medicine, and seeds of various Western fruits
and vegetables.

The first published report of the effort—officially called the "Agricultural Manual Labor School of Palestine"—was entitled *Meshullam! or, Tidings from Jerusalem*, a thin pamphlet full of messianic
hope. The group built at least one house at Artas and began to receive aid even from Jewish sources. Sir Moses Montefiore endorsed
the effort and counted its laborers as friends of the Jewish people.[6]
In the United States, the American Jewish weekly *The Occident* spoke
kindly of the colony's purposes. Mrs. Minor observed: "Our Jewish
brethren tell us, not infrequently, that our coming here is a sign that
the Messiah is near, and that He will bless the land. They love us
because we keep their Sabbath."[7]

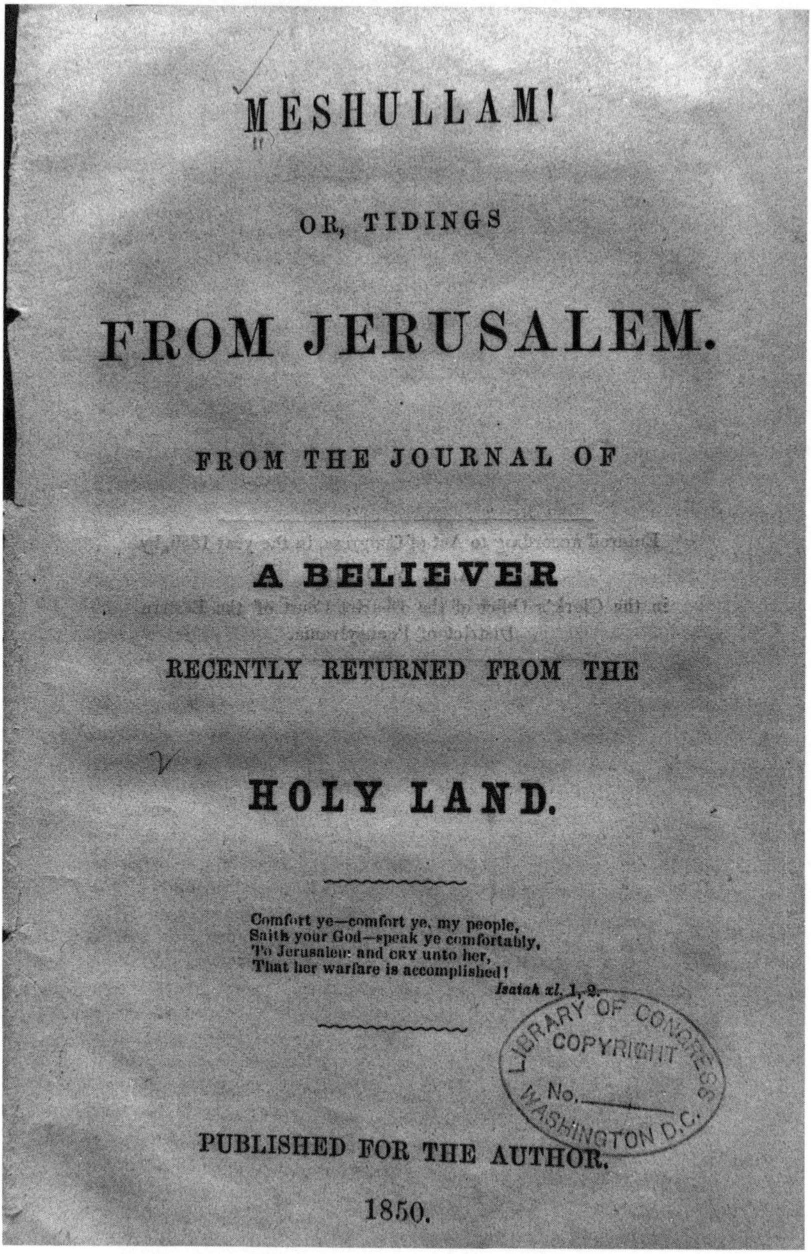

MESHULLAM!

OR, TIDINGS

FROM JERUSALEM.

FROM THE JOURNAL OF

A BELIEVER

RECENTLY RETURNED FROM THE

HOLY LAND.

Comfort ye—comfort ye, my people,
Saith your God—speak ye comfortably,
To Jerusalem and cry unto her,
That her warfare is accomplished!

Isaiah xl. 1, 2.

PUBLISHED FOR THE AUTHOR.

1850.

Fig. 21. TITLE PAGE OF CLORINDA MINOR'S TRACT *MESHULLAM!*
This messianic tract carried a report of Mrs. Minor's short-lived colony
in the valley of Artas, near Bethlehem. The colony was the first of several American attempts to establish permanent settlements in
nineteenth-century Palestine.

But Artas was a business venture with a religious purpose, and in the spiritually competitive atmosphere of Palestine the pressure for success in garnering adherents was too much for the outwardly idealistic plan. Troubles developed between the Americans and their interests and the interests of the British consul at Jerusalem, James Finn.[8] Finn had at one time been Meshullam's partner, and it was Finn who wanted to turn Artas into a refuge for apostate Jews because life in Jerusalem for such converts was socially unstable. The issue of American occupation of the site became so intense that the Americans eventually relocated their settlement farther to the west, on the Sharon Plain in an area near Jaffa renamed by the Americans as "Mount Hope."

The difficulties of reestablishing a settlement proved nearly fatal to the plans of the colonists. Moses Montefiore came to the group's rescue by purchasing an orange grove in the vicinity and turning it over to the colonists. But the colony (actually only a small group by then) dwindled even further. The death of Mrs. Minor on November 6, 1855, left only the son and an adopted daughter as remnants of the colony. For a time, however, the Minor scheme was perpetuated when it was incorporated into another colony, the American Agricultural Mission, which had originated with a New England family.

An American Agricultural Mission

Mrs. Minor's colony was an early flowering of the idea that the rebirth of the Holy Land, an event that was vital for the success of millennialist predictions, lay in better exploiting Palestine's agricultural resources. Another group of Americans tried to promote the same theory, and their efforts too ended before fruition.

On July 24, 1852, the *L.&A. Hobart*, a spritely bark, set sail from Boston with a young, idealistic New England couple on board. Mr. and Mrs. Phillip Dickson were on their way to the Promised Land as the anticipated vanguard of an independent settlement group confidently called "The American Agricultural Mission."[9] Their scheme was forthright and simple: They hoped to introduce the native populace of the Holy Land to three notions—Christianity, modern agriculture, and American ideals. But they had not counted on the difficulties of establishing their home in so foreign an environment. By April 25, 1853, Phillip was dead; a short time later, his widow was on her way back to New England. While at sea, and quite unknown to her, she passed her late husband's family sailing eastward toward Palestine to reinforce the original effort.

Walter Dickson (Phillip's father), his wife, and their daughters left Boston in mid-October 1853 aboard the *John Winthrop*. Arriving at Jaffa during the winter of 1854, they soon secured a small enclave for the proposed missionary work and farming, not far from the precincts of the port city, at the Mount Hope site. Before long, the enterprise attracted at least one German family, and two of Dickson's daughters married two of the other family's sons. The extended group constituted the "American Mission Colony."

Herman Melville, visiting the Holy Land in 1857, met the Dicksons and wrote in his journal that Deacon Dickson was "a thorough Yankee, about 60, with long oriental beard, blue Yankee coat, and Shaker waistcoat" and that Mrs. Dickson was "a respectable looking elderly woman." Melville asked the Dicksons if they had settled permanently in the Holy Land. Mr. Dickson replied "with a kind of dogged emphasis, 'Permanently settled on the soil of Zion, Sir.'" Melville asked whether the Dicksons employed any Jews and were told by Mr. Dickson, "No. Can't afford to hire them. Do my own work, with my son. Besides, the Jews are lazy & don't like to work." Melville asked whether Dickson thought the trait "a hindrance to making farmers of them," and Dickson replied, "That's it. The Gentile Christian must teach them better. The fact is the fullness of Time has come. The Gentile Christians must prepare the way." Melville reflected, "Old Dickson seems a man of Puritanic energy, and being inoculated with this preposterous Jew Mania, is resolved to carry his Quixotism through to the end. Mrs. D. dont seem to like it, but submits. The whole thing is half melancholy, half farcical— like the rest of the world."[10]

Despite their best intentions, relations between the colony and the local Arabs were strained. The comparatively independent Western women were subjected to insults, and the colony's livestock and property were frequently targets of thievery and vandalism. Trouble came to a head on the night of January 11, 1858, when the colony's compound was raided. During the fray, son-in-law Frederick Steinbeck was fatally shot and Walter Dickson was knocked unconscious. The women were raped and the colony was despoiled. In response to this outrage, the U.S. consul at Jerusalem, J. Warren Gorham, together with his Prussian colleague, demanded that the pasha take action. A 1,000 piaster reward was posted, although Gorham seemed dubious about the result because of the intense anti-Christian feelings of the Muslims. Yet it was not long before four Arabs were imprisoned and the family received more than $2,000 in damages from the authorities. The appearance of the U.S. steam frigate *Wabash* showing the colors off Jaffa harbor may have reinforced Turkish resolve to be of assistance. As for the survivors, by September 1858 the "American Agricultural Mission" was disbanded and the Dickson family was on its way back to the United States and the consoling familiarity of Groton, Massachusetts.[11] Eight years later another group of New Englanders would try their hand at settling the land near Jaffa in preparation for the Second Advent. That effort would become the grandest mistake of all.

Scandal at Jaffa

The newly built American bark *Nellie Chapin* landed 153 men, women, and children at Jaffa on September 22, 1866.[12] The group was composed of followers of George J. Adams, founder of the Church of the Messiah, a sect made up of former Millerites, Episcopalians, Baptists, Mormons, and Methodists. Because the group's colonizing efforts, known popularly as the Adams (or Jaffa) Colony, were widely reported in the United States, the colony provides a way to gauge the image of the Holy Land with regard to American settlement activities.

As with other, earlier settlers, the vision of the restoration of the land and the return of the Jews was part of a larger millennialist program. Millennialism, in the words of Robert Handy, had "helped Protestants through difficult times, revived their enthusiasm to do battle with unbelief and infidelity, to press into the western wilderness in search of souls, to redouble their missionary efforts in an effort to prepare the way for the Lord's coming."[13] The Civil War had been instrumental in raising the millennialist hopes of many Protestants to new heights, and in the elevated, rarified speculation a large dose of nineteenth-century romanticism was undeniably present. When viewed through such filters as these, the Holy Land became too alluring to resist; it beckoned the devout to take up the work of fomenting the End of Days. So the tenor of mid-nineteenth-century millennialist excitement struck an inspired chord in the fascinating but pitiful story of the American colony at Jaffa.

Millennialism was hardly the only factor behind the unusual events; there were also elements of greed, alcoholism, and duplicity, which made the affair so opprobrious. The key to the story lay in the personality of a single man, George Adams, a charismatic dreamer, controversial prophet, and opportunistic minister who believed that an American enclave in the Holy Land would give spiritual and material advantage once the Second Coming began.

George J. Adams was probably born in Oxford, New Jersey, in 1811. Growing up in a rural, out-of-the-way district, he was drawn into lay preaching among his fellow Methodists. Before long, he became ensnared by the "wildly competitive world of big-city evangelism,"[14] which allowed him to develop an acumen for the dramatic. A theater manager in Boston gave the evangelist a chance to emote Shakespeare before an audience, on the hunch that a draw is a draw, whether the backdrop be secular or spiritual. Although the run was short-lived, Adams acquired a taste for the stage and its seductions.

In New York City in February 1840, Adams attended a meeting at which Mormon missionary H. C. Kimball spoke about the growth and message of the newly emerging Church of Latter-Day Saints. Shortly thereafter Adams converted and became, rather presumptuously, a Mormon church elder and relocated to Illinois. Adams's fortunes among the Mormons were subject to the same pitfalls that later characterized his behavior during the Jaffa episode: He could not steer clear of liquor long enough to carry out his grand designs. He wanted to assume a key role in the hierarchy of the infant church, but his attempts were crippled by excesses of drink and charges of indiscretions and theft. In disgrace, Adams headed eastward to a remote area of Maine, where he could still traffic in religion and likely not be recognized.

George Adams claimed to have been called by God to preach the gospel and raise up a church to begin the work of colonizing the Holy Land, all to show the Jews that it was also their hour to return to the Promised Land, rebuild its fallen cities, and repopulate its countryside. This "Joshua's vision" for the settlement of Maine natives was remarkably enterprising, for he and his "Caleb," Abraham McKenzie of Indian River, had spied out the land firsthand in 1864, during the formative years of his Church of the Redeemer, and told his followers:

> We will raise wheat, barley, millet, cotton, castor oil, olive oil, wine, hemp, and all kinds of fruit, produce, and vegetables. Some will work as carpenters and boat builders. We'll run boarding houses and a stage line for the 30,000 European pilgrims that go each year. We don't expect to die for lack of employment.[15]

Fig. 22.   GEORGE ADAMS,
FOUNDER OF THE JAFFA
COLONY.   Adams was a
charismatic figure whose
vision of an American
presence in the Holy Land
fell victim to poor planning
and personal shortcomings.

When Adams and his flock arrived at Jaffa, they found that the
land an agent had been authorized to purchase was as yet un-
secured. Those early days saw the colonists camped out on the beach
north of Jaffa until all the lumber the party had brought from
Maine could be floated ashore and crude sheds were erected. The
colonists struggled in the harsh sun, unaccustomed to its strength.
As their first provisions began to disappear, the lack of food and
proper nutrition, combined with the climate, cost the lives of perhaps a score of adults and children before the end of the first
month.

With intense but underhanded deliberation, land was soon secured for a more permanent settlement, and the colony's carpenters

and mechanics set to work erecting New England–style houses on the sandy coastal plain. While awaiting the first produce of their gardens and fields, however, several more colonists perished. Even after the crops began to show a harvestable yield, they were scavenged at night. The colonists were bilked by local merchants because they did not know the language and trading customs of the land. And Adams became more dogmatic, more erratic, and more frequently drunk as time passed.

Meanwhile, the Ottoman authorities had issued a formal protest against the colony to the American minister at Constantinople, E. Joy Morris. The Turks declared, ineffectually and after the fact, that the Americans would not be able to colonize Palestine because foreigners would not be allowed to take possession of the "most fertile province." The land, they maintained, belonged to the natives who paid taxes and did military service. Should these natives be driven from their fields by a colony of Yankees, who would be subjects of another government and pay nothing and who might even be inclined, some day, to take possession of the country?[16]

Actually, the posturing by the Porte was probably nothing more than the opening charade in what was expected to become a business deal. Settlement of considerable numbers of foreigners was already facilitated by a recent Ottoman law (decreed June 10, 1867) that authorized foreigners to hold real estate anywhere in the Ottoman realms except the Hejaz, which contained the holy cities of Mecca and Medina. The privilege also carried with it the obligation that made the foreigner subject to Ottoman law instead of the consular law of their former homelands. The Ottoman posturing made sense because the right had not normally been extended to American citizens and would not be until 1874, when protocols between the two nations would be signed.[17]

When word began to circulate in the United States that something was amiss in the colony, reports began to surface about the character of the group's leader. An anonymous "gentleman in the vicinity of Machias, Maine," who escaped being lured into the venture himself, reported widely that Elder Adams was a scoundrel of long standing. His frequent changes of religion indicated as much, the "gentleman" said, noting that Adams had been at one time or another a Methodist, a Baptist, a Campbellite, a Mormon, and a Millerite. The writer went on to imply that Adams's stage experience was also condemnatory because Adams had "used the conclusion of his weekly ministerings in church to advertise his forthcoming theatrical schedule for that week." Others were quick to point out that "at his performance, he was frequently so intoxicated that he was unable even to say his lines."

His detractors painted Adams as having a considerable talent for deluding people. While in Maine, it was said, he had convinced more than one hundred people that he was a "true descendant of Ephraim and that he had been appointed of God to settle and revolutionize and Christianize a land which has for more than a century resisted the efforts of American missionaries." Right-thinking individuals had futilely warned those who had fallen under his spell about the outlandish impracticality of his scheme.

Before long, rumors began to circulate in the United States about conditions in the colony. Adams was said to have been arrested by the American consul, and other reports said Adams had been released when he pledged to rectify the colony's deterioration. With the group's fate seemingly in the balance, calls for U.S. government assistance in the affair were issued, and friends at home were reportedly planning to fit out a rescue vessel.

The various calls for aid for the Jaffa colonists had implications beyond the colony itself. Not only had the group apparently been duped by its scurrilous leader, but there was also the unvoiced imagery of proud New Englanders fighting a hostile environment far from the friendly, hospitable shores of home. That image reduced the colony to an updated version of the early settlement of America, only this time the Pilgrims had landed in the former Promised Land and found its promise hollow. This was, of course, highly appropriate. After all, hadn't that Old World place been usurped by the New Zion which was America?

In the United States the growing clamor for news of the colony touched off several controversies in the press. Some accounts had the colony on the verge of disaster, while other accounts tried to suppress the rising fears about the colony's fate. For example, the February 17, 1867, *New York Times* commented that most news from Jaffa on the Adams venture had been unfavorable from the beginning—particularly when reports dwelled on Adams's personal honesty and discretion. However, the *Times* also reprinted an item from the February 12, 1867, *Bangor Times*, which had called attention to several favorable letters the colonists had written.

In one letter, a J. B. Ames of the colony wrote to Captain C. E. Cobb of South Orrington, Maine, that the soil of Palestine was dark and rich, with no rocks, and that the colonists "can have just as much land as they want. Some of the grain crops were coming up and the colony suffered some sickness and the deaths of some children. The treatment by the locals had been generally good and thefts of the colony's property had been minimal." Ames also noted that only a few colonists had expressed a desire to return to the United States, and he excused their heresy as being due to nothing more than homesickness for the finer-quality products available in America.[18] In another letter, addressed to his brother and printed at the same time by the Bangor paper, Ames claimed that the colony's leader did not overrate anything about the venture. Those who were the most dissatisfied probably did not have enough faith in the scheme to begin with, he said. "They have forgotten what they came to this land for. I think it a glorious thing to live in a country where once dwelt the prophets, patriarchs, and the Messiah himself." Ames told his brother that the Americans were being favored by everybody, that local merchants had offered them whatever they needed, and that they could pay whenever they could. In stark contrast to the experience of the Dickson family only eight years before, Ames claimed that "the Arabs are our warmest friends." He also offered an optimistic prediction of the country's future prospects when he wrote that conditions might be changing in a year or two as a result of an anticipated French investment in new port facilities at Jaffa and a possible railway line to Jerusalem. In light of such changes, which appeared to be imminent, Ames was impatient with the colony's malcontents and called them "boobies" who growled and refused to labor from the first. He also conjectured that the sources of the bad news reports reaching America were the malicious lies spread by those same malcontents.[19]

In light of the contradictory information circulated about the Jaffa venture, and because of the increasing uneasiness of many Americans about the noble effort, pressure began to build in Washington for the federal government to intervene and clarify the status of the colonists. In response, Secretary of State William Seward appointed the Rev. Walter Bidwell, respected editor of *Eclectic Magazine*, to look into the affairs and prospects of the colony. Bidwell was accompanied on his mission by James P. Sanford, a *Chicago Evening Journal* correspondent whose interest in the matter lay in resolving the swirl of conflicting accounts over the colony's state of affairs.

The two men first heard Adams preach to his flock when they reached Jaffa on March 11, 1867. In an effort to understand why Adams's followers made the move to begin with, Bidwell and Sanford spoke with as many colonists as they could and reported that most of the colonists were relatively satisfied. In fact, when a mass meeting was held for the benefit of the two emissaries, a vote was taken on the level of satisfaction in the group as compared with the desire to return to America. Only one person, a "pale faced and decidedly intellectual-looking woman," voted to return home. Sanford confessed that he was somewhat sympathetic to this lone figure but nonetheless reported that he had been given a proper tour around the colony and had been briefed on the group's plans for future construction. He was also subjected to a theological discourse on the belief that Palestine was on the verge of an abundant flowering and rebirth. Finally, Sanford added that all members of the colony spoke highly of the kindness shown them by the native populace. In contrast, quite a number spoke out against "the unfairness of the American vice-consul at Jaffa, Mr. Lowenthal."[20] The Bidwell mission concluded on an ambiguous note.

By mid-August 1867, rumors about the colony's fate began to circulate again in the United States, bolstered by continued revelations about Adams's past. One anonymous report, for example, lamented the news that Jaffa colonists had been reduced to utter poverty and near-slavery by their leader. Being reduced to such a condition was to be expected, according to the anonymous source, who claimed to have had close business dealings with Adams some years before and to know something of the man's true character. Adams was called an "adventurer, a charlatan, and a scamp," and was fickle, opportunistic, and scandalous. As if these charges weren't enough, the accuser reviewed Adams's stage career and snubbed his talents as an actor: "Adams was so poor an actor as ever spoke, without doubt." It was no wonder that Adams had "so cruelly deceived and then so basely deserted the little band of New England men now starving at Jaffa."[21]

The August 20, 1867, *Boston Advertiser* reported the response of American consular personnel to what now appeared to be a genuine crisis for the colonists. U.S. Consul-General Hale in Egypt endorsed a call for help from some colonists. He noted that several groups of colonists had already been assisted, some through the charitable graces of passing American seamen and some—thirty-two in all, among whom there were eighteen destitute widows and children— were aided by the U.S. consul for Syria, J. Augustus Johnson, at his own expense. Johnson had earlier established personal contacts with Adams and his followers, and he said he could understand Adams's power over "illiterate men and women" after hearing some of his Sunday harangues. But Johnson also predicted that the hold Adams had over his followers would decrease as their experience with the world about them increased. The deteriorating affairs of the colony moved Johnson to act, he told his colleague Hale, because "he could not bear to see American citizens begging of Arabs in their misery to avoid dying of starvation in the streets of Jaffa."[22]

Johnson's attitude was full of implications for his ideas about the propriety of American affairs overseas, but his attitude is also revealing about the immediate condition of the Jaffa group, because Johnson was not an alarmist. Hale reported that the colonists' crops had failed and that there was literally nothing on which to support the remaining members. He also said that the die-hard colonists' verbal attacks on the consular personnel in the Levant region were unwarranted, especially in light of the generous financial assistance all consular officials had supplied. Still, Hale said that more aid was needed to bring home the disillusioned members of the colony who desperately wanted to leave but had no means. This call for aid was further strengthened by an appeal from the U.S. minister to Constantinople, E. Joy Morris.[23] Morris too stressed the pitiable condition of the colony and warned glumly that the approach of winter threatened to reduce the survivors to greater wretchedness.

However, even though most of the colonists had abandoned the dream on a large scale, some still persisted in their pursuit of the original scheme. On October 22, 1867, the *New York Times* reprinted a letter just received from one of the colonists addressed to a brother in Chicago; dated September 23, 1867, the letter appeared under the heading "The Jaffa Colony—A Favorable Report from a Member." In this sad apologetic, the colonist claimed that, contrary to rumors, the group was prospering, and he laid blame for whatever troubles they had encountered at the feet of the American vice-consul at Jaffa, Herman Lowenthal, who was also accused of having "cheated Mr. Adams out of more than five hundred pounds sterling." The author also told of deception by some of the original group, who turned out to have been "very bad men." He said, "They have done all they could to destroy Mr. Adams, but they have utterly failed. Those who have apostacized or seceded seem to be almost demons in human form." The writer also projected that new colonists would be joining the group later in the year: "The colony must succeed. Mr. Adams has the good-will of the Latins, the Greeks, the Armenians, the Maronites, the Turks, the Arabs, the Jews, and the Mahomedans. Can a man fail to succeed with such a host of friends? I answer, No!"[24]

Unlike the controversies raging over the colony in the press, the accounts of contemporary travelers are more revealing on the colony and on the reactions of uninvolved Americans to the Adams scheme. Charles W. Elliott, for example, reported on the colony in his travelogue *Remarkable Characters and Places of the Holy Land*. The immigrants had originally sailed from Maine, Elliott noted, to seek a home in the Holy Land, and to that end, they carried "their wives and children, their Bibles and their school house, their dexterous hands and their Yankee habits with them, while holding in their hearts a tender sentiment which made them hope they could once more make the Holy Land a place where Christians could live, olives flourish, and the rose tree bloom; where the love of Jesus might rule men's lives and the love of Mohammed might fade away." Despite the group's hope and courage, Elliott said, they lacked such essential elements as knowledge of the country's climate and cultural environment. Elliott, like Consul Johnson, viewed the plan as amounting to nothing less than an American attempt to emigrate backward: "They found it impossible, and the last report of them comes to us through the intelligent correspondent of the Tribune—it is sad, but it may teach the rest of us, that our own land is best for us."[25]

Like Johnson, Elliott was almost unforgiving because the colonists had voluntarily forsaken their American homeland for the Holy Land. The Jaffa group, he said, had learned from bitter experience "what it ought to have known before leaving America: that 'Jordan is a hard road to travel.'" Still, Elliott did not completely blame the group for its predicament; much had to be attributed to the delusive nature of the group's leadership. It is enlightening that the theme of "American/innocent led astray" is the motif of Elliott's thoughts:

> They wish to get back to America, and beg the ambassador to send a man-of-war to take them off. It is not characteristic of Americans to give up under such trials: but they undoubtedly feel that they have been deluded. In a strange land, where they are unprotected as they would be on a Texas frontier, without money, broken down by sickness, surrounded by those who speak only a strange language, and who look upon them as interlopers, it is not singular that their hearts should fail them. It is sad to think how many hearts have been broken by disappointment in that land, how many have deluded themselves into crusades to that land which we call the "Holy Land." When will the world learn that the Kingdom of Christ is a spiritual kingdom, and that the Jerusalem where he is to reign is a spiritual Jerusalem, and not the old, dirty Jewish city which once was (but not now) the type of a heavenly city.[26]

The classic message of Elliott's nineteenth-century moral is clear: Americans had no business recreating or retreating to their past shibboleths when there are new worlds for the Christians to conquer in the Western march of America's frontier.

Traveler John Franklin Swift, arising early in the morning on the day he was to depart for Jerusalem, was greeted on a Jaffa street in American English by colonists from the Adams settlement who recommended one over another of Jerusalem's two hotels. Swift called the recommendation "the American branch of industry known as hotel-running." Swift's first thoughts of the colony were that it must have been a "wonderful event":

> Not a colony of discontented and broken-down rebels, such as we have heard of seeking a new home in Mexico or Brazil, but a colony of genuine Yankees from New England, coming, as they say, with a new religion in one hand and American plows and reaping machines in the other, to regenerate the land on American principles. The whole movement had astonished the natives of the country as much as it must have amazed the people of America when they became informed of it.[27]

Swift visited the colony before departing for Jerusalem and reported that it had an airy appearance, with wide streets at right angles, squares, and neat cottages with green shutters. In speaking with a young boy there, Swift could not "detect any evidence of decadence of the race under the effect of the Syrian sun."[28] Some colonists Swift met conducted him to the home of the "President" Adams, where they were met by "Mrs. President Adams," a "large-sized lady with a decidedly military manner." Swift's session at the Adams home was quite revealing:

> We were soon seated in chairs placed in single file across a wide room, while the Presidentess stood in front making a speech, the substance of which, when stripped of a slight tendency to be grandiloquent, was, that the American eagle of freedom, after having perched for more than ninety years upon the rockbound coasts of his native land, had now for the first time found his pinions strong enough to sustain his weight, that with one grand swoop he had winged his glorious flight from the newest to the oldest land on earth, where, resting for a time upon the mountain peaks of Syria, he would soon gather renewed strength for still more mighty aerial ex-

ploits, that soon he would present to the astonished gaze of
the effete monarchs of the old world the wondrous spectacle
of a native people hitherto sunk in hopeless barbarism being
civilized through the precious truths of Christianity, conveyed
to them by means of the ingenious implements of agriculture,
that had already rendered our own country so famous.[29]

Mrs. Adams went on to tell her guests that England and France were
"becoming quite uneasy about, and anxious to know what was the
real design of the American colony in settling Palestine."[30] The
global nature of this intrigue was satisfying to a native of New
Hampshire, as Mrs. Adams admitted she was. She also boasted that
she was a granddaughter of a signer of the Declaration of Independence.

   At that point, Mr. Adams himself slipped quietly into the room.
He remained still until Mrs. Adams commenced a description of the
colony's theological underpinnings, at which point he joined in and
discussed his group. Adams said it had no creed except for faith in
the Bible, and he told how he had come to realize in 1859 that the
return of the Jews to "Canaan" and the reign of Jesus were imminent events, but that

      it was clear to every intelligent American that the country in
      its present condition was not a fit place for the residence of
      the Jews, nor for the reign of the Messiah; that it was not even
      reasonable to expect the Jews, with all their shrewdness, to
      return to a country such as was Palestine in its present state,
      nor was it quite certain that the Messiah himself would come
      unless great changes for the better were at least commenced;
      that his call was to plant the great and glorious institutions of
      our own land into the future home of the chosen people of
      God; that the true method of civilizing the benighted Arabs of
      the Sharon Valley was to teach them to turn up the soil with
      Johnson's patent shifting mold-board and gangplow; to plant
      grains with Smith's remarkable double-back-action drill, and
      to harvest the fruits of the earth with somebody else's wonder-
      ful combined self-adjusting reaping, thrashing, sacking,
      grinding, and bolting machines.[31]

   Mrs. Adams then resumed control of the interview, accounting the
small discontented number of colonists as troublemakers and describing the American consular agent at Jaffa, Mr. Lowenthal, as a

"monster in human form who had attempted in vain to stay the onward march of the new religion and the spread of agricultural improvements." She continued:

> Being a Jew, he of course opposed all Christian progress. Be-
> ing a foreigner and not an American, he naturally would ap-
> preciate neither the gang-plow of Johnson, the drill of Smith,
> nor the self-adjusting reaper, thrasher, sacker, grinder, and
> bolter of the other gentlemen. The wretch had from the first
> foreseen the good to the Christian cause to be produced by
> the movement, and had laid in plans to circumvent it. The
> plan of the wily Jew, it appeared, was in keeping with the
> commercial character of his people.

Swift had heard that Lowenthal had gained Mr. Adams's confidence
when Mrs. Adams was not around and that Lowenthal then convinced Adams to make him sole agent for the colony but instead
embezzled its funds. The colony suffered no sickness, Swift said,
only that "feigned" by discontented conspirators against Adams. But
seventeen of the group were murdered—poisoned—by one of Lowenthal's accomplices, who posed as a physician but was really a free-
love spiritualist.

After these racy discussions, Swift and his company were conducted around the colony and informed of its grandiose plans. Later
that day, Swift tried to pay a visit to Lowenthal, who was not at
home. Swift conjectured that, given the buildup to Lowenthal's reputation, perhaps "the facts in the end should prove him to be more
sinned against than sinning."[32] At a Franciscan convent, a brother
told Swift that conditions in the colony were pitiable, that members
sometimes came to beg bread, that Adams was a common drunkard
and his wife the real ruler of the group.

Henry Bellows, the Unitarian minister, found that Reverend
Adams and a much smaller group of followers were still holding on
in 1867 "full of faith and confidence," despite the colony's detrimen-
tal notoriety. Bellows wrote that he was received kindly by the
Adamses and that they "appeared to be living very comfortably." He
added that Adams explained his view of an imminent return of the
Jews to Palestine possibly under the kingship of one of the Roth-
schilds. According to Adams, the Jews would then recognize the validity of his "Church of the Messiah" after their return. Bellows observed that Adams "has the head of a religious fanatic, but not the
face. He is eminently secular in his manners but I should say he had

a very imperfect education, and a decided 'bee in his bonnet.'"³³
Adams told Bellows he had pledged to American consuls Hale and
Johnson that in the future he would recruit followers from Britain
and not America—likely because Adams was sensitive to the outlay
of personal funds by these consuls in shipping home disillusioned
colonists.

Samuel Clemens had some passing comments in *Innocents Abroad*
about the Adams colony, but more important, the cruise ship *Quaker
City* played a role of its own in the story of the colony's dissolution.
Clemens wrote that he found it difficult to understand the religious
faith of the colonists. He acknowledged that they believed in the
"long-prophecized assembly of the Jews in Palestine from the four
quarters of the world, and the restoration of their ancient power and
grandeur," but, he said,

> They do not make it appear that an immigration of Yankees
> to the Holy Land was contemplated by the old prophets as
> part of the programme; and now the Jews have not "swarmed,"
> yet one is left at a loss to understand why that circumstance
> should distress the American Colony of Mr. Adams. I can
> make neither head nor tail of this religion.³⁴

In spite of his puzzlement over the colonists' religion, Clemens was
impressed by a fellow passenger who helped a large number of the
stranded colonists to get home. Moses Beach, owner of the *New York
Sun* and a "warm admirer and friend" of Henry Ward Beecher, was
the *Quaker City* passenger who personally paid the $1,500 return fare
to Maine for some forty Adams colony refugees taken aboard the
cruise ship at Jaffa. Clemens hailed the deed as "an unselfish act of
benevolence."

With the last, large group of colonists abandoning their dream
and returning home, the tale of the Adams Colony was coming to an
end. Of the more than 150 people who had set out from Maine, only
20 to 25 diehards remained clustered around their prophet. Nearly
60 of the original party had succumbed to the trial and died away
from home. Some 70 more chose to go home broken and nearly
penniless,³⁵ and 40 of those were aboard the *Quaker City*, which took
them to Alexandria to secure passage directly home. Clemens aptly
branded the affair "one of the strangest chapters in American history," though from the perspective of our own time it was a precursor of events at Jonestown, Guyana, more than a century later.

The departure of most of the Jaffa colonists did not deter the small group of steadfast believers from pursuing the original vision. Among this group was Adams himself, who believed that American press reports of the enterprise were full of bitterness and venom because of rank falsehoods uttered against him by dissatisfied colonists. At one point, he said, these falsehoods had reached such a level that he was imprisoned by the consular court for a twelve-day period. Adams believed it was in the colony's interest to be rid of the unhappy colonists: "to recede and become United States paupers and beggars seemed with many of them to have become a kind of mania." Their departure raised to "glorious" levels the prospects for those who remained in the colony, and there were signs that Adams's original vision of an upbuilding of the country was already in evidence:

> A fine macadamized carriage road is being finished from Jaffa to Jerusalem, over 100 feet wide. Over 3,000 men are at work on it and over twelve miles of the road are already finished. It is to be completed in thirty days by order of the Sultan. This is no myth, but a reality. . . . Is not this a great step towards progression in this downtrodden land?

Contrary to other reports, Adams continued to claim that the band was at peace with the "Latins, Greeks, Armenians, Maronites, Turks, Arabs, and Mohammedans." Encouraged by such prospects, Adams boldly stated: "We, the colony, now stand free from every government on earth, and, as was our father Abraham, are strangers and pilgrims and sojourners on this earth."[36] This declaration of the colony's independence was no doubt the result of what Adams perceived as the failure of the U.S. consular authorities to provide protection for the group, though, in fact, Adams had a waiver foregoing such protection. Freedom from U.S. jurisdiction did not mean the remaining colonists no longer considered themselves Americans, however. Adams claimed that those who were left were still proud to fly the flag "every Lord's day."

One former Jaffa colonist, a Mrs. Norton, reflected freely on her experience to a *New York Times* correspondent and thereby provided an interesting counterweight to Adams's optimistic assessment of the colony's prospects since jettisoning its malcontents. Mrs. Norton said she would never forget the kindness of the "pleasure-seeking passengers of the *Quaker City*" in enabling her to return to the United States. She corroborated the reports of the "bad character" of Adams, saying that the leader had acted shamefully, was occasionally drunk, and had dishonestly misled the colony. And, she reported, the very night before the *Quaker City* departure, Adams had demonstrated his great love for his wife by locking her outside their home and letting her sleep "on the soft side of the ample doorstep." Mrs. Norton contradicted Adams's claims that the colony's relations with the locals were good, saying that the prejudice shown the Americans was a definite hindrance, especially in finding work through which the colonists might support themselves. The colonists themselves had built strong structures—several homes, a school, a store, and a hotel—but the store and hotel were useless, Mrs. Norton claimed, because there were no travelers for the hotel and no patrons for the store.

Appending his own opinion of the differences between the two sides of the controversy, the *Times* correspondent called the recently published reproach by Adams against those who had returned libelous. Their defense was obvious in light of the affair:

> Their only fault is in having made the mistake of going to Jaffa, under the leadership of such a man as Adams, and upon so visionary a mission. Once possessors of comfortable homes and well-to-do in the world, they are now bereft of both, and all that remains for them is to commence life over again and endeavor to retrieve their losses.[37]

The affair at Jaffa was a hectic and harrowing experience concentrated in the relatively short span of two years. Nevertheless, the size and scope of the venture made its failure a bigger fiasco than any of the previous colonial schemes. To be sure, it foundered because of simple human weakness and confusion, but like the other settlement efforts, it foundered also because the environment was not fully appreciated by the leaders. A compelling sense of purpose dominated the leaders' sense of reality and judgment. Even the preliminary visits to the Holy Land by the ventures' leaders did not jeopardize the reckless messianic compulsions. Once again, the image of the Holy Land as a promise for a better world had misled certain Americans in bizarre fashion. It must be emphasized, however, that the colony itself was not a futile venture. It did contribute to the story of Palestine's emergence, for it was a link in the chain of nineteenth-century colonial schemes that sought to improve conditions in the Holy Land.

Some Americans who remained at Jaffa after the Adams scheme was abandoned became involved in serving the tourist trade. The

British magazine *Leisure Hour*, for example, told how a wealthy Russian woman pilgrim, who was said to have lacked the "proper" side-saddle, instead hired an American wagon to transport her to Jerusalem.[38] The vehicle was an American-made springboard wagon driven by former colonist Rolla Floyd, who was one of the people so thoroughly convinced of the rightness of the colony's purpose that he decided to remain in the Holy Land. After mastering Arabic, Floyd was advised by members of the U.S. consular staff to go into the tour-guide/dragoman business. He did well for himself and gained a near-legendary reputation for his services, which after several years were complemented by a staff of guides, boatmen, and carriage drivers, as well as an array of furnishings to make any tour of the Holy Land a royal visit. President Grant was among the many dignitaries who enjoyed Floyd's services, and he thanked the guide for "the great assistance you have rendered us in our visit to all points of interest in and about the Holy City. Your thorough knowledge of Bible references, history & tradition of all points of interest in the Holy Land and your clear and concise explanation of the same has very much added to the interest and pleasure of our visit."[39]

Besides the few people left at Jaffa,[40] the colony's properties stood in mute testimony to the ambitiousness of the original plan. The mansion house erected for the prophet George Adams later became a hotel owned by a Russian nobleman, Baron Ustinov.[41] Most of the other properties were incorporated into the next colonial venture in the Holy Land.

German Templars and Their Relations with Americans

The demise of the Adams Colony leads immediately into the story of the Tempelgesellschaft, the Association of Templars, a predominantly German group that had several connections to the American Holy Land experience. The Tempel had its roots in Germany's Pietist movement of the seventeenth century, but is not to be confused with the earlier, medieval military orders, particularly the Knights Templar.[42] By the early nineteenth century, many Pietists were caught up in a millennialist fever that included the belief that all true Christians should migrate eastward. As a result, there was an exodus from several German states, which had already been depopulated by the ravages of the Napoleonic wars. In Württemberg, in an effort to stem the emigration, the king offered the Pietists an opportunity to establish autonomous communities within the framework of the state church.

Christoph Hoffman, son of the founder of the first of these autonomous communities, was the founder of the Templars. In the late 1840s he came to believe that the state church had failed in its mission, so he advocated acknowledgment of a "people of God" who could restore true Christianity and move humankind away from its liberal, revolutionary tendencies. Hoffman also believed that this new "people of God" were destined to replace the Jews of the Bible as inheritors of the Lord's land, and in 1854 he established an asso-

Fig. 23.   ADAMS COLONY AND GERMAN TEMPLAR REMNANTS TODAY.   A small number of Adams Colony buildings remain standing today in Jaffa. Pictured here is one of the better-preserved examples. The Lutheran church behind the building was constructed by German Templars after they took up residence at the Adams site.

ciation to oversee the resettling of Palestine. But this precursor group was subjected to official church and state pressures. By 1858 Hoffman and Georg David Hardegg, a former merchant, had visited Palestine but found that the time was not right for a mass resettlement of the country.

Back in Germany, continued repression of Hoffman's followers led to the establishment of the Tempel in 1861. Organizational restructuring was not enough, however. Government subjugation of the sect caused it to lose members continuously. In an effort to avoid total destruction, Hardegg proposed in 1867 that the resettlement scheme be implemented, despite the timing. Desire to get away from state repression, awareness of the efforts of the Maine colonists[43] and of Jewish plans for agricultural development, hope that the Tempel's beliefs would spread once reestablished in Palestine, and the promise of possible approval for the venture by the sultan were all factors that won support for the commencement of the move to the Holy Land.

In actuality, only a small proportion of the Tempel resettled. The group divided itself, settling at Haifa and Jaffa in 1868 and at other sites in subsequent years. At Jaffa the Templars bought up the properties of the abandoned Adams Colony, and in time they established themselves in several agricultural and commercial settlements throughout the country. Besides these rural settlements, communities of Templars were engaged in industrial and commercial pursuits (such as the tourist trade and the professions) in urban areas. As settlers they reached "a level of development unparalleled in Palestine. In planning, beauty, and organization, they had no equal in the country."[44]

Aside from their purchasing the Adams Colony's properties at Jaffa, the Templars had several other American connections. Some of the Templars were German-American citizens who had decided to rejoin their sect's enterprise in response to their leader's call. A large number of these German-Americans, for example, founded the Templar colony at Haifa. Because a need arose to provide consular service and protection to this group, John Baldwin Hay, then acting as consul-general in Beirut, nominated Jacob Schumacher to be the first American consular agent at Haifa. Schumacher was a naturalized American citizen, formerly of Buffalo, New York. He served in the post until 1891, when he was succeeded by his son, Gottlieb, who served until 1904. Gottlieb had an impressive reputation as an archaeologist and topographer[45] and did work for the competing British and German exploration societies: the Palestine Exploration Fund and the Deutscher Palästina Verein. His knowledge of the countryside and his correct dealings with Turks and Arabs made it easier for him to fulfill his dual occupation of consular agent and archaeologist.

Another member of the Templars was Ernest Hardegg, the long-tenured American vice-consul at Jaffa. Although Hardegg was a Prussian citizen, he favorably impressed American Consul Richard Beardsley by operating the "only good and respectable hotel at Jaffa."[46] Ernest Hardegg was appointed vice-consul in 1871 and served through 1910. Like Jacob Schumacher, Hardegg too was succeeded by his son, Jacob, who served the U.S. government until March 1917, one month before America entered World War I. The Hardegg family's role in American diplomatic affairs in the Holy Land is unique for its longevity.

When German and American settlement efforts are compared, it appears that the Germans also had a vision of the millennium in which the Holy Land was a key element. Typically, however, when leaders of American and German ventures first scouted the Holy Land, the Americans came away ready to begin as soon as possible but the Germans deferred, compelled to start their colonies only under the duress of persecution at home. The Germans probably had a keener sense of the Holy Land's demands. The German colony flourished until World War II, when the German presence in Palestine under a British mandate was not tolerated. Only one American colonial effort compared favorably with the longevity and success of the Templars. Devised in the tradition of American utopian pursuits, the "American Colony" at Jerusalem had strange and tragic beginnings.

The American Colony at Jerusalem

The words "Saved alone" on a cable shattered the world of Horatio Spafford. The successful Chicago lawyer, nearly ruined by the Great Chicago Fire of 1871, had struggled hard to rebuild his law practice and real-estate investments. With his wife, the former Anna Larssen, a daughter of Norwegian immigrants, he had led relief efforts to the point of exhaustion. When the opportunity to spend some relaxing time in Europe arose in 1873, Spafford decided to send his wife and

Fig. 24. EVIDENCE OF THE GERMAN TEMPLAR SETTLEMENT AT HAIFA. Architectural evidence of the German Templar colony as seen today on an abandoned building in Haifa. The passage is from Psalm 137: "If I forget thee, O Jerusalem, let my right hand forget its cunning." The Templars were able to achieve a greater degree of success with their colonies than the Americans, possibly because they had a more accurate idea of the realities of Ottoman Palestine.

four young daughters ahead while he concluded a business deal, so he saw his family depart on the *Ville du Havre,* one of the most luxurious steamships afloat at that time. Weeks later the cable arrived from Wales. Anna Spafford had miraculously been pulled from the cold Atlantic after the ship collided off the coast of Newfoundland in the early morning of November 22, 1873, with the English iron sailing ship *Lochearn.* The four Spafford girls were among the 230 passengers lost in the calamity. Later, on the sad journey across the Atlantic to join his wife, Spafford composed the words of a hymn still sung and beloved by many Christians today:

> When peace like a river attendeth my way,
> When sorrows like sea-billows roll,
> Whatever my lot, Thou hast taught me to say:
> "It is well, it is well with my soul."

The Spafford family began to grow again with the addition of a son born in 1876, and a daughter, Bertha, born in 1878. Scarlet fever attacked both children in 1880 and, tragically, only Bertha survived. A year later, another girl, Grace, was born. Despite the crushing trials, the Spaffords were steadfast in their faith, believing that their suffering indicated they had been marked for some divine purpose. Horatio was a close friend and supporter of the rising evangelist Dwight Moody, the man H. L. Mencken called "one of the most forceful and interesting Americans of his time . . . perhaps the greatest evangelist since John Wesley."[47] But Moody preached a doctrine —firmly established in the Spaffords' own church—that the couple found difficult to accept in light of their tragedies.

In the 1870s, elements of the orthodox Calvinist theology still had a strong hold over local Protestant pulpits, and evangelists frequently preached similar doctrines of divine wrath against sinners, divine punishment that was swiftly and everlastingly meted out. Moody called his preaching in this vein "shaking people over hell to make them good."[48] The Spaffords heard such doctrines preached, but they were preoccupied with burning questions that conventional theology did not answer. For example, the Spaffords rejected the notion that their suffering was God's way of punishing them for unfaithfulness; they rejected the idea of predetermined salvation or damnation; and they rejected the idea that private property could be held at the expense of the poor. The Spaffords' beliefs caused dissension in their local Presbyterian congregation and they, along with some like-minded friends, were soon asked to leave. Under Horatio's guidance, the group began holding its own meetings and soon was called "The Overcomers."

The break with their church was not a pleasant matter for the religiously and socially conscious Spaffords. In fact, it caused a controversy that "stirred Chicago" and was even reported in the papers. As a troubled Horatio Spafford began to seek peace of mind and a new perspective for his storm-tossed spirit, his thoughts gradually turned eastward to the Holy Land. His personal image of the Holy Land led him to believe that Jerusalem is "where my Lord lived, suffered, and conquered, and I wish to learn how to live, suffer, and especially to conquer." Spafford implied that the Holy Land held the key to great truths in an almost mystical way. Its reality could help him learn to cope with life's vicissitudes, much as it had enabled the historical figure of Jesus.

Spafford's plans to live in Jerusalem were apparently only temporary; he wanted to return to Chicago after an undetermined period.

His daughter Bertha revealed years later, "He and mother had no grandiose plans or expectations of what their going to Jerusalem could mean to anyone but themselves."[49] Regardless of their personal plans, the Spaffords' charisma attracted others, while spectacular rumors circulated among the curious about the "real" reasons the Overcomers were departing.

On August 17, 1881, Chicago newspapers reported that a party of eighteen was leaving for the Holy Land, including Bertha and Grace Spafford, the two surviving children of Horatio and Anna. By late September the group reached Jerusalem and rented a large house where they lived as a single "religious household while awaiting the fulfillment of biblical prophecy." Aside from utopian and eschatological motives, the little band took pleasure in their new home's association with the Bible. It was said, at one point, that these people of obvious wealth and culture "went every day to the Mount of Olives with tea and cakes, hoping to be the first to offer the Messiah refreshment"; years later Bertha confided that the trips were only ordinary picnics. Though considered odd, even among Jerusalem's diverse communities, the group soon became popular and accepted to a degree, and even served as hosts to a variety of Jerusalem's visitors.

One famous visitor was General Charles "Chinese" Gordon, the deeply religious British hero who spent almost a year's furlough in Jerusalem in 1882–83 fulfilling a lifelong desire to study biblical history and antiquities. Accompanying Gordon to the Holy Land was a young chaplain, the Rev. Herbert Drake. According to Bertha Spafford, the general was a frequent visitor to the colony and, though "Father did not agree with all the General's visionary ideas, . . . they were good friends."[50] But Gordon had personal reservations and private fears about the colony and the "extravagant American sect." Chaplain Drake had recklessly taken up with the group, and Gordon thought it would be best if he could get Drake home, away from the cult. But Gordon found talking to Drake difficult: "The Americans do not care for me to see Drake alone much."[51] While the general and the colony's adult leaders maneuvered subtly, five-year-old Bertha enjoyed the general's company, especially when she would creep up to the colony's flat roof—where the general could sometimes be found meditating—and be entertained by his stories. From the American colony's roof, incidentally, Gordon contemplated the "Garden Tomb" site, which he claimed was the true sepulchre of Jesus. The site eventually became known as "Gordon's Calvary," and its existence both stirred up the old arguments over the authenticity of the traditional sepulchre and provided an unadorned solace to disillusioned Protestants who were dismayed by the ornamental gaudiness of the traditional sepulchre site.

Gordon's association with the colony, and with Jerusalem itself, were terminated when he was sent by the khedive of Egypt to the Sudan, where a Muslim fundamentalist, the Mahdi, was stirring up a popular rebellion. Gordon died at Khartoum in 1885, beheaded by the Mahdi's troops. Drake, meanwhile, remained with the colony and assumed charge of the education of the colony's children.[52]

The American Colony, as the group came to be known, functioned like an early Christian commune, secure in the belief that the End of Days was near enough for all property to be shared and all work to be performed for the common good. The overriding importance of the group made marriage a conflicting value, so marriage was not considered practical for members. Even married couples were not encouraged to continue living together within the colony. These unusual features were not readily attractive to flocks of new adherents, and so the colony remained small during its early years.

While on a trip to the United States in 1895, Anna Spafford met an American-Swedish group that called itself the "Swedish Evangelical Church," a cluster of Swedish emigrant families living communally in Chicago and a related group of compatriots in Dalarna, Sweden. Lacking an academic theology (the church was led by a former sailor who had almost no formal schooling), the Chicago Swedish group was attracted to the idea of communal life at the site of Christianity's birth, in anticipation of the Second Coming. In November 1895 some thirty Chicago members left for the Holy Land, where they were quickly absorbed into the American Colony. Encouraging letters sent to the Dalarna branch soon enticed thirty-seven European Swedes to join the group. But when some of these newcomers fully comprehended their new surroundings—including the colony's utopian orientation and strictly regimented daily life—they decided to return home.

The American Colony was considerably aided by the additional newcomers who remained, even though the settlement took on a decidedly Swedish flavor. The skills many of the Swedes brought with them were immediately put to use, augmenting the colony's commercial base. For example, the colonists became known in the area for offering the best locally made occidental garments, the best blacksmithing and tinsmithing, and the best stonemasons and cabinetmakers. The colony eventually opened a girls' school, a photography shop that specialized in Holy Land views and biblical scenes, and a gift shop that sold souvenirs to the increasing number of tourists. On the suggestion of Baron Ustinov, the Jaffa hotelier, the colony also started offering accommodations to tourists during the busy season. With this broadened, practical economic base, the group's survival was ensured for years to come. In a sense, the Overcomers successfully "overcame" the unrealistic view of the Holy Land that had plagued earlier American settlers.

The controversy the Spaffords sought to escape in Chicago followed the American Colony to Jerusalem. Aside from some mistrust of the colony's motives—as evidenced by General Gordon's secret apprehensions—there was a deeper animosity between the colony and some of the resident American consuls stationed at Jerusalem, particularly Consul Selah Merrill. Merrill, who served at Jerusalem off and on over an eighteen-year period, was an Andover-trained Congregationalist minister who did not tolerate any deviation from Calvinist orthodoxy.

Merrill's first suspicions about the colony were fueled by a former colony member's vindictive tales as well as by unsolicited recollections of Spafford's heresy sent by his former enemies in Chicago. Merrill came to the conclusion that the colony was a manifestation of evil, based especially on the not-fully-understood attitudes of the colony toward marriage. Although he never visited, Merrill was convinced that free love, sex orgies, and adultery were advocated and practiced in the Colony, and his reports to the State Department shared those thoughts. He also let innocent tourists, who told him they wanted to see the American Colony, know what he thought of it.

The running feud between Merrill and the Spaffordites came to a ghastly head in 1887, after Horatio died. Merrill's substantial interests included the controversy over the authenticity of the Sepulchre and the placement of the lost Second Wall of the ancient city (the location of which would prove or disprove many theories about the city's growth). As was common in the archaeological efforts of untrained scholars, Merrill's diggings and explorations were oriented toward proving preconceived theories that, when verified, would enhance his personal reputation.

When trying to work at a site on the Mount of Olives that was supposed to have been the last place the Virgin Mary had been seen on earth, Merrill vigorously pursued his digging even though the spot was also the American Colony's burial ground. Merrill had his crews deposit all the exhumed remains into a mass grave. The grisly scene was discovered by Bertha Spafford, who claimed that she even recognized the remains of her father in the heap. In a city obsessed with the burial sites of the past, the outrage was the cause of deafening protest. The U.S. government dispatched an investigative committee, but Merrill was absolved of wrongdoing.

About ten years later Merrill involuntarily promoted a growing popular interest in the American-Swedish colonists. Selma Lagerlöf, the Swedish novelist destined to become the first woman to win the Nobel Prize for Literature, had been researching the Dalarna group and had come to Jerusalem to find out how its members were faring. Lagerlöf was met at her hotel one morning by Merrill, who tried to warn her of the colony's iniquitous state. The consul's vituperations had the opposite effect. Her interest stirred, Lagerlöf spent a good deal of time with the colony and then completed researching her novel *Jerusalem* in Sweden. Although ostensibly a work of fiction, *Jerusalem* sympathetically described in a thin disguise the state of the colony and its Swedish members.[53] In addition to Lagerlöf's positive work, published between 1901 and 1902, an article about the colony by Alexander Hume Ford appeared in the December 1906 *Appleton's Magazine*, blasting Merrill's performance with regard to the resident Americans.[54] Not long after that, the aging Merrill was reassigned to a forsaken post in steamy British Guiana (now Guyana).

The American Colony remained a viable religious group only as long as Anna Spafford was alive. When she died in 1923, dissensions within the group—especially a long-festering resentment over the division of labor between Americans and Swedes—led to the colony's gradual dissolution as a communal settlement. Bertha Spafford maintained the "American Colony Hotel" as a private enterprise, and it still exists in Jerusalem as a reminder of the city's quieter past (though it is no longer run by original colony descendants).

American efforts to colonize the Holy Land were, on the whole, aberrant, poignant, and illusory. Despite differences in the sizes of the ventures, and despite differences in the programs or relative successes, these efforts were based on an image of the Holy Land that was bathed in esoteric meaning. Each group expected to find conditions in the Holy Land at a low ebb, but their anticipations were keyed to an idealistic image of a potential biblical utopia, not to a realistic assessment of an Ottoman province. The colonial groups also arrived convinced that their enterprise would speedily restore the land and that the millennium would thereby be precipitated. While spiritually heartening, such beliefs were, however, irrelevant to the actual practical situations the settlers faced once they arrived.

Only the colonies that adapted to the new environment and were ready to adjust their mechanisms for survival ultimately prospered. The story of American settlement experiences in the Holy Land was therefore one of mixed folly and wonder and decidedly outside the conventional relations between nations and peoples. As a counterbalance to this ingredient, that most conventional form of relationship between America and the Holy Land, embodied in the American diplomatic experience, will be examined next.

CHAPTER 6

Diplomatic Prerogatives
The Consular Presence

I
\
n Room 244 of Chicago's Auditorium Hotel on
January 9, 1902, a group of pious laymen te-
diously reviewed the program of a Sunday School
Convention to be held the following June in Denver,
Colorado. The convention would be the tenth ecumenical gathering of Canadian and American Protestant Sunday school workers. As the session wore
on, it was suddenly enlivened by a digressing question about the yet undesignated location of the next
world gathering of Sunday school workers. The last
gathering, in London, was the third event of its kind
and was remembered just as fondly for its location as
for its inspiration. Each of the twelve men in the hotel room had an opinion on where and when the
next grand event should be held. When the group
turned to William N. Hartshorn, the bespectacled
publisher from Boston said softly, "Easter morning,
1904, at the Savior's Tomb, Jerusalem."

The idea was staggering. Before others had a
chance to recover, Hartshorn turned to Edward K.
Warren for support. Warren, a prosperous manu-
facturer and bank president from Michigan, had recently returned from the Holy Land. At Hartshorn's

The Burdens of Consulship

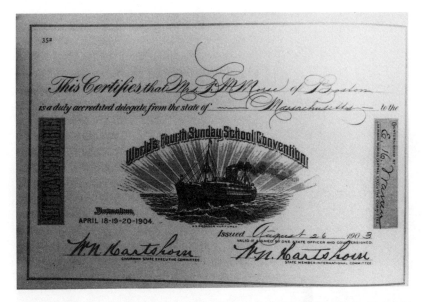

Fig. 25.   SUNDAY SCHOOL CONVENTION DELEGATE'S CERTIFICATE
OF ACCREDITATION.   The Grand Convention of Christian Sunday
school workers was held in Jerusalem in 1904. It was a success for the
organizers but a colossal headache for U.S. consular personnel.

nod, Warren quickly injected his impressions of the tomb and the
site of Calvary—not of the Holy Sepulchre, but of the more Pro-
testantly-acceptable site called "Gordon's Calvary"—and then he told
of some fondly recalled experiences in the Holy Land. One of the
company was moved to start singing a hymn, and soon the entire
group was enraptured with the idea. Warren was asked to investi-
gate its feasibility.

The following June, in Denver, the idea was submitted to the
gathered North American Sunday school workers. They heard Warren thoroughly review all the objections and all the attendant difficulties, then passed a resolution endorsing the plan. The idea was
visionary and stimulating:

> [It] received such hearty approbation that a large gathering is
> already assured. Even businessmen, not known to have been
> interested in Sunday school work, are writing to the Boston
> headquarters of the International Committee, saying that they
> are already making plans to go to the Holy Land in the year

named in order that they may attend the convention. The project has only sentiment behind it, but its approval shows that sentiment has a strong hold on the people.[1]

By April 2, 1904, two German liners were steaming through the Mediterranean carrying an army of Sunday school workers headed for Jerusalem. More than 1,500 strong, they would gather to promote the cause of Sunday school education within the context of Christianity's evangelical expansion.[2]

But for the American consul in Jerusalem, Selah Merrill, the prospect of yet another American tourist invasion of the Holy City was a recurrent nightmare. Only two years before, in March 1902, the steamer *Celtic* sailed into Jaffa with about 800 American tourists aboard, and it was only "at considerable trouble and some expense we were able to make this company of distinguished American tourists far more comfortable than they otherwise would have been. Facilities for handling and caring for such a large company are abundant in any American city, but here they are conspicuous by their absence." Merrill had to endure the grotesqueries of the Ottoman bureaucracy in order to secure a special detail of police. He called together all the city's carriage drivers (known for their imprudence) and warned them that they would be accountable for any accidents. He notified the local village sheikhs to rein in their "vicious youths," who made a habit of molesting tourists. And he arranged to have all known pickpockets and thieves rounded up and thrown out of the city and to have the city's normally dark streets lit at night and occasionally watered to keep down the dust. Despite all his behind-the-scenes efforts, however, Merrill lamented that "no one on the steamer knew what had been done by us."[3]

As consul, Merrill was aware of the situation in Palestine: "The conditions of weather, the precarious landing at Jaffa, the conditions of the country . . . reckless drivers, incompetent guides, poor and insufficient hotel accommodations, climate, food and other things combine to interfere with their comfort and happiness." In all, Merrill believed that "the coming of a great crowd of Americans to this city is always a matter of anxiety . . . and is to be deprecated."

The grand event took place anyway. Under Warren's chairmanship, it was accommodated in an enormous tent set up north of the city's walls, near the Damascus Gate. The Sunday school workers, joined by fellow evangelical Christians and missionaries from the region, were treated to a greeting from the Samaritan high priest, Jacob, son of Aaron—a bearded apparition in flowing robes and tur-

Fig. 26. SAMARITAN HIGH
PRIEST AT THE SUNDAY
SCHOOL CONVENTION. The
Samaritan High Priest, Jacob,
son of Aaron, stood outside the
assembly tent of the World Sunday School Convention in Jerusalem in 1904. With his flowing
robes and patriarchal appearance, the Samaritan leader provided conventioneers with a
tangible link to the biblical past.

ban who seemed to materialize directly from the pages of the Bible.
They also heard sermons from the renowned clergy in their midst,
toured the city of Jerusalem led by knowledgeable scholars, and
tried to see as much countryside as they could in the three weeks
that the chartered steamers lay off the Jaffa shore. When they left, it
was with feelings of satiety and confidence that the convention had
been successful.

Consul Merrill saw it from another perspective. "Diarrhea and
dysentery were quite prevalent among the visitors, but while in Jerusalem there were no deaths. There were some serious accidents, but
the wonder is that there were not very many when one considers the
conditions of living and traveling here and the inexperience of most

of the party."[4] The conventioneers were fulfilling a dream; Merrill was just doing his job.

A Job with Two Hats: Commercial and Official

American Consul Selah Merrill will be remembered for his feud with the Spaffordites and their "American Colony." A consul with a bumptious though practical outlook, he understood, for example, the chasm of difference between the reality of the Holy Land and the lure of Palestine as a tourist objective. He had observed the fortunes of Protestant missionaries laboring to bring a Western gospel of faith, democracy, and enterprise to Eastern hearts, and he had been enraged by the romantic compulsion of American Adventists to colonize the Promised Land. But as a civil servant charged with executing the duties of the American consulship abroad, Merrill had to look after the everyday affairs of his compatriots and thereby bridge

Fig. 27. U.S. AMERICAN CONSUL SELAH MERRILL. Merrill had a long and controversial career as Jerusalem's resident agent for the U.S. government. Like many consular appointees to the Holy Land post, his background included theological training and an interest in biblical studies.

the gap between their respective visions and the reality that the land presented.

In one respect this was the essence of the American consular experience in the Holy Land with regard to American imagery. Although the American consuls found themselves in the Holy Land for a variety of reasons, they were in the country primarily to assess commercial conditions, to look after American diplomatic affairs, and to adjudicate in legal matters involving Americans and persons claiming American protection. All of these activities were worldly-wise and made the consulship a burdensome proposition, and some of the Americans appointed to do the job could not contend with it.

Consul Albert Rhodes, for example, took a very dim view of consular service in the Holy Land. "Uneasy is the head that wears the consular crown," he wrote. "The responsibility of maintaining official dignity is oppressive, incompatible with mirth, and the bearing of such burdens any length of time generally develops a tendency to sadness. This is especially so with the American representative, whose quiet vegetation on Mount Zion is in such contrast to the aggressive life in America."[5] Rhodes's description made it seem as if the official representatives of the U.S. government were in exile from America rather than overseeing the nation's interests in the Holy Land. Many consuls felt the way Rhodes did, but others did not.

As a collective whole, American consular personnel illustrated another facet of the subtle interplay between myth and reality with respect to the Holy Land. These individuals entered the service of the U.S. government in Palestine for a variety of reasons. Some received the Jerusalem post reluctantly, settling for it as a mid-course solution to their original goals. Others actively sought Jerusalem and arrived with designs to use their experience for specific Holy Land–related purposes. Despite the circumstances of their arrival, all consuls came with a view of the Holy Land as place and past: they would be serving in the land of the Bible but dealing with Ottoman authorities in an Islamic milieu. The way the consuls reacted to and carried out their duties—simultaneously shaping the course of American diplomatic interest in Palestine—forged a significant aspect of America's Holy Land experience and further illustrated the impact geopiety had on American affairs through the influence and composition of the Holy Land's imagery in American culture.

Consular personnel were identified with two fundamental bonds between America and the Holy Land: diplomatic affairs and commercial relations. As official representatives of the United States, consuls were subject to instruction emanating from the foreign policy bureaucracy. They carried out American policy as formulated in Washington or in the American legation at Constantinople, and they created foreign policy by addressing or ignoring certain issues set before them. In general, before 1914, U.S. diplomatic concerns with the Holy Land were centered around the missionary, scholarly, and tourist interests of Americans. American diplomatic agents protected American travelers and induced the sultan to issue firmans that allowed archaeological expeditions.[6] In the words of Nadav Safran, they "afforded indispensable protection to the educational work of American missionaries which helped spark a cultural revival that marked the birth of Arab nationalism." They also

> provided protection to large numbers of Jerusalem Jews under the capitulation system, and American representatives in Constantinople wrestled with discriminatory laws against Jews because they affected the few hundred American Jews then residing in Palestine. . . . These activities derived from the concern of the American government that American citizens should not be discriminated against or placed under unjust laws, or they were taken out of humanitarian considerations in response to appeals of American Jews on behalf of their distressed brethren.[7]

In addition to these specific interests, the American diplomatic presence in the Holy Land, through the personages of the consuls, actualized the gradually accumulating perceptions, impressions, and opinions Americans held about the Holy Land. The American diplomatic presence condensed common American experiences and patterns of thought about Palestine and incorporated them into the manifest functioning of the federal government and its agents. The reason for this is the ultimate, popular base of American foreign policy. It is "not primarily the product of professional specialists in the State Department," writes Alan Geyer, but rather "the way in which the American people decide to confront or ignore the world around them."[8] In a sense, then, the foreign policy of the United States was the practical conception of national interest.[9] The factor that led the United States to establish relations with the Sublime Porte in the first place was trade.

Consular missions, although accredited by the government of one state to that of another, have been generally designed to serve the commercial interests of nations and only secondarily to serve the of-

ficial diplomatic interests of nations. Consuls have been used as public agents who promote and serve as guardians of the commercial
and industrial interests of the appointing state and its citizens and as
protectors of nationals traveling or resident in the foreign land.[10]

American trade with the Levant may have had obscure origins,
but it was significant enough to have been the target of an effort to
interrupt it. In the 1760s the British Acts of Trade attempted to
redirect most American commerce to British-controlled ports. Needless to say, the measure was resisted vigorously. Soon after the start
of the Revolution, trade between New England and the Levant was
resumed.[11] The need for expanded markets and the stability and
independence that commerce assured the new nation led President
John Adams to appoint an American mission to Turkey in 1799.
The mission was directed to negotiate a treaty of friendship, mutual
diplomatic relations, and trade. Together with developing missionary interest in the area, commercial interests and American concern
for the principles of independence and self-determination led to a
political desire to formalize American-Turkish relations,[12] thereby
paving the way for the establishment of formal diplomatic posts.
The bizarre nature of Ottoman bureaucracy, however, caused the
treaty negotiations to drag out for years. They were concluded as
late as 1830 with a treaty that gave Americans the same privileges
bestowed on Europeans as a result of the "capitulations." Vagaries in
and differing interpretations of the treaty led to disputes between
American and Turkish officials that continued for years, making the
job of American representatives more complex.

American relations with the Sublime Porte were preoccupied with
several unresolved or intricate matters of diplomacy, and the United
States displayed an even more remote interest in Turkey's fate than
did the European powers, even though American ministers in Constantinople frequently advised their government that the Ottoman
Empire was about to collapse. But the outstanding difficulties with
the treaty were paramount. One issue left unresolved, with compli-
cations already seen in the affairs of American colonists, concerned
the Turkish protocol on landownership by foreign nationals and the
Turkish right to tax such property. An even thornier issue had to do
with the extent of American protection and jurisdiction over naturalized citizens and the consular courts. Because there were an unusually high number of Americans living or sojourning in Palestine
(as opposed to other regions of the Ottoman Empire), and a large
number of Jews in Palestine who claimed to be naturalized Americans or who sought U.S. protection because they lacked the security

of being protégés of other consuls, both those issues caused great consternation among American consuls in the Holy Land. Merrill was right when he indicated the consul had a thankless job.

A Faltering Start

The American consular presence in the Holy Land was divided unequally among three locations: Jerusalem, Jaffa, and Acre/Haifa. While Jaffa and Acre/Haifa were staffed by consular agents, the Jerusalem post was a full-fledged consulate after 1857, occupied by a consul, an occasional assistant, a dragoman, and a *kevass*, an exotically costumed consular guard supplied by the pasha. Consular agents were simply individuals responsible for seeing to American interests; they were not necessarily Americans, or even Europeans. The Jaffa agency, after a time, became the post of an assistant consul. Although an American consular agency at Acre dated from 1843, it soon relocated to Haifa after the influx of German and German-American Templars in the 1870s. Because of the jurisdictional configuration of the Ottoman Levant, the Haifa agency was part of the Beirut consulate and was not associated with the American consulate at Jerusalem.

The first appointed U.S. consular agent for Jaffa and Jerusalem was David Darmon, a Jew who claimed to be a naturalized citizen of France. Darmon had been recommended to Commodore David Porter, head of the American legation in Constantinople, by an American Jewish traveler passing through the Turkish capital on the way back from a trip to the Holy Land in 1831. But Darmon soon began to overstep the bounds of his role as agent, first by dealing directly with the State Department (instead of following channels through his direct superiors) and next by proposing several schemes that Porter found odious, such as elevating Darmon with the title "Consul for Palestine" or having the United States seize the island of Cyprus. Although Darmon's activities and proposals irked him, Porter delayed requesting the man's ouster because Porter knew the State Department had been asked to create a central, salaried consular post in Jerusalem with subsidiary agencies at Jaffa and Beirut.[13] But Washington was slower to act than Porter anticipated, vacillating about whether to have a post at the remote station.

Porter's discontent eventually shifted into action as a result of the cruise of the USS *Delaware* to the Holy Land in 1834. Although Darmon had followed consular practice by extending courtesies to the ship's company, Commodore Patterson of the *Delaware* found his reception objectionable. In a letter to Porter, Patterson painted an unsavory portrait of the man who would be America's representative. The word of a fellow naval officer was enough for Porter, and he rescinded Darmon's appointment. Darmon believed that the American Board missionaries at Jerusalem had instigated Porter's actions because Darmon had proudly withstood conversion efforts. His letter of appeal was typically levantine for the time, described as "an admixture of humble submission, pleas for forgiveness, flattery, demands for money to cover the extraordinary expenses incurred by his receptions in the line of duty, and pointed threats that unless he received satisfaction from Porter, he would appeal over his head to the President."[14] Darmon's appeal was rejected by Porter, and the Jerusalem-Jaffa post remained unoccupied until 1844.

Early in May 1844 a letter arrived on the desk of Secretary of State John C. Calhoun. It was written by Philadelphia Congressman Edward J. Morris, recently returned from his trip through the Levant, and introduced a Mr. Warder Cresson of Philadelphia, who desired appointment as American consul at Jerusalem. Morris wrote Calhoun that, from his own observation, he knew what a great convenience a consulate would be to American travelers, since consulates afford official "protection and comfort." Morris observed that because Jerusalem "is now much frequented by Americans" a consulate there would be most useful, and he concluded with the unsubtle hint that Cresson "was a gentleman of capacity & probity & intended to make Jerusalem his place of residence."[15]

Apparently, the idea of a consulate made available through the preferential residence of an American citizen—and costing the federal government little capital outlay—appealed to Calhoun, who in turn commissioned Cresson as the first American consul to Jerusalem on May 17, 1844. On that same day, Cresson was confirmed by the Senate. Shortly after notice of the appointment appeared in the press, Samuel D. Ingham, a former congressman and secretary of the treasury under President Jackson, wrote to Calhoun. Ingham noted the appointment of Cresson but wrote that "the appointment is made a theme of ridicule by all who know him. I cannot make allowance for the gross imposition practiced on the appointing power."[16] Ingham claimed that Cresson "has been laboring under aberration of mind for many years," that "his mania is of the religious species"—or at least serious enough to impugn Cresson's credentials as an American representative. Calhoun reconsidered the appointment and on June 22 sent Cresson a letter: "I am instructed by the President to inform you that, having reconsidered the proposal to establish a consulate at Jerusalem, he is of the opinion it is not called for by the public service and therefore declines to establish it at present."[17] The letter was sent to Cresson at Philadelphia, but Cresson had already departed for Jerusalem unaware of the change. By December 1844 word reached the American legation at Constantinople that an American citizen who was thoroughly convinced that the ingathering of the Jews was imminent was passing himself off as the American consul at Jerusalem and, among other things, "giving papers of protection to Jews and others not citizens of the United States."[18]

The American minister to Turkey, Dabney Carr, dismissed Cresson as a madman and disavowed him to the Ottoman authorities. When Cresson finally received Calhoun's retraction, he stepped aside, but maintained his residence at Jerusalem until 1848. In March of that year the spiritually hungry Cresson converted to Judaism, and in September he returned to Philadelphia to liquidate his affairs. Once back in the United States, Cresson (who had assumed the name Michael Boaz Israel) was met by a hostile and disconsolate family who sought to have him declared insane in a jury trial. By 1850 another trial reversed the findings, and two years later Cresson returned to the Holy Land as an observant Jew who proposed the founding of a Jewish agricultural settlement near Jerusalem and thereby assumed a peculiar rank among the proto-Zionists of the early nineteenth century.

In 1856 the United States finally did establish a full consulate at Jerusalem with the appointment of a Boston physician, John Warren Gorham, to the newly created and salaried post, replacing a string of vice-consuls and agents who acted on instructions from Beirut. Gorham, who arrived in Jerusalem in March 1857, delayed raising his nation's flag over the Holy City until the Fourth of July, but the affair was not without incident. With the pasha out of town at Nablus, the garrison commander at first refused to honor the flag, as customary, with a twenty-one-gun salute because the banner represented a nation ruled by a mere president and not a king. After a night of frantically exchanged notes culminating with Gorham's threat to appeal to the sultan himself, the commander yielded. At 10:00 A.M. the American flag was hoisted over the U.S. consulate within the walled city of Jerusalem for the first time and received its due homage and official welcome.[19]

The undesirability of the Jerusalem post became evident through the rapid succession of consuls. Gorham lasted until September 1860, when he had to be removed because of alcoholism exacerbated

Fig. 28.   THE FIRST AMERICAN CONSULATE IN JERUSALEM.   This building is still located within the Old City's walls, near the Jaffa Gate. A flag overhead and an eagle plaque above the doorway identified its function both for Ottoman authorities garrisoned in the Citadel across the street and for residents and tourists.

by boredom. His successor, William R. Page of Maine, served until November 1861, when he left outraged "over the promiscuous issuance of letters of protection in Constantinople to what he called "hordes of spurious Americans"—namely, Jews seeking the protection of an enlightened diplomat. Page was followed by New Yorker Franklin Olcott, who served between 1861 and 1862; Isaac Van Etten of Minnesota, who served in 1863; and Albert Rhodes of Pennsylvania, who stayed at his post from 1863 to 1865. Each quickly grew bored and tired of the remote post and its unique though trying demands. The next consul would find the post no different.

Bureaucrats in Jerusalem

Victor Beauboucher, who had emigrated from Belgium to America, held antislavery beliefs that led him to fight for the Union cause. A volunteer with the 28th Massachusetts Regiment, he lost a leg at the Battle of Cold Harbor in 1864. Assistant Secretary of War and former newspaper editor Charles A. Dana recommended the estimable Beauboucher to Secretary of State Seward for overseas assignment, and Beauboucher won appointment to the Jerusalem consulate in August 1865. Beauboucher quickly became disappointed with the post and distressed by his worsening health as a result of his wounds, made no less bearable by the exasperating affairs of Adams at the Jaffa Colony.

Beauboucher saw the Jerusalem consulate as having little commercial importance to the United States, and instead of the customary trade-related duties of most consuls, he found himself largely concerned with protection of the considerable number of American travelers who were passing through Palestine as a result of the cessation of the "Late Unpleasantness" and the holding of the Universal Exposition in Paris. Beauboucher was proud to report that "a trip through Palestine can be accomplished with the utmost safety and tranquility relative to brigandage" because he had ensured that local authorities would protect tourists and pilgrims.

Besides the Adams Colony affair and the protection of American tourists, Beauboucher soon became embroiled with affairs in Jerusalem's Jewish community. His involvement with that community illustrates the complexities of the capitulatory system and how much consular prerogative that system gave foreign governmental representatives. It also demonstrates how American officials dealt with an element of the Holy Land population.

In 1868 Beauboucher innocently intervened in a matter that involved the Jewish community's sensitivity to attempts by Christian missionaries to convert Jews. As a targeted population for missionary work, the Jews had communal feelings against evangelical activities that ran extremely deep. For example, the London Jews' Society, a major British missionary group, spent considerable money and effort to establish a foothold in Jerusalem. Through their highly regarded hospitals, they tried to subtly introduce patients to Christianity by leaving religious works at the bedsides of the unconverted. Despite the hospital's concessions to Jewish ritual needs, such as serving kosher food to patients, the Jewish community leaders fought the proselytizing attempts vigorously, excommunicating members who used the hospitals; attacking patients being discharged, and smashing their medicines; and bitterly fighting with the British consul, whom they saw as protecting the interests of his own compatriots.[20] Perhaps this incident involving Beauboucher

would not have had such international repercussions if the city had
been any other than Jerusalem or if the incident had not taken place
within the memory of the infamous Mortara Affair of 1858, when
an Italian Jewish child was secretly baptized by its nurse and a custody battle ensued with the Roman Catholic church.[21] More than
likely, Beauboucher just did not fully appreciate or understand the
concern of the Jewish community over missionary activity. He had,
after all, received a warm reception from the Jewish community, bolstered perhaps by the appointment of Jewish merchant Herman
Lowenthal to head the Jaffa arm of the agency and by adoption of
the European system of noncitizen protégés, which ensured that the
insecure Jews would have a measure of influence because their interests were looked after by a foreign power.

The incident that caused the stir between the Jewish community
and the American consul involved the status of a thirteen-year-old
girl named Sarah Steinberg. Sarah, an orphan, had been under the
charge of her older brother. When the brother died, Sarah's guardianship became an issue between Rabbi Ari Marcus, head of Jerusalem's Grand Synagogue and a chief communal leader, and Sarah's
older sister, who had previously converted to Protestantism. The
rabbi, a Prussian protégé, claimed that the Jewish community had
the right to guardianship over Sarah in order to protect her from
conversion, so, moving speedily after the brother's death, the rabbi
"abducted" Steinberg. The child's sister then appealed to Beauboucher for help lest the rabbi arrange a hasty marriage for the
child in order to reestablish legal guardianship. Drawn into the fray,
Beauboucher in turn demanded that the acting Prussian consul get
the girl back from Rabbi Marcus, but no action was taken—out of
the Prussian's prudent experience. Impulsively, Beauboucher
stormed off, with his *kevass* in tow, in search of the girl at the home
of Rabbi Marcus. It was a Friday afternoon, and, with the Sabbath
impending, a fight ensued between the consular *kevass* and the
rabbi's followers (the girl was not at the rabbi's home). Eventually,
the rabbi was dragged off to the pasha's residence, where Beauboucher called for justice. Because the rabbi was under Prussian
protection, no action could be taken except by the Prussian consul,
who was away at Beirut. Beauboucher was forceful enough to have
the consul telegraphed, and instructions were returned to the acting
consul, ordering that the rabbi be imprisoned in the consular jail.

While Beauboucher saw his action as humane in the face of religious fanaticism, to Jews around the world it was bureaucratically
overbearing. Soon the U.S. government began receiving outraged

messages from Jerusalem's Jews telling about the unjust physical attack on the rabbi, who had only been defending a Jewish soul in
peril. Beauboucher's administrative superiors reacted swiftly, and
messages of concern came streaming in from all over, especially
from Washington. That the story became somewhat garbled and
overblown did not help either. One version had Beauboucher recovering the girl only to run off with her himself! What seems likely is
that the girl ended up in Alexandria, Egypt, either at the home of an
uncle or as a child bride.

The taxing incident pushed the ailing Beauboucher beyond en-
durance of the demands of his post, and he requested a transfer,
which was approved.[22] In the United States, the incident had the
effect of promoting the mission of a Rabbi Hayim Sneersohn, who
was collecting money for Jerusalem's charities. Sneersohn himself
appealed to the federal government to appoint "consuls friendly to
our race," and he took satisfaction in Beauboucher's replacement
even though the replacing consul also assumed a bureaucratic posture in his post.[23]

Actually, very early in his tenure Beauboucher was upset with his
assignment and desired a more agreeable post. He thought Naples
would be better for his health, and the passengers of the *Quaker City*
cruise pressed the State Department to transfer him according to his
wishes. But the aggravation of the Jerusalem tenure followed Beauboucher down through the years. As late as 1886, he was still pursuing his claims on the U.S. government for repayment of out-of-
pocket expenses related to the Jaffa Colony affair.

Richard Beardsley, Jerusalem's consul between 1870 and 1873,
was a member of the University of Michigan's class of 1859 who had
served the Union as a naval paymaster, though the action he saw was
limited to the bombardment of several ports below New Orleans.
After the war, Beardsley traveled for a time in Europe and Africa,
and like Beauboucher he sought a Mediterranean post for health
reasons and also preferred an assignment to Naples. But the government was not quick to act on his request for an appointment. Growing impatient, Beardsley wrote to Secretary of State Hamilton Fish,
appealing to his sympathies and telling Fish that if he remained in
the United States any longer it would be at great peril to his life—at
least so his physician told him. The U.S. government apparently decided not to imperil Beardsley any further, for on January 13, 1870,
Beardsley was appointed to Jerusalem.

Perhaps the much-heralded completion of the Suez Canal made
assignment to the Levant region seem suddenly more attractive.[24]

Certainly Beardsley's first reports from Jerusalem were hopeful in tone and expressed his optimistic view that

> with her climate, soil, and geographical position, Palestine un-
> der favorable circumstances would become one of the most
> prosperous states on the Mediterranean. What she requires is
> a wise and just government which will protect instead of plun-
> der her people, internal improvement such as roads and
> bridges to render her different parts of easy access and aque-
> ducts to irrigate her thirsty soil, and above all in patriotic
> spirit and national aspiration among her people. This last
> would naturally result in the course of time from a good gov-
> ernment and then would commence the resurrection and re-
> juvenation of Palestine. She would rapidly advance in wealth
> and prosperity. Her desert wastes would again blossom as the
> rose and she would soon become one of the most favored
> countries in the world.[25]

Beardsley informed Washington that, in his view, the Jordan Valley in the vicinity of Jericho appeared "remarkably well-adapted for the growth of every tropical product." Quoting Josephus, he called the area potentially "equaling in fertility the most luxuriating gardens of other countries." Although the greater part of the area's fertile plain was little more than desert, "all the elements of its former prosperity are still there, and whenever the smallest attention is given to its cultivation, its fertility is wonderful."[26]

Beardsley's overall assessment was sober and remarkably free of theological underpinnings or pessimism. The resources of the coun-try, he believed, were underdeveloped; agriculture was frequently primitive, and simple neglect and mismanagement had caused the naturally rich and fertile soil to be barren. He postulated that if the ruling authorities rendered the country safe and secure from the nominally subservient bedouin tribes, sufficient capital could be mustered for further development. But with a government that made no move to improve the country's wretched roads, little could be expected for the time being. He concluded: "There can be no doubt that Palestine, with her resources fully developed, her agri-cultural capabilities utilized, and under the rule of a wise and just government, would soon have a population many times larger than at present, and become one of the most wealthy and prosperous countries on the Mediterranean."[27]

In April 1871 Consul Beardsley informed the State Department that the number of American travelers was triple that of the number of other nationalities passing through Jerusalem thus far that year and that most of these tourists seemed to be coming to Palestine by way of China and India. Beardsley also advised, "It would be well if our countrymen knew that to travel in Palestine and the East it is not necessary or wise to join large parties" and recommended parties of five or six travelers.[28] Underscoring the still dangerous aspects of travel in the Holy Land was an incident that involved two daughters of Yale University President Theodore Dwight Woolsey in 1870. Traveling to Jerusalem from Beirut, the two girls contracted dysentery and died en route. Despite the crushing blow, Woolsey wrote a letter of support and thanks for the services Consul Beardsley had rendered under trying circumstances.[29]

On February 10, 1872, Beardsley wrote Secretary of State Fish that he wanted to be considered for the consul-general's post at Alexandria, or, if not there, at Marseilles, Lyon, or Bordeaux. His wish to be stationed elsewhere than Jerusalem stemmed from a desire for more duties and responsibilities than he had in the Holy Land— and, incidently, more pay, for the pay of the Jerusalem post was inadequate for his expenses. By 1873, Consul Beardsley was gone.

Ordained Consulship

With Beardsley's departure, the Jerusalem consulate appeared to enter a new phase. It had already changed from the undeveloped post in an undesirable backwater that the consuls before Beauboucher found it to be and had become a mercurial bureaucratic post through the attitudes and labors of Beauboucher and Beardsley. But Jerusalem remained an unusual assignment encumbered by uniquely sensitive circumstances. In response to these circumstances a pattern of appointments seemed to unfold, and the post frequently became identified with religion and/or antiquarian interests. Most likely due to the perception of the Holy Land as both place and past, the Jerusalem consulate began to emerge as a place best suited for a particular type of official. In the years between 1873 and 1917 the consular post was occupied for the most part by Protestant clergymen—most of whom actively sought the Jerusalem position, unlike some of their predecessors.

Consul Beardsley's successor, Frank DeHass of New York City, lobbied hard for an appointment to the Jerusalem post. On Septem-

Fig. 29.   U.S. CONSUL AND AUTHOR FRANK DEHASS. DeHass made it clear from the start that he viewed his appointment to the Holy Land as an opportunity to pursue his interest in biblical research and antiquities.

ber 2, 1872, he wrote to President Grant asking to be made consul at Jerusalem because he wanted to "complete a work on biblical archaeology and make further researches as a member of the American Palestine Exploration Society." A former pastor of the Metropolitan Church in Washington, D.C., DeHass had become obsessed with studying the Holy Land. Failing to receive a reply to his first letter, he brashly handed an application to President Grant while the president was vacationing at Long Branch, New Jersey. In a still later letter, DeHass added to his request the familiar refrain that the post was desired for health reasons, though in this particular case the health was that of his wife. A few weeks later DeHass sent word to Secretary of State Hamilton Fish, on June 18, 1873, reiterating his impatient desire for appointment to Jerusalem and noting that he wanted to do additional research in biblical archaeology, "something I think can be better prosecuted under the auspices of the Government in an official capacity." DeHass also suggested to Fish that he believed the consular position at Jerusalem would be well suited to keeping an eye on the sultan's illegal slave trade. "It is for the cause of science and humanity I ask the appointment, not for any pecuniary benefit as I should have to resign a position of $6,000 per year to accept the office." The request was not made for political reasons, either, though DeHass let Fish know that he had sent out ten thousand circulars to American clergymen, urging support for Grant and damning some scandalous reports against the Grant administration. After a while, the administration relented, and DeHass was off for Jerusalem to work on his book.

It is not unfair to say that DeHass used his appointment to his best advantage. As he himself admitted, his "object in accepting an appointment under the United States Government and making his home for several years in Palestine was not the honor or emoluments of Office, but a desire to visit the lands of the Bible, so that he might examine and see for himself how far the manners, customs, and traditions of the people and topography of those countries agree with the inspired word."[30] But DeHass made no mistake about his position. While serving at Jerusalem, he attended properly to his diplomatic and commercial responsibilities. For instance, he had to use his good offices to compensate the owner of a donkey killed by a shore party from U.S. sloop of war *Alaska* when the sailors were roaming Jaffa's alleyways in drunken merriment.[31]

But DeHass, and most of the consuls who followed him,[32] also kept an eye on the land of antiquity and had, perhaps, an enhanced appreciation of their situation because of it. Straddling both worlds, a consul with a good sense of humor would relish the scene created by many Eastern practices. Edwin S. Wallace, consul from 1893 through 1898, provided a good example when he wrote of the figure of the scimitar-wielding *kevass*:

> A smile is not out of place on the face of an American as he sees his military escort conducting him through the streets of the Holy City, and imagines what a sensation he would create were he to pass along any street of any city in his own land similarly conducted. But he is now in Turkey where nothing is done as other people do it.[33]

Consular personalities in the period before 1918 began assuming proportions more appropriate to the place. Those who were clergymen usually represented the liberal, humane tradition of their faith and acted accordingly when exercising their duties. Henry Gillman, although not a clergyman, exemplified this liberal, enlightened approach to his duties when in the late 1880s he became involved in protesting and resisting Turkish efforts to expel recently emigrated

Russian Jews from the country as they were arriving in larger numbers than ever before. According to Frank E. Manuel, Gillman "saw himself as the agent of Divine Providence, ordained to facilitate the entrance into the land of Jews who were being driven out of Russia by its harsh decrees."[34] Some undoubtedly had odious attitudes about what they were doing. For example, Selah Merrill, an adherent of old-line Calvinist orthodoxy, was haughty and disdainful of the growing numbers of Jews who sought his protection, but even so, he applied many of the same policies his predecessors had. As for their observations on the contemporary state of the country, consuls were perceptive and often pessimistic, in that they were disappointed that the land's potential was not being achieved under the Turks.

An Untapped Potential

In the minds of many consuls, the Holy Land was simply not a promising commercial site. Victor Beauboucher observed that Jaffa, the available entry port, provided only inconvenient anchorage offshore, which was dangerous in the winter months. Palestine's exports were limited to small amounts of grain, sesame, and oranges annually. Communication with the country's interior was nonexistent beyond the limitations of a horse and rider. A proposal for a carriage road to Jerusalem was bureaucratically delayed, and the first of a series of proposals for a rail line in the country was abandoned in exasperation.[35] Beauboucher reported that there were few travelers during the hot summer months and suggested that the best time to visit the Holy Land was in the spring. Nonetheless, he estimated that in the eighteen months before July 1867 an astonishing five hundred Americans had made the Holy Land trip.

Economic conditions in Palestine during Beauboucher's term were bleak. Harvests in two successive years (1865 and 1866) had been devoured by locusts, and the price of provisions had quadrupled. Taxes had been raised to keep the government's excesses on par, and Beauboucher appraised the poor peasantry, "reduced to the most frightful misery," as understanding "nothing of civilization beyond exactions" and reduced to the level of productive animals rather than human beings. Beauboucher saw the Jews of Palestine as the only European element permanently established in the country; he perceived its commerce as being conducted by Christian Arabs, or "Greeks," and severely limited by the overall state of affairs and lack of diversity in produce or goods.

Consul-General J. Augustus Johnson, reporting from Beirut in October 1866, wrote to the State Department that commerce between Syria and the United States "has not received that impetus which was expected as a consequence of the close of the war." Only one American ship stopped at Beirut for commercial purposes during 1865. It is ironic from the perspective of the late twentieth century that Johnson anticipated at least one vessel from Boston via Alexandria, Egypt, to stop at Beirut soon with a cargo of American petroleum: "Beirut and Damascus use this oil in preference to the olive oil of Syria because of its superior quality and cheapness and its use is becoming more general throughout the country."[36] In 1868 Johnson wrote from Beirut that he was more hopeful about trade prospects, calling the State Department's attention to the fact that "commerce between Syria and the United States has gained considerably during the year 1868 and it is hoped that henceforth it will be conducted on a wider basis."[37] He reported that again Syria's chief import from the United States during the period was petroleum and that it continued to replace olive oil as a fuel source in the East. The turning away from olive oil to petroleum was with good cause in the nineteenth century. Excessive Ottoman taxation policies, to the point of levying duties on the produce of individual trees, tended to discourage the cultivation of olives and figs. This policy was unfortunate not only because it repressed a native industry but also because it discouraged reforestation and general planting.

The nature of affairs in Ottoman Palestine even made it difficult on occasion for consuls to assess the state of trade. For example, Consul Beardsley explained in his second annual report on trade, filed in November 1871, that he believed commercial information for Palestine would best be supplied through the records of the Jaffa customs house since all the exports and imports for the province were entered for duties at Jaffa. His explanation to Washington of attempts to secure this data provide a picture of the Turkish bureaucracy in action:

> I have endeavored to obtain copies of the custom-house records at Jaffa. With that object in view, I applied some months ago to the Ottoman authorities of Palestine for permission to examine the official registers at Jaffa, and was answered that an order from the chief officer of the customs at Beirut was necessary. I then applied to Beirut for such an order, and was

informed that the desired information could only be given in obedience to an order from the chief of customs at Constantinople. As it was then too late to obtain the desired order and have copies made of the records in time for this year's commercial reports, I endeavored to obtain the required information from private sources. After waiting several weeks for the promised statistics, I have at last received certain tabular statements purporting to be the returns of the commerce of the port of Jaffa during the past eighteen months, but which are in reality a confused mass of figures manifestly unreliable and almost unintelligible. I can make no use of them except to embody in this general report some of the items which appear to be most correct.[38]

Beardsley thought that Jerusalem, for its size and importance as the principal town of the province, was "one of the least industrial and commercial [centers] in the world."[39] Most manufactured and staple goods were imported from Europe, while only petroleum and lumber were the principal American imports. The chief exports of the city were soap and "Jerusalem ware"—crucifixes, beads, crosses, and ornaments made mostly of olive wood and mother-of-pearl. Only the soap was traded locally (to Egypt); the Jerusalem ware went primarily to the local pilgrim trade and for export. Between September 1870 and September 1871 Beardsley certified five orders of such material for shipment to the United States.

Beardsley also noted that demand for American lumber was "considerable and gradually increasing," and he could foresee present conditions offering an inducement for other American products to be sent to the Holy Land as well. He suggested too that several local products might be exported to America with some profit. For instance, he claimed that the local soap was of an excellent quality and would even soon be exported to Britain, where it could compete successfully with English soap. Exports of olive oil, cotton (though produced in then-insignificant quantities), fruits, and sesame could also be profitable ventures, given some enterprise.

American enterprise occasionally sought to exploit Palestine's resources, but in ways that were instructive about American business perceptions of the Holy Land. If the Holy Land's sacred association was an inescapable feature, then an untapped market already existed and only capital and a good idea were needed to make some money. In the autumn of 1906, Selah Merrill offered his good services to Colonel Clifford Nadaud of Covington, Kentucky. The colonel, who claimed to be on the staff of Kentucky's governor, was president of the International River Jordan Water Company of New York.

The company intended to make available to the American public freshly bottled water from the "sacred river of Judea." Nadaud, who arrived in Jerusalem with letters of recommendation from the U.S. legation in Constantinople, secured several wagons and a staff of workers in the Holy City. He commissioned the construction of fifty-three giant casks and set up a purification center at the traditional site of Jesus' baptism. The water, more than thirty-four tons of it in the initial shipment, was boiled, cooled, and poured into the casks from large cauldrons. In addition to the certifying stamps of the company, the pasha, and the patriarch of Jerusalem, Merrill saw fit to add the consular stamp, a step Washington later deemed improper. Merrill contended, however, that "the company has been well launched by men of character, capital, and energy, its purpose is unique, novel and well becoming American enterprise and it deserves to succeed."[40] Regardless of the propriety of Merrill's involvement, his attitude showed his belief in the capacity of progress and enterprise to advance civilization, a belief many of Merrill's fellow consuls held. In the Holy Land, this belief was in contrast to perceived Eastern stagnation, regressiveness, or depravity.

The idea that Turkish rule over Palestine was corrupt and confused was reinforced, for example, by reports from American Consul Willson, who declared the state of Turkish rule was totally disorganized and unimproved despite the efforts of Great Britain to sponsor reform. The biggest single question, Willson wrote, was what will happen to Turkey once its government falls. As examples of the decay rampant in Palestine on account of Turkish misrule, Willson called Jericho a "dead" city and said Tiberias might as well be the same. In contrast, Willson claimed that conditions in Nazareth and Bethlehem were improving as a result of increased Christian tourism.[41]

Perhaps the best summary of the consular position, bridging the gap between expectations and realities, was made by Selah Merrill, the consul who served officially at Jerusalem for more than fourteen years and who resided in the area for almost thirty years, having come originally to work for the American Palestine Exploration Society. Merrill wrote his superiors that many of the expressions of interest the consulate received about business possibilities in the Holy Land lacked a sound knowledge of the state of the country and were inconsistent with reality:

The number of business letters received making inquiries about business matters is large, if I could be authorized to decline about half of them because the questions become absurd when asked in view of the conditions existing in this country, our postage bill will be lessened by a few dollars each quarter.[42]

For some American officials, the gap between image and reality had narrowed appreciably. They merely had to contend with fellow citizens who still labored under misconceptions that were expressions of geopiety.

American missionaries and colonists were compelled to experience the Holy Land firsthand on account of their endemic beliefs, and American tourists were drawn to the land by its cultural and spiritual mystique. These groups were free to assimilate only the parts of Ottoman reality that would allow them to cope with their strongly held agendas, but the consuls had to deal with the entire "package": the land and its condition, its political environment, its various peoples, commercial affairs, and so forth. It is not surprising that the consuls had their most extensive connections with another group of Americans that experienced the Holy Land, scholars—curiously, the most past-oriented of Americans most familiar with the Holy Land.

CHAPTER 7

From Faith to Treasure to Truth
The Toils of Scholarship

F ranklin Hoskins, an early-twentieth-century American missionary associated with the Syria mission at Beirut, once related an apocryphal story about a peculiar gap in knowledge about the Holy Land. He told of the visit a young woman paid to an older lady friend who loved the Bible and who read it frequently from cover to cover. The younger woman related excitedly that she was about to depart for the Holy Land and would be touring Jerusalem, Bethlehem, Galilee, and all the other famous sites connected with the life of Jesus. The older woman listened silently and then "put down her work, removed her silver-rimmed spectacles and exclaimed: 'Well now! I know all these places were in the Bible, but I never thought of them being on the earth.'"[1] That telling remark accentuates the chasm between the Holy Land of scriptural faith and the Holy Land of everyday reality. It also implicates the role the Bible played in shaping the extent of knowledge of the land.

The sampling of American experiences in the Holy Land during the Ottoman years has shown that, whatever the activity, for many Americans the Holy Land retained its image as faraway place and remote past, though perhaps not to the degree expressed by the older woman of Hoskins's story. Travelers and missionaries, and colonists and consuls, were propelled to the Holy Land by an assortment of reasons, and all pursued a variety of ambitions and programs once they arrived. Simply, the travelers wanted to see the land and its peoples; the missionaries came to change the land's peoples; the colonists came to change the world in which they settled; and the consuls had the job of dealing with practical, everyday affairs. But in the course of their activities, all demonstrated a perception of lapsed time, and this may be seen in their various expressions about the reality of Ottoman Palestine.

This perception permeated these Americans to various degrees, and the pattern held true even for the most intentionally past-oriented group of Americans to encounter Palestine: those who methodically sought to understand the country's past and to rationally probe its antiquity. This group may be categorized loosely as "scholars" because of their general commitment to serious, systematic study. It includes people of various theological outlooks and dogmatic postures who were engaged in such labors as exploration, excavation, biblical, Semitic, and philological studies. Because the rubric of scholarship can be quite broad, we shall concentrate on one of its many manifestations, the gradual emergence of a detached, scientific mode for the study of the Holy Land's past: archaeology.

To Know the Land

The romance of archaeology is a naturally appealing theme. In connection with American experiences in the Holy Land, it was a subject buttressed by visions of adventure, images of esoteric scholarship, practical skill, and the potential for finding treasure or magically and precisely recreating the forgotten and mythic past. Americans' antiquarian interest in the Holy Land was centered around the land's association with biblical lore and spiritual attachments. The Holy Land's reality was most often the subject of conjectures about how extensive those remnants of the past were.

The gradual, modern "rediscovery" of the Holy Land by enlightened nineteenth-century minds was a topic that vividly caught and held the American imagination through various stages. Americans felt a certain pride and responsibility for the emergence of formal scientific study of the Holy Land, having supposedly led the way in opening up the Holy Land to scientific exploration in the first half of the nineteenth century. When surface exploration evolved into scientific excavation during the century's second half, American work came to be measured against the standards established by European scholars, notably British, French, and German. Yet Americans continued to maintain an influential presence, particularly through the work of several well-regarded personalities associated with the British. Americans repossessed a central role in the field during the British Mandatory era, after World War I, when the "golden age of American Near Eastern archaeology"[2] commenced, dominated by the towering intellect and "paramount role"[3] of William Foxwell Albright. Albright served as professor of Near East studies at Johns Hopkins University and for more than forty years was a guiding figure at the American Schools of Oriental Research at Jerusalem. In 1970 the school was renamed the Albright Institute in his honor.[4]

American interest in Holy Land archaeology also includes elements of the dramatic conflict between science and religion. As an emerging discipline, archaeology provided a perhaps unique arena in which the forces of religious conviction could discourse openly with the spirits of humanistic modernism, logical objectivity, and reasoned doubt that challenged conventional patterns of faith. During the course of archaeology's development, many of the Americans who labored in and contributed to the field had clerical training in their background, and many too held a deep and religiously inspired interest and respect for the Bible.[5] Yet most of these American participants were also committed to studying the Holy Land by applying the same rational, scientific methods that produced Darwinism and its secular offspring. The clash of these forces frequently took place within the hearts of individuals, and the way this conflict was resolved can tell us much about both American religion and American science.[6] The individual thoughts and motives that produced this momentous conflict would be subject enough for a separate work. We shall concentrate here instead on the broader history of American activity in this area.

Although archaeology today implies investigation through excavation, it is conventionally assumed that knowledge of the surface of the landscape precedes and is an integral part of such excavation. The reason for this emphasis in the history of Palestinian archaeology was the critical need for accurate site identification in the Holy Land. For this reason, the work of scientific surface explorers or observers, who used precise and systematic methods, is conventionally considered part of the story of archaeological endeavors.

Albright's study, *The Archaeology of Palestine and the Bible*, divided the scientific work done in the Holy Land prior to the 1930s into three phases: 1838 to 1890, when scientific exploration and excavation began; 1890 to 1914, when material was collected and published but inaccurately dated and classified; and after 1917, when the scientific method of Holy Land archaeology truly matured (Holy Land archaeology entered other phases in subsequent years, but they are beyond the scope of this analysis). Albright observed about the importance of the development of scientific knowledge of the Holy Land's past:

> Except for the work of the last century, and especially of the last generation, it would be impossible to reconstruct the ancient social, political, or religious history, material civilization, arts and crafts, etc., since our chief documentary source, the Bible, invariably requires archaeological elucidation before it becomes completely intelligible from any of these points of view.[7]

It is also clear that scientific interest in the Holy Land's past, on the part of Americans and others, is rooted in the singular association of the land with the events described in the Bible. In fact, as a geographic area of specialty within the discipline of archaeology, Palestinian archaeology has acquired a name that expresses this cultural-literary association best: biblical archaeology.

Scholarly study of the Holy Land, in terms relevant to the history of archaeology, probably dates from the time of the Roman emperor Constantine and his mother, Queen Helena. At the first ecumenical council of the Christian church in the year 325 at Nicaea, which the emperor and Jerusalem's Bishop Macarius attended, Macarius made the acquaintance of Constantine's mother and proceeded to tell her about the condition of the sites associated with the life of Jesus.[8] The queen was moved by Macarius's plea that the sites be preserved, and the following year she journeyed to Jerusalem and, with the bishop, ranged over the country and gave her lasting imprimatur to the identification of the various sites. Although Helena's interest in the sites was primarily religious, and the inspired manner through which she identified many of the sites was less than scientific, her interest nevertheless ignited the flame of pilgrimage to the Holy Land and, along with it, an abiding interest in the sacred sites.

Shortly thereafter a pilgrim from Bordeaux, in Gaul, made the trek to Jerusalem in the year 333.[9] The role of the pilgrim in relation to the state of scholarly knowledge about the Holy Land down through at least the nineteenth century should not be minimized. Even though pilgrim aims in visiting the land were spiritual, the pilgrims who recorded their impressions down through the centuries have prevented "too serious [a] loss of knowledge about the country."[10]

Changes wrought in the Holy Land in the years following the advent of Islam, together with conditions in Europe, caused a hiatus in Western scholarly observations of Holy Land geography. This condition changed, however, as a result of the Crusades. The Crusades left Europe with a progressive interest in the Holy Land, and the resulting lucrative pilgrim traffic was too alluring for Palestine's Muslim rulers to halt it. The Holy Land literature produced by Englishmen formed part of America's legacy related to the Holy Land, and several of these works made important contributions toward furthering knowledge about Palestine. In 1703 the English Protestant Henry Maundrell produced his exemplary traveler's account, which was quite popular among English-speaking readers. Bishop Richard Pococke journeyed through the Holy Land in 1738, often leaving the beaten pilgrim track. He subsequently published more plans, drawings, and copies of inscriptions than any of his predecessors.

The birth of modern antiquarian interest in the Middle East can be dated to Napoleon's efforts at establishing a French presence astride the British-Indian trade route in 1799. When Napoleon invaded Egypt, he brought along with him men of science and culture, whose purpose was to form a special commission that would fathom the richness of the past and propose the outline for a grand restoration of former Egyptian glories. The period between 1801 and 1812 saw the curious work of an adventurous Swiss citizen, Johann Burckhardt. Burckhardt traveled throughout the Holy Land and was the first modern scholar to record Arabic place names accurately. The romance of the East and his explorations prompted him to become a Muslim, and he traveled under the name "Sheikh Ibrahim" in relative safety and freedom. Burckhardt was one of the first modern Europeans to rediscover the rock-city of Petra and gain access to other sites on the eastern side of the Jordan. During the same period, from 1805 to 1807, a German, Ulrich Jasper Seetzen, became the first person to explore scientifically such other important sites as Caesarea Philippi near the headwaters of the Jordan, Amman, and Jerash, on the eastern side of the Jordan.

"Yet for all this accumulated activity, the Land of Israel was virtually a *terra incognita* from a scientific point of view,"[11] a fact not mitigated by Ottoman suspicions of Western interests, scientific and otherwise. The Turks were not without cause. Exploratory and archaeological interest in the Holy Land during the nineteenth century thinly veiled the nationalistic and imperialistic thrusts of major European powers.[12] However, as a result of internal divisions within the empire in the 1830s, and the unsettling conditions and late reforms brought about by Mehemet Ali, Palestine's generally unfriendly environment was altered.

Americans Take the Field

The years of Egyptian occupation of Palestine were marked by the rarity of a strong, centralized government that was tolerant of minorities and intolerant of local corruption and that enforced greater security within its borders. The period of Egyptian rule thus saw a marked increase in the exposure of Palestine to Westerners, and this was never more true than with the arrival of the singular figure who would become "the founder of biblical archaeology," the American, Edward Robinson.

American entry into the field of biblical geographical research was a natural result of the special relationship Americans had with the Holy Land that had been promoted by the Bible's popularity.[13] Bible reading had made Americans intensely familiar with Holy Land geography,[14] and news of contemporary journeys to biblical sites made the Bible even more real and reaffirmed its hold on the American mind. It was not a coincidence that Edward Robinson was also "recognized as the foremost American biblical scholar of his day"[15] with regard to linguistics and interpretation.

Edward Robinson's reputation has been enhanced rather than diminished by passing of time. Robinson went from farm labor to law to the study and teaching of Greek and Hebrew at Andover Theological Seminary in Massachusetts, before his curiosity and abilities led him abroad for study in Germany under the finest critical minds of the time. Upon his return to the United States, he continued his association with Andover until he was invited to New York's Union Theological Seminary in 1837, which granted him an immediate three-year leave of absence to pursue his research in the Holy Land. He was then forty-four years old.

Together with Eli Smith, an American Board missionary stationed in Beirut who knew the local language, people, and customs, Robinson roamed over Palestine for months during 1838 and subjected it to the first trained, critical study of its surface features and an analysis of its Arabic place names. He then returned to Berlin to sort out and transcribe his data. The result was the scientific location of scores of biblical sites and the publication in 1841 of the monumental *Biblical Researches in Palestine, Mount Sinai, and Arabia Petrea*.[16] Later, in 1852, Robinson and Smith returned to the field, and the result was publication of *Later Biblical Researches in Palestine and the Adjacent Regions*.[17] Titus Tobler, a Swiss doctor who began his own research three years before Robinson's initial journey, wrote in 1867: "The works of Robinson and Smith alone surpass the total of all previous contributions to Palestinian geography from the time of Eusebius and Jerome to the early nineteenth century."[18] Robinson's critical approach gave his work its "epochal importance," to the extent that all surface explorations that followed were only gleanings in comparison.[19]

Robinson's work was not free from controversy. Probably due more to his "uncompromising desire to uncover truth"[20] than to a Puritan-inspired theological hostility toward Catholicism, Robinson found much fault with a number of traditions associated with sites and religious orders in the Holy Land. In particular, he conjectured that the acknowledged site of Jesus' sepulchre was probably wrong because it was determined under circumstances that promoted Bishop Macarius and were therefore of suspect honesty—a "pious fraud," according to Robinson. This opinion enraged George Williams, a former chaplain to the first Anglican bishop in Jerusalem and at the time dean of King's College, Cambridge. Williams was the author of a detailed study of the topography of Jerusalem published in 1845, *The Holy City*,[21] in which he defended the traditional site based on topographical evidence. Williams claimed that many of Robinson's conclusions were fallacies, "argued out often on insufficient premises, or in contravention of historical or topographical phenomena." Although the controversy was never resolved, a later edition of Williams's work retracted the personal tone of his attack on Robinson.[22]

Ten years after Robinson's initial venture, the American minister to the Sublime Porte requested a firman to allow an American naval party "to circumnavigate and explore the Dead Sea and its entire coast . . . in the interest of science and for the gratification of enlightened curiosity." The request was considered so important that it was sent to the sultan for a decision. The sultan's approval, in an

Fig. 30. JERUSALEM'S CHURCH OF THE SEPULCHRE. The Church of the Sepulchre was the focus of Christian pilgrimage and controversy involving Americans in the nineteenth century. A visit to this shrine was the highlight of many American tourists' itineraries. Others, including scholar Edward Robinson, regarded the site as being inauthentic because it did not meet preconceived expectations or reasoned evidence.

Fig. 31. U.S. NAVAL EXPEDITION ENCAMPMENT. Encampment of the U.S. Navy's Jordan River and Dead Sea expedition. Under the command of Lieutenant Lynch, the expedition was bolstered by Lynch's strong will and unwavering Christian faith. It was the first successful endeavor in modern times to circumnavigate the Dead Sea.

atmosphere still wary of foreign military ventures within the Turkish domain, indicated the high level of "Ottoman confidence in American good will that no strategic designs" were behind the move.[23]

Lieutenant William Francis Lynch, "an earnest Christian and lover of adventure,"[24] led a handpicked U.S. naval party of "young, muscular, native-born Americans, of sober habits"[25] in an expedition of five officers and nine seamen down the Jordan River from the Sea of Galilee, to and around the Dead Sea in 1848. Using two metal boats dragged inland from Acre, Lynch and his men took soundings, drew navigational charts, and corroborated the recently offered claim that the Dead Sea was actually below sea level. The expedition weighed anchor from the Brooklyn Navy Yard in November 1847 and returned in December 1848, suffering the loss of one officer, Lieutenant J. B. Dale, to sickness. The trying circumstances of the expedition and the sickness that plagued the party made Lynch almost regret the effort. "As I looked upon my companions drooping around me, many and bitter were my self-reproaches for having ever proposed the undertaking."[26] The results were published in official and popular versions, with the latter going through numerous editions and reprintings. Lynch, according to historian David Finnie,

> sums up a great deal that we have observed in other Americans. . . . Like the missionaries, he was a Godly man steeped in fundamentalist doctrine and Old Testament lore. His excessive zeal for showing (literally) the flag was shared by many another American. His self-appointed mission to be explorer of the Jordan and Dead Sea combined pioneering spirit with religious sentiment. . . . What Lynch did could hardly have been attempted or accomplished by a man of any other nationality of his time. Unlike the French, the Russians, or the English, the motives of his government in authorizing the expedition were utterly unpolitical. Lynch simply got a bee in his bonnet, persuaded the Navy to back him, did what he set out to do without fuss, wrote it all up (in a rather ponderous way) and vanished from the scene. William Francis Lynch was pure pioneer.[27]

After these initial scientific ventures, the tempo of Palestine exploration increased, although the Europeans now dominated the field. The quality of work, however, was not of the caliber established by Robinson. For example, Titus Tobler, Robinson's contemporary who has come to be regarded as the founder of the German school of

Palestine exploration, relished the idea of heightened competition in the field because it served to further knowledge. But Tobler himself was "awed by the scope of Robinson's researches" and even "feared that the gifted man had robbed him of his life's ambition."[28] Victor Guerin, a Frenchman who explored Palestine, also tried to identify biblical sites, producing seven weighty volumes on his effort. His works were largely discounted later by scholars because they lacked critical acumen and because "he failed to grasp that the country's many tells cover the sites of ancient cities,"[29] in retrospect an error almost beyond comprehension.

Another French explorer, Félicien de Saulcy, journeyed to Palestine in the 1850s and performed the first modern excavations of a Palestinian site, the uncovering of the "Tombs of the Kings" outside Jerusalem. De Saulcy, whom Albright characterized as a man whose "enterprise exceeded his knowledge and his vanity exceeded both,"[30] erroneously pegged the tomb as belonging to the age of the Judean monarchs, largely because there was as yet little knowledge of the history of architectural details and epigraphy in Palestine. The tombs actually dated from the years 50 to 70 of the Christian Era, prior to the destruction of Herod's temple.

Popular interest and awareness of the exploratory work being done in the Holy Land was high in the 1860s, stirred perhaps by the tone of nationalistic competition as British, French, and German "schools" of Palestinology began to take shape. Lacking a sustained American presence, popular American interest was instinctively drawn to the field's newest stars, the British, whose Palestine Exploration Fund (P.E.F.) was founded in 1865. In no small way, the exchanges between British and American periodicals sustained the interest, and the P.E.F. was readily adopted as a field representative for the Americans, at least for a time.

Deferral Again to the British

The Palestine Exploration Fund of Great Britain did much to reawaken American interest in Palestinian antiquity in the late 1860s. Americans shared a sense of commonality with the British when the Fund came to the Holy Land. Their perspectives were as Anglo-Saxon Protestants, and as such, they saw as much difference between themselves and the Latin and Greek Christians as they did with the Muslims. They shared a heritage of Holy Land lore as Anglo-Saxon

Protestants. English pilgrimage literature was just as much a part of the American literary heritage as it was of the British heritage. Yet it was not only a sense of shared language, or even a sense of shared history as transmitted from the era of the Crusades, that gave the British and Americans a measure of closeness. Their Protestant traditions also had a good deal of bearing on the public's receptivity to missionary efforts, the guardianship of holy sites, and even the historical viewpoint on biblical events and figures. Perhaps with no other European people did Americans share so much in common when it came to the Holy Land.

The Palestine Exploration Fund grew out of a literary society founded in Jerusalem in 1847 by British Consul James Finn and his wife, Elizabeth.[31] In 1867 the Fund sent Charles Warren, a young lieutenant in the Ordnance Corps, on a mission to excavate Jerusalem. Although Warren was amply funded, the task was far greater than anyone had anticipated. Because he worked at a time when there was no reliable criterion for dating masonry and pottery, he dated the masonry of the great retaining wall of the Temple Mount as coming from the time of Solomon instead of the reign of Herod. On the other hand, Warren dated the remains of a Maccabean fortress at Gibeah as being the work of Crusaders. Inaccuracies made Warren's work less useful to subsequent, more sophisticated archaeologists, but he did much useful site clearance and, together with the Ordnance Survey completed by Captain Charles Wilson shortly thereafter, laid the foundations for all subsequent work on topography and history in Jerusalem.[32]

It is significant that reports of Warren's work of shaft-sinking and vault-passageway exploration explicitly recognized that "ancient Jerusalem lied buried beneath enormous masses of debris. Underneath the pavements of the modern street lies the old Sacred City of Zion, as little revealed by the contour of the surface as were the monuments under the same mounds of Mosul." This was in sharp contrast to the belief of many that the streets of nineteenth-century Jerusalem were virtually the same as those trodden by Jesus. It was expected that work would continue at Jerusalem that would "result in discoveries of immense value and interest to the Christian world, as throwing light on scriptural references to the ancient city of Jerusalem, and the later history of the last Jewish struggle against the Romans."[33]

The work of the Palestine Exploration Fund was frequently promoted in American newspapers and journals. A letter from the Fund secretary to the editor of the *New York Times* reported some of the Fund's recent work, particularly the work of Lieutenant Warren:

The interest which at present exists in America in the Exploration Fund is chiefly confined to that comparatively small class who have actually visited Jerusalem. These carry away with them a lively recollection of the importance, actual and possible, of the work and of the difficulties under which they are carried on. That great class comprehending all Americans—that is all who are interested in the elucidation and illustration of Scripture, or in the verification of truth, and detecting falsehood in history—who should show interest in us, have not as yet done so, because they have never yet been directly appealed to and are generally ignorant of the very existence of our Society.[34]

The Fund, the Secretary noted, wanted to conduct a thorough and complete exploration of Palestine: to determine, once and for all, the exact locations of sacred sites; to study Palestinian flora, fauna, meteorology, and climate; and to excavate the vast accumulations of rubbish in order to settle the many questions raised by archaeological lore. The secretary also wanted to maintain contact with "those Americans—not by any means a small number"—who had visited Warren and descended into his shafts, feeling their ways along the passages and galleries he had excavated under the Holy City. The secretary teased his readers with some of the more provocative findings, alluding to the locating of Solomonic ruins around the Temple Mount and passageways of unknown and intriguing origin and purposes.

   A follow-up appeal from the new secretary of the Fund, Walter Besant, appeared one year later in another letter to the editor of the *Times*: "Our work has become more largely known in the States, partly through the accounts of travelers, partly through the efforts of individual gentlemen. Especially, Rev. Dr. Patten of Chicago, Rev. Dr. Budington of New York, Rev. Dr. Bidwell, Rev. J. W. Hubbell, and others." Besant's appeal was direct, as it was aimed at the religious and nationalistic sentiments of the readers:

   The countrymen of Dr. Robinson and Dr. Smith need not be informed that Palestine has been less explored and is less well known than any country in England, or any district in Europe. They know that the city of Jerusalem has no sites fixed, no localities certain. Where the Savior stood before Pilate; where the Temple was in which he taught; where the Sepulchre in which he was buried; where the Calvary where he suffered—these are all points which have yet to be cleared up.

> ... And I have the honour to invite travelers in Palestine who have observed anything new or have remarked anything which throws light on the sacred books, or who can suggest any steps in the way of exploration, to make this [the Fund's] journal . . . their medium.[35]

The author of an article in the widely read magazine *Leisure Hour* told of the work of the Palestine Exploration Fund, presuming that the readers were already aware of the association's work. The author remarked that he trusted

> the honour and privilege of prosecuting the accurate and systematic investigation of the archaeology, topography, etc., of the Holy Land, for biblical illustration, may be reserved for England and America, now peculiarly the Lands of the Bible, and between whom there is no religious jealousy, but a willing and ready cooperation in all labors that tend to throw light around the sacred volume.[36]

Even news of an attack by a mob of three hundred Algerian Muslims on the camp of the British crew completing its survey of Palestine in the Galilee hills was carried with much interest in the United States, further enhancing the popular view of Palestine as a wild and dangerous place.

The December 11, 1868, issue of the *New York Times* reported on a local meeting of the Long Island Historical Society at which a Rev. W. J. Budington, D.D., spoke on the recent findings and operations of the Palestine Exploration Fund. Budington recognized that "much of the evidence which was to settle many disputes was to be brought from beneath the soil." In a comment that spoke legions about the inauguration of scientific work, Budington noted that Warren commenced work determined to take nothing for granted. Budington predicted that the "Christian world of this or of the next generation was likely to have grand solutions of truth made to them."

At the same lecture, a William H. Thomson, M.D., "who said he was a native of the land . . . and was as familiar with the region as many of the audience were with Brooklyn and New York," related observations relative to more ancient civilizations in the region.[37] A Rev. A. P. Putnam expressed gratitude for the discoveries already made and "for the encouraging promise of more to come. He seconded the proposition of Dr. Budington that aid be sent to their British friends who were prosecuting this work, for out of it were to

come great and grand things—treasures of knowledge—the reconstruction of history." And Rev. R. S. Storres, D.D., offered his conception of Jerusalem and its surroundings "without ever having
been there in person." He characterized the city as being "a little
tongue of land occupying less ground than there was in Prospect
Park. It was about 1,200 years older than Rome. It signified 'peace'
and yet, since David defended it against the Jebusites there was not a
spot on earth on which there had been more scenes of blood and
carnage."[38]

By the summer of 1872, it was reported, the British were pushing
on with their explorations and the British Fund was out of debt. The
income of the P.E.F. was said to be nearly $15,000 a year, a sum
that went a long way in supporting the work in Palestine. Captains
Warren and Stewart were replaced at Jerusalem by Captain Claude
Conder.[39]

At a meeting of the British Society on July 10, 1872, a Thomas
Mooney made "an animated harangue of an adverse sort," declaring
that there was enough work exploring London's misery, crime, and
ignorance without going to Palestine. He then proposed an amendment to a resolution repledging the society to its founding purpose.
The amendment read: "All moneys raised by the Society should be
devoted to discovering the 'ruins of humanity' in London." It was
not seconded, and someone pointed out that Mooney was not even a
member of the Society. The Archbishop of York did respond, however, that money was being sent toward charitable purposes and
these were quite independent from the Fund's sources:

> Such criticism as Mr. Mooney's are often heard, and although
> manifestly unsound, are sufficiently plausible to be worth oc-
> casional refutation. They are applied most frequently to the
> labors of missionaries and sometimes perhaps with more pro-
> priety than to the exploration of Palestine. Yet apart from the
> obvious absurdity of assuming that because evil exists in any
> one place, good should not be attempted in any other, the
> bearing of missions on the prospective condition of the home
> poor should disarm hostile comment. Quite apart from reli-
> gious considerations, the tendency of missions is to open up
> fresh areas for the surplus industries at home, to create new
> and attractive centers for emigration and prosperity. The dis-
> coveries promised in the Holy Land are of vast moment to all
> Christians as confirmation of their faith, while the work of the
> missionaries possess an industrial and social as well as theo-
> logical significance. Neither, we may be sure, deserve the

sweeping condemnation of Mr. Mooney and his kind, who, failing to see an inch beyond their noses, are unable to perceive that what they censure may be calculated to favor the truest and best good of the classes whose interests they appear to protect.[40]

From 1872 to 1878 the Palestine Exploration Fund sponsored the making of an inch-by-inch survey of "Western" Palestine under the leadership of C. R. Conder and H. H. Kitchener. Although the survey was superseded in following years by more accurate works, it remains even today an indispensable tool for archaeologists and topographers. In the judgment of William F. Albright, "it is surprising how few significant ruins were overlooked by the surveyors of the expedition. To be sure, many of the identifications by which Conder, in particular, thought that the topography of biblical Palestine was settled for good, have proved to be wrong. But errors and omissions are remarkably few when we consider the scope and speed of the undertaking."[41]

The Fund's survey of Western Palestine did not preclude future topographical work, but rather stimulated it because

> . . . there are many omissions, certain districts were not carefully studied, while the archaeological importance of the telul (plural of tell) was only imperfectly understood at first, and many were omitted from the maps; there are also many errors of orthography, which are generally the fault of the native scribe who was employed to write the names in Arabic. Moreover, no idea of the date of the ruins described could then be given, since the surveyors were army men, whose knowledge of archaeology was very limited. Nor can they be blamed for their ignorance, since the most important criteria, especially the use of potsherds for dating, were not yet discovered.[42]

The work of the British, motivated as much by strategic as scientific concerns, needed to be supplemented in some way. In the United States, people were ready to lend this support, and an American effort paralleling that of the British began to take shape.

An American Palestine Exploration Society

The *New York Times* of September 18, 1871, noted that its readers were well aware that the British Palestine Exploration Fund's work has been "of so great importance as to attract the attention of the whole Christian world." An account of the Fund's work, *The Recovery of Jerusalem*, had been republished quite successfully in this country and was "widely used here." The newspaper commented, significantly:

> One result of this publication has been the formation of a "Palestine Exploration Society" in this country at the head of which is Rev. Joseph P. Thompson, while among the members of the Committee are such men as Profs. Hitchcock and Henry B. Smith, Rev. Drs. John Cotton Smith, Washburn, and Vincent, Profs. Hackett, Kendrick, James Strong, and Day, Rev. D. Stuart, Dodge, Howard Patten, W. C. Prime, William A. Booth, Dr. Willis James and others eminent in various walks of life. The Palestine Exploration Society proposes to undertake a part of the work of research in the Holy Land, not in rivalry with or upon the same ground already occupied by the English Society, but in harmony with its labors, and in a different district. The two societies have been in correspondence and . . . in our own Society propose, if it can sufficiently interest the public to send out an expedition to explore east of the Jordan, in ground equally interesting and important. . . . To our countrymen belongs the credit of having given the first impulse towards the exploration of Palestine in recent times. Dr. Edward Robinson, Dr. Eli Smith, Lieut. Lynch . . . Dr. Barclay, author of *The City of the Great King*; Prof. Hackett, Dr. Thomson, whose work *The Land and the Book* is famous, Mr. Osborn, and other Americans have worked in this field, mostly at their own expense, but in a manner which secured most important results. It is fit, therefore, that Americans should not refrain now, when a work so welcome to all Christian men and women, so interesting and important, is prosecuted for the first time with adequate means by an English society.[43]

The effect of the establishment of the British Palestine Exploration Fund, and the wide distribution that news of the Fund's work received in the United States, did cause the Americans eventually to establish their own similar association. In 1870 the American Palestine Exploration Society was organized in New York. The two associations maintained close contact and to a degree even coordinated their efforts.

By the spring of 1873, the American Society was ready to field a party for the exploration of the east side of the Jordan. The first party was composed of a military officer, a college professor, and two ministers, together with a number of assistants and bearers. The group set out from Beirut, where a local advisory committee had been formed, on direction from New York. The advisory committee consisted of members of the Beirut mission station of the American Board and faculty of the Board's Beirut College. The expedition was instructed to maintain close ties to this Beirut extension, even to the degree of clearing preliminary reports and plans through it.

Beginning in February 1873, reports of the progress of the American Society's expedition began to reach the United States. The casts and inscriptions that were made excited the scholarly community, and teasing notes of field exploits in exotic locales held the interest of the general reading public. The work in Moab and on the eastern side of the Jordan were considered particularly desirable at that time, and in any case, the Americans were not resigned to having lost their prerogative on the western side of the Jordan just because of the British activity. The allure of the eastern side was the Moabite Stone, a remarkable treasure that offered the first independent corroboration of the biblical narrative and the chance that some additional finds of a sensational nature might quickly be found in the relatively unexplored region.

The end of the first season of the expedition and the return of its leader, Lieutenant Steever, were heralded as occasions for the Society to make further plans and to trumpet "the magnitude and importance of this great American enterprise,"[44] to the general public. A lack of funds, however, stalled any further effort for the time being.

The Society's work after its first expedition was suspended because of a lack of funds and "other reasons," notably involving personnel. However, "a few months ago a new interest was awakened in its behalf by the earnest efforts of Charles Stewart Smith of this City (New York), whose subscription of $1,000 to the fund and friendly challenge to other gentlemen of wealth and culture in this city and Boston to do likewise have resulted in a large addition to the funds of the society."[45] With the infusion of new monies, a second exploring party was commissioned by the Society, under the command of Colonel James C. Lang, and it arrived in London and received much attention and a cordial greeting from their British counterparts. As composed, the party also included the Rev. John A. Paine of Tarrytown, New York, and a Mr. Rudolf Meyer, an engineer.[46] An executive committee meeting held on November 18, 1874, heard Dr.

Howard Crosby discuss Paine's work and appointed the Rev. Selah
Merrill to be Paine's associate. One result of Paine's work was his
identification of the biblical Pisgah.[47] As for Merrill, in the judgment
of William F. Albright, "he was no Robinson, much less a Clermont-
Ganneau, and the results of his work were also insignificant."[48]

At first, in terms of the American-British cooperative effort, reaction to the American work was quite positive. The British Foreign
Office, with its interests in the region intensifying because of the
recent acquisition of Cyprus and the opening of the Suez Canal, was
especially appreciative of the savings that the American Society's
mapping work would mean to the British field teams working on the
western side of the Jordan. Both the Foreign Office and the War
Office welcomed a modern large-scale map of Palestine, and both
English and American societies produced their maps simultaneously.
In 1879, the thirteen-sheet American map reached the British government via the British Society, but a copy of the American map was
already on file in the War Office's Intelligence Department, where
several officers of the Royal Engineers examined the American work
and declared it "a most valuable addition to the geographical knowledge hitherto very imperfect of the countries lying between the Jordan and the Euphrates."[49]

Apparently, the Americans were aware of the interest in their
product. The American map covered about five hundred square
miles per each of twelve of its sheets, and the thirteenth sheet gave
the results of topographic triangulation as well as the results of the
archaeological and surface explorations. The whole included 150
geographic names that had hitherto not appeared on other modern
maps. In a letter to the British Society that assessed the map's value,
the Americans wrote: "Whether accepted or not as final, our map at
all events is much better than any compilation of existing maps
would be, and we offer it to the English society on condition that we
receive say 50 copies of the larger map and 800 of the smaller when
published."[50] Only after a long look at the map of the Americans did
the British have second thoughts about its quality. Several inaccuracies were found, enough that the British informed the Americans that while their map was "a distinct step in advance . . . [it was]
inadvisable and injudicious to place [such an] inexact and incomplete
[map] beside exact work." This amounted to an outright rejection of
the American effort, and in February 1881 the British decided to re-
map for themselves the territory surveyed by the Americans. The
British commissioned Lieutenant Conder to lead the mapping party,
which was composed of commissioned and noncommissioned offi-

cers of the Royal Engineers. The liberality of the War Office in sharing its personnel for the effort indicated the level of priority attached to the expedition by Her Majesty's government. The Conder expedition began work in the spring of 1881 and completed the job in 1882. The Fund published the results of the expedition in 1883 under the title *Survey of Eastern Palestine*. As for the American Palestine Exploration Society, it slipped into oblivion after publishing only four statements.

The American effort to emulate the British had been a dismal failure. Nevertheless, it served as a conduit for American interests and highlighted the activities of some Americans in connection with the Holy Land's archaeological exploration. One of these Americans was Howard Crosby, the Society's secretary. Crosby was both a scholar and a man of public affairs. The great-grandson of a signer of the Declaration of Independence, Crosby grew up in wealthy surroundings bequeathed to his family by an uncle, Colonel Henry Rutgers, for whom Rutgers College was named. Crosby started learning Greek at six years of age, and he graduated from New York University at age eighteen. He was one of the early organizers of New York's Young Men's Christian Association. Beginning his career at Rutgers as a professor of Greek, Crosby soon was ordained in the Presbyterian church and assumed the pulpit of churches first in New Brunswick, New Jersey, and then in New York.

Crosby was not in any sense a narrow cleric—his interests were humane, informed, and broad. He served as Chancellor of the City University of New York from 1870 to 1881; delivered the Yale lectures on preaching between 1879 and 1880; founded the Society for the Prevention of Crime; was active in the temperance movement; and was also interested in creation of an international copyright law. Before publishing his first book, *Lands of the Moslem*, in 1851, Crosby toured the Levant. His interest in the development of the American Society may also have been rooted in his activities as a member of the New Testament Company of the American Revision Committee from 1872 to 1880, a group that sought to revise the translation of the Bible in popular use at the time.

The work of the Palestine Exploration Fund was clearly scientific in nature, though closely coordinated with the growing strategic interests of the British Empire in the region. The reasons behind much of the popular interest in Holy Land exploration and archaeology, however, continued to remain linked to the possibility of spectacular discoveries and the acquisition of priceless artifacts.

Treasures and Frauds

As the Palestine Exploration Fund's first expedition was being organized, in the years between 1865 and 1870, a young French scholar began working in the Holy Land and made numerous discoveries on his own, without the benefit of extensive support from a home constituency. Charles Clermont-Ganneau arrived in the Holy Land as a twenty-one-year-old employee of the French consular service. In 1870, after only three years in the Holy Land, he was involved in the successful recovery of the Moabite Stone from bedouins.

In 1868 a German minister associated with the British Church Missionary Society discovered a black basalt stele in the ruins of a biblical-age city in Moab on the east side of the Jordan. The stele was covered with inscriptions in the old style of Semitic script and, after some deciphering, with the help of Charles Clermont-Ganneau and Captain Charles Warren of the British Palestine Exploration Fund, the stele was described as relating the victory of Moabite King Mesha over the Israelite kingdom of Omri during the ninth century B.C.E. This remarkable find received an appropriate ovation in the Western world, where rationalistic tendencies of modern thought were casting doubt on the historicity of the biblical narrative. "Here at last was a quite independent confirmation of the essential truth of the Scriptural account."[51] Although the stele itself was smashed into fragments by suspicious bedouins, enough pieces and copied segments were salvaged to later forward to the Louvre, where it was reconstructed and in whose collections it remains today.

American Consul Beardsley was quick to note the discovery of the Moabite Stone. In a dispatch to Washington that included a report of the event by the Prussian consul Mr. Peterman, Beardsley called the event "of so much interest to the scientific world."[52] In 1871 Clermont-Ganneau discovered the famous inscription that had once adorned a wall of the Second Temple. The inscription warned Gentiles not to enter the Temple's inner courts. William F. Albright evaluated Clermont-Ganneau's contributions, saying,

> [He] made numerous brilliant discoveries as well as a great many minor finds, on his own account. His career, like that of Robinson, illustrated the fact that a single man of genius may advance the sum of knowledge in a given field more than a whole generation of inferior investigation or a treasury full of money for a costly series of undertakings.[53]

The Frenchman demonstrated a sureness of method and penetration that surpassed the most advanced archaeological and topographic knowledge of the Holy Land that had accumulated to that time. For example, it was Clermont-Ganneau who opposed accepting the authenticity of the Shapira manuscript, countering the opinions of the leading German orientalists of the day. The manuscript was promoted as being the original manuscript of Deuteronomy, written by the hand of Moses himself. Clermont-Ganneau called it a fraud and won over public opinion, though from the perspective of subsequent knowledge the manuscript was probably contemporaneous with the Dead Sea Scrolls.[54]

The years after the Civil War were a period of unprecedented American interest in antiquities. During that time, the U.S. government, particularly through the Navy, became heavily involved in the trafficking in such antiquities. The involvement started innocently enough. The pasha of Tripoli recovered the anchor of the U.S. frigate *Philadelphia* in 1871 and presented it to the American government. The ship was lost during one of the most dramatic moments of the Tripolitan War at the start of the nineteenth century. That same year, the ship *Shenandoah* was dispatched to Mersin, the seaport of Tarsus, to load a three-ton sarcophagus exhumed by the local U.S. consular agent. The sarcophagus later ended up in the Metropolitan Museum of Art, in New York City.

The link between the Navy and the Metropolitan Museum was embodied in Italian expatriate, General Luigi Cesnola. Cesnola had emigrated to the United States and married the daughter of an American privateer before serving with distinction in the Civil War. After the war, he was appointed U.S. Consul on Cyprus. Self-trained in archaeology, Cesnola carried on a series of successful excavations at ancient burial sites, and in 1871 the Navy retrieved a box of his curiosities for the Smithsonian Institution. In 1875 the Navy ship *Congress* transported the remainder of his finds to New York, where they became an integral part of the Metropolitan's collections. Shortly afterward, Cesnola himself was installed as the museum's director. Behind the Metropolitan's Fifth Avenue structure today stands perhaps the last and greatest example of federal government involvement in the trafficking in antiquities. In 1879 the American consul-general for Egypt successfully negotiated, on behalf of the city of New York, the acquisition of an Alexandrian obelisk called "Cleopatra's Needle." As before, the Navy cooperated to the extent that supervision of the obelisk's lowering and loading was under the direction of a U.S. naval officer.[55]

Many American consuls were archaeology buffs, and some even
contributed to the advancement of archaeological knowledge, but
most did so in an indirect way. Because of their positions, they were
frequently called on to make appropriate legal arrangements for expeditions and to report to the State Department any unusual or significant finds by archaeologists in the Holy Land. Of course, some
consuls were not as intrigued by antiquities as others. Albert Rhodes,
for example, poked fun at the passion for antiquities popular among
the foreign consuls at Jerusalem whenever they would gather for
their social teas:

> Every society has its fashion, and the fashion of this Jerusalem
> coterie is to talk learnedly on archaeology. Hence at these en-
> tertainments it rains stones—Moresque, Byzantine, Roman,
> and every other kind of stone ever used in Jerusalem con-
> struction. This bombardment goes on at every tea, until those
> present mutually persuade themselves that they are archae-
> ologists.[56]

The consul who was perhaps the most persuaded of his own scholarship was Selah Merrill, although in Merrill's case there was a measure of justification. Merrill arrived in the Holy Land originally as
part of the American Palestine Exploration Society. Staying on long
after the Society's demise, he authored a large body of material, both
popular and scholarly, that raised the level of American interest in
the Holy Land's past. But Merrill had no scholarly training in an
archaeological sense, and his lack of training was responsible for an
attitude of defensiveness about his general performance and position as Jerusalem's American consul over such a long span (he was
reassigned to Georgetown, Guyana, in 1907). To twentieth-century
archaeologist George Ernest Wright, Merrill had compromised himself beyond redemption when he gave permission for his name to be
used in connection "with the most famous forgery in Near Eastern
history," the Shapira manuscript, in the wake of the authentic excitement over the Moabite Stone.[57]

Spirit of the Age

Inevitable change was taking place in scholarly research in the Holy
Land, and American readers eagerly consumed news of such

changes. The *Theological Eclectic*, which characterized itself as "a repository, chiefly of foreign theological literature," reprinted portions
of an article from the October 1867 issue of the *British Quarterly Review* on recent researches in Jerusalem. The extensive article covered several topics of interest to Americans.[58] It noted that, until
recently, access to the broad plateau atop the Temple Mount, called
the Haram es Sharif, could be achieved only by stealth or under
severe restrictions that hindered full topographical examination.
But, the article went on, "fanaticism has yielded to court favor or
bakshish, and many parts of the Haram may be visited, measured,
sketched, and photographed with freedom."[59] The suggestion was
that there was now a new scientific spirit of the age and that access
and expanded knowledge could alter the more strange theories or
other so-called infallible ecclesiastical traditions. Also, new examinations would lead moderate and open-minded thinkers to a common
central conception of Jerusalem's topography.

The same article reviewed the findings of the Count Melchior de
Vogue as reported in his *Le Temple de Jerusalem*, published in Paris in
1864. The count's work was generally accepted, especially with regard to the subterranean portions of the Temple Mount, which had
cisterns, archways, and passages lacing the area below ground. However, accumulations of rubbish and debris were said to clutter many
sites more than previously realized. The article called for carrying
out and completing excavation until the topography of the city became fully elucidated. It noted that the time was opportune—especially because the Turkish sultan was planning to visit Christian
lands—to remove old prejudices and subdue fanatical feelings so
that "ere long a flood of light will be thrown on some of the most
interesting points of sacred topography and archaeology."[60]

Topographic questions continued to appear in reports through
the end of the nineteenth century, although excavation activities
gradually began to dominate readers' attentions. An article in *Eclectic
Magazine* announced that "scientific expeditions were taking the
place of amateur travelers" and that while surface investigations
were being carried out in more systematic fashion, the number of
excavations was increasing "and the long-buried monuments of past
ages are being brought to the light of day." One change slowly taking place was the replacement of surface exploration with the art of
excavation. "A week's work with spade and pickaxe would in most
parts of the Holy Land, do more to supply information still required
than years of learned research or volumes of keen controversy."[61]

Before 1890, expeditions to the Holy Land generally did not have any way to date whatever archaeological finds were made—the only exception being, perhaps, inscriptions. But even there, masonry was undatable, and the inscriptions themselves could be the subject of dispute. "Until there was a science of stratigraphy there was no hope for a scientific archaeology," William Albright observed.[62] Palestinologists largely ignored Schliemann's discovery at Troy that mounds were actually artificial accumulations of layers of occupation at a given site. It was not until the 1890s that the idea of using pottery as a dating tool was seriously considered in the Holy Land.

At the age of thirty-seven, Englishman William Flinders-Petrie appeared on Palestine's archaeological scene in 1890. Having worked during the 1880s in Egypt, he came to Palestinian archaeology with the rudiments of a scientific archaeological method. He was careful to record systematically all finds at excavations, and he began to use pottery as a means of dating. In 1900 he discovered "the fundamental principle of sequence-dating," which enabled an extension of "relative chronology into periods where there are no stratified remains for direct comparison." Flinders-Petrie worked for six weeks at the mound of Tel el-Hesi in southeastern Palestine, and as a result of this work "he was able to state positively that each period had its own typical pottery, which could be distinguished by a trained eye from corresponding pottery of earlier or later periods."[63] In addition to this major breakthrough, Flinders-Petrie related some of his findings to those he had come across in Egypt, further strengthening his arguments.

Reaction to Flinders-Petrie's breakthrough was hardly supportive. The Palestine Exploration Fund surveyor Claude Conder scoffed at the new dating criterion that pottery provided. But Flinders-Petrie's findings were soon verified in subsequent work at Tel el-Hesi between 1891 and 1893 for the Palestine Exploration Fund by American Frederick Jones Bliss. Bliss was a son of Daniel Bliss, the founder and president of the American Syrian Protestant College, the old American Board school at Beirut that later evolved into the American University of Beirut.[64]

With the advent of sequence-dating came a new era in the archaeological study of the Holy Land. Once the technique became established, the age of the dilettante archaeologist declined and the age of ultra-scientific study began in earnest. One practitioner of the new approach was American George Andrew Reisner, who began his career, like Flinders-Petrie, in Egypt. Unlike others of the time, Reisner had neither theological school education nor a background directly associated with religion. Born in Indianapolis in 1867, he was the son of a shoestore clerk and the grandson of a Napoleonic sol-

dier who emigrated to the United States from Alsace. Reisner was a
Harvard graduate with strong interest in Semitic languages and history that led him to study at Göttingen and Berlin. He originally
went to Egypt in 1897 as part of a commission to catalog antiquities
for the Cairo Museum. Once there, he was enrolled as head of a
University of California expedition financed by Mrs. Phoebe Hearst,
whom he met in Cairo. Aside from affirming Flinders-Petrie's system of pottery typology, Reisner refined the application of careful
stratigraphic study to site excavations. He brought "amazing energy
and capacity for hard work" to his fieldwork, and "utter devotion to
scholarship."[65] Although preoccupied with Egypt, Reisner did super-
vise a Harvard University excavation at Samaria between 1908 and
1910 that has been called "one of the few truly scientific excavations
in Palestine prior to World War I."[66]

The Harvard expedition to Samaria was noteworthy too for the
quality of its other American staff. The expedition's architect was
Clarence Stanley Fisher, a Philadelphia native who, like Reisner, had
no theological training (he was a practicing Lutheran and his wife
was the daughter of a Baptist minister). Fisher was a shy but high-
strung man, which made it difficult for others to work with him. But
Fisher was a thorough investigator. He was associated with the University of Pennsylvania Museum both before and after his work at
Samaria. With Reisner's work in Egypt ongoing during the Samaria
expedition, much of the actual fieldwork fell to Fisher and David
Gordon Lyon. Fisher applied Reisner's techniques of observation to
the extent that every particular of work at Samaria was recorded in
exacting detail. This methodology became the standard of correct
archaeological practice from that time on.

Lyon too was an exacting scholar, and by the time he was working
at Samaria he had already achieved distinction as founder and director of Harvard's Semitic Museum. Lyon's background was an interesting counterpoint to that of Reisner and of Fisher. Born in ante-
bellum Alabama, Lyon came from a family of devout Southern
Baptists. Though never formerly ordained, Lyon even used to
preach on occasion. Beginning his interest in Semitic languages at
the Southern Baptist Seminary in Louisville, Kentucky, Lyon went
abroad to receive his doctorate in Assyriology from the University of
Leipzig. He held the post of director of the American School of
Oriental Research in Jerusalem in 1906–7, before joining Gottlieb
Schumacher at Samaria in 1908. When the Samaria project was
adopted by Harvard, Lyon became its director until Reisner assumed the position.

During the new age of scientific precision an entirely objective

Fig. 32. FIRST SITE OF THE AMERICAN SCHOOL OF ORIENTAL
RESEARCH, JERUSALEM.   Contemporary view of the old Grand New
Hotel, site in 1901 of the first home of the American School. The
school was designed to provide a permanent milieu of higher learning
in which American scholars could work. It still functions as the
Albright Institute, renamed in honor of its most revered director, biblical archaeologist William F. Albright.

outlet for American archaeological interest in the Holy Land
emerged: the American School of Oriental Research at Jerusalem.[67]
The American School grew out of the determined efforts of several
American groups in 1895 to rejoin the scholarly efforts at excavating
the Holy Land. Led by Harvard Bible professor Joseph Henry
Thayer and other members of the Society of Biblical Literature, several universities and learned societies formed a corporation for the
establishment and support of the School. Interest in the institution
did not, however, grow solely out of a desire to dig. As the nineteenth century came to a close, American scholarship in biblical and
cognate studies (such as the study of the languages of the ancient
Near East) achieved new levels of respectability. William Rainey Harper, a Yale Hebraist who became president of the University of Chicago, was particularly influential in the growth of American Near

East studies, both for his own teaching as well as for the quality of his appointments at Chicago. For example, Harper brought James Henry Breasted, America's premier Egyptologist, to Chicago, and Breasted became director of Chicago's prestigious Oriental Institute.

It was in such an atmosphere that the American School of Jerusalem began. The School was designed to be a permanent institution of advanced learning that would serve as the focal point of American scholarly work in the Holy Land. It was to be headed by a director appointed yearly, thereby giving numerous scholars the opportunity to work under its auspices. Its first director, Yale Professor Charles C. Torrey, opened the School in 1901 and received much assistance from Selah Merrill in setting up operations in a room of the Grand New Hotel, just inside the Jaffa Gate area of Jerusalem. Merrill played another important role with regard to the School when his pottery collection was purchased in 1906 by then director Benjamin W. Bacon, acting astutely in light of the importance of pottery typology. Bacon wrote to justify the purchase, "The very alphabet of the modern excavator is the study of pottery, and is a science which can only be studied in object lessons."[68]

Within the context of the American School, scholars were free to probe Palestine's past in a rational, nonsentimental manner. Although this did not mean that scholars of the American School were free from confronting the reality of Ottoman Palestine, it does mean that their expressed thoughts and published reflections became much more specific to their primary purpose of being in the Holy Land. American archaeology achieved a level of scientific objectivity without compromising the pattern set by earlier nineteenth-century American scholars in terms of the Holy Land's image—that is, the idea of the Holy Land to American archaeologists remained firmly bound with the Bible. Their organizations and their interests were centered around the Bible as document and key to the physical setting of Palestine. As the next chapter shows, some scholars explored the connection between the Bible and its place and arrived at intriguing though misleading conclusions.[69] Nevertheless, in terms of the training received by scholars and their dependence on methodical study and review rather than solely on faith or doctrine, the scholars as a class were perhaps better favored than other Americans to also see and analyze the reality of their surroundings in Ottoman Palestine.

CHAPTER 8

Meet Me in St. Louis

The view is an astounding one: the Temple Mount with its Dome of the Rock bathed in bright sunlight. Tourists are scattered about its plaza, marveling over the place and its sacred associations. In the foreground, the solemn eastern wall of the Holy City looks like stone yet is somewhat more uniform than expected; it is bedecked with huge block letters gratuitously announcing: "Jerusalem." As if to temper reverence with levity, an enormous ferris wheel looms over the scene.

The sky is Missouri's, not the Holy Land's; the view is of the Jerusalem exhibit at the 1904 St. Louis World's Fair, a spectacle that epitomized the popular appeal of the Holy Land for earlier Americans.[1] In a ten-acre space at the very center of the fairgrounds, the Jerusalem Exhibit Company, a Fair concessionaire, reproduced the principal features and life of Jerusalem on an unprecedented scale. The site was contoured to replicate hills and valleys; it was then enclosed in a reproduction of the city's ancient walls complete with gates. Inside, such structures as the Church of the Sepulchre, the Temple Mount, Solomon's Stables, the Golden Gate, the Via Dolorosa, and the Wailing Wall were erected to full scale and arranged in a manner that more or less approxi-

Fig. 33. STEREOGRAPHIC SLIDE VIEW OF 1904 JERUSALEM
EXHIBIT. The Temple Mount area of the exhibit at the St. Louis
World's Fair. The full-scale model of portions of the city of Jerusalem
was an enormous undertaking that captured the imagination of fairgoers. Although it was one of several fair exhibits of exotic locales, it
was hailed as a spiritualizing and educational experience.

mated their placement in reality. Compacted, narrow streets with
shops, peopled with native Jerusalemites and livestock, portrayed
life in the Holy City for fairgoers. Religious services and ceremonies
of the various faiths and ethnic groups were staged as pageants. Lectures on picturesque Palestine and its peoples were delivered to
troops of Sunday school masters and pupils.

Golden Dome and Ferris Wheel

The Jerusalem exhibit was a massive and expensive undertaking, but
it had broad support from an advisory board composed of clergy
representing twenty-seven religious groups of Protestants, Catholics,
and Jews. The affair was presided over by the Rev. W. B. Palmore, a
Southern Methodist, and managed by Alexander Konta, a St. Louis
businessman who had visited the Holy Land on several occasions
and had good relations with the Turkish authorities. The investment
prospectus issued by the Exhibit Company made it clear that the
project was intended to create for the visitor a "vision and a dream"
that would educate, enlighten, and spiritualize.

The display will, in short, be Jerusalem itself. It is intended that there shall be at least three hundred natives to make the scene realistic. When the visitor enters the gates of the city he shall be made to feel as though he were in actual Jerusalem, with its streets, bazaars, buildings, and people forming a picture of supreme interest to those who have never been there and surprisingly familiar to those who have. There will be peasant women who will vend from native baskets the luscious oranges, lemons, dates, and grapes which so attracted the spies of Israel. These peasants will be seen in their tattered, yet picturesque, garments. The native merchant will offer you from his bazaar such goods as he sells the Frank from across the seas, and unless he looks far beyond the confines of the street where his shop is located, he will see nothing unfamiliar to his eyes. There will be Bedouins from the desert, with their camel's hair fillets, bound round their heads, native Christians in blue dresses and embroidered veils, Copts, Moslems, Turks, and priests. . . . This display . . . shall be free from anything which will in the least detract from its dignity and solemnity.[2]

Theodore Roosevelt commended the project for securing "prominence to the religious side of the world's development" in connection with the World's Fair.[3] Others saw it as "exercising a powerful influence toward the advancement of Christianity," and some incorruptible moralists welcomed it as "counteracting to some extent influences of the 'midway' sort" that were inevitably present at such gatherings and for being a respectable "antidote to much that will make no contribution to intelligence nor good morals"[4] (meaning those things that were just plain fun). To the Rev. E. Morris Ferguson, general secretary of the New Jersey Sunday-School Association, the Jerusalem exhibit represented an opportunity for thousands of scholars and teachers who were unable to attend the World Sunday School Convention in the real Jerusalem that same year to make a pilgrimage to St. Louis of equal educational and spiritual value[5] because, as the exhibit's promoters claimed, "it is a remarkable fact that Palestine has changed little since the days of Christ, and in some respects but little, if any, since the days of Abraham. This will be vividly impressed upon the visitor to the Jerusalem exhibit."[6] The image/reality mode of perception, present at Chautauqua and in the stereoscopic tour of Hurlbut and Kent, was consummately evident at the fairgrounds in St. Louis.

The Defined Image and Geopiety

Perhaps more than any other single geographical idea, the Holy
Land sparked this curious fusion of image and reality in the minds
and hearts of Americans. Ottoman Palestine was everlastingly the
Land of the Bible, a segment of the Turkish realm wherein the
drama of Christianity began. It was both fetid Oriental wasteland
and resplendent biblical garden. It was a tourist attraction and a
place to see, a mission field and place to evangelize, a Promised
Land and a place to colonize, a wilderness, an outpost, a treasure
chest of antiquity.

To Americans, the Holy Land as concept was inextricably bound
to the dual contexts of place and past, and this in turn affected the
nature of the popular image of the Holy Land in America. We have
already called the process of fusing place and past in the viewer's
mind that of "image/reality" and the phenomenon of expressing this
special regard for the Holy Land "geopiety." As for the composite
image itself, we have already seen its outline intimated through certain features, qualities that circumscribed it and defined its chief
characteristics. To be specific, the first of these has been the idea
that the Holy Land existed in a quasi-utopian and sentimental form
—distorted, removed, and elevated above the reality that actually
existed. Some Americans saw the Holy Land as simply an unearthly
abstraction; as the older woman in the story told by missionary
Franklin Hoskins, it just never seemed to register in the minds of
some that the locales of the Bible might actually be real places on
earth. The Holy Land's transformation from transcendent concept
to physical reality proved to be a necessary but difficult notion for
many Americans to comprehend, especially Americans who had only
heard and read of the Holy Land and never actually experienced it.
Yet surprisingly the transformation was difficult—and disillusioning
too—for many of the Americans who did visit the Holy Land.

In so many accounts by Americans who traveled around the Holy
Land, we have seen a pattern: an unconscious attempt to evade what
they actually saw by instead trying to find vestiges of the primitive
that would be in accord with notions of what the country and its
inhabitants were "supposed" to look like. A typical example was traveler John Franklin Swift, who, stopping at a fountain outside Ramleh on the road to Jerusalem in 1867, mused about a scene of native
women gathered around, drawing water: "twenty Rebeccas stood before us," he insisted.[7] Such scenes were immediately satisfying to

Fig. 34. AN ATTEMPT TO SAIL THE SEA OF GALILEE. Mark Twain's party of pilgrims attempted to enjoy a biblically reminiscent sail across the Sea of Galilee, only to be put off by an outrageous price quote for the service by local boatmen. The humorous incident from *Innocents Abroad* illustrates metaphorically the conflict between image and reality as it existed in nineteenth-century American relations with the Holy Land. Illustration from *Innocents Abroad*.

some—or at least reassuring. Being reassured at matching biblical dioramas with everyday sights—or, conversely, being disappointed at not finding them—was a further indication that Americans were thinking about the Holy Land in a special fashion.

Americans who found it impossible to avoid the profane reality of an everyday country were soberly disappointed. A small but interesting book entitled *Palestine*, written by the Rev. J. I. Boswell in 1883 as part of a popular home-study series, recalled a number of these typically negative reactions to the Holy Land. Under the heading "Jerusalem as It Is," Boswell wrote: "The first sight of the city is disappointing. The streets are only narrow lanes, badly paved and dirty. The stone houses are unattractive and the people, for the most part, poor and degraded. Such is not the city which the imagination paints." Plainly, Boswell, like so many others, had an image that was

not in accord with reality and had to rely on his historical consciousness to make the scene appealing, as he continued: "But as one re-
calls its history, and the influence which has gone out of it through
all the world, he sees beauty even in its desolation, and wanders
among its ruins with ever-increasing interest."[8]

Most of the remainder of Boswell's short work is predictably devoted to ancient history rather than the country's contemporary
state. But Boswell did add a classic caution against a catalog of fallacies we have seen others hold about the Holy Land:

> That Palestine is a large land, because it occupies so large a
> space in the history of the world. Our historic glasses are mag-
> nifying ones. That the land is fair and fertile. It once was, but
> is not so now. The terraces are broken down, the water-
> courses are few, the groves of palms and oaks have long since
> disappeared. The fact is, the people are few and dispirited,
> and the towns are not attractive save for their historical asso-
> ciations. Many books of travel are written by those who have
> glowing imaginations. Palestine could be made to support
> from six to ten times its present population. To do this, it
> must have (1) good government (2) capital and (3) industry
> guided by intelligence. As it is, Palestine stands a visible mon-
> ument to the historic truth of the Holy Scriptures.[9]

Boswell's program for improving conditions in the Holy Land was a
typical prescription by a Gilded Age missionary of the American
democratic faith, pushing the gospels of enlightened politics, fi-
nance, and technology. His conclusion—that the disillusioning present of the country was evidence of prophetic accuracy—was the reaction of one whose personal beliefs were reinforced by the gap
between the Bible's glowing description of the Holy Land and the
seamy reality of Palestine under Ottoman rule. The land bore witness to biblical truth, specifically to the record of divine threats to
punish the land and its inhabitants for miscreancy. Here was yet
another dimension to the image of the Holy Land, and it was a dimension that did not exclude the notoriously sacrilegious either.
"Palestine sits in sackcloth and ashes," Clemens professed in *Innocents Abroad*. "Over it broods the spell of a curse that has withered its
fields and fettered its energies. . . . Palestine is desolate and unlovely.
And why should it be otherwise? Can the curse of the Deity beautify
a land? Palestine is no more of this workday world. It is sacred to
poetry and tradition—it is dreamland."[10]

The image of the Holy Land could also be seen in the peculiar and extraordinary activities on the part of some Americans themselves. Such activities, despite their unusualness, have provided us with a window on the effects of the Holy Land's impact. This was demonstrated by several of the settlement ventures, but even on an individual level this was so. For example, a British vicar named Alexander Boddy who traveled in the Holy Land at the close of the nineteenth century related a story he had heard from the British consul at Jerusalem. The consul told of a "strange being" who arrived in the Holy City one day bareheaded and who claimed to have walked from Port Said across the desert to meet "Christus Secondus" on a certain day at the Mount of Olives. The man was reportedly an American.[11] Although the American connection in Boddy's story remains unconfirmed, such unusual behavior—motivated by the image and associations of the Holy Land—was well within the realm of American activity.[12]

The various reactions to the image of the Holy Land display for us in the broadest terms the nature of the bi-form imagery of the Holy Land as a place inseparable from a shared past. From the failure of an old woman to associate the place with everyday reality, to a tourist's search for elements of culturally induced preconceptions when confronted by a specific scene (the Rebeccas at the well), to the uninhibited search for the land that just was not there (the bareheaded wanderer)—these examples were manifestations of the effects of American perceptions as they refocused through the lens of myth. They all, in a way, reflected the idea that the Holy Land was a place remote in time as well as space.

The element of remoteness in America's image of the Holy Land can be tied directly to Protestant concern with the historical figure of Jesus and the importance of the Bible. Although the influence of Protestantism in the formation of the American image of the Holy Land was decisive, the image itself was not always affected by changes and forces that altered American Protestantism during the latter nineteenth century. Darwinism, for example, had little direct impact on the Holy Land's image, but biblical criticism certainly did—in positive and negative ways. On the positive side, criticism gave rise to a more intensively scientific interest in the Holy Land. Recall, for example, Edward Robinson's feud over the reliability of tradition in identifying popularly assumed sacred sites. On the negative side, biblical criticism eroded the level of popular belief in the Bible, and many Americans turned aside, becoming estranged from Scripture altogether, losing their former familiarity with Holy Land figures, locales, and events. The American image of the Holy Land was remote; it was romantic; it was easily put at odds with the physical reality that actually presented itself. It was also frequently mythical, being couched in terms that would not or could not be applied to any other land. It was past-oriented, even to the extent that conjectures about the land's future were made within the framework of the land's past.

For example, on January 20, 1879, the *New York Times* carried a notice on the progress of a project to buy Palestine reputedly under way in Britain and led by a group of Jewish figures that included members of the Rothschild and Montefiore families. The project was reported near completion, and the financiers were described as confident that it would be successful and welcomed by Jews the world over. The article went on to say that those familiar with Palestine would know that it is not a particularly desirable place and not extensive in size, and that therefore it should be quite a bargain at an inexpensive price. The country's most fertile area, the coastal plain, had been producing the same succession of crops "year after year for 40 centuries without artificial aid." As for the remainder of the land, the article painted a dim view:

> Many tourists have such numberless associations with Palestine that they have idealized it prodigiously (but to a man who views it without bias, it is a dreary, disagreeable land, its undulating surface, rounded hills separated by narrow glens, and its crevasses striking the eye monotonously and unpleasantly). So much has been said for generations of the Jews regaining possession of Jerusalem, that it is agreeable to think that they are likely to do so at last. They certainly deserve Jerusalem.

Evidently, even in the years before Jewish nationalist aspirations gelled into the formal Zionist movement of the late 1890s, the difference between the image and the reality of the Holy Land was already coloring responses to rumored Jewish efforts to regain the land.

The Holy Land's image also correlated with another concept commonly held in American thought: the "myth of the new beginning." According to cultural historian Stephen Ausband, "Myths are tales that are accepted, on the whole, as either true to historical fact or as reinforcing and demonstrating a society's understanding of the truth about natural phenomena, and which are treated seriously by most members of the society."[13] Myths, according to Ausband, provide meaning and order to the world. People use myths in order to think about the world, "to give direction and coherency to the world."[14] "Americans tend to cherish and believe in their myths, both the religious or quasi-religious and the purely secular, as zealously as any society has ever protected its own system of ordering the world."[15]

The "new beginning" is in essence a whole category of American myth. Though largely secular, it parallels some of the ways Americans tended to view the Holy Land. The "myth of the new beginning" "includes primarily the belief that the essence of the American experience is the fresh start, the chance to escape from the mistakes and shortcomings of past societies."[16] While largely derived from connections to the Judeo-Christian tradition, the view of the Holy Land held by Americans was inextricably bound to the myth that the American was the New Man from the New Eden,[17] an idea of obvious lineage to sixteenth-century Puritan thought that America was the New Zion. We have seen the application of this myth to the disastrous settlement scheme of the Adams Colony, when it was echoed in the sentiment that the Yankee colonists had no business marching backward to the Old World when they should have been advancing westward in the New.

The way Ottoman Turkey was generally viewed is also a good example of how the myth of the new beginning was applied in conventional American thought about the Holy Land. Turkey and its rulers appeared cruel and barbaric both to Europeans and to Americans,[18] and the Holy Land was inescapably part of this vast, corrupt empire. As the land of Jesus and the Bible, Palestine was a captured, enthralled domain of the Turks, and yet it was somehow different from the rest of Turkey: Its desolation was seen as the result of divine intent; it just happened to be in Turkish hands. The Holy Land was the fateful land; the Turks just happened to be its temporal oppressors at the time.

Aside from the "myth of the new beginning," the theme of Palestine's abandonment after its former glories was popular in the literature of travel during the nineteenth century, and most American travelers understood it in the vein of prophetic fulfillment. As David Landes pointed out in his thoughtful essay "Palestine Before the Zionists," "This was the general opinion, the conventional wisdom of a still believing world: that the Holy Land, Terra Sancta, was holy because it was cursed and cursed because it was holy; and that it bore witness by its sterility and devastation to the unpardonable, inexpiable crime of deicide."[19]

As a result of changes in the volume and style of travel literature, the proliferation of more intense archaeological work, and simply increased news from that part of the world, Americans gradually began to think of the Holy Land in more realistic terms. However, expectations unrelated to current realities remained and were frequently couched in biblical/religious terminology. The Holy Land was the ultimate land of history, the land of the oldest familiar story —be that story an article of faith or merely a cultural inheritance. When confronting this land of history, the reactions of Americans differed only with regard to the viewers' orientation, level of belief, and sights seen. To some, the vista presented by the land was authentically biblical, not varying from the context they recalled from their readings or summoned in their imaginations. To others, the land was a curious sham, a disappointment, because it did not match preconceived expectations.

American interest in the Holy Land was an outcome of Protestant American religious sensibilities affected by the primary forces within American religion, common touches that brushed all American churches. As such, the American image of the Holy Land was an emotional one. America had been, after all, the New Canaan of the Puritans, the best hope of the world, an almost messianic assumption. Study of the Holy Land came in the religious and emotional climate of family Bible readings or church education. Because of this emotional foundation, the American image of the Holy Land through 1918 continued to remain romantic, nostalgic, perhaps somewhat unnatural, and certainly to a degree unreal.

The myth of the Holy Land as place and past in the consciousness of Americans cannot be judged as either a right or wrong mode of perception. It was simply an adaptive feature applied, through public discourse in one form or another, by influential segments of the American population. The image of the Holy Land (or "myth" of the Holy Land, in the terminology of Smith's *Virgin Land*) had a ubiquitous role in the normal affairs of Americans related to the Holy Land. Americans were led to the Holy Land as a destination for travel enjoyment and edification. They wanted to see the Holy Land, and experience it, during pilgrimages they hoped would recapture and manifest scenes they could only imagine when reading the Bible. Americans were led to the Holy Land by a zeal to spread Protestantism, a faith they believed was the most progressive form of religion and the form compatible with their equally cherished democratic ideals—ideals that were, coincidently, held to be the highest expression of advanced civilization. Americans were led to the Holy

Land by its ascribed role in the foreseen millennium. Some even sought to settle there and be present for the events predicted in millennialist eschatology. Americans were led to the Holy Land by academic interests rooted in the Bible. Some were also led by the desire to see the Bible proved correct, because one of the foundations of the Protestant faith was a return to the Bible as a primary force. And finally, Americans found themselves in the Holy Land in response to the land's increasing importance and accessibility—an importance in the political affairs of Western nations and an accessibility that allowed large numbers of Americans to disembark on the Holy Land's shores. In brief, the affairs of Americans through their tourist, missionary, colonial, consular, and archaeological experiences revealed their images of the Holy Land.

The assembled sample of American experiences in the Holy Land generated a certain momentum of their own—that is, a sort of evolutionary theater is apparent in the stories of missionary, colonial, consular, and scholarly interests, despite their frequently episodic natures. There was even a corresponding evolution in traveler experiences, though in a much more subtle way. That evolution was a function of increased exposure, though it did not necessarily result in clearer understanding.

The activities of some Americans indicated a sort of compensation for the effects of the bi-form myth of the Holy Land. These Americans accepted their perceptions of the land as place and past without compromising the manner in which they confronted the reality of Ottoman Palestine. The Christian and Missionary Alliance, Jerusalem's American Colony, the Americans associated with the Templars, the "ordained" consuls, and the American School of Oriental Research at Jerusalem were all to a degree successful, or at least long-lasting, perhaps because they recognized the unique place of the Holy Land and appreciated their own perspectives of its meaning in relation to their particular goals. Parsons, Fisk, the American Board, the Adams Colony, the early consular appointees, and the American Palestine Exploration Society were in the same way failures (in the sense of not being able to satisfy their various ambitions), perhaps because they did not compensate for the powerful influence of the Holy Land's magnetic imagery.

In order to successfully classify American Christian attachment to the Holy Land as an expression of geopiety, we must correlate it first with the concepts of perception and values. Any perceptual behavior exhibits three processes: selection of the perceived subject, accentuation of certain of its features, and, last, the preferential retention of certain of these features. Also, the degree to which any individual selects, accentuates, and retains aspects of a perceived subject will be determined by personally held beliefs and values, the results of education in the broadest sense. An individual's value orientation will sensitize the person into accepting the results of having responded to certain values and objects more readily than others. Value orientation contributes to selection and accentuates certain percepts in favor of others while erecting barriers against percepts and ideas that are incongruent with or threatening to the individual's values.[20]

Changing an individual's values is a complex process that depends on the person's previously held assumptions and the degree to which the person holds the values. Simply, weakly held values change easily, strongly held values resist change.[21] In terms of Christian attachment to the Holy Land, the combination of land and sacred association was enhanced by a selectivity in perceiving facts, especially when those facts conflicted with strongly held values. Thus the imagery of the Holy Land as Zion—as a part of a meaningful past—was retained tenaciously, while at the same time the image of the Holy Land as a place came into clearer focus. This was how the combination of perception and values produced a geopious awareness of the Holy Land.

The past, wrote geographer David Lowenthal, "is needed to cope with the present landscape." He maintained that people selectively perceive what they are accustomed to seeing:

> Features and patterns in the landscape make sense to us because we share a history with them. Every object, every grouping, every view is intelligible partly because we are already familiar with it, through our own past and through tales heard, books read, pictures viewed. We see things simultaneously as they are and as we viewed them before; previous experience suffuses all present perception. Each scene and object is invested with a history of real or imagined involvements, their perceived identities stem from past acts and expectations. . . . But it is not simply nostalgia that makes the past so powerful. Hindsight and overview enable us to comprehend past environments in ways that elude us when we deal with the shifting present. The new visitor is most apt to read the past into the present.[22]

We have seen this demonstrated in American reflections on the Holy Land.

It is easy to assume that Americans would neglect the past in light of the awesomeness of the raw wilderness present of the North American continent. But Americans were neglectful only to the extent that they were more concerned with the future. In fact, "attachment to the future provided both a rationale and a substitute for the rejected past."[23] Lowenthal observed:

> If the character of the place is gone in reality, it remains preserved in the mind's eye of the visitor, formed by historical imagination, untarnished by rude social facts. The enduring streets and buildings persuade him that the past is present. We also require more conscious and particular evidence of the past—features and structures we believe to be old, previous, or durable. The intimate continuity of past with present is a source of general comfort.[24]

Evidence of this searching for continuity, in the context of the Holy Land, was abundant in the experiences of Americans.

In another, perhaps more cogent sense, the vast changes taking place in America as the nineteenth century came to a close served to enhance the image of an unchanged Holy Land. As Kevin Lynch, author of *What Time Is This Place?* noted, "those who lack continuity at home often search for it abroad. . . . Most Americans go away from home to Europe to feel at home in time."[25] If this were so for Europe, how much more so for the land of ultimate antiquity, where age was enhanced by sacredness. This searching need to feel at home in time was epitomized by Herman Melville.

Clarel, the protagonist of Melville's lengthy poem of a pilgrimage to the Holy Land, arrived in Palestine seeking revelation and reaffirmation. But instead of finding the sublime and inspiring Rose of Sharon, which would have supplied Melville with the reassuring answers to his questions of his place in the world, he found only disillusionment and none of the rearming tools he thought he needed to cope with a wavering faith. "Jerusalem touches a deeper note. It is not a mere geographical expression; it is an idea, a hope, a city of the spirit. No wonder that devout souls have shrunk from visiting the actual Jerusalem, fearing a reality so far removed from their ideals."[26]

Americans had an attachment to the Holy Land that was unlike their collective attachments to any other "Old World" locale. Yet there was also a streak of ambivalence in the connection because, just as Christianity seemed to have replaced other religious traditions,

the Holy Land as a focus of geopietistic sentiment was partially supplanted by the new Promised Land, America. American reaction to
the physical presence of Zion might have implied a contradiction
with the idea of America being the new place where humankind was
to get a fresh start amid unspoiled nature.[27] It did not contradict the
idea, but rather complemented it. The Holy Land represented all
that had come before the advent of the American Eden. America
represented the bright future of humanity. Subscription to the idea
of an American Eden frequently meant nodding, respectful assent to
that of a pristine Holy Land. As romantically charged notions rooted
in the earlier traditions of nineteenth-century thought, they gradually became sublimated in the face of the naturalistic, scientific tradition that ushered in the twentieth century.

The Consequences of the Image

Several patterns in American perceptions of the Holy Land are now
clear. The first is the perception of the land as being one unit of the
larger Turkish entity, existing under the negative domination and
yet unable to take any action, for the time being at least, that would
change the status quo. Another perception was that change—derived from apocalyptic, political, or cultural sources—was certain to
take place at some time in the future, at which point there would be
a drastic reassertion of the country's identity. For some observers,
this reassertion would be linked to the land's Jewish past. For others,
the reassertion would be by those described as the land's only true,
long-standing inhabitants: its native peasantry or native Christian
populace. This particular outgrowth of the myth of the Holy Land
had profound implications for developments after the close of Ottoman rule in Palestine in 1918.

As already posited, the image of the Holy Land manifested itself
in the practical affairs of Americans. One clear manifestation saw
the image of the Holy Land coloring American responses to the social and political changes taking place in the Holy Land during the
latter part of the nineteenth century. American attitudes about the
Holy Land existed in a framework of evolving intellectual, social,
religious, and political conditions, yet these attitudes demonstrated a
somewhat dissociated tone—that is, they were removed from everyday reality. This was because, as we have seen, the image of the Holy
Land in the American mind was formed from two distinct actuali-

ties: American perceptions of the Holy Land as a corporeality, and American preconceptions of the country as the land of Bible—preconceptions that had been fixed by America's cultural and religious heritage. The enmeshed singular image of the Holy Land was dominated by the myth of the past, with its biblical, primitive associations, and this was an imposing, ubiquitous specter in the minds of Americans when contemplating the Holy Land. The geopiety context of the sacred "presence of a past" harbored a variety of implications for unfolding social and political developments. Changes taking place in the Holy Land's Jewish community provide a good illustration of how American reactions reflected this "baggage."

The Anglo-Saxon heritage of dealings with Jews was a strong factor in the formation of the American image of Jews. Stereotypes of Jews, which tended to promote Christianity at the expense of Judaism, were part of this heritage.[28] Within American Protestantism, there were occasions when medieval Christian images of Jews were readily adopted and even intensified.[29] In English and American literature, the Jew himself existed—at least through the start of the twentieth century—in two perspectives: one evil and the other noble.[30] This image of the Jew, with both its dark and its light aspects, became part of the picture of Palestine's Jewish settlement, and in spite of the changes taking place in the composition of Palestine's Jewish community. The attitude was often reflected in American observations of Palestinian Jewish society and politics.

The author of a series of travel reports on the Holy Land, which appeared in the popular magazine *Leisure Hour*, reported that he had met "one of their rabbis, a man perhaps of fifty, but so dirty and grizzled that it was difficult to tell his age," who took a party of tourists up to his room to exhibit a thirty-eight-volume edition of the Talmud. As they were leaving, the headmistress of a local mission school pointed out a young girl sitting in the passageway as being the rabbi's latest wife, one of a series who would probably soon be cast off for "some frivolous reason" and end up in the care of the school. The headmistress claimed she had charge of five or six of these unfortunate women already. Incensed by the allegation, the author wrote: "If these idle, worthless men claim the protection of the different European governments to which they profess to belong, we naturally asked why they are allowed to set at naught the authorities of these countries by violating all laws of civilization."[31]

The protection the author cited was the welcome adoption of Jewish interests, especially by the consular officials of Great Britain and the United States. Based solely on prejudices and negative imagery,

there was open questioning about whether the Jewish community
needed the protection at all. What was misunderstood was the nature of the Ottoman reality that fostered such a system of client
groups.

In another example, a letter signed by "Oscanyon" was published
in the *New York Times* on April 28, 1869, offering an opinion on the
recent cause for the visit of a Holy Land rabbi to America. The rabbi
had come to entreat the U.S. government to intercede with the sultan on behalf of Holy Land Jews. "Oscanyon" wrote, with obvious
impatience, that the Jews had fled to the Turkish realm in the first
place because they sought refuge from the persecution of a Catholic
country (i.e., Spain). The implication was that Jews were never satisfied even though they had cause to be:

> The stigma which Christianity itself has inflicted upon the
> Jewish race, has hitherto made the Jew a by-word in all lands.
> But the Christianity of the nineteenth century exhales an at-
> mosphere of liberality and equality which pervades the world,
> and Jews and Gentiles, Turks and Greeks are invigorated into
> a new consciousness of humanity and life, and all those ap-
> peals to freedom are but the throes of regeneration. Hence it
> is unjust to say the present condition of the Israelites in Tur-
> key is the fault of the Government. Moreover, the Israelites of
> Turkey, of whom there are about 20,000 in Palestine and
> 150,000 in the whole Empire, are not fair representatives of
> the race. Unlike their brethren in Europe and America, they
> are ignorant, bigoted, and treacherous. If the friends, them-
> selves, of these miserable and "suffering" people are truly de-
> sirous of doing them practical good, they should leave imagi-
> nary grievances aside, and at once endeavor to educate them.
> In doing so, they will not only contribute towards their wel-
> fare, but also second the efforts of the Government itself,
> whose liberal policy extends to all the varied nationalities
> which compose the Empire.

Implicit in the remarks of "Oscanyon" on Palestinian Jews (as opposed to the "Western" Jews) was the ignoble image of Jews as malcontents, expressed in terms that made the Jews sound parasitic.

An interesting counterpoint to such negativism was the famous
"Blackstone Memorial." William Blackstone, born in 1841 in Adams,
New York, was a devout Chicago businessman who claimed to have
once "wrestled with God" during an especially intense religious ex-

perience. The experience redirected Blackstone's interests toward evangelism. After a pilgrimage to the Holy Land in 1888, he began to ask "What shall be done for the Russian Jews?" whose treatment under czarist rule was progressively worsening. By March 5, 1891, Blackstone had gathered 413 signatures in a "Memorial," which he presented to President Harrison and Secretary of State Blaine. In answer to the question of where the Russian Jews should go, Blackstone proposed: "Why not give Palestine back to them again? According to God's distribution of nations it is their home—an inalienable possession from which they were expelled by force." The petition was not the pre-Zionist meanderings of a Warder Cresson. It was signed by some of America's most elite citizens, among them the Speaker of the U.S. House of Representatives, the Chief Justice of the Supreme Court, John D. Rockefeller, J. Pierpont Morgan, Cyrus McCormick, Charles Scribner.[32]

Whether derived from negative or positive imagery, the point is that such examples show that Americans brought certain preexisting conceptions into the process of forming an image of the Holy Land. Some of these conceptions were positive, optimistic, and liberal; others were negative and stereotypical.[33] But they all contributed to the weight of the "baggage" carried to the Holy Land by those Americans who wrote about it, its affairs, and its peoples. It is naturally presumed that Americans who wrote most about the Holy Land were likely to be those who interacted with it firsthand, and for the best example we turn again to the category of biblical scholars.

In the nineteenth century, with regard to the native peasantry and native Christian peoples of Palestine, there arose two schools of thought that tried to connect contemporary Arabic culture with the biblical, pre-Hellenistic Near East. The first of these schools was the "Pan-Babylonian movement" of Hugo Winckler, a German scholar who saw many reflections of ancient Near Eastern culture in the literature and folklore of Islamic Arabia. Winckler's thought was largely rejected by most scholars of Islamic studies and was championed by only a few romantic Arabists. The second school was founded by the American biblical scholar, Samuel Ives Curtiss. According to William F. Albright, Curtiss's influence "on European and American thought has been very great indeed," though his views probably represented more a scholarly formulation of popular thought than an original, groundbreaking study.[34] Nonetheless, the work of Curtiss was carefully scientific and unemotional, which made him a pioneer.

In fact, Albright compared Curtiss to Edward Robinson, the father of biblical archaeology: "Like Robinson, Curtiss was trained in

Germany; like Robinson, he was accompanied by a missionary (Rev. J. S. Crawford, whose Arabic was superior to Eli Smith's); and as in the case of Robinson, his book (*Primitive Semitic Religion Today*) appeared in German as well as in English."[35] Albright admitted to being "strongly affected" by Curtiss's views when he first began researching in the Holy Land, though he denied being a member of Curtiss's school. It was after fifteen years of Near Eastern research that Albright became convinced that Curtiss's "main conclusions with regard to the historical significance of his results were entirely erroneous." To have sparked this response from Albright, Curtiss's formulations must have been remarkable.

The misleading postulations presented by Curtiss in his *Primitive Semitic Religion Today*[36] were based on a belief in the essential continuity of race and culture in Palestine during millennia of population change. Curtiss first cited George Adam Smith's opinion in *The Historical Geography of the Holy Land*,[37] saying that "the population of Syria has always been essentially Semitic." "There are few lands," he continued, "into which so many divers races have come. . . . But all these have scarcely ever been grafted on this, and the stock is Semitic." To Curtiss, therefore, "the conquered race allied with high places and seats of primeval worship can maintain themselves against every Oriental conqueror."[38] Curtiss went on to assert that "all the inhabitants of Syria and Palestine, except Protestant Christians, who have been mostly shamed out of the ancient beliefs, are for the purposes of our investigations, modern Semites. Even in towns which have been mostly fully Europeanized, there are traces of ancient superstition and usages coming down from primitive Semitism."[39] Thus, according to Curtiss, the Arab populace most nearly represented the people and culture of the Bible; they were at the core of the "unchanging East."

Albright contradicted this thinking. He maintained that over the past five thousand years there had broadly been three different phases of civilized life in the Middle East: the Ancient Orient, the Hellenistic-Roman Orient, and the Islamic Orient. "Both the historian of civilization and the historian of ideas must, however, emphatically reject the conception of an 'unchanging East,' a conception which has no support in the facts of history."[40] To Albright, the affinity between the first two phases was materially less than between the second and third phases. In other words, Islam was as much an offshoot of Hellenistic culture as it was of Judeo-Christian religion. "Not to recognize this fact and its implications is to misinterpret the course of history and misunderstand Near Eastern life and thought." Albright summarized his opinion that

there is a mass of evidence in favor of the relatively recent
date of most concrete elements in Islamic religion and culture. . . . The gap which separates Greco-Roman civilization
from Ancient Oriental is much greater than that which di-
vides Islam from Hellenism. Religiously, Islam is an integral
part of the Judeo-Christian tradition and owes very little directly to the religions of the Ancient Orient.[41]

Nonetheless, Curtiss's ideas were given enormous credence in the
early twentieth century, and the concept he espoused was portentous
for the growing politicization of the Middle East. Just how much so
was shown by another scholar.

Archaeologist and biblical scholar Lewis Bayles Paton was a well-
respected faculty member of the Hartford Theological Seminary
and director, in 1903, of the American School of Oriental Research
in Jerusalem. As an acknowledged expert on the Near East, Paton
was consulted by the Inquiry, a prototype think tank formed by
President Woodrow Wilson to anticipate the consequences of the
end of World War I.[42] In a report prepared for the federal govern-

Fig. 35. WILLIAM BAYLES
PATON, BIBLICAL SCHOLAR.
Paton was an American
biblical scholar, an early
director of the American
School of Oriental Research
at Jerusalem, and a con-
temporary of Samuel Ives
Curtiss. Paton's attitudes, like
those of Curtiss, typified the
impact that certain views of
the Holy Land and its peoples
had on the development of
U.S. policy after World War I.

ment, Paton underscored that the "Syrian race" of Palestine, who were largely identified as being Orthodox Christians in religion, were descendants of the original peoples of the Holy Land and that it was nomadic Arabs who emerged from Arabia with Muhammad. He classified Palestine's Jews as being largely of European or Western origin, with no continuous claim to the land.[43] The effects of such a position might have had far-reaching results with regard to U.S. policy, in response, say, to the Balfour Declaration in 1917.

Another archaeologist and scholar, Elihu Grant, eventually took the lead in producing anti-Zionist polemics that were entrenched in the idea that the Holy Land's native populace were the direct descendants of the land's original inhabitants. Grant, who was first connected with the Ramallah mission of the Society of Friends and later with Haverford College, wrote much of his material during the later period of the British Mandate, but it stemmed from his early study *The Peasantry of Palestine* (1907) and was based on his observations of Palestinian village life. To Grant, the early Hebrews of the Holy Land were far removed from present-day Jewry, and Jewish involvement with Zionism was degrading to Judaism: "To grab and develop [Palestine's] water power, its salts, and its industrial possibilities is questionable, from the point of view of religion, morals, or politics."[44] Grant saw the Arab populace as either Christian ("the native remainder of the early Church") or Muslim (formerly Christian Palestinians before converting to Islam). As for the country's Jews, Grant declared that, while they may be racially descended from the Hebrews and Israelites of the Bible, they have no claim to the land because their religion developed much later, in his view.[45]

Similarly strong orientations were evident among other Protestants, though in less consequential ways. Missionary William Loring Worcester wrote several short stories for Sunday school children in which Jesus' youthful contemporaries were assigned names like Ali, Ahmed, Khalil, and Ibrahim, even though they were supposed to have been residents of first-century Judea, where the predominant languages were Greek, Hebrew, Aramaic, and Latin.[46]

The idea that the Holy Land's Christian Arabs are descended from the land's original inhabitants still exists today.[47] With contemporary Arab/Israeli issues focusing on the ownership of title to the land, such an assumption gives the Christian Arabs, the traditional ally of American Christian missionaries' interest in the area, the fullest claim to inherit the land. Of course, the view that the land retained its essentially biblical character had the biggest effect on receptivity to the Zionist program and its aims in the Holy Land. That program, and the growing level of political awareness, were part of the changes that thrust the region into a new, violent age.

Happy Descent into a Growing Maelstrom

The accumulated tensions of fierce nationalistic competition among the Western powers, intensified by a furious arms race and exacerbated by a multitude of geopolitical confrontation points, pushed the world into a generalized war in the summer of 1914. Germany successfully maneuvered Turkey into an alliance, and the Turks were dragged into the fray. They occupied a position from which it was possible to damage Britain's vital colonial lifeline at Suez; they controlled Palestine. The British foresaw a threat to their interests and had steadily strengthened their position in Egypt. Nonetheless, Suez was too strategic a target to be ignored by the war. The Young Turks, who in 1908 had supplanted the sultanate at the political helm of the empire, dispatched one of their leaders, Djemal Pasha, to Jerusalem to set up a regional military command. Djemal Pasha turned Palestine into an occupied camp. He conscripted troops, requisitioned supplies, and exiled or jailed individuals on the merest suspicion. Conditions in Palestine changed from unfavorable to precarious.

One of the earliest conditions caused by the war was the lack of authentic, factual news about events: "The Turks published the wildest accounts of defeats of the Allies; an Arabic paper gravely stated that a Zeppelin, armed with an electromagnet, had visited Petrograd and drawn up the Czar out of his palace, and that it had dealt similarly with the President of the French Republic, and with King George!"[48] From the start, the war caused disruptions in American activities in the Holy Land. Tourism dropped off dramatically, archaeologists and university-sponsored field expeditions were suspended. The American consul, Otis Glazebrook, found himself using his good offices to assist a broad range of stranded people. Among them were the five British Church Missionary Society missionaries who had remained in Palestine to close the affairs of Britain's missionary establishment in the country. As might have been presumed, the American Christian and Missionary Alliance missionaries also fell victim to the dislocations caused by the outbreak of World War I. When hostilities were declared between Britain and Turkey, only three women were left to run the Jerusalem mission:

M. Best, Mary Butterfield, and Miss A. Gunmore. Their fellow missionaries

> had been evacuated amidst scenes of confusion and danger
> and the ladies were left with all the activities of the work in-
> tensified by the troublous times. Mail was censored and irreg-
> ular. Funds were uncertain; both because of fluctuating ex-
> change and because of local currency troubles. Hoarded
> supplies dwindled to the vanishing point and the petition for
> daily bread became a very real and timely prayer.[49]

Conditions were deteriorating in large measure because of a crip-
plingly effective British blockade of Palestine. Yet even during the
blockade, Americans continued to maintain a connection with the
Holy Land.

> American naval vessels helped evacuate Palestinian Jews ex-
> pelled by the Turks from Jaffa to Alexandria and were com-
> missioned to transport food, petrol, medicines, money, and
> other relief to the Jews of the Holy Land, cut off from their
> sources of aid in the rest of the world by the British blockade
> and abandoned to their fate by the Turks.[50]

The strategic importance of Suez was too great an objective for the
Germans to leave solely in the hands of the Turks, so a joint Turk-
ish-German command was established, and early in 1915 the first of
several attacks against the British were launched across the Sinai.
Turkish failures to take the canal were no consolation to the British,
however. With Palestine remaining in Turkish hands, the threat was
persistent. In December 1916 the British mounted a counterattack
into Palestine, along the same coastal invasion route that Napoleon
had used. But the British drive was halted at Gaza, and repeated
attempts to take the town failed. An impatient British High Command reassigned the dogged soldier Edmund Allenby from the
Western Front to Egypt, with instructions to break the deadlock.
When the United States entered the war in 1917, Consul Glazebrook, who had been on friendly terms with the authorities, arranged to have the three Alliance women evacuated. The Turks,
who were generally kind to the ladies, even helped them catch the
train from Jerusalem on May 17, 1917. Unfortunately, the women's
railroad car was diverted overnight to a munitions dump that was
frequently the target of French aerial sorties. Half a world away that

night, at a session of the annual Council of the Alliance being held in Nyack, New York, "a delegate suddenly burdened for the ladies at Jerusalem urgently requested special prayers on their behalf." The Council prayed and, coincidentally, no bombing runs were conducted that night, though the levantine sky was clear and beautiful.

By the autumn of 1917, Allenby was ready to move. Feinting another attack at Gaza, Allenby instead swung inland and outflanked the Turks at Beersheba. He then turned around and stormed besieged Gaza successfully. The break in the stalemate and the swiftness of the operations caused the Turks to panic in their retreat. With Turkish and German troops heading north, the British forces were able to take Jerusalem without a major engagement. Ironically, the end of four centuries of Turkish rule over the Holy City came when the mayor of the city (holding a bedsheet someone gave him at the American Colony) approached two British skirmishers and told them about the city's surrender.

When news of the capture of Jerusalem reached Dr. A. B. Simpson, founder of the Christian and Missionary Alliance, he was in Chicago on a convention tour. Simpson immediately returned to his hotel room. Overcome with emotion, he dropped to his knees and prayed that the redemption of the Jews was also at hand, since the fall of the city portended great and miraculous events. Recovering his composure, Simpson left the hotel and went on to address a crowd at the Moody Tabernacle.[51] The idea that the city had been captured by Christian forces burned in his heart, and he continued for weeks after to inspire large crowds with impressions on the exciting times. Like Dr. Simpson, most Americans knew intuitively that a new era had commenced with the fall of Jerusalem, and they were quite hopeful.

By that December, most Americans were aware of the British effort to court Jewish opinion through the issuance of a pro-Zionist understanding on the disposition of Palestine. After protracted negotiations with British Zionists, the Balfour Declaration in favor of a Jewish national home in Palestine was issued on November 2, 1917. Now the country was under British military control, and its final disposition was yet to be decided. The age of Palestine's increasing politicization had commenced. Yale geographer Ellsworth Huntington, among the scholars of the time, wrote:

> Our philanthropists, our educators, and our missionaries have done more for Syria and other parts of the Turkish Empire than have the peoples of any other nation. We have done our

best to inspire them with the love of freedom and with aspirations for progress. We cannot leave them in the lurch until we know that they are safely under the guardianship of some wise, strong power like Great Britain.[52]

That guardianship was finalized by the Council of the League of Nations on September 29, 1922, and the Holy Land's image in the American mind was never quite the same again.

Notes

INTRODUCTION

1. Jesse Lyman Hurlbut, *The Story of Chautauqua* (New York: Putnam, 1921), p. x. Other useful looks at Chautauqua are Theodore Morrison's *Chautauqua: A Center for Education, Religion, and the Arts in America* (Chicago: University of Chicago Press, 1974); Joseph Gould's *The Chautauqua Movement* (New York: State University of New York, 1961); E. E. Snyder's "The Chautauqua Movement in Popular Culture: A Sociological Analysis," *Journal of American Culture* 8 (1985): 79. See also, to a lesser degree, Irene DaBoll's *Recollections of the Lyceum and Chautauqua Circuits* (Freeport, Maine: Bond Wheelwright, 1969); Harry Harrison's *Culture Under Canvass* (1958; reprint, Westport, Conn.: Greenwood Press, 1978); and Richard Campen's *Chautauqua Impressions* (Chagrin Falls, Ohio: West Summit Press, 1984).

2. Rudyard Kipling, *Abaft the Funnel* (New York: B. W. Dodge, 1909), p. 188. This work is actually a collection of earlier pieces, most of which were written as a correspondent for the Indian paper *The Pioneer Mail*. Kipling's original piece on Chautauqua appeared in the April 2, 1890, issue. For more information on Kipling's first U.S. visit, see Lord Birkenhead, *Rudyard Kipling* (New York: Random House, 1978), pp. 90–91; and Martin Fido, *Rudyard Kipling* (New York: Viking, 1974), pp. 56–58.

3. Victoria and Robert Case, *We Called It Culture* (Garden City, N.Y.: Doubleday, 1948), p. 12.

4. Morrison, *Chautauqua*, p. 12. Morrison includes two marvelous photographs of Chautauqua's Palestine Park in his book. In one, the Chautauqua Choir is arrayed down the slopes of "Mount Hermon," the model's largest hillock. The other view of the park, from below the "Dead Sea" area, gives some idea of the size and complexity of the model.

5. Morrison, *Chautauqua*, p. 35.

6. John H. Vincent, *The Chautauqua Movement* (1885; reprint, Freeport, N.Y.: Books for Libraries Press, 1971), p. 264. In a biography of Vincent, the whole Chautauqua movement was characterized as "no other than a gigantic Palestine class." See Robert Handy, ed., *The Holy Land in American Protestant Life, 1800–1948: A Documentary History* (New York: Arno Press, 1981), p. xiii; the quotation is from Leon Vincent, *John Heyl Vincent: A Biographical Sketch* (New York: Macmillan, 1925), p. 91.

7. Kipling, *Abaft the Funnel*, p. 195.

8. J. B. Deregowski, "Pictorial Perception and Culture," *Scientific American* 227 (1972): 82; R. Serpell, "How Perception Differs Among Cultures," *New Society* 20 (1972): 620; B. Bernstein, "Some Sociological Determinants of Perception: An In-

quiry into Sub-Cultural Differences," *British Journal of Sociology* 9 (1958): 159; M. H.
Segall, *The Influence of Culture on Visual Perception* (Indianapolis: Bobbs-Merrill, 1966).

   9. Leo Postman, Jerome Bruner, and Elliot McGinnies, "Personal Values as Selective Factors in Perception," *Journal of Abnormal and Social Psychology* 43 (1958): 142.
For the specific topic of environmental perception, see P. M. Dansereau, *Inscape and
Landscape: The Human Perception of the Environment* (1973; reprint, New York: Columbia University Press, 1975); and *Environmental Perception and Behavior*, ed. David Lowenthal (Chicago: University of Chicago, Department of Geography, 1967).

   10. Henry Steele Commager, *The American Mind* (New Haven: Yale University
Press, 1950), p. vii.

   11. Rivka Demsky and Ora Zimmer have made an estimable contribution toward
the control of this large body of material in their "America and the Holy Land: A
Select Bibliography of Publications in English," *Jerusalem Cathedra* 3 (1983): 327. Also,
the published proceedings of the series of America–Holy Land Colloquia are useful
in citing extraneous works as well as for pointing up the need for a comprehensive
bibliographical tool to control this material. See *America and the Holy Land: A Colloquium* (Jerusalem: Hebrew University, Institute for Contemporary Jewry, 1972); *With
Eyes Toward Zion: Scholars Colloquium on America–Holy Land Studies* (New York: Arno
Press, 1977); *With Eyes Toward Zion II: Themes and Sources in the Archives of the United
States, Great Britain, Turkey, and Israel* (New York: Praeger, 1986); and *With Eyes Toward Zion III: Western Societies and the Holy Land* (New York: Praeger, 1991). Other
works that are useful for understanding the scope of America–Holy Land materials
are the splendid reprint series, "America and the Holy Land," issued in 1977 by Arno
Press in more than seventy volumes; Robert Handy's compilation, *The Holy Land in
American Protestant Life, 1800–1948: A Documentary History* (New York: Arno Press,
1981); V. Lipman's nearly parallel compilation, *Americans and the Holy Land Through
British Eyes, 1820–1917: A Documentary History* (London: Published by the author,
1989); and Gershon Greenberg's projected study *Holy Lands and Religious America*
(forthcoming).

   12. Charles W. Elliott, *Remarkable Characters and Places of the Holy Land* (Hartford,
Conn.: J. B. Burr, 1867), p. 390.

   13. Frank S. DeHass, *Buried Cities Recovered* (Philadelphia: Bradley, 1885), p. 10.

   14. Former President Jimmy Carter, for example, termed this area "the most volatile and coveted region in the world, one whose instability is almost certainly the
greatest threat to world peace." Jimmy Carter, *The Blood of Abraham* (Boston:
Houghton Mifflin, 1985), p. 4.

   15. For this very reason, contemporary interpretive studies on aspects of the
America–Holy Land relationship are most often drawn around politically charged
themes. To illustrate, Frank Manuel's classic *Realities of America-Palestine Relations*
(1949; reprint, Westport, Conn.: Greenwood Press, 1975) traced the history of American diplomatic efforts on behalf of Palestine's growing Jewish population, efforts that
were precursory to eventual American political recognition. Hertzel Fishman's *American Protestantism and a Jewish State* (Detroit: Wayne State University Press, 1973) analyzed liberal Protestant reaction to the gradual fruition of Zionist work between 1917
and 1948. Esther Feldblum wrote about American Catholic reaction to a Jewish State
from 1917 to 1959 in *The American Catholic Press and a Jewish State* (New York: Ktav,
1977). David Rausch has written about American Protestant fundamentalism and its
receptivity to Zionism between 1878 and 1918 in his *Zionism Within Early American
Fundamentalism* (New York: Edwin Mellon Press, 1979). More recent is Peter Grose's
examination of the idea of Jewish restoration as it matured in an American setting:

Israel in the Mind of America (New York: Knopf, 1983). All these works imply a substantial cultural underpinning between Christian Americans, popular American tradition, and the Holy Land. Unfortunately, this broader cultural connection receives only cursory treatment in these works.

Where the connection is raised in other studies, it is predictably only a minor part of the story of American Christian contacts with the larger Middle East region. Such works as John DeNovo's *American Interests and Policies in the Middle East, 1900–1939* (Minneapolis: University of Minnesota Press, 1963); Abdul Tibawi's *American Interests in Syria, 1800–1901* (Oxford: Clarendon Press, 1966); David Finnie's *Pioneers East* (Cambridge, Mass.: Harvard University Press, 1967); James Field's *America and the Mediterranean World, 1776–1882* (Princeton, N.J.: Princeton University Press, 1969); Robert Daniel's *American Philanthropy in the Near East, 1820–1960* (Athens, Ohio: Ohio University Press, 1970); James Grabill's *Protestant Diplomacy and the Near East* (Minneapolis: University of Minnesota Press, 1971); and Thomas Bryson's *American Diplomatic Relations with the Middle East, 1784–1975* (Metuchen, N.J.: Scarecrow Press, 1977), while all worthy analyses that incorporate elements essential to an understanding of the American Christian relationship with the Holy Land do not satisfactorily dwell on the unique attraction the Holy Land held for Americans and their culture. Last, some studies have focused on the country's attraction, but not in an exclusively American context. Naomi Shepherd's *The Zealous Intruders: The Western Rediscovery of Palestine* (San Francisco: Harper & Row, 1987) and Neil Silberman's *Digging for God and Country* (New York: Knopf, 1982) are examples of such a focus.

16. Yehoshua Ben-Arieh, "Perceptions and Images of the Holy Land," in *The Land That Became Israel: Studies in Historical Geography*, ed. Ruth Kark (New Haven, Conn.: Yale University Press, 1989), p. 37. Ben-Arieh does me the honor of citing my earlier work, "Zion as Place and Past," in his thoughtful essay.

17. For an examination of the importance of the domestic setting in a cultural sense, see Maxine Van de Wetering, "The Popular Concept of 'Home' in Nineteenth-Century America," *Journal of American Studies* 18 (1984): 5.

18. See R. S. Dilly, "Tourist Brochures and Tourist Images," *Canadian Geographer* 30 (1986): 59, for a discussion of this concept in another geographical setting.

19. See Merle Miller, *Plain Speaking: An Oral Biography of Harry S. Truman* (New York: Berkeley Publishing, 1974), pp. 230–32, for an easily accessible example of Truman's reflection. Carter's analysis of the regional Middle East conflict is especially rich in retaining the Holy Land's biblical imagery. During a visit to Israel in May 1973, Carter reported that he arose early in the mornings to catch a glimpse of Jerusalem coming alive "when few tourists were about, and to catch a flavor of how it might have been two thousand years earlier, when Jesus strolled the same streets." In a similar fashion, he reported that he and his wife discovered that urban areas "were often so different from what we expected. They seemed buried, closed in, tinseled, and highly commercial, not simple and primitive as we had imagined." Carter, *The Blood of Abraham*, p. 24. Examples of similar imagery may also be found in the writings of other U.S. presidents as well.

20. Henry Nash Smith, *Virgin Land: The American West as Symbol and Myth* (Cambridge, Mass.: Harvard University Press, 1950). See also Smith's "The West as an Image of the American Past," *University of Kansas City Review* 18 (1951): 29; B. Marks's "The Concept of Myth in *Virgin Land*," *American Quarterly* 5 (1953): 71; R. Bridgman's "The American Studies of Henry Nash Smith," *American Scholar* 56 (1987): 259; and A. Trachtenberg's "Myth and Symbol," *Massachusetts Review* 25 (1984): 667.

21. John Kirkland Wright, *Human Nature in Geography* (Cambridge, Mass.: Harvard University Press, 1965), pp. 250–85.

22. Yi-Fu Tuan, "Geopiety: A Theme in Man's Attachment to Nature and Place," in *Geographies of the Mind* (New York: Oxford University Press, 1976), pp. 11–12.

23. Ibid., p. 13.

24. Samuel Purchas, *Hakluytus Posthumous; or, Purchas, His Pilgrimes*, quoted in Barbara Tuchman's *Bible and Sword* (New York: New York University Press, 1956), p. 104.

25. Yi-Fu Tuan in *Geographies of the Mind*, p. 29.

26. Ibid., p. 30.

27. Harold F. Jenkins, *Two Points of View: The History of the Parlor Stereoscope* (Uniontown, Pa.: E. G. Warman, 1973), p. 44. See also J. Jones's *Wonders of the Stereoscope* (New York: Knopf, 1976); and W. C. Darrah's *Stereo Views: A History of Stereographs in America and Their Collection* (Gettysburg, Pa.: Published by the author, 1964). Of special interest on the topic of the Holy Land in nineteenth-century photography are Y. Nir's *The Bible and the Image: The History of Photography in the Holy Land, 1839–1899* (Philadelphia: University of Pennsylvania Press, 1985) and his "Cultural Predisposition in Early Photography: The Case of the Holy Land," *Journal of Communication* 35 (1985): 32.

28. Jesse Lyman Hurlbut and Charles Foster Kent, *Palestine Through the Stereoscope* (New York: Underwood & Underwood, 1914). An earlier edition of the work, by Hurlbut alone, was published by Underwood & Underwood in 1900 under the title *Traveling in the Holy Land Through the Stereoscope*.

29. "Charles Foster Kent," *Journal of Biblical Literature* 45 (1926): 5.

30. Hurlbut and Kent, *Palestine Through the Stereoscope*, pp. 5–7.

CHAPTER 1

1. George A. Barrois, *Twentieth-Century Encyclopedia of Religious Knowledge* (Grand Rapids, Mich.: Baker Book House, 1955), p. 523.

2. Two articles by Gideon Biger are especially noteworthy regarding borders: "Where Is Palestine? Pre–World War I Perceptions," *Area* 13 (1981): 153; and "The Names and Boundaries of Eretz-Israel (Palestine) as Reflections of Stages in Its History," in *The Land That Became Israel: Studies in Historical Geography*, ed. Ruth Kark (New Haven, Conn.: Yale University Press, 1989).

3. George A. Barton, *Archeology and the Bible* (Philadelphia: American Sunday-School Union, 1916), p. 94. The idea stems from the Bible itself; see Deuteronomy 11:10–12.

4. "Holy (The Sacred)," in *Dictionary of the History of Ideas*, ed. Philip P. Wiener (New York: Scribner, 1973), 2:511.

5. O. R. Jones, *The Concept of Holiness* (New York: Macmillan, 1961). See also R. Cooper, "The Unifying Structure of the Experience of the Holy," *Philosophy Today* 32 (1988): 54; and Q. Smith, "An Analysis of Holiness," *Religious Studies* 24 (1988): 511.

6. Rudolf Otto, *The Idea of the Holy* (Oxford: Oxford University Press, 1936), p. 13.

7. Jones, *The Concept of Holiness*, p. 52.

8. Mircea Eliade, *The Sacred and the Profane* (New York: Harcourt, Brace, 1959), p. 26.

9. For the merest of examples, see the opening commentary of the classic medieval Jewish commentator Rabbi Shlomo Yitshaki (Rashi) on Genesis 1:1, as well as the Mishnaic text in *Kelim* 1:6. For summary discussions, see *Zion in Jewish Literature*, ed. A. S. Halkin (New York: Herzl Press, 1961), esp. chaps. 1 and 2, on Zion in biblical and rabbinic literature respectively. Also useful is *The Land of Israel: Jewish Perspectives*, ed. Lawrence A. Hoffman (Notre Dame, Ind.: University of Notre Dame Press, 1986), and Zev Vilnay's *Legends of Palestine* (Philadelphia: Jewish Publication Society, 1932), pp. 3–19.

10. The covenant between people, land, and God is specified early in the Bible (cf. Genesis 13:14–18 and esp. 15:18–21) and then carried throughout subsequent biblical narrative: The land is a gift to a particular people as part of a covenantal contract. While endowed with natural richness and irresistible features ("flowing with milk and honey"), it is also clearly a land that lies at the disposal of divine will. An elaborate burden of responsibility is enumerated in the biblical text: To remain attached to the land, the people must guard and observe its holiness. Harry M. Orlinsky, "The Biblical Concept of the Land of Israel: Cornerstone of the Covenant Between God and Israel," in *The Land of Israel: Jewish Perspectives*, p. 27.

11. W. D. Davies has produced several works especially relevant to the theme of the comparative places of land and territoriality in Christianity and Judaism. See his *The Gospel and the Land* (Berkeley and Los Angeles: University of California Press, 1974) and *The Territorial Dimension of Judaism* (Berkeley and Los Angeles: University of California Press, 1982) as well as W. Brueggemann's *The Land as Gift, Promise, and Challenge in Biblical Faith* (Philadelphia: Fortress Press, 1977).

12. George L. Robinson, *The Biblical Doctrine of Holiness* (Chicago: Winona Publishing Co., 1903), p. 34.

13. See K. P. Prior, *The Way of Holiness: The Christian Doctrine of Sanctification* (Chicago: Intervarsity Press, 1967).

14. This urge to travel for sacred purposes evolved into one of the mainstays of the modern world's economy: tourism. See J. M. Theilmann, "Medieval Pilgrims and the Origins of Tourism," *Journal of Popular Culture* 20 (1987): 93.

15. Frank H. Epp, *Whose Land Is Palestine* (1970; reprint, Grand Rapids, Mich.: Eerdmans Publishing Co., 1974), p. 87.

16. Henry Van Dyke, *Out-of-Doors in the Holy Land* (1908; reprint, New York: Scribner, 1911).

17. Stanford Shaw, *History of the Ottoman Empire and Modern Turkey* (Cambridge: Cambridge University Press, 1976–77). See also *The Ottoman State and Its Place in World History*, ed. Kemal Karpat (Leiden: Brill, 1974); Zev Vilnay, *Toldot ha-'Arvim veha-Muslamim be-Erets Yisra'el* (History of the Arabs and Moslems in the Land of Israel) (Tel Aviv: A. Y. Shtibel, 1931/1932).

18. Characterization of the Ottoman Empire as "sick man of Europe" may derive from Russian Czar Nicholas I, who in a series of conversations with British Ambassador Sir Hamilton Seymour in 1853 said, "We have a sick man on our hands—a man gravely ill. It will be a grave misfortune if one of these days he slips through our hands, especially before the necessary arrangements are made." See Lord Kinross's *The Ottoman Centuries: The Rise and Fall of the Turkish Empire* (New York: Morrow Quill Paperbacks, 1977), p. 483.

19. See James Field's *America and the Mediterranean World, 1776–1882* (Princeton, N.J.: Princeton University Press, 1969); David Finnie's *Pioneers East* (Cambridge, Mass.: Harvard University Press, 1967); and Abdul Tibawi's *American Interests in Syria, 1800–1901* (Oxford: Clarendon Press, 1966).

20. Anthony Alderson, *The Structure of the Ottoman Dynasty* (Oxford: Clarendon Press, 1956); and Halil Inalcik, *The Ottoman Empire* (London: Variorum Reprints, 1978). See also Noel Barber, *The Sultans* (New York: Simon & Schuster, 1973).

21. Abdul Tibawi, *A Modern History of Syria, Including Lebanon and Palestine* (New York: St. Martin's Press, 1969), p. 23.

22. D. Kushner, "The Ottoman Governors of Palestine, 1864–1914," *Middle Eastern Studies* 23 (1987): 274.

23. Amnon Cohen, *Palestine in the Eighteenth Century* (Jerusalem: Magnes Press, 1973).

24. S. Pamuk, "The Decline and Resistance of Ottoman Cotton Textiles, 1820–1913," *Explorations in Economic History* 23 (1986): 205. See also Pamuk's *The Ottoman Empire and European Capitalism, 1820–1913: Trade, Investment, and Production* (Cambridge: Cambridge University Press, 1987).

25. Chaim Wardi, "The Question of the Holy Places in Ottoman Times," in *Studies on Palestine During the Ottoman Period*, ed. Moshe Ma'oz (Jerusalem: Magnes Press, 1975), pp. 31–48; hereafter cited as *Studies on Palestine*.

26. John Marlowe, *Perfidious Albion* (London: Elek, 1971).

27. Nelson was redressing an earlier stroke of bad luck: his failure to engage the French (and contain them) outside Toulon on account of bad weather. J. Christopher Herold, *Bonaparte in Egypt* (New York: Harper & Row, 1962).

28. Of the numerous secondary sources on the venture, probably Herold's *Bonaparte in Egypt* is best, although other useful works include P. G. Elgood's *Bonaparte's Adventure in Egypt* (London: Oxford University Press, 1931) and Christopher Lloyd's *The Nile Campaign* (New York: Barnes & Noble, 1973). For the siege of Acre, see Mordechai Gihon, "Matsor Napole'on 'al 'Ako" (Napoleon's Siege at Acre), which appeared in the proceedings of the 19th Archeological Convention of the Israel Exploration Society published under the title *Ma'aravo shel Galil ve-hof ha-Galil* (Western Galilee and the Galilee Coast) (Jerusalem: The Society, 1965); and also Stanford Shaw, *Between Old and New: The Ottoman Empire Under Sultan Selim III, 1789–1807* (Cambridge, Mass.: Harvard University Press, 1971). As part of his campaign, Napoleon had tried to arouse the popular support of non-Muslims by appealing to sectarian interests. Some Christian groups in Galilee, and some Maronites, precipitously heeded his calls. Tibawi, *A Modern History of Syria*, p. 37.

29. Alfred Bonne, *The Economic Development of the Middle East* (New York: Oxford University Press, 1945), p. 10. Estimations of Palestine's population during the Ottoman period are generally subject to question because of the lack of reliable census data. Other means of estimating the size of the population—such as relying on the observations of Western travelers—are even more unreliable. Perhaps the most frequent and veracious observation was that the country was underpopulated, though many reports express this in terms of the country's "devastation" or "abandonedness." See Fred Gottheil, "The Population of Palestine, Circa 1875," *Middle Eastern Studies* 15 (1979): 310; Yehoshua Ben-Arieh, "The Population of the Larger Towns in Palestine During the First Eighty Years of the Nineteenth Century, According to Western Sources," in *Studies on Palestine*, pp. 49–69. Ben-Arieh lists the twelve most populous towns in the order of their relative sizes: Jerusalem, Acre, Gaza, and Nablus; Safed and Hebron; Tiberias, Jaffa, and Ramleh; Haifa, Nazareth, and Bethlehem. Jerusalem retained its status as largest urban center through the end of Ottoman rule, while Jaffa and Haifa grew into the status of second and third largest centers.

30. Salman Farah, "A History of the Druze Settlements in Palestine During the Ottoman Period," in *Studies on Palestine*, pp. 31–48.

31. A. D. Crown's *Bibliography of the Samaritans* (Metuchen, N.J.: Scarecrow Press, 1984) is very comprehensive and useful for further information regarding this unique Holy Land community.

32. See Derek Hopwood, *The Russian Presence in Syria and Palestine, 1843–1914* (Oxford: Clarendon Press, 1969), for a treatment of the Russian exertions. Particularly useful with regard to British and American interests are A. Tibawi's *British Interests in Palestine, 1800–1901* (London: Oxford University Press, 1961) and *American Interests in Syria, 1800–1901*; *The British Consulate in Jerusalem in Relation to the Jews of Palestine, 1838–1914*, ed. Albert Hyamson (New York: AMS Press, 1975), which is a reprint of the 1939–40 edition; and Frank Manuel's *The Realities of American-Palestine Relations* (1949; reprint, Westport, Conn.: Greenwood Press, 1975).

33. Moshe Ma'oz, "Changes in the Position of the Jewish Communities of Palestine and Syria in the Mid-Nineteenth Century," in *Studies on Palestine*, p. 143.

34. In addition to Vilnay, see Aryeh Horshi, *Toldot ha-Yehudim be-Erets Yisra'el Tahat Shilton ha-Muslamim* (History of the Jews in the Land of Israel under Moslem Administration) (Jerusalem: Yad Ben-Zvi, 1975).

35. Jere L. Bacharach, *A Middle East Studies Handbook* (1984; reprint, Seattle: University of Washington Press, 1989), p. 135. See also Bat Ye'or, *The Dhimmi: A Historical Survey of Jews and Christians Under Islam* (Rutherford, N.J.: Fairleigh Dickinson University Press, 1984); and *Christians and Jews in the Ottoman Empire: The Functioning of a Plural Society*, ed. B. Braude and B. Lewis (New York: Holmes & Meier, 1982).

36. Tibawi, *A Modern History of Syria*, p. 29.

37. James Finn, a British consul, provided examples of the power and influence of the agents in his *Stirring Times* (London: C. K. Paul, 1878) and *A View From Jerusalem, 1849–1858*, ed. Arnold Blumberg (Rutherford, N.J.: Fairleigh Dickinson University Press, 1980).

38. A. Granott, *The Land System in Palestine* (London: Eyre & Spottiswoode, 1952). The terms for taxes on non-Muslims were often used interchangeably, but the taxes themselves applied to specific purposes. The traditional, ecclesiastically rooted *jizya* was a more specialized tax than the *kharaj* which, after the *Tanzimat* reforms of 1856, were abolished in favor of a tax in lieu of military service. See entries "Kharadj" and "Djizya" in *The Encyclopaedia of Islam*, new ed., ed. E. von Donzel et al. (Leiden: E. J. Brill, 1978). See also Ruth Kark's "Changing Patterns of Land Ownership in Nineteenth-Century Palestine: The European Influence," *Journal of Historical Geography* 10 (1984): 357.

39. Tibawi, *A Modern History of Syria*, p. 29.

40. Without the centralized control, native sheikhs, amirs, and chieftains had the chance to aggrandize their local domains and wage neighborhood campaigns against one another, further upsetting the civil order.

41. Tibawi, *A Modern History of Syria*, pp. 65–69; see also J. Marlowe's *Perfidious Albion*.

42. Yitshak Hofman, "The Administration of Syria and Palestine Under Egyptian Rule, 1831–1840," in *Studies on Palestine*, pp. 311–33.

43. Ma'oz, "Changes in the Position of the Jewish Communities," in *Studies on Palestine*, pp. 142–63.

44. Shmuel Avitsur, "The Influence of Western Technology on the Economy of Palestine During the Nineteenth Century," in *Studies on Palestine*, pp. 485–94. See also

his *Haye Yom-yom be-Erets Yisra'el be-Me'ah ha-Tesha Asarah* (Everyday Life in the Land of Israel in the Nineteenth Century) (Tel Aviv: 'Am ha-Sefer, 1972).

45. Roderic Davison, *Reform in the Ottoman Empire, 1856–1876* (Princeton, N.J.: Princeton University Press, 1963); Bernard Lewis, "The Ottoman Empire in the Mid-Nineteenth Century: A Review," *Middle Eastern Studies* 1 (1965): 283; Moshe Ma'oz, *Ottoman Reform in Syria and Palestine, 1840–1861* (Oxford: Oxford University Press, 1968). For developments taking place in specific cities during the nineteenth century the following works are useful: Ruth Kark, *Jaffa: A City in Evolution, 1799–1917* (Jerusalem: Yad Izhak Ben-Zvi Press, 1990); Helga Dudman, *Tiberias* (Jerusalem: Carta, 1988); Yehoshua Ben-Arieh's monumental two-volume study of the Old and New sections of Jerusalem, *Jerusalem in the Nineteenth Century* (New York: St. Martin's Press, 1986); Martin Gilbert, *Jerusalem: Rebirth of a City* (New York: Viking, 1985); Jeff Halper, "On the Way: The Transition of Jerusalem from a Ritual to Colonial City, 1800–1917," *Urban Anthropology* 13 (1984): 1.

46. Alexis de Tocqueville, *Democracy in America* (New York: Knopf, 1945), 1:303. See also W. A. Galston, "Tocqueville on Liberalism and Religion," *Social Research* 54 (1987): 499.

47. See V. L. Brereton's *Training God's Army: The American Bible School, 1880–1940* (Bloomington: Indiana University Press, 1990).

48. Winthrop Hudson, *American Protestantism* (Chicago: University of Chicago Press, 1961), pp. vi–vii.

49. Ibid., p. 109.

50. This is so with regard to other areas of the globe besides the Holy Land. The early presence of America in the Middle East region, for example, was due solely to the pursuit of commercial and missionary activities—economic and spiritual "outreach" so to speak. Both these activities can be linked in some way to the influence of American Protestantism: from the reputed predilection of Protestantism toward commercial enterprise and work, as proffered by sociologist Max Weber, to the glaringly obvious evangelical fervency and sense of mission Protestantism fostered. See Finnie, *Pioneers East*; and Field, *America and the Mediterranean World*.

51. Congregationalists, Episcopalians, Presbyterians, Methodists, Baptists, and Lutherans. See Edwin S. Gaustad, *Historical Atlas of Religion in America* (New York: Harper & Row, 1962); and Frank S. Mead, *Handbook of Denominations in the United States* (New York: Abingdon Press, 1961). Also of use is R. Finke and R. Stark, "Turning Pews into People: Estimating Nineteenth-Century Church Membership," *Journal of the Scientific Study of Religion* 25 (1986): 180.

52. Hudson, *American Protestantism*, p. 2.

53. Max Lerner, *America as a Civilization* (New York: Simon & Schuster, 1957), pp. 704–5.

54. Tocqueville, *Democracy in America*, 2:152.

55. See M. A. Noll, "The Bible in America," *Journal of Biblical Literature* 106 (1987): 493.

56. *With Eyes Toward Zion: Scholars' Colloquium on America–Holy Land Studies* (New York: Arno Press, 1977), p. 246; and John Leighly, "Biblical Place-Names in the United States," *Names: Journal of the American Name Society* 27 (1979): 46.

57. Harold Fisch, *Jerusalem and Albion: The Hebraic Factor in Seventeenth-Century Literature* (New York: Schocken Books, 1964).

58. Edward Robinson, *Biblical Researches in Palestine, Mount Sinai, and Arabia Petrea* (London: Crocker & Brewster, 1841), 1:46. For background on the growth and influence of Sunday school education in America, see A. M. Boylan's *Sunday School: The*

Formation of an American Institution, 1790–1880 (New Haven, Conn.: Yale University Press, 1988).

59. George Phillips, *The American Republic and Human Liberty Foreshadowed in Scriptures* (Cincinnati: Poe & Hitchcock, 1864). Phillips's work was part of a tradition established early in American literature. For example, Timothy Dwight's epic poem *The Conquest of Canaan* (Hartford: E. Babcock, 1785) retold the story of Joshua in a transparent allegory where it was really George Washington leading his people to their destiny rather than Moses' successor. Perhaps Phillips was moved by the parallel divisions of the Jewish and American commonwealths into two sovereign states. In any case, Phillips's discourse on mission fits neatly with such studies as Ralph Gabriel's *The Course of American Democratic Thought* (New York: Ronald Press, 1949) and Edward Burns's *The American Idea of Mission* (New Brunswick, N.J.: Rutgers University Press, 1957). For the treatment of a similar theme, see *The American Republic and Ancient Israel* (New York: Arno Press, 1977).

60. Temperance too was easily associated with the Bible; see J. L. Merrill's "The Bible and the American Temperance Movement: Text, Context, and Pretext," *Harvard Theological Review* 81 (1988): 145.

61. Vernon Parrington, *American Dreamers* (New York: Russell & Russell, 1964), p. 8. See also S. Bercovitch's "Rhetoric as Authority: Puritanism, the Bible, and the Myth of America," *Social Science Information* 21 (1982): 5, and his *The Puritan Origins of the American Self* (New Haven: Yale University Press, 1975); and J. R. Knott's *The Sword and the Spirit: Puritan Responses to the Bible* (Chicago: University of Chicago Press, 1980). Mason Lowance's *The Language of Canaan* (Cambridge, Mass.: Harvard University Press, 1980) is an excellent study of the use of biblical imagery as symbol and metaphor in New England society, beginning with the Puritans and ending with the nineteenth-century Transcendentalists.

62. On the elasticity of biblical interpretation during the Middle Ages, see Beryl Smalley's dated *The Study of the Bible in the Middle Ages* (Oxford: Clarendon Press, 1941) and M. T. Gibson's more recent "The Study of the Bible in the Middle Ages," *Journal of Ecclesiastical History* 39 (1988): 230.

63. Ferenc M. Szasz, *The Divided Mind of Protestant America, 1880–1930* (University, Ala.: University of Alabama Press, 1982), p. 16.

64. Gaillard Hunt, *The History of the Great Seal of the United States* (Washington, D.C.: U.S. Department of State, 1909). "It had taken as long to settle upon a design as it had to win the war: the committee to prepare the seal had been set up by Congressional resolution late in the afternoon of the Fourth of July, 1776." The seal was eventually approved (in the form now appearing on one dollar bills) on June 20, 1782. Quoted in Field, *America and the Mediterranean World*, p. 3. See also *With Eyes Toward Zion*, plate 2 following p. 138, for the rejected entry.

65. Samuel Levine, "Changing Concepts of Palestine in American Literature to 1867" (Ph.D. diss., New York University, 1953). A condensed version of Levine's work, "Palestine in the Literature of the United States," appeared in *Early History of Zionism in America*, ed. Isidore Meyer (1958; reprint, New York: Arno Press, 1977), pp. 21–38. Levine's work proved to be an especially useful prequel to the present study, as he approached the subject from a cultural perspective.

66. William Dinsmoor, "Early American Studies of Mediterranean Archaeology," *Proceedings of the American Philosophical Society* 87 (1943): 71.

67. On the Levant Company, see Mortimer Epstein, *The Early History of the Levant Company* (New York: A. M. Kelly, 1968); and Alfred Wood, *A History of the Levant Company* (Oxford: Oxford University Press, 1935).

68. See Barbara Tuchman's *Bible and Sword* (New York: New York University Press, 1956) for a discussion of these links. Tuchman mentions, for example, the fabled connections between Britons and Holy Landers, such as the possible Mediterranean ancestry of pre-Celtic Britain, contacts with Phoenicians, the shared mantle of Roman rule, Joseph of Arimathea as legendary apostle to Britain, and the important heritage of the Crusades.

69. Richard B. Davis, *George Sandys, Poet-Adventurer* (New York: Columbia University Press, 1955), p. 43.

70. Tuchman, *Bible and Sword*, p. 74.

71. Originally published in London in 1615, the work went through eight English, one German, and two Dutch editions during the seventeenth century. The edition quoted here is the seventh, which was published under the title *Sandys Travels* (London, 1673).

72. Ibid., prelim. p. ii.

73. Ibid., p. 124.

74. Tuchman, *Bible and Sword*, p. 79.

75. Sandys, *Sandys Travels*, p. 114.

76. Dinsmoor, "Early American Studies of Mediterranean Archaeology," p. 71.

77. H. M. Sayre, "Surveying the Vast Profound: The Panoramic Landscape in American Consciousness," *Massachusetts Review* 24 (1983): 723. The following works on American artists and the Holy Land and/or Middle East are quite useful: J. Davis, "Frederick Church's 'Sacred Geography,'" *Smithsonian Studies in American Art* 1 (1987): 79; D. D. Thompson, "American Artists in North Africa and the Middle East, 1797–1914," *Antiques* 126 (August 1984): 303; and V. W. Von Hagen, "Artist of a Buried World," *American Heritage* 12 (1961): 8, which is about Frederick Catherwood, who exhibited an acclaimed panorama of Jerusalem in New York City in the late 1830s.

78. For example, the role of a select few American theological schools is pronounced in the America–Holy Land relationship because a significant number of Holy-Land–experienced figures received their training in them or were otherwise provided an intellectual/spiritual environment by them. Among these institutions, Andover, Hartford, Princeton, Chicago, and Union Theological seminaries are especially conspicuous. For the role of Bible schools in shaping religious outlook, see Brereton's *Training God's Army*.

79. See R. Lerner et al., "Christian Religious Elites," *Public Opinion* 11 (1989): 54; and *The Rich, the Well Born, and the Powerful: Elites and Upper Classes in History*, ed. F. C. Jaher (Urbana: University of Illinois Press, 1973).

80. See Robert Handy's source compilation, *The Holy Land in American Protestant Life, 1800–1948* (New York: Arno Press, 1977), for a concise survey. Using documentary extracts, Handy reveals how the Holy Land became known to Americans between 1800 and 1948. The various groups had been identified by Handy in his earlier discussions of the extent of America–Holy Land relations. See also his "Studies in the Interrelationship Between America and the Holy Land," *Journal of Church and State* 13 (1971): 283, and his definitive contributions to the America–Holy Land conferences.

81. See George Antonius, *The Arab Awakening* (1946; reprint, New York: Paragon Books, 1979).

82. Henry F. May, *The End of American Innocence: A Study of the First Years of Our Time, 1912–1917* (New York: Knopf, 1959).

CHAPTER 2

1. Mary Todd Lincoln to James Smith, December 17, 1866; quoted in *Mary Todd Lincoln: Her Life and Letters*, ed. Justin G. Turner and Linda T. Turner (New York: Knopf, 1972), pp. 218, 400.

2. H. Sivan, "Holy Land Pilgrimage and Western Audiences: Some Reflections on Egeria and Her Circle," *Classical Quarterly* 38 (1988): 528; V. Wheeler, "Travelers' Tales: Observations on the Travel Book and Ethnography," *Anthropological Quarterly* 59 (1986): 52.

3. The Holy Land–related works produced by these authors were Stephens's *Incidents of Travel in Egypt, Arabia Petrea, and the Holy Land* (New York: Harper, 1838); Curtis's *The Howadji in Syria* (New York: Harper, 1852); Taylor's *The Lands of the Saracen* (New York: Putnam, 1856); De Forest's *Oriental Acquaintance* (New York: Dix, Edwards, 1856); Bryant's *Letters From the East* (New York: Putnam, 1869); Browne's *Yusef; or, The Journey of the Frangi, a Crusade in the East* (New York: Harper, 1853); and Melville's *Clarel: A Poem and Pilgrimage in the Holy Land*, ed. W. E. Bezanson (New York: Hendricks House, 1960).

4. For treatments of this period, see David Finnie's *Pioneers East* (Cambridge, Mass.: Harvard University Press, 1967); James Field's *America and the Mediterranean World, 1776–1882* (Princeton, N.J.: Princeton University Press, 1969); Samuel Levine's "Changing Concepts of Palestine in American Literature to 1867" (Ph.D. diss., School of Education, New York University, 1953); Yehoshua Ben-Arieh's *The Rediscovery of the Holy Land in the Nineteenth Century* (Jerusalem: Magnes Press, 1979); Ahmed Metwalli's "The Lure of the Levant: The American Literary Experience in Egypt and the Holy Land, 1800–1865" (Ph.D. diss., Department of English, State University of New York at Albany, 1971); David Klatzker's "American Catholic Travelers to the Holy Land, 1861–1929," *Catholic Historical Review* 74 (1988): 55, and his "American Christian Travelers to the Holy Land, 1821–1939" (Ph.D. diss., Temple University, 1987); M. Obeidat's "Lured to the Exotic Levant: The Muslim East to American Travelers of the Nineteenth Century," *Islamic Quarterly* 31 (1987): 167; E. F. VandeBilt's "Proximity and Distance: American Travelers to the Middle East, 1819–1918" (Ph.D. diss., Cornell University, 1985); and R. W. Stookey's "The Holy Land: The American Experience, the Christian Concern," *Middle East Journal* 30 (1976): 351. Also useful is the popular account given by Neil Silberman, *Digging for God and Country: Exploration, Archaeology, and the Secret Struggle for the Holy Land, 1799–1917* (New York: Knopf, 1982).

5. Seward had actually been to the Holy Land once before, in 1859. Completion of his term of office gave him the opportunity for an around-the-world tour that included a stay in the Holy Land for a second time, in 1871. Grant embarked on a grand tour of Europe and the East that included a stop in the Holy Land during the winter of 1878.

6. Samuel Clemens, *Mark Twain's Notebook*, ed. Albert Bigelow Paine (New York: Harper, 1935), pp. 32–54.

7. Leon Dickinson, "Mark Twain's *Innocents Abroad*: Its Origins, Composition, and Popularity" (Ph.D. diss., University of Chicago, 1945), p. 1. See also Dickinson's two articles, "Mark Twain's Revisions in Writing the *Innocents Abroad*," *American Literature* 19 (1947): 139, and "Marketing a Bestseller: Mark Twain's *Innocents Abroad*," *Papers of the Bibliographical Society of America* 41 (1947): 107.

8. The transcontinental rail link was still three years away; hence the circuitous route.

9. *Alta California*, April 9, 1867.

10. Stephen Morrell Griswold, *Sixty Years with Plymouth Church* (New York: Revell, 1907), pp. 153–66.

11. *New York Sun*, June 8, 1867; quoted in L. Dickinson, "Mark Twain's *Innocents Abroad*," pp. 4–5.

12. Mary Fairbanks, "The Cruise of the *Quaker City*, with Chance Recollections of Mark Twain," *Chautauquan* 14 (1892): 429.

13. The substantial number of studies of *Innocents Abroad* does not detract from its usefulness as a centerpiece for the study of America's Holy Land imagery and the American tourist/pilgrim. On the contrary, given its status as an American literary classic, its position is natural. Holding the works and impressions of other travelers up to comparison in terms of experiences and motivations—but not literary style, of course—produces a summary of the American tourist experience that is honest in its proportions. See also A. Gibben, "The Importance of Mark Twain," *American Quarterly* 37 (1985): 30; F. G. Robinson, "Patterns of Consciousness in the *Innocents Abroad*," *American Literature* 58 (1986): 46; J. Steinbrink, "Why the Innocents Went Abroad: Mark Twain and American Tourism in the Late Nineteenth Century," *American Literary Realism* 16 (1983): 278; S. Clemens, *Traveling With the Innocents Abroad*, ed. D. M. McKeithan (Norman: University of Oklahoma Press, 1958); and D. Ganzel, *Mark Twain Abroad: The Cruise of the "Quaker City"* (Chicago: University of Chicago Press, 1968).

14. Samuel Clemens, *The Innocents Abroad; or, The New Pilgrim s Progress*, with an introduction by A. Kazin (New York: Bantam Books, 1964), p. v.

15. Daniel Boorstin, *America and the Image of Europe* (New York: Meridian Books, 1960). For further discussion of the image of Europe in the American mind, see Cushing Strout, *The American Image of the Old World* (New York: Harper & Row, 1963); and Philip Rahv, *Discovery of Europe* (Garden City, N.Y.: Anchor Books, 1960). For an interesting turnabout on Middle Eastern views of America, see A. Ayalon, "The Arab Discovery of America in the Nineteenth Century," *Middle Eastern Studies* 20 (1984): 5; and M. A. Farah, "The United States Identity from Its Origin to 1876 in Syria" (Ph.D. diss., New York University, 1977).

16. Clemens, *Mark Twain's Notebook*, p. 106.

17. Clemens, *The Innocents Abroad*, p. ix.

18. Samuel Clemens, *The Travels of Mark Twain* (New York: Coward, McCann, 1961), p. 15. For the discussion between Clemens and Elisha Bliss on selection of a title, see also Clemens's *Mark Twain's Letters to His Publishers, 1867–1894*, ed. Hamlin Hill (Berkeley and Los Angeles: University of California Press, 1974), pp. 18–20.

19. Clemens, *The Innocents Abroad*, p. vi.

20. Franklin Walker, *Irreverent Pilgrims* (Seattle: University of Washington Press, 1974), p. 7.

21. *Dictionary of American Biography* (New York: American Council of Learned Societies, 1928–37), vol. 1.

22. Ibid. Bellows died in 1882.

23. Henry Whitney Bellows, *The Old World in Its New Face* (New York: Harper, 1868–69).

24. John Franklin Swift, *Going to Jericho* (New York: A. Roman, 1868), pp. 6–7.

25. Charles W. Elliott, *Remarkable Characters and Places of the Holy Land* (Hartford, Conn.: J. B. Burr, 1867), p. vi.

26. Nathaniel Clark Burt, *The Land and Its Story* (New York: D. Appleton, 1869), p. 3.

27. Ibid., p. 5.

28. William L. Gage, *The Land of Sacred Mystery* (Chicago: J. A. Stoddard, 1871), p. 14.

29. Jacob Freese, *The Old World* (Philadelphia: Lippincott, 1869), p. 2.

30. Joseph I. Taylor, *A Gyre Thro' the Orient* (Princeton, Ill.: Republican Book & Job Printing Office, 1869), p. 4.

31. Ibid., p. 5.

32. Ibid., p. 7.

33. David McCullough, *Mornings on Horseback* (New York: Simon & Schuster, 1981), p. 118.

34. Theodore Roosevelt, *Theodore Roosevelt's Diaries of Boyhood and Youth* (New York: Scribner, 1928), p. 312.

35. *Professor Park and His Pupils* (Boston: S. Usher, 1899), p. 90.

36. Ibid., p. 35.

37. Philip Schaff, *Through Bible Lands* (New York: American Tract Society, 1878), p. 1.

38. Thomas DeWitt Talmage, Diary, December 1889–January 1890, Manuscript Division, Library of Congress. Talmage's diary of his Holy Land trip was expanded in a series of sermons delivered to his Brooklyn (N.Y.) Tabernacle. The sermons, in turn, were published as *Talmage on Palestine* (Springfield, Ohio: Nast, Crowell & Kirkpatrick, 1890).

39. Henry Van Dyke, *Out-of-Doors in the Holy Land* (1908; reprint, New York: Arno Press, 1977), p. ix. Trips to the East, especially to the Levant and the Holy Land, were customarily viewed by Westerners as being able to salve personal crises. "I can hardly tell why it should be, but there is a longing for the East very commonly felt by proud-hearted people, when goaded by sorrow," Alexander Kinglake wrote in reference to Lady Hester Stanhope. According to Franklin Walker, the same remark was applicable to Herman Melville. See Walker, *Irreverent Pilgrims*, p. 4. Kinglake's remarks are from his *Eothen* (New York: D. Appleton, 1898), p. 68.

40. James D. McCabe, *A Tour Around the World by General Grant* (Philadelphia: National Publishing Co., 1879), p. 20.

41. Ibid., p. 21.

42. William S. McFeely, *Grant* (New York: Norton, 1981), p. 450.

43. W. R. Siddall, "Transportation and the Experience of Travel," *Geographical Review* 77 (1987): 309.

44. J. Augustus Johnson, "The Colonization of Palestine," *The Century* 2 (1882): 293.

45. Taylor, *A Gyre Thro' the Orient*, p. 304.

46. Swift, *Going to Jericho*, p. 201.

47. Bellows, *The Old World in Its New Face*, p. 304.

48. Freese, *The Old World*, p. 20.

49. Ibid., p. 67.

50. Willis A. Sutton, Jr., "Travel and Understanding," *International Journal of Comparative Sociology* 8 (1967): 223.

51. A. A. Murphy, "Homiletic Advantages of a Trip to the Holy Land," *Homiletic Review* 21 (1891): 86.

52. For a more detailed analysis of the phases and composition of the sojourn as a

sociological phenomenon, see Eugene H. Jacobson, "Sojourn Research: A Definition of the Field," *Journal of Social Issues* 19 (1963): 123.

CHAPTER 3

1. Samuel Clemens, *The Innocents Abroad; or, The New Pilgrim's Progress*, with an introduction by A. Kazin (New York: Bantam Books, 1964), p. 310.
2. Ibid., p. 311.
3. Samuel Clemens, *Mark Twain's Notebook*, ed. Albert Bigelow Paine (New York: Harper, 1935), p. 84.
4. Clemens, *The Innocents Abroad*, p. 313.
5. Samuel Clemens, *Traveling With the Innocents Abroad*, ed. D. M. McKeithan (Norman: University of Oklahoma Press, 1958), pp. 186–87.
6. Emily Severance, *Journal Letters, Quaker City, 1867* (Cleveland: Gates Press, 1938), p. 161.
7. John Franklin Swift, *Going to Jericho* (New York: A. Roman, 1868), p. 211.
8. *New York Times*, May 21, 1874.
9. Clemens, *The Innocents Abroad*, p. 436.
10. Swift, *Going to Jericho*, p. 211.
11. Joseph I. Taylor, *A Gyre Thro' the Orient* (Princeton, Ill.: Republican Book & Job Printing Office, 1869), p. 131.
12. Clemens, *Mark Twain's Notebook*, p. 100.
13. Severance, *Journal Letters*, p. 164.
14. Ibid., p. 170.
15. Clemens, *The Innocents Abroad*, p. 344.
16. Clemens, *Mark Twain's Notebook*, p. 90.
17. Clara E. Waters, *A Simple Story of What One of Your Lady Friends Saw in the East* (Boston: Privately printed, 1869), p. 76.
18. Ibid., p. 5.
19. Henry Whitney Bellows, *The Old World in Its New Face* (New York: Harper, 1868–69), pp. 249–50.
20. Clemens, *Mark Twain's Notebook*, p. 90.
21. Taylor, *A Gyre Thro' the Orient*, p. 287.
22. Ibid., pp. 263–64.
23. Waters, *A Simple Story*, p. 44.
24. Theodore Roosevelt, *Theodore Roosevelt's Diaries of Boyhood and Youth* (New York: Scribner, 1928), p. 311.
25. Swift, *Going to Jericho*, p. 206.
26. J. B. Devins, "Americanization of the Holy Land," *Woman's Home Companion* 32 (1905): 18.
27. T. Roosevelt, *Theodore Roosevelt's Diaries of Boyhood and Youth*, p. 312.
28. Clemens, *The Innocents Abroad*, p. 310.
29. Ibid., p. 342. Physician Jacob Freese noted that the horsemanship of the Arab and his love for the animal were two characteristics that were apparent to everyone who travels the Holy Land. Either Clemens was going out of his way to debunk a myth, or Freese was going out of his way to maintain one. See Jacob Freese, *The Old World* (Philadelphia: Lippincott, 1869), p. 105.
30. *New York Times*, April 14, 1878.

31. Clemens, *Traveling with the Innocents Abroad*, p. 264.

32. Clemens, *The Innocents Abroad*, p. 344.

33. Ibid., p. 345.

34. William C. Prime, *Tent Life in the Holy Land* (New York: Harper, 1857). Whatever Clemens may have felt about Prime's book, it was undoubtedly one of the more significant travel books about the Holy Land produced by an American during the nineteenth century.

35. Clemens, *Traveling With the Innocents Abroad*, p. 265.

36. Freese, *The Old World*, p. 143.

37. Bellows, *The Old World in Its New Face*, p. 282.

38. Taylor, *A Gyre Thro' the Orient*, p. 288.

39. Roosevelt, *Theodore Roosevelt's Diaries of Boyhood and Youth*, p. 313.

40. Clemens, *Traveling With the Innocents Abroad*, pp. 305–6.

41. Freese, *The Old World*, p. 99.

42. Roosevelt, *Theodore Roosevelt's Diaries of Boyhood and Youth*, p. 316.

43. Clemens, *Traveling With the Innocents Abroad*, p. 185.

44. Ibid., p. 302.

45. Waters, *A Simple Story*, p. 74.

46. Nathaniel Clark Burt, *The Land and Its Story* (New York: D. Appleton, 1869), p. 45.

47. Ibid., p. 39. In contrast, Clemens observed at Tiberias that between there and Damascus he saw no country capable of "supporting any such population as one gathers from the Bible. The people in this region in the Bible were just as they are now—ignorant, depraved, superstitious, dirty, lousy, thieving vagabonds." See Clemens, *Mark Twain's Notebook*, p. 100.

48. Charles W. Elliott, *Remarkable Characters and Places of the Holy Land* (Hartford, Conn.: J. B. Burr, 1867), pp. 353–54.

49. Ibid., p. 341.

50. Bellows, *The Old World in Its New Face*, p. 251.

51. Ibid., p. 265.

52. Freese, *The Old World*, p. 223.

53. Clemens, *Traveling With the Innocents Abroad*, pp. 303–4.

54. Severance, *Journal Letters*, p. 162.

55. The "moment of commitment" is one of the nine phases in the sojourn sequence proposed by Eugene Jacobson; see his "Sojourn Research: A Definition of the Field," *Journal of Social Issues* 19 (1963): 124.

56. Severance, *Journal Letters*, p. 165.

57. Clemens, *Mark Twain's Notebook*, p. 99.

58. Clemens, *The Innocents Abroad*, p. 340.

59. William Dinsmoor, "Early American Studies of Mediterranean Archaeology," *Proceedings of the American Philosophical Society* 87 (1943): 77.

60. Taylor, *A Gyre Thro' the Orient*, p. 217.

61. M. R. Parkman, Diary, March 5–April 23, 1871, New York Public Library.

62. Severance, *Journal Letters*, p. 173.

63. Ibid., p. 161.

64. Taylor, *A Gyre Thro' the Orient*, p. 246.

65. Ibid., p. 126.

66. Ibid., pp. 358–59.

67. Clemens, *Traveling with the Innocents Abroad*, p. 186.

68. Swift, *Going to Jericho*, p. 243.

69. Ibid., p. 245.

70. Ibid., p. 247.

71. Ibid., p. 250.

72. Taylor, *A Gyre Thro' the Orient*, p. 317.

73. Ibid., p. 318.

74. Clemens, *Mark Twain's Notebook*, p. 100.

75. Swift, *Going to Jericho*, p. 249.

76. Parkman Diary.

77. Burt, *The Land and Its Story*, p. 232.

78. Elliott, *Remarkable Characters*, p. 395.

79. Ibid., p. 349.

80. Freese, *The Old World*, p. 81.

81. Ibid., p. 140.

82. Roosevelt, *Theodore Roosevelt's Diaries of Boyhood and Youth*, p. 316.

83. Taylor, *A Gyre Thro' the Orient*, pp. 275–76.

84. Parkman Diary.

85. Freese, *The Old World*, pp. 65–66.

86. Clemens, *Mark Twain's Notebook*, p. 98.

87. Roosevelt, *Theodore Roosevelt's Diaries of Boyhood and Youth*, p. 313.

88. Waters, *A Simple Story*, p. 53.

89. William S. McFeely, *Grant* (New York: Norton, 1981), p. 450. See also Julia Dent Grant, *Personal Memoirs*, ed. John Y. Simon (New York: Putnam, 1975), pp. 213–36.

90. John Russell Young, *Around the World with General Grant* (New York: American News Co., 1879), p. 467.

91. Taylor, *A Gyre Thro' the Orient*, p. 281.

92. See Joshua 8:30–35.

93. Parkman Diary.

94. Swift, *Going to Jericho*, pp. 236–37.

95. Eliza Bush, *My Pilgrimage to Eastern Shrines* (London: Hurst & Blackett, 1867), pp. 86–87.

96. Ibid., p. 281. For a survey of British views of the range of American Holy Land activities, see V. Lipman's *Americans and the Holy Land Through British Eyes, 1820–1917: A Documentary History* (London: Published by the author, 1989).

97. John MacGregor, *The Rob Roy on the Jordan* (New York: Harper, 1875), p. 358.

98. Freese, *The Old World*, p. 77.

99. Waters, *A Simple Story*, p. 12.

100. Clemens, *The Innocents Abroad*, p. 338.

101. Taylor, *A Gyre Thro' the Orient*, p. 164.

102. A. A. Boddy, *Days in Galilee and Scenes in Judea* (London: Gay & Bird, 1900), pp. 326–27.

103. Alexander Wallace, *The Desert and the Holy Land* (Edinburgh: W. Oliphant, 1868), p. 153.

104. Freese, *The Old World*, p. 79.

105. Ibid., pp. 135–36.

106. Taylor, *A Gyre Thro' the Orient*, p. 369.

107. For further works on the interplay between tourism, pilgrimage, travel, and perceptions, see J. F. Sears, *Sacred Places: American Tourist Attractions in the Nineteenth Century* (New York: Oxford University Press, 1989); B. N. Aziz, "Personal Dimensions of the Sacred Journey: What Pilgrims Say," *Religious Studies* 23 (1987): 247; C. B.

Firestone, *The Coasts of Illusion: A Study of Travel Tales* (New York: Harper, 1924); and T. Hiss, *The Experience of Place* (New York: Knopf, 1990).

CHAPTER 4

1. M. R. Parkman, Diary, March 5–April 23, 1871, New York Public Library.

2. Emma R. Pitman, *Mission Life in Greece and Palestine* (London: Cassell, Pelter, Galpin, 1882), p. 1.

3. See Abdul L. Tibawi, *American Interests in Syria, 1800–1901* (Oxford: Clarendon Press, 1966), p. 9; Saul P. Colbi, *Christianity in the Holy Land: Past and Present* (Tel Aviv: Am Hassefer, 1969), pp. 85–94.

4. Kenneth S. Latourette, *Missions and the American Mind* (Indianapolis: National Foundation Press, 1949), p. 28.

5. The link between faith and secular mission was tellingly illustrated by Herman Melville in his novel *White Jacket* when he wrote: "We Americans are the peculiar, chosen people . . . the Israel of our time; we bear the Ark of the liberties of the world." Herman Melville, *White-Jacket; or, The World in a Man-of-War* (Boston: L.C. Page, 1892), p. 144. Along with democracy came the motive for commerce too; see A. N. Porter, "'Commerce and Christianity': The Rise and Fall of a Nineteenth-Century Slogan," *The Historical Journal* 28 (1985): 597.

6. Abdul L. Tibawi, *British Interests in Palestine, 1800–1901* (Oxford: Oxford University Press, 1961), pp. 8–9.

7. Joseph L. Grabill, *Protestant Diplomacy and the New East: Missionary Influences on American Policy, 1810–1927* (Minneapolis: University of Minnesota Press, 1971), p. 7.

8. Levi Parsons, *The Dereliction and Restoration of the Jews* (Boston: S. T. Armstrong, 1819), p. 19.

9. Pliny Fisk, *The Holy Land, an Interesting Field of Missionary Enterprise* (Boston: S. T. Armstrong, 1819), p. 37. The works of both Parsons and Fisk appear in *Holy Land Missions and Missionaries* (New York: Arno Press, 1977).

10. L. Fawaz, "The City and the Mountain: Beirut's Political Radius in the Nineteenth Century as Revealed in the Crisis of 1860," *International Journal of Middle East Studies* 16 (1984): 489.

11. Grabill, *Protestant Diplomacy and the Near East*, p. 7.

12. Yehoshua Ben-Arieh, *The Rediscovery of the Holy Land in the Nineteenth Century* (Jerusalem: Magnes Press, 1979), p. 167.

13. Henry Whitney Bellows, *The Old World in Its New Face* (New York: Harper, 1868–69), p. 292.

14. Joseph I. Taylor, *A Gyre Thro' the Orient* (Princeton, Ill.: Republican Book & Job Printing Office, 1869), p. 272.

15. Charles G. Gordon to R. H. Barnes, June 6, 1883, Boston Public Library.

16. Barclay was one of the occupiers of Monticello after Jefferson, although his upkeep of Jefferson's neoclassical homestead was abysmal—to the point of near-ruin. See Mary Cable and Annabelle Prager, "The Levys of Monticello," *American Heritage* 29 (February–March 1978): 33.

17. D. S. Burnet, *The Jerusalem Mission* (New York: Arno Press, 1977).

18. *The Holy Land in American Protestant Life, 1800–1948: A Documentary History*, ed. R. Handy (New York: Arno Press, 1977), p. 83.

19. Ibid.

20. James T. Barclay, *The City of the Great King* (New York: Arno Press, 1977), p. 477.

21. For more extensive discussion of the influence of the American Board on the foreign policy of the United States in the period after World War I, see Grabill, *Protestant Diplomacy and the Near East*; John A. DeNovo, *American Interests and Policies in the Middle East, 1900–1939* (Minneapolis: University of Minnesota Press, 1963); and Robert L. Daniel, *American Philanthropy in the Near East, 1820–1960* (Athens: Ohio University Press, 1970).

22. Ben-Arieh, *The Rediscovery of the Holy Land*, p. 163.

23. Christina H. Jones, *American Friends in World Missions* (Elgin, Ill.: Brethren Publishing House, 1946).

24. Julius Richter, *A History of Protestant Missions in the Near East* (New York: AMS Press, 1970), p. 207.

25. Anna R. Gracey, *Eminent Missionary Women* (New York: Eaton & Mains, 1898), p. 72. See also R. Pierce Beaver, "Pioneer Single Women Missionaries," *Missionary Research Library Occasional Bulletin*, September 30, 1953; Barbara Welter, "She Hath Done What She Could: Protestant Women's Missionary Careers in Nineteenth Century America," *American Quarterly* 30 (1978): 624; and A. White, "Counting the Cost of Faith: America's Early Female Missionaries," *Church History* 57 (1988): 19.

26. Pitman, *Mission Life in Greece and Palestine*, p. 6.

27. Ibid., p. 9.

28. *Spirit of Missions* 34 (1869): 492.

29. Tibawi, *British Interests in Palestine*, p. 161.

30. *Spirit of Missions* 40 (1875): 57.

31. Ibid., 39 (1874): 42.

32. Ibid., 171.

33. Ibid., 43 (1878): 487.

34. Ibid., p. 30.

35. Angus C. MacInnes, *The Episcopal Church and the Middle East* (New York: Morehouse-Gorham, 1958), p. 13.

36. Kenneth Scott Latourette, *A History of the Expansion of Christianity* (Grand Rapids, Mich.: Zondervan, 1970), 4:76. See also W. R. Hutchinson's *Errand to the World: American Protestant Thought and Foreign Missions* (Chicago: University of Chicago Press, 1987); and H. F. May's "Missionaries and Their Doubts," *Reviews in American History* 16 (1988): 55.

37. Grabill, *Protestant Diplomacy and the Near East*, p. 6. See also Latourette's *Christianity in a Revolutionary Age* (New York: Harper, 1958–62), 1:viii–ix.

38. Kenneth Scott Latourette, *World Service* (New York: Association Press, 1957), p. 35.

39. Ibid., p. 30.

40. Grabill, *Protestant Diplomacy and the Near East*, p. ix.

41. *The Jerusalem Young Men's and Women's Christian Association* (Jerusalem: The Association, 1933), pp. 352–53. See also Latourette, *World Service*, pp. 352–53.

42. Basil Matthews, *John R. Mott* (New York: Harper, 1934); John R. Mott, *Addresses and Papers* (New York: Association Press, 1947); Charles H. Hopkins, *John R. Mott, 1865–1955* (Grand Rapids, Mich.: Eerdmans, 1978); R. V. Pierard, "John R. Mott and the Rift in the Ecumenical Movement During World War I," *Journal of Ecumenical Studies* 23 (1986): 601.

43. Ramsey, "College Evangelists and Foreign Missions: The Student Volunteer Movement, 1886–1920" (Ph.D., diss., University of California at Davis, 1988).

44. S. M. Zwemer, "The Evangelization of the Mohammedan World in This Generation," in *Students and the Modern Missionary Crusade* (New York: Student Volunteer Movement, 1906), p. 462.

45. Commission on Appraisal, Laymen's Foreign Missions Inquiry, *Rethinking Missions* (New York: Harper, 1932), p. 290.

46. See E. G. Wilson, "The Christian and Missionary Alliance: Development and Modification of Its Original Objectives" (Ph.D. diss., New York University, 1984).

47. Albert E. Thompson, *The Life of A. B. Simpson* (Brooklyn, N.Y.: Christian Alliance Publishing Co., 1920), p. 114.

48. *After Fifty Years* (Harrisburg, Pa.: Christian Publications, 1939), p. 278.

49. *World Statistics of Christian Missions* (New York: Committee of Reference and Counsel of the Foreign Missions Conference of North America, 1916).

50. Edward M. Earle, "American Missions in the Near East," *Foreign Affairs* 7 (1929): 399.

51. For the residual effect on the native populace, see A. Abu-Ghazaleh, "American Missions in Syria: A Study of American Missionary Contributions to Arab Nationalism in Nineteenth Century Syria," *Journal for Arab and Islamic Studies* 3 (1982): 5; and Joseph Grabill, "Protestant Diplomacy and Arab Nationalism, 1914–1948," *American Presbyterian* 64 (1986): 113.

52. Nelson R. Burr, *A Critical Bibliography of Religion in America* (Princeton, N.J.: Princeton University Press, 1961), pp. 404–5. This point is further embellished by James S. Udy, "Attitudes Within Protestant Churches of the Occident Towards Propagation of Christianity in the Orient" (Ph.D. diss., Boston University, 1952); and Kenneth Scott Latourette, "The Effect of the Missionary Enterprise Upon the American Mind," *Religion in Life* 13 (1944): 53.

53. Charles C. Starbuck, "A General View of Missions: The Turkish Empire," *Andover Review* 11 (1889): 97.

54. Grabill, *Protestant Diplomacy and the Near East*, p. 7.

55. Philip E. Schoenberg, "Palestine in the Year 1914" (Ph.D. diss., New York University, 1978), p. 58.

56. Latourette, *Missions and the American Mind*, p. 31.

57. Clifton Jackson Phillips, *Protestant America and the Pagan World* (Cambridge, Mass.: East Asian Research Center, Harvard University, 1969), p. vii.

58. John K. Fairbank, "Assignment for the 1970s," *American Historical Review* 74 (1969): 877.

59. Latourette, *Missions and the American Mind*, p. 33.

60. Grabill, *Protestant Diplomacy and the Near East*, p. 4.

61. Latourette, *Missions and the American Mind*, p. 34.

62. Alan Geyer, *Piety and Politics* (Richmond, Va.: John Knox Press, 1963), p. 13.

63. Grabill, *Protestant Diplomacy and the Near East*, p. 3.

64. Frank E. Manuel, *The Realities of America-Palestine Relations* (1949; reprint, Westport, Conn.: Greenwood Press, 1975), p. 3. The struggle between missionaries and Zionists in the postwar years, especially at the Paris Peace Conference, was not a two-way battle. Manuel notes that anti-Zionist Jews and American Catholics also "preferred to veto Jewish control in the land where their most sacred relics rested." Together with American business interests, these special groups collided in Paris and

had varying degrees of success in influencing American foreign policy away from Zionist interests.

CHAPTER 5

1. James Field, *America and the Mediterranean World, 1776–1882* (Princeton, N.J.: Princeton University Press, 1969), p. 81.

2. J. Augustus Johnson, "The Colonization of Palestine," *The Century* 2 (1882): 293.

3. Neil A. Silberman, *Digging for God and Country* (New York: Knopf, 1982), pp. 24–27.

4. Edward Robinson, *Later Biblical Researches in Palestine and in the Adjacent Regions* (Boston: Crocker & Brewster, 1856), p. 156.

5. The episode of the Millerites and the Minor Colony is derived from several sources, the most useful of which is the series of four articles written by Jane Marsh Parker under the title "A Fanatic and Her Mission: A Story Historical," which appeared in *The Churchman* on October 10, 17, 24, and 31, 1896. Parker wrote that her information was based on letters, notes, and miscellaneous materials compiled for a projected biography of Clorinda Minor that was never published. Parker had inherited the materials and used them instead in the articles. Also of interest is Minor's own work, *Meshullam! or, Tidings from Jerusalem* (Philadelphia: Published by the author, 1850). Also useful are Ruth Kark's "Millenarism and Agricultural Settlement in the Holy Land in the Nineteenth Century," *Journal of Historical Geography* 9 (1983): 47; and V. Lipman's *Americans and the Holy Land Through British Eyes, 1820–1917: A Documentary History* (London: Published by the author, 1989). For the Millerites, see *The Disappointed: Millerism and Millenarianism in the Nineteenth Century*, ed. Ronald L. Numbers and Jonathan M. Butler (Bloomington: Indiana University Press, 1987).

6. See Lipman, *Americans and the Holy Land Through British Eyes*, pp. 127–33.

7. Clorinda Minor, "Letter from Palestine," *The Occident* 12 (1854): 200.

8. See James Finn, *A View from Jerusalem, 1849–1858: The Consular Diary of James and Elizabeth Anne Finn*, ed. Arnold Blumberg (Rutherford, N.J.: Fairleigh Dickinson University Press, 1980).

9. According to British scholar V. Lipman, the Dicksons were Seventh-Day Baptists who were inspired by Mrs. Minor's letters as published in Philadelphia and other papers. See Lipman, *Americans and the Holy Land Through British Eyes*, p. 134. Although the Dicksons resided at Mount Hope with Mrs. Minor until the latter's death in 1855, I have decided to treat their effort as separate because their intentions differed somewhat from Mrs. Minor's original plan.

10. Herman Melville, *The Melville Log*, ed. John Leyda (New York: Harcourt, Brace, 1951), 2:548–49.

11. Finn, *A View from Jerusalem*, pp. 281, 304, 310. See also George W. Chamberlain, "A New England Crusade," *New England Magazine* 36 (1907): 195. There is at least one report that a descendant of the survivors was American novelist John Steinbeck.

12. There are several useful works on the Adams Colony, some of which have already been cited as bearing on the broader America–Holy Land relationship, such as J. Field's *America and the Mediterranean World*, David Finnie's *Pioneers East: The Early American Experience in the Middle East* (Cambridge, Mass.: Harvard University Press,

1963). In addition to J. A. Johnson's "The Colonization of Palestine," see Peter Amann's "Prophet in Zion: The Saga of George J. Adams," *New England Quarterly* 37 (1964): 477; H. Davis's "The Jaffa Colonists from Downeast," *American Quarterly* 3 (1951): 344; S. Eidelberg's "The Adams Colony in Jaffa, 1866–1869," *Midstream* 3 (1957): 52; and perhaps the most complete monographic treatment, Reed Holmes's *The Forerunners* (Independence, Mo.: Herald Publishing House, 1981).

13. Robert T. Handy, *A History of the Churches in the United States and Canada* (Oxford: Oxford University Press, 1976), p. 156.

14. Amann, "Prophet in Zion," p. 449.

15. Holmes, *The Forerunners*, p. 128.

16. Charles W. Elliott, *Remarkable Characters and Places of the Holy Land* (Hartford, Conn.: J. B. Burr, 1867), p. 586.

17. Abdul L. Tibawi, *American Interests in Syria, 1800–1901* (Oxford: Clarendon Press, 1966), p. 189.

18. *New York Times*, March 20, 1867, p. 2.

19. *New York Times*, February 17, 1867, p. 5.

20. *New York Times*, April 15, 1867, p. 5.

21. *New York Times*, August 19, 1867, p. 6.

22. *New York Times*, August 22, 1867, p. 3.

23. *New York Times*, September 2, 1867, p. 4.

24. *New York Times*, October 22, 1867, p. 2.

25. Elliott, *Remarkable Characters and Places of the Holy Land*, p. 584.

26. Ibid., p. 585.

27. John Franklin Swift, *Going to Jericho* (New York: A. Roman, 1868), p. 193.

28. Ibid., p. 197.

29. Ibid., p. 198.

30. Ibid., p. 199.

31. Ibid., p. 200.

32. Ibid., p. 204.

33. Henry Whitney Bellows, *The Old World in Its New Face* (New York: Harper, 1868–69), p. 263.

34. From a letter that appeared in the *New York Tribune* on November 2, 1867, quoted in Samuel Clemens, *Traveling with the Innocents Abroad: Mark Twain's Original Reports from Europe and the Holy Land*, ed. D. M. McKeithan (Norman: University of Oklahoma Press, 1958), p. 307.

35. *New York Times*, November 14, 1867, p. 1.

36. Letter to the *Washington Chronicle*, reprinted in the *New York Times*, January 25, 1868, p. 3.

37. *New York Times*, February 2, 1868, p. 8.

38. *Leisure Hour* 18 (1869): 506.

39. U. S. Grant to Rolla Floyd, February 17, 1878; reprinted in Holmes, *The Forerunners*, p. 254.

40. Another former colonist was Herbert Clark, who later became the Thomas Cook travel agent in Palestine and an American vice-consul. Holmes, *The Forerunners*, pp. 257–58.

41. Ustinov was the grandfather of popular British actor Peter Ustinov. Peter Ustinov, *Dear Me* (New York: Penguin Books, 1983), p. 20.

42. The medieval military orders associated with the Latin Kingdom of Jerusalem and the Crusades are unrelated to the Templars of the nineteenth century. Of the three most powerful orders (the Teutonic Knights, the Knights Hospitalers and the

Knights Templars), the Templars, or Poor Knights of Christ and of the Temple of Solomon, were founded in 1120 as a religious community pledged to the protection of Christian pilgrims in the Holy Land and who swore allegiance to the Latin Patriarch of Jerusalem.

43. The fortunes of the colony had been followed in the German weekly *Die Suddeutsche Warte*. See *Palästina-Chronik, 1853 bis 1882*, compiled by Alex Carmel (Ulm: Vaas, 1978).

44. Alex Carmel, "The German Settlers in Palestine and Their Relations with the Local Arab Population and the Jewish Community, 1868–1918," in *Studies on Palestine During the Ottoman Period*, ed. M. Maoz (Jerusalem: Magnes Press, 1975), pp. 442–65.

45. William F. Albright, *The Archaeology of Palestine* (Baltimore: Penguin Books, 1961), p. 28.

46. U.S. Consular Files, Haifa, National Archives.

47. *American Mercury* 21 (1930): 124.

48. Bertha Spafford Vester, *Our Jerusalem* (1950; reprint, New York: Arno Press, 1977), p. 25.

49. Ibid., p. 56.

50. Ibid., p. 99.

51. Charles Gordon to R. H. Barnes, June 6, 1883, Boston Public Library.

52. Vester, *Our Jerusalem*, p. 99.

53. Selma Lagerlof, *Jerusalem* (1903; reprint, Westport, Conn.: Greenwood Press, 1970).

54. Alexander Hume Ford, "Our American Colony at Jerusalem," *Appleton's Magazine* 8 (1906): 643.

CHAPTER 6

1. "Proposed Convention at Jerusalem," *The Chautauquan* 36 (1902): 11.

2. Charles G. Brumball, *A Pilgrimage to Jerusalem* (Philadelphia: Sunday School Times Co., 1905), pp. xxiii–xxiv. See also *Glimpses of Bible Lands: The Cruise of the Eight Hundred* (Boston: Central Committee, World's Fourth Sunday-school Convention, 1905); John B. Devins, "The International Sunday-School Invasion of the Holy Land," *Woman's Home Companion* 32 (February 1905): 3. The American contingent was made up of 701 people from the United States and 63 from Canada. This group sailed from Hoboken, New Jersey, on March 8, 1904, aboard the German liner *Grösser Kurfurst*. A European contingent of 258 people sailed from Marseilles on April 2, 1904, aboard the *Augusta Victoria*. The two groups met at Jerusalem in a gathering that was augmented by 491 others, putting the total attendance at over 1,500 people. See also V. Lipman, *Americans and the Holy Land Through British Eyes, 1820–1917: A Documentary History* (London: Published by the author, 1989), pp. 223–24.

3. Selah Merrill to Herbert Pierce, Dispatch 50, March 17, 1902, U.S. Consular Records, Jerusalem, National Archives.

4. Selah Merrill to Francis Loomis, Dispatch 82, May 5, 1904, U.S. Consular Records, Jerusalem, National Archives.

5. Albert Rhodes, "Our Consul at Jerusalem," *The Galaxy* 14 (1872): 437.

6. Frank E. Manuel, *The Realities of America-Palestine Relations* (1949; reprint, Westport, Conn.: Greenwood Press, 1975), p. 8.

7. Nadav Safran, *The United States and Israel* (Cambridge, Mass.: Harvard University Press, 1963), p. 36.

8. Alan Geyer, *Piety and Politics* (Richmond, Va.: John Knox Press, 1963), p. 13.

9. Charles Beard, *The Idea of National Interest* (1934; reprint, Chicago: Quadrangle Paperbacks, 1966), p. 1.

10. Elmer Plischke, *Conduct of American Diplomacy* (Princeton, N.J.: Van Nostrand Co., 1961), p. 305.

11. Leland J. Gordon, *American Relations with Turkey, 1830–1913: An Economic Interpretation* (Philadelphia: University of Pennsylvania Press, 1932); W. L. Wright, Jr., "American Relations with Turkey to 1831" (Ph.D. diss., Princeton University, 1928).

12. James A. Field, "Trade, Skills, and Sympathy: The First Century and a Half of Commerce with the Near East," *Annals of the American Academy of Political and Social Science* 401 (1972): 1.

13. The American Board had been lobbying for establishing such a consulate at Jerusalem as early as 1834. See Abdul L. Tibawi, *American Interests in Syria, 1800–1901* (Oxford: Clarendon Press, 1966), p. 189.

14. Manuel, *The Realities of America-Palestine Relations*, p. 10.

15. Abraham J. Karp, "The Zionism of Warder Cresson," *Early History of Zionism in America*, ed. Isadore S. Meyer (New York: American Jewish Historical Society, 1958), p. 3.

16. Ibid., p. 4.

17. Ibid.

18. Manuel, *The Realities of America-Palestine Relations*, p. 10.

19. James Finn, *A View from Jerusalem, 1849–1858: The Consular Diaries of James and Elizabeth Anne Finn*, ed. A. Blumberg (Rutherford, N.J.: Fairleigh Dickinson University Press, 1980), p. 277.

20. This was not a baseless charge. The British consulate had extensive entanglements with Protestant and evangelical interests. Christ Church, the first established Protestant church in the city, began as the British consul's "personal chapel" in order to circumvent local objections to the building of a new Christian structure within Jerusalem's walls. The evangelical activities of consul James Finn were another example, although by 1868, Noel Temple Moore, successor to the ebullient Finn, was pursuing a more traditional role as political protector of British interests. See Lipman, *Americans and the Holy Land Through British Eyes*, pp. 14–18; and C. E. Farah, "Protestantism and British Diplomacy in Syria," *International Journal of Middle East Studies* 7 (1976): 321.

21. Cecil Roth, *The History of the Jews of Italy* (Philadelphia: Jewish Publication Society, 1946), pp. 471–72.

22. Manuel, *The Realities of America-Palestine Relations*, pp. 26–31.

23. Hayim Tsvi Sneersohn, *Palestine and Roumania* (1872; reprint, New York: Arno Press, 1977). See also Norton B. Stern and William M. Kramer, "A Pre-Israeli Diplomat on an American Mission, 1869–1870," *Western States Jewish Historical Quarterly* 8 (1976): 232.

24. The proximity of Egypt naturally made developments there of interest to Americans in the Levant. Aside from the opening of the Suez Canal there was another, lesser known sidelight of U.S. relations with Egypt: the presence of veteran Civil War officers from North and South, employed by Egypt's Khedive Ismail for the purpose of nurturing independent Egyptian military power. See James Field, *America and the Mediterranean World, 1776–1880* (Princeton, N.J.: Princeton University Press, 1969), pp. 389–435; W. B. Hesseltine and H. C. Wolf, *The Blue and the Gray on the Nile*

(Chicago: University of Chicago Press, 1961); and P. Carbitès, *Americans in the Egyptian Army* (London: Routledge, 1938).

25. Manuel, *The Realities of America-Palestine Relations*, p. 14.

26. *U.S. Consular Reports* (1871), 1117.

27. Ibid., p. 1119.

28. Dispatch 30, April 20, 1871, U.S. Consular Records, Jerusalem, National Archives.

29. Dispatch 14, November 14, 1870, U.S. Consular Records, Jerusalem, National Archives. See also letter from Woolsey dated March 1, 1871.

30. Frank S. DeHass, *Buried Cities Recovered* (Philadelphia: Bradley, Garretson, 1882), p. 9.

31. Dispatch no. 19, November 6, 1874, U.S. Consular Records, Jerusalem, National Archives.

32. DeHass's term ended in 1877; he was followed by Joseph G. Willson (of Iowa), who served from 1877 to 1882; Selah Merrill, who served during the years 1882–85, 1891–93, and 1898–1907; Nageeb J. Arbeely (an Arab-American appointee from Tennessee), who served in 1885; Henry Gillman (a Michigan man of broad scientific interests and former head of the Detroit Public Library), who served from 1886 to 1891; Presbyterian minister Edwin S. Wallace, who served from 1893 to 1898; Thomas R. Wallace, who served from 1907 to 1910; William Coffin (a merchant and professional diplomat), who served from 1910 to 1913; and Episcopal clergyman Otis Glazebrook, who served from 1914 to 1917.

33. Edwin S. Wallace, *Jerusalem the Holy* (New York: Revell, 1898), pp. 152–53.

34. Manuel, *The Realities of America-Palestine Relations*, p. 67.

35. U.S. Department of State, *Annual Report on Foreign Commerce* (Washington, D.C., 1866), pp. 422–23.

36. Although the postwar period saw a rise in American exports to the Levant ("by 1868 illuminating oil had become America's chief export to Syria and Egypt" and "even the sacred lamps over the Prophets' tomb in Mecca are fed with oil from Pennsylvania"), still most goods were being carried aboard foreign-flag vessels and not on U.S. merchant ships. See J. Field, *America and the Mediterranean World*, pp. 311–13.

37. *U.S. Consular Reports* (1868): 591.

38. *U.S. Consular Reports* (1871): 1115.

39. Ibid.

40. "The River Jordan Water Company," November 12, 1906, U.S. Consular Reports, National Archives. It does not appear, from information in the consular archives, that the venture was very successful.

41. *New York Times*, November 14, 1879, p. 1.

42. Unnumbered report, June 24, 1905. Quoted in Clark Clifford, *The Palestine Question in American History* (New York: Arno Press, 1978), p. 4.

CHAPTER 7

1. Franklin Hoskins, *From the Nile to Nebo* (Philadelphia: Sunday School Times, 1912), p. 15. Hoskins traveled from Egypt through Sinai and up into Palestine in the spring of 1909. He traveled in the company (and through the generosity) of the Rev. John F. Goucher, founder of Baltimore's Goucher College (see Figure 2).

2. James Field, *America and the Mediterranean World, 1776–1882* (Princeton, N.J.: Princeton University Press, 1969), p. 45.

3. *Near Eastern Studies in Honor of William Foxwell Albright*, ed. Hans Goedicke (Baltimore: Johns Hopkins University Press, 1971), p. xi.

4. Born in Chile in 1891 to Methodist missionaries, Albright was indeed a legendary figure. Extremely nearsighted and with a crippled hand, Albright grew up consumed with a passion for reading and history. After undergraduate studies at Upper Iowa University, Albright literally "rode the rails" eastward to Johns Hopkins University and a stellar career as Orientalist. Albright was once described as "the world's outstanding authority on old things." See David Noel Freedman's *The Published Works of William Foxwell Albright: A Comprehensive Bibliography* (Cambridge, Mass.: American Schools of Oriental Research, 1975), p. 11.

5. See William G. Dever, *Archaeology and Biblical Studies* (Evanston, Ill.: Seabury-Western Theological Seminary, 1974); and G. Ernest Wright, "The Phenomenon of American Archaeology in the Near East," in *Near Eastern Archaeology in the Twentieth Century*, ed. James A. Sanders (Garden City, N.Y.: Doubleday, 1970).

6. See Paul A. Carter's *The Spiritual Crisis of the Gilded Age* (DeKalb: Northern Illinois University Press, 1971) for a treatment of the effects Darwinism had on the Protestant churches in industrialized, post–Civil War America; see also H. Hovenkamp's *Science and Religion in America, 1800–1860* (Philadelphia: University of Pennsylvania Press, 1978).

7. William F. Albright, *The Archaeology of Palestine and the Bible* (Cambridge, Mass.: American Schools of Oriental Research, 1974), pp. 17–18.

8. Teddy Kollek and Moshe Pearlman, *Pilgrims to the Holy Land* (New York: Harper & Row, 1970), pp. 33–34.

9. *Itinerary from Bordeaux to Jerusalem*, trans. Aubrey Stewart, annotated by C. W. Wilson (London: Palestine Pilgrims' Text Society, 1887).

10. George A. Barton, *Archaeology and the Bible* (Philadelphia: American Sunday School Union, 1937), p. 95.

11. Yehoshua Ben-Arieh, *The Rediscovery of the Holy Land in the Nineteenth Century* (Jerusalem: Magnes Press, 1974), p. 5.

12. Neil Silberman's *Digging for God and Country* (New York: Knopf, 1982) discusses this theme at length.

13. Unlike the slowly developing American interest in other areas of Near Eastern and Mediterranean culture, fields that were associated more with the heritage of Western civilization. Interest in the art and archaeology of other Mediterranean lands was confined through much of the nineteenth century to better-educated Americans, whereas Bible knowledge was almost universal. William B. Dinsmoor, "Early American Studies of Mediterranean Archaeology," in *Proceedings of the American Philosophical Society* 87 (1943): 70.

14. Field, *America and the Mediterranean World*, p. 102.

15. William F. Albright, *The Archaeology of Palestine* (London: Penguin Books, 1954), p. 19.

16. Edward Robinson and Eli Smith, *Biblical Researches in Palestine, Mount Sinai, and Arabia Petrea* (London: Crocker & Brewster, 1841).

17. Edward Robinson, *Later Biblical Research in Palestine and in the Adjacent Regions* (1856; reprint, New York: Arno Press, 1977).

18. Albright, *The Archaeology of Palestine*, p. 25.

19. Ibid., p. 20.

20. Ben-Arieh, *The Rediscovery of Palestine in the Nineteenth Century*, p. 90.

21. George Williams, *The Holy City: Historical, Topographical, and Antiquarian Notices of Jerusalem* (London: J. W. Parker, 1849).

22. See Ben-Arieh, *The Rediscovery of the Holy Land in the Nineteenth Century*, p. 133, and the source extracts and comments in V. Lipman, *Americans and the Holy Land Through British Eyes, 1820–1917: A Documentary History* (London: Published by the author, 1989), pp. 35–42.

23. Abdul L. Tibawi, *American Interests in Syria, 1800–1901* (Oxford: Clarendon Press, 1966), p. 229. Circumnavigation of the Dead Sea was a feat not yet accomplished in modern times, until Lynch's expedition. For example, Christopher Costigan, an Irishman, attempted the effort and failed, losing his life to heat stroke for the attempt in the year 1835. For earlier, unsuccessful Dead Sea attempts, see B. Kreiger's *Living Waters: Myth, History, and Politics of the Dead Sea* (New York: Continuum, 1988).

24. "Lynch, William Francis," *Dictionary of American Biography*, ed. A. Johnson et al. (New York: Scribner, 1946–58).

25. William F. Lynch, *Narrative of the United States' Expedition to the River Jordan and the Dead Sea* (Philadelphia: Lea & Blanchard, 1849), pp. 13–14. The *Narrative* was Lynch's attempt to publish a less formal account than the one presented in his *Official Report of the United States Expedition to Explore the Dead Sea and the River Jordan* (Baltimore: J. Murphy, 1852). He also wanted to be sure that his observations as head of the expedition received early and popular exposure, in order to compete with the narrative published under the editorship of E. P. Montague, *Narrative of the Late Expedition to the Dead Sea, from a Diary by One of the Party* (Philadelphia: Carey & Hart, 1849).

26. Lynch, *Narrative*, p. 502.

27. David Finnie, *Pioneers East: The Early American Experience in the Middle East* (Cambridge, Mass.: Harvard University Press, 1967), pp. 269–70.

28. Ben-Arieh, *The Rediscovery of the Holy Land in the Nineteenth Century*, p. 74.

29. Ibid., p. 183.

30. Albright, *The Archaeology of Palestine*, p. 26.

31. Elizabeth Finn, *Reminiscences of Mrs. Finn* (London: Marshall, Morgan & Scott, 1929), p. 252.

32. Albright, *The Archaeology of Palestine*, pp. 26–27.

33. *New York Times*, May 16, 1869, p. 3.

34. *New York Times*, October 6, 1868, p. 4.

35. *New York Times*, October 24, 1869, p. 3.

36. "Two Months in Palestine," *Leisure Hour* 18 (1869): 615.

37. This was William Hanna Thomson, son of American Board missionary William McClure Thomson. The elder Thomson was author of the immensely popular *The Land and the Book* (1885; reprint, Hartford, Conn.: S. S. Scranton, 1907), discussed in Chapter 4. From the age of nine, William H. Thomson was schooled in the United States, and he became a physician with the goal of eventually serving as a medical missionary. An outbreak of violence in Syria in 1859 thwarted his plans to return to the Near East, and he remained in New York City. As an Army medical examiner during the Civil War, Thomson was engaged in examining draftees in his Manhattan office when he was attacked in a melee that tumbled out into the streets and spread out of control, becoming known as the infamous New York City Draft Riots in July 1863 (cf. *The National Cyclopedia of American Biography* [Clifton, N.J.: J. T. White, 1898–1984], 23:321).

38. *New York Times*, December 11, 1868, p. 3.

39. Many of the Fund's personnel went on to other posts and assignments for the British government. In Warren's case, one of his later assignments was as chief commissioner of Scotland Yard, where he played an important role in the case of "Jack the Ripper." See Silberman, *Digging for God and Country*, p. 126.

40. *New York Times*, July 10, 1872, p. 4.

41. Albright, *The Archaeology of Palestine*, pp. 27–28.

42. Albright, *The Archaeology of Palestine and the Bible*, p. 22.

43. *New York Times*, September 18, 1883, p. 4.

44. *New York Times*, November 25, 1873, p. 2.

45. *New York Times*, July 18, 1875, p. 12.

46. Barton, *Archaeology and the Bible*, pp. 96–97.

47. John A. Paine, "Identification of Pisgah," *American Palestine Exploration Society Statement*, 1870.

48. Albright, *The Archaeology of Palestine*, p. 28.

49. Palestine Exploration Fund, Minutes of the Executive Committee, quoted in A. L. Tibawi, *American Interests in Syria*, p. 231.

50. Ibid.

51. John M. Allegro, *The Shapira Affair* (Garden City, N.Y.: Doubleday, 1965), p. 29.

52. Dispatch 32, April 28, 1871, U.S. Consular Records, National Archives.

53. Albright, *The Archaeology of Palestine*, p. 27. See also Albright's *The Archaeology of Palestine and the Bible*, p. 21.

54. See Allegro's *The Shapira Affair* and Silberman's *Digging for God and Country* for discussion of this fascinating incident. The affair ended tragically when Shapira, owner of the manuscript, was accused of forgery and deception as he tried to sell the relic to the British Museum for one million pounds. When the sale fell through, the overextended and utterly defamed Shapira committed suicide; the manuscript itself disappeared when it was in the custody of the museum.

55. Field, *America and the Mediterranean World*, pp. 336–37.

56. Albert Rhodes, "Our Consul at Jerusalem," *Galaxy* 14 (1872): 438.

57. George Ernest Wright, "The Phenomenon of American Archaeology in the Near East," *Near Eastern Archaeology in the Twentieth Century*, ed. J. A. Sanders (Garden City, N.Y.: Doubleday, 1970), p. 10.

58. Two "grand points of interest" in Jerusalem remained the special focus of readers' attentions, the site of the Temple and the Holy Sepulchre; other sites were regarded as subsidiary. Certainty about the site of the Sepulchre was considered unachievable. Only if the course of the elusive second city wall could be established would there be an indication as to whether the site was at one time outside of the city. Only then could it be said that perhaps the site was authentic. This was not so with the Temple site. Its general location within the Haram was unquestioned because of the existence of the defining retaining walls from the time of Herod and perhaps earlier. Only specific aspects, such as where the courts and buildings were in relation to the Haram's present structures, were still in question. For a contemporary view of how the Temple Mount discussion continues, see Leen Ritmeyer, "Locating the Original Temple Mount," *Biblical Archaeology Review* 18 (1992): 24.

59. "Recent Researches in Jerusalem," *Theological Eclectic* 5 (1867): 387.

60. Ibid., p. 396.

61. "Recent Researches in Palestine," *Eclectic Magazine* 6 (1867): 641. The article first appeared in the *British Quarterly* and probably was of British authorship.

62. Albright, *The Archaeology of Palestine*, p. 29.

63. Ibid.

64. Frederick Bliss's connections with the school remained strong throughout his career, since his brother Howard succeeded their father as president.

65. "Reisner, George Andrew," in *Dictionary of American Biography*, ed. A. Johnson et al. (New York: Scribner, 1946–58).

66. Henry O. Thompson, *Biblical Archaeology: The World, the Mediterranean, the Bible* (New York: Paragon House, 1987), p. 91.

67. For a historical overview of the school, see Philip J. King's *American Archaeology in the Mideast* (Philadelphia: American Schools of Oriental Research, 1983).

68. Ibid., p. 38.

69. Samuel Ives Curtiss's *Primitive Semitic Religion Today* (Chicago: Revell, 1902) is a prime example. Curtiss will be discussed further in the next chapter.

CHAPTER 8

1. "Walls of Jerusalem and the Ferris Wheel . . . Louisiana Purchase Exposition, St. Louis, U.S.A. No. 8503," stereographic slide (Bennington, Vt.: H. White, 1904).

2. Jerusalem Exhibit Company, *Prospectus* (St. Louis: The Company, 1903), p. 10. My thanks to Dr. Rechav Rubin for generously sharing with me this prospectus and other information about the Jerusalem model at St. Louis. While information about the St. Louis Fair is plentiful, information about the model, which was supposed to be dismantled after the Fair and sent on tour, has been scarce. It should also be noted that the St. Louis Fair—like many other fairs before and since—had elaborate exhibits on other geographical themes and reproductions of faraway sites. Given the nature of the image of the Holy Land, however, Jerusalem's sacred sites were inevitable as a feature of Palestine.

3. Ibid., p. 23.

4. Ibid., pp. 26–27.

5. Ibid., p. 27.

6. Ibid., p. 14.

7. John Franklin Swift, *Going to Jericho* (New York: A. Roman, 1868), p. 210.

8. J. I. Boswell, *Palestine* (New York: Philips & Hunt, 1883), p. 1. The series was designed for use by young and old, for independent study or in Lyceum Reading Unions or Chautauqua Literary and Scientific Circles.

9. Ibid., p. 16

10. Samuel Clemens, *The Innocents Abroad* (New York: New American Library, 1980), pp. 441–42.

11. Alexander Boddy, *Days in Galilee and Scenes in Judea* (London: Gay & Bird, 1900), p. 334.

12. In recent years Israeli psychologists have been exploring a phenomenon known as "Jerusalem Syndrome," a temporary aberration of mind that occurs in otherwise normal individuals who visit the Holy Land and have difficulty coping with reality. The syndrome was found to be most prevalent among American Protestants, of all the other groups of tourists visiting Israel. See, for example, *The Baltimore Sun*, April 26, 1987, p. 9A.

13. Stephen C. Ausband, *Myth and Meanings, Myth and Order* (Macon, Ga.: Mercer University Press, 1983), p. 6.

14. Ibid., p. 15.

15. Ibid., p. 51.

16. Ibid., p. 54.

17. For a discussion of this theme, see R.W.B. Lewis, *The American Adam: Innocence, Tragedy, and Tradition in the Nineteenth Century* (Chicago: University of Chicago Press, 1955).

18. Noel Barber, *The Sultans* (New York: Simon & Schuster, 1973), p. 158.

19. David Landes, "Palestine Before the Zionists," *Commentary* 61 (1976): 50.

20. Leo Postman, "Personal Values as Selective Factors in Perception," *Journal of Abnormal and Social Psychology* 43 (1948): 152.

21. C. F. Osgood and P. H. Tannenbaum, "The Principles of Congruity in the Prediction of Attitude Change," *Psychological Review* 62 (1955): 42.

22. David Lowenthal, "Past Time, Present Place: Landscape and Memory," *Geographical Review* 65 (1975): 5.

23. David Lowenthal, "The Place of the Past in the American Landscapes," in *Geographies of the Mind: Essays in Historical Geosophy in Honor of John Kirtland Wright*, ed. D. Lowenthal (New York: Oxford University Press, 1976), p. 96.

24. Lowenthal, "Past Time, Present Place," p. 8.

25. Kevin Lynch, *What Time Is This Place?* (Cambridge, Mass.: MIT Press, 1972), p. 40.

26. Vincent Kenny, *Herman Melville's "Clarel"* (Hamden, Conn.: Archon Books, 1973), p. 70.

27. Roderick Nash, *Wilderness and the American Mind* (New Haven: Yale University Press, 1974).

28. For a detailed look at the earlier English heritage, see Bernard Glassman, *Anti-Semitic Stereotypes Without Jews: Images of Jews in England, 1290–1700* (Detroit: Wayne State University Press, 1975).

29. Martin Marty, *Protestantism* (New York: Holt, Rinehart & Winston, 1972), p. 191.

30. See Harold Frisch, *The Dual Image: The Figure of the Jew in English and American Literature* (New York: Ktav, 1971).

31. "Two Months in Palestine," *Leisure Hour* 18 (1869): 636.

32. For the text of the petition, see *Christian Protagonists for Jewish Restoration*, ed. Moshe Davis (New York: Arno Press, 1977). For further information about the Blackstone Memorial as an expression of Christian Zionism, see Lawrence Epstein's *Zion's Call: Christian Contributions to the Origin and Development of Israel* (Lanham, Md.: University Press of America, 1984); Anita Lebeson's "Zionism Comes to Chicago," in *Early History of Zionism in America*, ed. I. Meyer (New York: American Jewish Historical Society, 1958); Michael Pragai's *Faith and Fulfilment: Christians and the Return to the Promised Land* (London: Valentine, Mitchell, 1985); Peter Grose's *Israel in the Mind of America* (New York: Knopf, 1983); and David Rausch's *Zionism Within Early American Fundamentalism, 1878–1918* (New York: Edwin Mellon Press, 1979).

33. For an extensive, provocative study of how similar stereotypes were applied to Islamic and Arab culture, see Edward W. Said, *Orientalism* (New York: Vintage Books, 1979).

34. William F. Albright, *History, Archaeology, and Christian Humanism* (New York: McGraw-Hill, 1964), p. 159.

35. Ibid., p. 160.

36. Samuel Ives Curtiss, *Primitive Semitic Religion Today* (Chicago: F. Revell, 1902).

37. George Adam Smith, *The Historical Geography of the Holy Land* (New York: Hodder & Stoughton, 1895).

38. Curtiss, *Primitive Semitic Religion Today*, p. 59.

39. Ibid., p. 62.

40. Albright, *History, Archaeology, and Christian Humanism*, p. 158.

41. Ibid., p. 175.

42. See Lawrence Gelfand's *The Inquiry: American Preparations for Peace, 1917–1919* (New Haven, Conn.: Yale University Press, 1963).

43. Lewis Bayles Paton, "Report on the Geography, History, Ethnology, Religions, Economics, Domestic Life, and Government of the Land of Palestine," Document 459, April 15, 1918, The Inquiry, National Archives.

44. Elihu Grant, *Palestine Our Holy Land* (Baltimore: Author, 1940), p. 3.

45. Elihu Grant, *The People of Palestine* (Philadelphia: Lippincott, 1921), which was an enlarged edition of Grant's *The Peasantry of Palestine: Life, Manners, and Customs of the Village* (Boston: Pilgrim Press, 1907).

46. William Loring Worcester, *Children of Gospel Days* (Philadelphia: American New Church Tract and Publication Society, 1897).

47. For an example, see Steven Runciman, *The Historic Role of the Christian Arabs in Palestine* (London: Longmans, for the University of Essex, 1970). Runciman appends the notion to the idea that Palestine's Christian Arabs were "enriched" by Crusader blood, a thought with obvious racial overtones.

48. H. G. Harding, *The Land of Promise* (London: Church Missionary Society, 1919), p. 111.

49. *After Fifty Years: A Record of God's Working Through the Christian and Missionary Alliance* (Harrisburg, Pa.: Christian Publications, 1939), p. 145.

50. Nadav Safran, *The United States and Israel* (Cambridge, Mass.: Harvard University Press, 1963), p. 36.

51. A. E. Thompson, *The Life of A. B. Simpson* (Brooklyn, N.Y.: Christian Alliance Publishing Co., 1920), p. 276.

52. Ellsworth Huntington, "The Future of Palestine," *Geographical Review* 7 (1919): 24. Huntington, an ordained Congregationalist minister and professor of geography at Yale, was famous for analyzing Palestine and its civilization in light of climatic change. See his *Palestine and Its Transformation* (Boston: Houghton Mifflin, 1911).

America's Holy Land, 1610–1918: A Selective Bibliography

The purpose of this extensive bibliography, and its organization, is to draw attention to the scope and depth of the relationship between Americans and the Holy Land. It updates, for the 1610–1918 period, the bibliographies previously published in this field. This bibliography has been organized into units that parallel the topical arrangement of the text. Entries have been alphabetized by author and/or title, following relevant cataloging rules used by most libraries—that is, entries for edited works are alphabetized by title, not by editor or editors.

American Backgrounds

Abell, A. I. *The Urban Impact on American Protestantism, 1865–1900.* 1943. Reprint. Hamden, Conn.: Archon Books, 1962.

Alsaeed, I. H. "The Origins and Meaning of America's Special Relationship with Israel." Ph.D. diss., University of Houston, 1989.

America and the Holy Land: A Colloquium. Jerusalem: Hebrew University, Institute for Contemporary Jewry, 1972.

American Puritan Imagination: Essays in Revaluation. Compiled by S. Bercovitch. New York: Cambridge University Press, 1974.

American Republic and Ancient Israel. New York: Arno Press, 1977.

Angeles, P. A. *Dictionary of Christian Theology.* New York: Harper & Row, 1985.

Arabs in America: Myths and Realities. Edited by B. Abu-Laban and F. T. Zeady. Wilmette, Ill.: Medina University Press International, 1975.

Arabs in the New World: Studies on Arab-American Communities. Edited by S. Y. Abraham and N. Abraham. Detroit: Wayne State University Press, 1983.

Bailyn, B. *The New England Merchants in the Seventeenth Century.* Cambridge, Mass.: Harvard University Press, 1955.

Baltzell, E. D. *The Protestant Establishment: Aristocracy and Caste in America.* New York: Random House, 1964.

Baritz, L. *City on a Hill: A History of Ideas and Myths in America*. New York: Wiley, 1964.
Barker, C. A. *American Convictions: Cycles of Public Thought, 1600–1850*. Philadelphia: Lippincott, 1970.
Bartlett, I. H. *The American Mind in the Mid-Nineteenth Century*. New York: Crowell, 1967.
Bass, C. B. *Backgrounds to Dispensationalism*. Grand Rapids, Mich.: Eerdmans, 1960.
Beale, Howard K. *Theodore Roosevelt and the Rise of America to World Power*. Baltimore: Johns Hopkins University Press, 1984.
Bellah, R. "Civil Religion in America." *Daedalus* 1 (1967): 1.
Bercovitch, S. "Rhetoric as Authority: Puritanism, the Bible, and the Myth of America." *Social Science Information* 21 (1982): 5.
———. "The Typology of America's Mission." *American Quarterly* 30 (1978): 135.
Berger, P. L. *The Noise of Solemn Assemblies*. Garden City, N.Y.: Doubleday, 1961.
Berkof, H. "Israel as a Theological Problem in the Christian Church." *Journal of Ecumenical Studies* 6 (1969): 329.
Between Belief and Transgression: Structuralist Essays in Religion, History, and Myth. Edited by M. Izard and P. Smith. Chicago: University of Chicago Press, 1982.
The Bible as a Document of the University. Edited by H. D. Betz. Chico, Calif.: Scholars Press, 1981.
The Bible in America: Essays in Cultural History. Edited by N. O. Hatch and M. A. Noll. New York: Oxford University Press, 1982.
Bible in the Medieval World: Essays in Memory of Beryl Smalley. Edited by K. Walsh and D. Wood. New York: Published for the Ecclesiastical History Society by Blackwell, 1985.
Billington, R. A. *American History After 1865*. Totowa, N.J.: Littlefield, Adams, 1974.
Bloomfield, M. H. *Alarms and Diversions: The American Mind Through American Magazines, 1900–1914*. The Hague: Mouton, 1967.
Blumenberg, H. *Work on Myth*. Cambridge, Mass.: MIT Press, 1985.
Boylan, A. M. *Sunday School: The Formation of an American Institution, 1790–1880*. New Haven: Yale University Press, 1988.
Brereton, V. L. *Training God's Army: The American Bible School, 1880–1940*. Bloomington: Indiana University Press, 1990.
Bridgman, R. "The American Studies of Henry Nash Smith." *American Scholar* 56 (1987): 259.
Brill, E. H. *The Creative Edge of American Protestantism*. New York: Seabury Press, 1966.
Brooks, C. "Notes on American Mythology." *Partisan Review* 55 (1988): 309.
Burns, E. M. *The American Idea of Mission*. New Brunswick, N.J.: Rutgers University Press, 1957.
Burton, W. L. "Protestant America and the Rebirth of Israel." *Jewish Social Studies* 26 (1964): 203.
Butler, J. *Awash in a Sea of Faith: Christianizing the American People*. Cambridge, Mass.: Harvard University Press, 1990.

Caillois, R. *Man and the Sacred*. Glencoe, Ill.: The Free Press, 1960.

Campbell, E. E. *Establishing Zion: The Mormon Church in the American West, 1847–1869*. Salt Lake City, Utah: Signature Books, 1988.

Campen, R. N. *Chautauqua Impressions: Architecture and Ambience*. Chagrin Falls, Ohio: West Summit Press, 1984.

Carter, P. A. *The Spiritual Crisis of the Gilded Age*. DeKalb, Ill.: Northern Illinois University Press, 1971.

Case, V., and R. Case. *We Called It Culture*. Garden City, N.Y.: Doubleday, 1948.

Cauthen, W. K. *The Impact of American Religious Liberalism*. New York: Harper & Row, 1962.

Chavchavadze, M. *Man's Concern with Holiness*. London: Hodder & Stoughton, 1970.

Clebsch, W. A. *American Religious Thought: A History*. Chicago: University of Chicago Press, 1973.

———. *From Sacred to Profane America*. New York: Harper & Row, 1968.

Cole, W. S. *An Interpretive History of American Foreign Relations*. Homewood, Ill.: Dorsey Press, 1974.

Coleman, R. J. *Issues of Theological Warfare: Evangelicals and Liberals*. Grand Rapids, Mich.: Eerdmans, 1972.

Collins, R. M. "David Potter's *People of Plenty* and the Recycling of Consensus History." *Reviews in American History* 16 (1988): 321.

Commager, H. S. *The American Mind*. New Haven: Yale University Press, 1950.

Crossan, D. "Antisemitism and the Gospel." *Theological Studies* 26 (1965): 193.

Crossing the Waters: Arabic-Speaking Immigrants to the United States Before 1940. Edited by E. J. Hoogland. Washington, D.C.: Smithsonian Institution Press, 1987.

Cutcliffe, S. H.; J. A. Mistichelli; and C. M. Roysdon. *Technology and Values in American Civilization: A Guide to Information Sources*. Detroit: Gale Research, 1980.

DaBoll, I. B. *Recollections of the Lyceum and Chautauqua Circuits*. Freeport, Maine: Bond Wheelwright, 1969.

Daniel, N. *Islam and the West: The Making of an Image*. Edinburgh: University Press, 1960.

Daniel, R. L. "American Influences in the Near East Before 1861." *American Quarterly* 16 (1964): 72.

Darrah, W. C. *Stereo Views: A History of Stereographs in America and Their Collection*. Gettysburg, Pa.: Author, 1964.

Davies, W. D. *The Gospel and the Land: Early Christianity and Jewish Territorial Doctrine*. Berkeley and Los Angeles: University of California Press, 1974.

———. *The Territorial Dimension of Judaism*. Berkeley and Los Angeles: University of California Press, 1981.

Demsky, R., and O. Zimmer. "America and the Holy Land: A Select Bibliography." *Jerusalem Cathedra* 3 (1983): 327.

DeNovo, J. A. *American Interests and Policies in the Middle East, 1900–1939*. Minneapolis: University of Minnesota Press, 1963.

DeYoung, J. C. *Jerusalem in the New Testament*. Kampen: J. H. Kok, 1960.

Dictionary of American Biography. Edited by A. Johnson et al. New York: Scribner, 1946–58.

Dobschutz, E. *The Influence of the Bible on Civilization*. New York: F. Ungar, 1959.

Dorfman, J. *The Economic Mind in American Civilization*. 1946–59. Reprint. New York: A. M. Kelly, 1966–69.

Dwight, T. *The Conquest of Canaan: A Poem in Eleven Books*. New York: AMS Press, 1971. Reprint of the 1785 edition published by E. Babcock, Hartford.

The Education of American Ministers. New York: Institute of Social and Religious Research, 1934.

Encyclopedia of Theology: A Concise Sacramentum Mundi. Edited by K. Rahner. London: Burns & Cates, 1975.

Epstein, L. J. *Zion's Call: Christian Contributions to the Origins and Development of Israel*. Lanham, Md.: University Press of America, 1984.

Epstein, M. *The Early History of the Levant Company*. 1908. Reprint. New York: A. M. Kelly, 1968.

Feldman, E. Y. *The American Catholic Press and the Jewish State, 1917–1959*. New York: Ktav, 1977.

Ferst, B. "The Chronicles of Bible-Science: A Short History of People Who Take the Good Book for a Science Textbook." *Journal of American Culture* 8 (1985): 27.

Field, J. *America and the Mediterranean World, 1776–1882*. Princeton: Princeton University Press, 1969.

Fink, R. *America and Palestine*. New York: American Zionist Emergency Council, 1944.

Finke, R., and R. Stark. "Turning Pews into People: Estimating Nineteenth-Century Church Membership." *Journal of the Scientific Study of Religion* 25 (1986): 180.

Finnie, D. H. *Pioneers East: The Early American Experience in the Middle East*. Cambridge, Mass.: Harvard University Press, 1967.

Fisch, H. *The Dual Image: The Figure of the Jew in English and American Literature*. New York: Ktav, 1971.

Fishman, H. *American Protestantism and a Jewish State*. Detroit: Wayne State University Press, 1973.

Foster, F. H. *The Modern Movement in American Theology*. 1939. Reprint. Freeport, N.Y.: Books for Libraries Press, 1969.

Francaviglia, R. V. *The Mormon Landscape: Existence, Creation, and Perception of a Unique Image in the American West*. New York: AMS Press, 1978.

Franklin, J. H. *Reconstruction: After the Civil War*. Chicago: University of Chicago Press, 1961.

Freitag, R. S. *The Star of Bethlehem: A List of References*. Washington, D.C.: Library of Congress, 1979.

Friedman, J. *The Most Ancient Testimony: Sixteenth-Century Christian-Hebraica in the Age of Renaissance Nostalgia*. Athens, Ohio: Ohio University Press, 1983.

Gabriel, R. H. *Christianity and Modern Thought*. New Haven: Yale University Press, 1924.

———. *The Course of American Democratic Thought*. New York: Ronald Press, 1956.

Gaer, J., and B. Siegel. *The Puritan Heritage: America's Roots in the Bible.* New York: New American Library, 1964.

Galston, W. A. "Tocqueville on Liberalism and Religion." *Social Research* 54 (1987): 499.

Garraty, J. A. *The Transformation of American Society, 1870–1890.* New York: Harper & Row, 1968.

Garrison, W. E. *The March of Faith: The Story of Religion in America Since 1865.* 1933. Reprint. Westport, Conn.: Greenwood Press, 1971.

Gaston, P. L. *No Stone on Another: Studies in the Significance of the Fall of Jerusalem in the Synoptic Gospels.* Leiden: Brill, 1970.

———. "Text and Textbook: The Bible as Literature." *Papers on Language and Literature* 23 (1987): 104.

Gaustad, E. S. *A Religious History of America.* New York: Harper & Row, 1966.

Geyer, A. F. *Piety and Politics.* Richmond, Va.: John Knox Press, 1963.

Gibson, M. T. "The Study of the Bible in the Middle Ages." *Journal of Ecclesiastical History* 39 (1988): 230.

The Gilded Age and After. Edited by J. A. DeNovo. New York: Scribner, 1972.

Ginger, R. *The Age of Excess: The United States from 1877 to 1914.* New York: Macmillan, 1975.

Gordh, G. R. *Christian Faith and Its Cultural Expression.* Englewood Cliffs, N.J.: Prentice-Hall, 1962.

Gould, J. E. *The Chautauqua Movement: An Episode in the Continuing American Revolution.* New York: State University of New York, 1961.

Grant, F. C. "Bible and Civilization." *Religion in Life* 22 (1953): 431.

Greven, P. *The Protestant Temperament: Patterns of Child-Rearing, Religious Experience, and the Self in Early America.* 1977. Reprint. Chicago: University of Chicago Press, 1988.

Grose, P. *Israel in the Mind of America.* New York: Knopf, 1983.

Guide to America–Holy Land Studies. Edited by N. Kaganoff et al. New York: Arno Press and Praeger Publishers, 1980–84.

Gunn, G. *The Interpretation of Otherness: Literature, Religion, and the American Imagination.* New York: Oxford University Press, 1979.

Hall, D. B. *Worlds of Wonder, Days of Judgment: Popular Religious Belief in Early New England.* New York: Knopf, 1989.

Hals, R. M. "The Promise and the Land." In *Speaking of God Today: Jews and Lutherans in Conversation,* edited by P. D. Opsahl and M. H. Tanenbaum. Philadelphia: Fortress Press, 1974.

Hamilton, G. E. *Oliver Wendell Holmes: His Pioneer Stereoscope and the Later Industry.* New York: Newcomen Society of North America, 1949.

Handy, R. *A Christian America: Protestant Hopes and Historical Realities.* New York: Oxford University Press, 1984.

———. *A History of the Churches in the United States and Canada.* Oxford: Oxford University Press, 1976.

———. "Studies in the Interrelationships Between America and the Holy Land." *Journal of Church History* 13 (1971): 283.

Harap, L. *The Image of the Jew in American Literature: From Early Republic to Mass Immigration.* Philadelphia: Jewish Publication Society, 1974.

Hardon, J. A. *The Spirit and Origins of American Protestantism.* Dayton, Ohio: Pflaum Press, 1968.

272   A Selective Bibliography

Harrison, H. P. *Culture Under Canvass: The Story of Tent Chautauqua*. West-port, Conn.: Greenwood Press, 1978. Reprint of the 1958 edition published by Hastings House, New York.
Hatch, N. O. *The Democratization of American Christianity*. New Haven: Yale University Press, 1989.
Hayes, T. W. "Nicholas of Cusa and Popular Literacy in Seventeenth-Century England." *Studies in Philology* 84 (1987): 80.
Hays, S. P. *The Response to Industrialism, 1885–1914*. Chicago: University of Chicago Press, 1957.
Hesseltine, W. *The Blue and the Gray on the Nile*. Chicago: University of Chicago Press, 1961.
Higgs, R. *The Transformation of the American Economy, 1865–1914*. New York: Wiley, 1971.
Hill, D. S. *The Education and Problems of the Protestant Ministry*. Worcester, Mass.: Clark University Press, 1908.
Hillers, D. R. *Covenant: The History of a Biblical Idea*. Baltimore: Johns Hopkins University Press, 1969.
Himes, C. F. *Theory, History, and Construction of the Stereoscope*. Philadelphia: Franklin Institute, 1872.
Hoge, D. R. *Division in the Protestant House*. Philadelphia: Westminster Press, 1976.
Holmes, Oliver W. *The Stereoscope and Stereoscopic Photographs*. New York: Underwood & Underwood, 1899.
Holstun, J. *A Rational Millennium: Puritan Utopias of Seventeenth-Century England and America*. New York: Oxford University Press, 1987.
The Holy Land in American Protestant Life, 1800–1948: A Documentary History. Edited by R. Handy. New York: Arno Press, 1981.
Hood, Louis. "The Ancient and Modern Jew." *New Englander* 37 (1878): 674.
Hopkins, C. H. *The Rise of the Social Gospel in American Protestantism, 1865–1915*. New Haven: Yale University Press, 1940.
Hudson, W. *American Protestantism*. Chicago: University of Chicago Press, 1961.
Hughes, R. T., and C. L. Allen. *Illusions of Innocence: Protestant Primitivism in America, 1630–1875*. Chicago: University of Chicago Press, 1988.
Hunt, G. *The History of the Great Seal of the United States*. Washington, D.C.: U.S. Department of State, 1909.
Hurlbut, Jesse L. *The Story of Chautauqua*. New York: Putnam, 1921.
Hutchinson, W. R. *The Modernist Impulse in American Protestantism*. Cambridge, Mass.: Harvard University Press, 1976.
In the Great Tradition: Essays on Pluralism, Voluntarism, and Revivalism. Valley Forge, Pa.: Judson Press, 1982.
Irwin, A. L. *Three Taps of the Gavel: The Chautauqua Story*. Chautauqua, N.Y.: Chautauqua Institution, 1977.
Isaac, J. *The Teaching of Contempt*. New York: Holt, Rinehart & Winston, 1964.
Israel: Its Role in Civilization. Edited by M. Davis. New York: Harper, 1956.
Jenkins, H. F. *Two Points of View: The History of the Parlor Stereoscope*. Uniontown, Pa.: Warman, 1973.

Jones, H. M. *The Age of Energy: Varieties of American Experience, 1865–1915*. New York: Viking Press, 1971.

Jones, J. *Wonders of the Stereoscope*. New York: Knopf, 1976.

Jones, O. R. *The Concept of Holiness*. New York: Macmillan, 1961.

Kammen, M. *People of Paradox: An Inquiry Concerning the Origins of American Civilization*. Ithaca, N.Y.: Cornell University Press, 1972.

Katsh, A. I. *Hebraic Contributions to American Life*. New York: New York University Bookstore, 1941.

Kelly, R. L. *Theological Education in America*. New York: George H. Doran, 1924.

Kipling, Rudyard. *Abaft the Funnel*. New York: B. W. Dodge, 1909.

Kirkland, E. C. *Dream and Thought in the Business Community, 1860–1900*. Ithaca, N.Y.: Cornell University Press, 1956.

Klein, C. *Anti-Judaism in Christian Theology*. Philadelphia: Fortress Press, 1978.

Knott, J. R. *The Sword of the Spirit: Puritan Responses to the Bible*. Chicago: University of Chicago Press, 1980.

Kraft, W. F. *The Search for the Holy*. Philadelphia: Westminster Press, 1971.

Kuklick, B. "Myth and Symbol in American Studies." *American Quarterly* 24 (1972): 435.

La Haye, T. F. *The Bible's Influence on American History*. San Diego: Master Books, 1976.

Langley, L. D. "Jacksonian America and the Ottoman Empire." *Muslim World* 68 (1978): 46.

Lankard, F. G. *The Bible and the Life and Ideals of the English-speaking People*. New York: American Bible Society, 1936.

Leighly, J. "Biblical Place Names in the United States." *Names* 27 (1979): 46.

Lerner, M. *America as a Civilization*. New York: Simon & Schuster, 1957.

Lerner, R. et al. "Christian Religious Elites." *Public Opinion* 11 (1989): 54.

Levine, L. W. *Highbrow/Lowbrow: The Emergence of Cultural Hierarchy in America*. Cambridge, Mass.: Harvard University Press, 1988.

Levine, S. H. "Changing Concepts of Palestine in American Literature to 1867." Ph.D. diss., New York University, 1953.

Lewis, R. W. *The American Adam: Innocence, Tragedy, and Tradition in the Nineteenth Century*. Chicago: University of Chicago Press, 1955.

Liljegren, S. B. *The Revolt Against Romanticism in American Literature as Evidenced in the Works of S. L. Clemens*. New York: Haskell House, 1964.

Lipman, V. *Americans and the Holy Land Through British Eyes, 1820–1917: A Documentary History*. London: Author, 1989.

Littell, F. H. *From State Church to Pluralism*. New York: Macmillan, 1971.

Louisiana Purchase Exposition (St. Louis, Mo., 1904). *The Greatest of Expositions Completely Illustrated*. St. Louis: Official Photographic Co., 1904.

Lowance, M. I. *The Language of Canaan: Metaphor and Symbol in New England from the Puritans to the Transcendentalists*. Cambridge, Mass.: Harvard University Press, 1980.

Lowenberg, B. J. "Darwinism Comes to America, 1859–1900." *Mississippi Valley Historical Review* 28 (1941): 339.

Lynes, R. *The Domesticated Americans*. New York: Harper & Row, 1963.

McClure, J. G. *The Supreme Book of Mankind: The Origin and Influence of the English Bible*. New York: Scribner, 1930.

274   A Selective Bibliography

McFaden, J. D. *Our Bible, Our Church, and Our Country*. Philadelphia: Brethren Tract Society, 1889.
MacGillivray, J. D. *Bible Studies on Sanctification and Holiness*. Chicago: Revell, 1889.
McKelvey, B. *The Urbanization of America, 1860–1915*. New Brunswick, N.J.: Rutgers University Press, 1963.
McLoughlin, W. G. "Pietism and the American Character." *American Quarterly* 17 (1965): 163.
———. *Revivals, Awakenings, and Reform*. Chicago: University of Chicago Press, 1978.
Maddow, B. *A Sunday Between Wars: The Course of American Life from 1865 to 1917*. New York: Norton, 1979.
Mahler, R. "The Historical Background of Pre-Zionism in America and Its Continuity." In *A Bicentennial Festschrift for Jacob Rader Marcus*, edited by B. Korn. New York: Ktav, 1976.
Malachy, Y. *American Fundamentalism and Israel*. Jerusalem: Hebrew University, Institute of Contemporary Jewry, 1978.
Marsden, G. M. *Fundamentalism and American Culture: The Shaping of Twentieth-Century Evangelicalism, 1870–1925*. New York: Oxford University Press, 1980.
Marty, M. E. *Modern American Religion*. Chicago: University of Chicago Press, 1986–91.
———. *Protestantism*. New York: Holt, Rinehart & Winston, 1962.
———. *Righteous Empire*. New York: Dial Press, 1970.
May, H. F. *The End of American Innocence: A Study of the First Years of Our Own Time, 1912–1917*. New York: Knopf, 1959.
———. *Ideas, Faiths, and Feelings: Essays on American Intellectual and Religious History, 1952–1982*. New York: Oxford University Press, 1983.
———. *Protestant Churches and Industrial America*. 1949. Reprint. New York: Octagon Books, 1963.
Mead, F. S. *See These Banners Go: The Study of the Protestant Churches in America*. Indianapolis: Bobbs-Merrill, 1936.
Mead, S. E. "Denominationalism: The Shape of Protestantism in America." *Church History* 23 (1954): 291.
———. *The Lively Experiment: The Shaping of Christianity in America*. New York: Harper & Row, 1963.
Mendenhall, G. E. *The Tenth Generation: The Origins of the Biblical Tradition*. Baltimore: Johns Hopkins University Press, 1973.
Merrill, J. L. "The Bible and the American Temperance Movement: Text, Context, and Pretext." *Harvard Theological Review* 81 (1988): 145.
Millenarianism and Messianism in English Literature and Thought, 1650–1800. Edited by R. H. Popkin. New York: E. J. Brill, 1988.
Miller, W. L. *The Protestant and Politics*. Philadelphia: Westminster Press, 1958.
Mirsky, D. "Hebrew in the United States." *Herzl Yearbook* 5 (1963): 83.
Miyakawa, T. S. "American Frontier and Protestantism." Ph.D. diss., Columbia University, 1952.
Moore, R. L. *Religious Outsiders and the Making of Americans*. New York: Oxford University Press, 1986.

Moorhead, J. H. "Perry Miller's Jeremiad Against Nineteenth-Century Protestantism." *South Atlantic Quarterly* 86 (1987): 312.

Morey, A. J. "American Myth and Biblical Interpretation in the Fiction of Harriet Beecher Stowe and Mary E. Wilkens Freeman." *Journal of the American Academy of Religion* 55 (1987): 471.

Morrison, T. *Chautauqua: A Center for Education, Religion, and the Arts in America*. Chicago: University of Chicago Press, 1974.

Morsy, S. A. "The Bad, the Ugly, the Super-Rich, and the Exceptional Moderate: U.S. Popular Images of the Arabs." *Journal of Popular Culture* 20 (1986): 13.

Morton, T. *New English Canaan*. New York: Da Capo Press, 1969. Reprint of the 1637 edition published by J. F. Stam, Amsterdam.

Mousa, I. S. "The Arab Image: The *New York Times*, 1916–1948." *Gazette: International Journal for Mass Communication Studies* 40 (1987): 101.

Myers, G. *History of Bigotry in the United States*. New York: Random House, 1943.

The Myths We Live By. Edited by R. Samuel and P. Thompson. New York: Routledge, 1990.

Nelson, L. E. *Our Roving Bible: Tracking Its Influence Through English and American Life*. New York: Abingdon-Cokesbury, 1945.

Nevins, A. *The Emergence of Modern America, 1865–1878*. New York: Macmillan, 1927.

Newman, L. I. *Anglo-Saxon and Jew*. New York: Block, 1923.

Nichols, J. H. *Romanticism in American Theology*. Chicago: University of Chicago Press, 1961.

Noble, D. W. *The Progressive Mind, 1890–1917*. Chicago: Rand McNally, 1970.

———. "Religion of Progress in America, 1890–1914." *Social Research* 22 (1955): 417.

Noll, M. A. *Between Faith and Criticism: Evangelicals, Scholarship, and the Bible in America*. New York: Harper & Row, 1986.

———. "The Bible in America." *Journal of Biblical Literature* 106 (1987): 493.

Norton, W. *Church and Newspaper*. New York: Macmillan, 1930.

Obeidat, M. "The Muslim Orient in the American Literary Scene: A Bibliographical Note." *American Studies International* 26 (1988): 25.

O'Brien, C. C. *God Land: Reflections on Religion and Nationalism*. Cambridge, Mass.: Harvard University Press, 1988.

Ost, Axel B. *The Bible and Our National Life*. Minneapolis: Minneapolis Veckoblad, 1921.

Palestine: Mohammedan Holy Land. Edited by C. D. Matthews. 1949. Reprint. New York: AMS Press, 1980.

Parkes, J. N. *The Conflict of the Church and the Synagogue*. New York: Hermon Press, 1974.

Parrington, V. L. *Main Currents in American Thought*. New York: Harcourt Press, 1939.

Peckham, M. *Romanticism: The Culture of the Nineteenth Century*. New York: G. Braziller, 1965.

Penn, M. J., and D. E. Schoen. "American Attitudes Toward the Middle East." *Public Opinion* 11 (1988): 45.

Perry, B. *The American Mind.* 1912. Reprint. Port Washington, N.Y.: Kennikat Press, 1968.

Pierard, R. V. *Civil Religion and the Presidency.* Grand Rapids, Mich.: Academie Books, 1988.

"Present Knowledge and Influence of the Bible." *Biblical World* 21 (1903): 243.

Reading in America: Literature and Social History. Edited by C. N. Davidson. Baltimore: Johns Hopkins University Press, 1989.

Readings on Concepts of Zion. Edited by P. A. Wellington. Independence, Mo.: Herald, 1973.

The Rich, the Well Born, and the Powerful: Elites and Upper Classes in History. Edited by F. C. Jaher. Urbana: University of Illinois Press, 1973.

Roberts, W. H. *The Reaction of American Protestant Churches to the Darwinian Philosophy, 1860–1900.* Chicago: Author, 1938.

Robinson, D. *American Apocalypses: The Image of the End of the World in American Literature.* Baltimore: Johns Hopkins University Press, 1985.

Rosedale, H. G. *Queen Elizabeth and the Levant Company.* London: H. Froude, 1904.

Rosenberg, C. E. *No Other Gods: On Science and American Thought.* Baltimore: Johns Hopkins University Press, 1976.

Roston, M. *Prophet and Poet: The Bible and the Growth of Romanticism.* Evanston, Ill.: Northwestern University Press, 1965.

Rowe, H. K. *History of Andover Theological Seminary.* Newton, Mass.: Andover Theological Seminary, 1933.

Roy, R. L. *Apostles of Discord.* Boston: Beacon Press, 1953.

Rudisill, R. *Mirror Image: The Influence of the Daguerreotype on American Society.* Albuquerque: University of New Mexico Press, 1971.

Rust, J. B. *Modernism and the Reformation.* New York: Revell, 1914.

Sandeen, E. R. *The Roots of Fundamentalism: British and American Millenarianism, 1800–1930.* Chicago: University of Chicago Press, 1970.

Sayre, H. M. "Surveying the Vast Profound: The Panoramic Landscape in American Consciousness." *Massachusetts Review* 24 (1983): 723.

Schlesinger, A. M. *The Rise of the City, 1878–1898.* 1933. Reprint. Chicago: Quadrangle Books, 1971.

Schneidau, H. N. *Sacred Discontent: The Bible and Western Tradition.* Berkeley and Los Angeles: University of California Press, 1977.

Shaban, F. *Islam and Arabs in Early American Thought: Roots of Orientalism in America.* Durham, N.C.: Acorn Press, 1991.

Shriver, W. P. *Immigrant Forces.* New York: Missionary Education Movement of the United States and Canada, 1913.

Simms, P. M. *The Bible in America.* New York: Wilson-Erikson, 1936.

Sivan, G. *The Bible and Civilization.* Jerusalem: Keter, 1973.

Smalley, B. *The Study of the Bible in the Middle Ages.* Oxford: Oxford University Press, 1941.

Smith, P. "Anglo-American Religion and Hegemonic Change in the World System, 1870–1980." *British Journal of Sociology* 37 (1986): 88.

Smith, T. L. "Protestant Schooling and American Nationality, 1800–1850." *Journal of American History* 53 (1967): 679.

———. *Revivalism and Social Reform: American Protestantism on the Eve of the Civil War.* Baltimore: Johns Hopkins University Press, 1980.

Snyder, E. E. "The Chautauqua Movement in Popular Culture: A Sociological Analysis." *Journal of American Culture* 8 (1985): 79.

Solberg, W. U. *Redeem the Time: The Puritan Sabbath in Early America.* Cambridge, Mass.: Harvard University Press, 1977.

"Some Influences of Hebraic Culture on Modern Social Organization." *American Journal of Sociology* 71 (1966): 384.

Spears, M. K. "Tocqueville in 1989." *Hudson Review* 42 (1989): 369.

Stavely, K.W.F. *Puritan Legacies: Paradise Lost and the New England Tradition, 1630–1890.* Ithaca, N.Y.: Cornell University Press, 1987.

Stedman, Murray S. *Religion and Politics in America.* New York: Harcourt, Brace & World, 1964.

Stevenson, L. L. *Scholarly Means to Evangelical Ends: The New Haven Scholars and the Transformation of Higher Learning in America, 1830–1890.* Baltimore: Johns Hopkins University Press, 1986.

Stokes, A. P., and L. Pfeffer. *Church and State in the United States.* New York: Harper & Row, 1964.

Stookey, R. W. *America and the Arab States: An Uneasy Encounter.* New York: Wiley, 1975.

———. "The Holy Land: The American Experience, the Christian Concern." *Middle East Journal* 30 (1976): 351.

Suleiman, M. W. *The Arabs in the Mind of America.* Brattleboro, Vt.: Amana Books, 1988.

Szasz, F. M. *The Divided Mind of Protestant America, 1880–1930.* University, Ala.: University of Alabama Press, 1982.

Tarshish, A. "Jew and Christian in a New Society: Some Aspects of Jewish-Christian Relationships in the United States, 1848–1881." In *A Bicentennial Festschrift for Jacob Rader Marcus,* edited by B. Korn. New York: Ktav, 1976.

Tiplady, T. *The Influence of the Bible on History, Literature, and Oratory.* New York: Revell, 1924.

Tocqueville, A. *Democracy in America.* New York: Knopf, 1945.

Trachtenberg, A. "Myth and Symbol." *Massachusetts Review* 25 (1984): 667.

Trumbull, H. C. *Sunday School: Its Origin, Mission, Methods, and Auxiliaries.* Philadelphia: J. D. Wattles, 1893.

Tuchman, B. *Bible and Sword.* New York: New York University Press, 1956.

Turner, J. C. *Without God, Without Creed: The Origins of Unbelief in America.* Baltimore: Johns Hopkins University Press, 1985.

Tuveson, E. L. *Redeemer Nation: The Idea of America's Millennial Role.* Chicago: University of Chicago Press, 1968.

Upchurch, H. M. *Toward the Study of Communities of Americans Overseas.* Alexandria, Va.: Human Resources Research Organization, 1970.

Valentine, A. C. *1913: America Between Two Worlds.* New York: Macmillan, 1962.

Van de Wetering, M. "The Popular Concept of 'Home' in Nineteenth-Century America." *Journal of American Studies* 18 (1984): 5.

Van Rooden, P. T. *Theology, Biblical Scholarship, and Rabbinical Studies in the Seventeenth Century.* New York: E. J. Brill, 1989.

Verite, M. "Restoration of the Jews in English Protestant Thought, 1790–1840." *Middle Eastern Studies* 8 (1972): 2.

Vincent, John H. *The Chautauqua Movement*. 1885. Reprint. Freeport, N.Y.: Books for Libraries Press, 1971.

Vincent, L. *John Heyl Vincent: A Biographical Sketch*. New York: Macmillan, 1925.

Vogt, V. O. *Cult and Culture*. New York: Macmillan, 1951.

Walker, P. *Holy City, Holy Places? Christian Attitudes to Jerusalem and the Holy Land in the Fourth Century*. New York: Oxford University Press, 1990.

Ward, D. *Cities and Immigrants: A Geography of Change in Nineteenth-Century America*. New York: Oxford University Press, 1971.

Weber, T. P. *Living in the Shadow of the Second Coming: American Premillennialism, 1875–1982*. Chicago: University of Chicago Press, 1987.

Weinfeld, M. *The Promise of the Land: The Inheritance of the Land of Canaan by the Israelites*. Berkeley and Los Angeles: University of California Press, 1992.

Weisburger, F. P. *Ordeal of Faith: The Crisis of Church-going America, 1865–1900*. New York: Philosophical Library, 1959.

Welch, C. *Protestant Thought in the Nineteenth Century*. New Haven: Yale University Press, 1972–85.

Werblowsky, R.J.Z. *The Meaning of Jerusalem to Jews, Christians, and Muslims*. Jerusalem: Israel Universities Study Group for Middle Eastern Affairs, 1978.

Wiebe, R. H. *The Search for Order, 1877–1920*. New York: Hill & Wang, 1967.

Williams, P. W. *Popular Religion in America: Symbolic Change and the Modernization Process in Historical Perspective*. Urbana: University of Illinois Press, 1989.

Williams, W. A. *The Roots of Modern American Empire*. New York: Random House, 1969.

Wilson, J. F. *Public Religion in American Culture*. Philadelphia: Temple University Press, 1979.

Wilson, W. *The Bible and Progress*. New York: Globe Lithographing, 1911.

Wish, H. *The American Historian: A Social-Intellectual History of the Writing of the American Past*. 1960. Reprint. Westport, Conn.: Greenwood Press, 1983.

With Eyes Toward Zion: Scholars Colloquium on America–Holy Land Studies. Edited by M. Davis. Papers presented at the colloquium, Washington, D.C., 1975. New York: Arno Press, 1977.

With Eyes Toward Zion II: Themes and Sources in the Archives of the United States, Great Britain, Turkey, and Israel. Edited by M. Davis. Papers presented at the Second International Scholars Colloquium on America–Holy Land Studies, Washington, D.C., 1983. New York: Praeger, 1986.

With Eyes Toward Zion–III: Western Societies and the Holy Land. Papers from the July 1990 Workshop of the International Center for University Teaching of Jewish Civilization, held in Jerusalem. Edited by M. Davis and Y. Ben-Arieh. New York: Praeger, 1991.

Wood, A. C. *A History of the Levant Company*. New York: Barnes & Noble, 1964.

Wood, I. F., and E. Grant. *The Bible as Literature*. New York: Abingdon Press, 1914.

Wright, L. C. *United States Policy Toward Egypt, 1830–1914*. New York: Exposition Press, 1969.

Holy Land Realities

Aaronsohn, A. "Saifna Ahmar, Ya Sultan." *Atlantic* 118 (1916): 1.
———. *With the Turks in Palestine*. Boston: Houghton Mifflin, 1916.
Abu-Lughod, I. A. *Arab Rediscovery of Europe: A Study in Cultural Encounters*. Princeton: Princeton University Press, 1963.
Ader, J. H. *Histoire de l'expedition d'Egypte et de Syrie*. Paris: A. Dupont, 1826.
Adler, F. "State and Prospects of the Jews." *North American Review* 125 (1877): 133.
Ahmed, A. S. *Discovering Islam: Making Sense of Muslim History and Society*. New York: Routledge & Kegan Paul, 1988.
Ahmed, F. *The Young Turks*. Oxford: Clarendon Press, 1969.
Alderson, A. D. *The Structure of the Ottoman Dynasty*. Oxford: Clarendon Press, 1956.
Alexander, E. "Where Is Zion?" *Commentary* 86 (September 1988): 47.
Allenby, E. H. "Jerusalem Campaign." *Current History Magazine* 8 (1918): 153.
Anderson, M. S. *The Eastern Question, 1774–1923*. London: Macmillan, 1966.
Antonius, G. *The Arab Awakening*. 1946. Reprint. New York: Paragon Books, 1979.
Avitsur, S. *Haye Yom-yom be-Erets Yisra'el be-Me'ah ha-Tisha Esreh*. Tel Aviv: Am ha-Sefer, 1972.
Ayalon, A. "The Arab Discovery of America in the Nineteenth Century." *Middle Eastern Studies* 20 (1984): 5.
Badeau, J. S. *The American Approach to the Arab World*. New York: Published for the Council on Foreign Relations by Harper & Row, 1968.
Barber, N. *The Sultans*. New York: Simon & Schuster, 1973.
Baron, S. W. "The Jewish Question in the Nineteenth Century." *Journal of Modern History* 10 (1938): 51.
———. "Palestinian Messengers in America, 1849–1879: A Record of Four Journeys." *Jewish Social Studies* 5 (1943): 115.
Baroni, A. "General Allenby in Palestine." *Asia* 18 (1918): 899.
Bat Ye'or. *The Dhimmi: A Historical Survey of Jews and Christians Under Islam*. Rutherford, N.J.: Fairleigh Dickinson University Press, 1984.
Beckingham, C. F. "A Jewish Franciscan in the Ottoman Empire." *Asian Affairs* 18 (1987): 257.
Bein, A. *The Return to the Soil: A History of Jewish Settlement in Israel*. Jerusalem: Youth and Hechalutz Department of the Zionist Organization, 1952.
Ben-Arieh, Y. "The Growth of Jerusalem in the Nineteenth Century." *Annals of the Association of American Geographers* 65 (1975): 254.
———. *Jerusalem in the Nineteenth Century: Emergence of the New City*. Jerusalem: Yad Izhak Ben-Zvi Institute, 1986.
———. *Jerusalem in the Nineteenth Century: The Old City*. Jerusalem: Yad Izhak Ben-Zvi Institute, 1984.

Bensinger, G. J. "Palestine in German Thought and Action, 1871–1914." Ph.D. diss., Loyola University of Chicago, 1971.

Ben-Zvi, Y. *Erets-Yisra'el ve-Yishuvah bi-Yeme ha-Shilton ha-Otmani.* Jerusalem: Yad Izhak Ben-Zvi Institute, 1975.

Bernoyer, F. M. *Avec Bonaparte en Egypte et en Syrie.* Abbeville: Les Presses francaises, 1976.

Bijlefeld, W. A. "European Christians and the World of the Mamluks." *Muslim World* 73 (1983): 208.

Black, D. *Red Dust: An Australian Trooper in Palestine.* London: J. Cape, 1931.

Bluett, A. *With Our Army in Palestine.* London: A. Melrose, 1919.

Blumberg, A. *Zion Before Zionism, 1838–1880.* Syracuse, N.Y.: Syracuse University Press, 1985.

Blumgarten, S. *The Feet of the Messenger.* 1923. Reprint. New York: Arno Press, 1977.

Brereton, F. S. *With Allenby in Palestine: A Story of the Latest Crusade.* London: Blackie, 1920.

Brigham, C. H. "Jews in Palestine." *North American Review* 95 (1862): 331.

Burrell, D. B. "Journeys of Faith in the Holy Land." *America* 152 (1985): 229.

Burstein, M. *Self-Government of the Jews in Palestine Since 1904.* 1934. Reprint. Westport, Conn.: Hyperion Press, 1976.

Burton, W. L. "Protestant America and the Rebirth of Israel." *Jewish Social Studies* 26 (1964): 203.

Call to America to Build Zion. New York: Arno Press, 1977.

Canaan, T. *Mohammedan Saints and Sanctuaries in Palestine.* 1927. Reprint. Jerusalem: Ariel, c.1980.

Canton, W. *Dawn in Palestine.* London: Society for Promoting Christian Knowledge, 1918.

Carmel, A. *Toldot Hefah bi-Yeme ha-Turkim.* Jerusalem: Yad Izhak Ben-Zvi Institute, 1977.

Christians and Jews in the Ottoman Empire: The Functioning of a Plural Society. Edited by B. Braude and B. Lewis. New York: Holmes & Meier, 1982.

"Christmas in Redeemed Jerusalem." *Literary Digest* 55 (1917): 24.

"Classic Battleground." *Nation* 105 (1917): 683.

Cohen, A. *Palestine in the Eighteenth Century.* Jerusalem: Magnes Press, 1973.

Cohen, E. "Vision of Zion, the Vision of Palestine: Dreams That Clash." *Christianity and Crisis* 37 (1977): 81.

Coldicott, R. *London Men in Palestine and How They Marched to Jerusalem.* London: E. Arnold, 1919.

Constantini, P. D. *Bonaparte en Palestine.* Paris: Halluin, 1967.

Davey, R. P. *The Sultan and His Subjects.* London: Chapman & Hall, 1897.

Davison, R. H. *Reform in the Ottoman Empire, 1856–1876.* 1963. Reprint. New York: Gordian Press, 1973.

————. "Turkish Attitudes Concerning Christian-Muslim Equality in the Nineteenth Century." *American Historical Review* 59 (1953): 844.

DeHaas, J. *History of Palestine.* New York: Macmillan, 1933.

"Delivery of Jerusalem." *Current History Magazine* 8 (1918): 163.

Dominian, L. "The Arab Problem in Relation to Syria, Palestine, Mesopotamia." *Inquiry Document 285*, April 15, 1918. U.S. National Archives.

Dudman, H. *Tiberias*. Jerusalem: Carta, 1988.

Early History of Zionism in America. Edited by I. S. Meyer. 1958. Reprint. New York: Arno Press, 1977.

Egypt and Palestine: A Millennium of Association, 868–1948. Edited by A. Cohen and G. Baer. New York: St. Martin's Press, 1984.

Elgood, P. G. *Bonaparte's Adventure in Egypt*. London: Oxford University Press, 1931.

Epstein, L. J. *Zion's Call: Christian Contributions to the Origins and Development of Israel*. Lanham, Md.: University Press of America, 1984.

"Fall of Jerusalem." *Living Age* 296 (1918): 242.

Falls, C. B. *Armageddon, 1918*. Philadelphia: Lippincott, 1964.

"Fate of Palestine After the War." *Current Opinion* 60 (1916): 422.

Fawaz, L. "The City and the Mountain: Beirut's Political Radius in the Nineteenth Century as Revealed in the Crisis of 1860." *International Journal of Middle East Studies* 16 (1984): 489.

Fitzgerald, W. "Holy Places of Palestine in History and Politics." *International Affairs* 26 (1950): 1.

Fox, F. *The History of the Royal Gloucestershire Hussars Yeomanry, 1898–1922: The Great Cavalry Campaign in Palestine*. London: P. Allam, 1923.

Friedman, I. "Lord Palmerston and the Protection of the Jews in Palestine, 1839–1851." *Jewish Social Studies* 30 (1968): 23.

Friedman, S. S. *Land of Dust: Palestine at the Turn of the Century*. Washington, D.C.: University Press of America, 1982.

Gelfand, L. E. *The Inquiry: American Preparations for Peace, 1917–1919*. New Haven: Yale University Press, 1963.

Gerber, H., and N. Gross. "Inflation or Deflation in Nineteenth-Century Syria and Palestine." *Journal of Economic History* 40 (1980): 351.

Gibb, H. A. *Islamic Society and the West*. London: Oxford University Press, 1950.

Gilbert, M. *Jerusalem: Rebirth of a City*. Jerusalem: Domino Press, 1985.

Gilbert, V. *The Romance of the Last Crusade: With Allenby to Jerusalem*. New York: Appleton, 1926.

Gilboa, E. "Terrorism and Trust: How We See the Middle East." *Public Opinion* 9 (1986): 52.

Glasse, C. *The Concise Encyclopedia of Islam*. New York: Harper & Row, 1989.

Gordon, B. L. *New Judea: Jewish Life in Modern Palestine and Egypt*. Philadelphia: J. H. Greenstone, 1919.

Gottheil, F. M. "The Population of Palestine: Circa 1875." *Middle Eastern Studies* 15 (1979): 310.

Gottheil, R. "Palestine Under the New Turkish Regime." *Independent* 69 (1910): 1,369.

Graham, S. "Jerusalem and the War." *Collier's Magazine* 50 (1912): 38.

Graham-Brown, S. *Palestinians and Their Society, 1880–1946*. London: Quartet Books, 1980.

Granott, A. *The Land System in Palestine*. London: Spottiswoode, 1952.

Gullett, H. S. *The Australian Imperial Force in Sinai and Palestine, 1914–1918*. Sydney: Angus & Robertson, 1923.

Halkin, A. S. *Zion in Jewish Literature*. New York: Herzl Press, 1961.

Hallberg, C. W. *The Suez Canal: Its History and Diplomatic Importance*. 1931. Reprint. New York: Octagon Books, 1974.

Halper, J. "On the Way: The Transition of Jerusalem from a Ritual to Colonial City, 1800–1917." *Urban Anthropology* 13 (1984): 1.

Haslip, J. *The Sultan: The Life of Abdul-Hamid II.* 1958. Reprint. New York: Holt, Rinehart & Winston, 1973.

Hermassi, E. "The French Revolution and the Arab World." *International Social Science Journal* 41 (1989): 33.

Herold, J. C. *Bonaparte in Egypt.* New York: Harper & Row, 1962.

Hitti, P. H. "The Impact of the West on Syria and Lebanon in the Nineteenth Century." *Journal of World History* 2 (1954): 608.

———. *A Short History of Lebanon.* New York: St. Martin's Press, 1965.

———. *The Syrians in America.* New York: Doran, 1924.

Hopgood, D. *The Russian Presence in Syria and Palestine, 1843–1914.* Oxford: Clarendon Press, 1969.

Horshi, A. *Toldot ha-Yehudim be-Erets Yisra'el Tahat Shilton ha-Muslamim.* Tel Aviv: Sefarim Yesod, 1979.

Hoskins, H. *British Route to India.* New York: Octagon Books, 1966.

Hughes, C. E. *Above and Beyond Palestine: An Account of the Work of the East Indies and Egypt Seaplane Squadron, 1916–1918.* London: E. Benn, 1930.

Inalcik, H. *The Ottoman Empire: Conquest, Organization, and Economy.* London: Variorum Reprints, 1978.

Isaacs, S. H. *The True Boundaries of the Holy Land.* New York: Arno Press, 1977. Reprint of the 1917 edition published in Chicago.

Issawi, C. P. *The Economic History of the Middle East, 1800–1914.* Chicago: University of Chicago Press, 1966.

Izkowitz, N. *Ottoman Empire and Islamic Tradition.* New York: Knopf, 1972.

Jannaway, F. G. *Palestine and the Powers.* London: E. Stock, 1918.

"Jerusalem Freed from the Moslem Yoke." *Current Opinion* 64 (1918): 6–7.

"Jerusalem Taken with Bayonets to Save the Holy Places from Shellfire." *Literary Digest* 55 (1917): 94.

Jews and Arabs in Palestine: Studies in a National and Colonial Problem. Edited by E. Sereni and R. E. Ashery. Westport, Conn.: Hyperion Press, 1976. Reprint of the 1936 edition published by Hechalutz Press, New York.

"Jews in Jerusalem." *Hogg's Weekly Instructor* 4 (1850): 288.

Kaleel, M. J. *When I Was a Boy in Palestine.* Boston: Lothrop, Lee & Shepard, 1914.

Kamen, C. S. *Little Common Ground: Arab Agriculture and Jewish Settlement in Palestine, 1920–1948.* Pittsburgh, Pa.: University of Pittsburgh Press, 1991.

Kark, R. "Changing Patterns of Land Ownership in Nineteenth-Century Palestine: The European Influence." *Journal of Historical Geography* 10 (1984): 357.

———. *Jaffa: A City in Evolution, 1799–1917.* Jerusalem: Yad Izhak Ben-Zvi Press, 1990.

Karpat, K. H. "The Ottoman Emigration to America, 1860–1914." *International Journal of Middle East Studies* 17 (1985): 175.

Khalidi, W. *Before Their Diaspora: A Photographic History of the Palestinians, 1876–1948.* Washington, D.C.: Institute for Palestine Studies, 1984.

Kinross, J. *The Ottoman Centuries: The Rise and Fall of the Turkish Empire.* New York: Morrow Quill Paperbacks, 1977.

Knee, S. E. *The Concept of Zionist Dissent in the American Mind, 1917–1941.* New York: Robert Speller, 1979.

———. "The King-Crane Commission of 1919: The Articulation of Political Anti-Zionism." *American Jewish Archives* 29 (1977): 22.

Kobler, F. *The Vision Was There: A History of the British Movement for the Restoration of the Jews to Palestine.* London: Published for the World Jewish Congress, British Section, by Lincolns-Prager, 1956.

Kohn, H. *Western Civilization in the Near East.* New York: Columbia University Press, 1936.

Kreiger, B. *Living Waters: Myth, History, and Politics of the Dead Sea.* New York: Continuum, 1988.

Kushner, D. "The Ottoman Governors of Palestine, 1864–1914." *Middle East Studies* 23 (1987): 274.

The Land That Became Israel: Studies in Historical Geography. Edited by Ruth Kark. New Haven: Yale University Press, 1990.

Landau, J. M. *Abdul-Hamid's Palestine.* London: Andre Deutsch, 1979.

Landes, D. S. "Palestine Before the Zionists." *Commentary* 61 (1976): 47.

Lazar, H. *Kibush Yafo.* Tel Aviv: Shelah, 1951.

Lewis, B. "The Return of Islam." *Commentary* 61 (1976): 39.

Lewis, R. *Everyday Life in Ottoman Turkey.* New York: Putnam, 1971.

Li-fene heyot ha-Tsiyonut: Le-toldot ha-ra'yon ha-le'umi ha-Yehudi u-she'elat Erets Yisra'el. Edited by S. Almog. Jerusalem: Merkaz Zalman Shazar, 1981.

Lloyd, C. *The Nile Campaign: Nelson and Napoleon in Egypt.* New York: Barnes & Noble, 1973.

Lock, H. O. *With the British Army in the Holy Land.* London: R. Scott, 1919.

Lockhart, J. G. *Palestine Days and Nights: Sketches of the Campaign in the Holy Land.* London: R. Scott, 1920.

Magie, D. "Palestine." *Inquiry Document 364,* n.d. U.S. National Archives.

Mandell, N. J. *The Arabs and Zionism Before World War I.* Berkeley and Los Angeles: University of California Press, 1976.

———. "Ottoman Policy and Restrictions on Jewish Settlement in Palestine, 1881–1908." *Middle Eastern Studies* 10 (1974): 312.

———. "Ottoman Practice as Regards Jewish Settlement in Palestine, 1881–1908." *Middle Eastern Studies* 11 (1975): 31.

———. "Turks, Arabs, and Jewish Immigration into Palestine, 1882–1914." *Middle Eastern Affairs* 4 (1965): 77.

Maoz, M. *Ottoman Reform in Syria and Palestine, 1840–1861.* Oxford: Clarendon Press, 1968.

Marlowe, J. *The Making of the Suez Canal.* London: Cresset Press, 1964.

———. *Perfidious Albion: The Origins of Anglo-French Rivalry in the Levant.* London: Elek, 1971.

Marmorstein, E. "European Jews in Muslim Palestine." *Middle Eastern Studies* 11 (1975): 74.

Massey, W. T. *How Jerusalem Was Won.* London: Constable, 1919.

Masterman, E.W.G. *The Deliverance of Jerusalem.* New York: H. Doran, 1918.

Maxwell, D. *The Last Crusade.* New York: J. Lane, 1920.

Meinertzhagen, R. *Middle East Diary, 1917–1956.* New York: Yoseloff, 1960.

Meyer, M. A. "Jewish Colonies in Palestine." *Independent* 54 (1902): 2,347.
Miller, W. *Ottoman Empire and Its Successors, 1801–1927.* 1927. Reprint. New York: Octagon Books, 1966.
Miot, J. F. *Memoires pour Servir à l'Histoire des Expeditions en Egypte et en Syrie.* Paris: Normant, 1814.
Moore, A. B. *The Mounted Riflemen in Sinai and Palestine: The Story of New Zealand's Crusaders.* Aukland: Whitcombe & Tombs, 1920.
More, J. N. *With Allenby's Crusaders.* London: Heath, Cranton, 1923.
Morrison, J. L. *Allenby's First Attempt on Jerusalem.* Kingston, Ont.: Jackson Press, 1919.
Muslih, M. Y. *The Origins of Palestinian Nationalism.* New York: Columbia University Press, 1988.
Palästina-Chronik, 1853 bis 1882. Edited by A. Carmel. Ulm: Vaas, 1978.
Palestine and Israel in the Nineteenth and Twentieth Centuries. Edited by E. Kedourie and S. G. Haim. Totowa, N.J.: F. Cass, 1982.
Palestine in the Late Ottoman Period: Political, Social, and Economic Transformation. Edited by D. Kushner. Jerusalem: Yad Izhak Ben-Zvi, 1986.
Pamuk, S. "The Decline and Resistance of Ottoman Cotton Textiles, 1820–1913." *Explorations in Economic History* 23 (1986): 205.
———. *The Ottoman Empire and European Capitalism, 1820–1913: Trade, Investment, and Production.* Cambridge: Cambridge University Press, 1987.
———. "The Ottoman Empire in the 'Great Depression' of 1873–1896." *Journal of Economic History* 44 (1984): 107.
Patai, R. *The Arab Mind.* New York: Scribner, 1976.
———. *Golden River to Golden Road: Society, Culture and Change in the Middle East.* Philadelphia: University of Pennsylvania Press, 1969.
———. *On Culture Contact and Its Working in Modern Palestine.* Menasha, Wis.: American Anthropological Association, 1947.
Penslar, D. J. "Zionism, Colonialism, and Technology: Otto Warburg and the Commission for the Exploration of Palestine, 1903–1907." *Journal of Contemporary History* 25 (1990): 143.
Perez, N. N. *Focus East: Early Photography in the Near East, 1839–1885.* New York: Abrams, 1988.
Peters, F. E. *Jerusalem and Mecca: The Typology of the Holy City in the Near East.* New York: New York University Press, 1986.
———. *Jerusalem: Holy City, Holy Places.* New York: Hagop Kevorkian Center for Near Eastern Studies, 1983.
———. *Jerusalem: The Holy City in the Eyes of Chroniclers, Visitors, Pilgrims, and Prophets from the Days of Abraham to the Beginnings of Modern Times.* Princeton: Princeton University Press, 1985.
———. "The Procession That Never Was: The Painful Way in Jerusalem." *Drama Review* 29 (1985): 31.
Peters, J. *From Time Immemorial: The Origins of the Arab-Jewish Conflict Over Palestine.* New York: Harper & Row, 1984.
Pipes, D., and A. M. Garfinkle. "Is Jordan Palestine?" *Commentary* 86 (October 1988): 35; and 87 (February 1989): 2.
Plesur, M. "Zionism in the General Press, 1897–1914." *Herzl Yearbook* 5 (1963): 127.

The Political Awakening in the Middle East. Edited by G. Lenczowski. Englewood Cliffs, N.J.: Prentice-Hall, 1970.

Polk, W. R. *The Arab World.* Cambridge, Mass.: Harvard University Press, 1980.

Pragai, M. *Faith and Fulfilment: Christians and the Return to the Promised Land.* London: Vallentine, Mitchell, 1985.

Prince, A. E. *Palestine in Transition from War to Peace.* Kingston, Ont.: Jackson Press, 1921.

Raanan, U. *The Frontiers of a Nation: A Re-Examination of the Forces Which Created the Palestine Mandate and Determined Its Territorial Shape.* London: Batchworth Press, 1955.

Ramasaur, E. E. *The Young Turks: Prelude to the Revolution of 1908.* Princeton: Princeton University Press, 1957.

Rausch, D. A. "The Evangelicals and Zionists." *Midstream* 31 (1985): 13.

————. "Our Hope: Protofundamentalism's Attitude Toward Zionism, 1894–1897." *Jewish Social Studies* 40 (1978): 239.

————. *Zionism Within Early American Fundamentalism, 1878–1918.* New York: Edwin Mellon Press, 1979.

Ravid, Z. "The Yishuv in Palestine in the Nineteenth Century as Reflected in Its Hebrew Literature." Ph.D. diss., Yeshiva University, 1960.

"Recent Jewish Progress in Palestine." *Nation* 103 (1916): 220.

"Redeeming the Holy Land from Turk Mis-Rule." *Literary Digest* 57 (1918): 66.

"Relief and Reconstruction in the Holy Land." *Review of Reviews* 58 (1918): 537.

"The Restoration of the Jews." *Appleton's Journal* 23 (1880): 276.

Rise of Israel: From Precursors of Zionism to Herzl. Edited by I. Friedman. New York: Garland, 1987.

Robertson, J. *With the Crusaders in Palestine.* Dunedin, N.Z.: A. H. and A. W. Reed, 1938.

Robinson, T. H. *Palestine in General History.* London: Oxford University Press, 1929.

Root, M. L. "Jewish Flight from Palestine to Egypt." *Review of Reviews* 51 (1915): 709.

Rose, N. A. *The Gentile Zionists: A Study in Anglo-Zionist Diplomacy, 1929–1939.* London: Cass, 1973.

Rosenberg, A. "Condition of Palestine." *Fraser's Magazine* 92 (1875): 123.

————. "Regeneration of Palestine." *Gentleman's Magazine* 16 (1876): 573.

Rowley, G. *Israel into Palestine.* New York: Mansell, 1984.

Runciman, S. *The Historic Role of the Christian Arabs of Palestine.* Harlow, Eng.: Longmans, 1970.

Ruppin, A. *The Agricultural Colonisation of the Zionist Organisation in Palestine.* London: M. Hopkinson, 1926.

Sachar, H. M. *The Emergence of the Middle East, 1914–1924.* New York: Knopf, 1969.

————. *A History of Israel: From the Rise of Zionism to Our Time.* New York: Knopf, 1976.

Said, E. W. "Conspiracy of Praise." *Nation* 241 (19 October 1985): 381.

————. "Interpreting Palestine." *Harper's Magazine* 274 (1987): 19.

Sanders, C. L. "Gospel Goes to the Holy Land." *Ebony Magazine* 39 (December 1983): 36.

Sarton, G. *The Incubation of Western Culture in the Middle East.* Washington, D.C.: Library of Congress, 1951.

Schick, R. "Christian Life in Palestine During the Early Islamic Period." *Biblical Archaeologist* 51 (1988): 218.

Schoenberg, P. E. "Palestine in the Year 1914." Ph.D. diss., New York University, 1978.

Schur, N. *History of the Samaritans.* New York: P. Lang, 1989.

Scott-Montcrieff, C. E. *On the Track of Our Troops in Palestine.* London: Skeffington, 1918.

Segal, H. E. "Perceptions of U.S. Policy in Israel's Pre-State Period: The Shaping of Anxiety." *Middle East Studies* 24 (1988): 473.

Sharif, R. S. *Non-Jewish Zionism: Its Roots in Western History.* London: Zed Press, 1983.

Shaw, S. J. *Between Old and New: The Ottoman Empire Under Sultan Selim III, 1789–1807.* Cambridge, Mass.: Harvard University Press, 1971.

———. *History of the Ottoman Empire and Modern Turkey.* New York: Cambridge University Press, 1976–77.

Shepherd, N. *The Zealous Intruders: The Western Rediscovery of Palestine.* New York: Harper & Row, 1987.

Sneersohn, H. *Palestine and Roumania.* New York: Hebrew Orphan Asylum Printing Establishment, 1872.

Sokolow, N. *History of Zionism, 1600–1918.* 1919. Reprint. New York: Ktav, 1969.

Steiner, Z. "The Promising Land." *History* 69 (1984): 238.

Stern, N. B., and W. M. Kramer. "A Pre-Israeli Diplomat on an American Mission, 1869–1870." *Western States Jewish Historical Quarterly* 8 (1976): 232.

Still, W. N. *American Sea Power in the Old World: The United States Navy in European and Near Eastern Waters, 1865–1917.* Westport, Conn.: Greenwood Press, 1980.

Stockton, R. R. "Christian Zionism: Prophecy and Public Opinion." *Middle East Journal* 41 (1987): 234.

Stone, J. S. *The Taking of Jerusalem.* Chicago: Daughaday, 1918.

Studia Palaestina: Studies in Honour of Constantine K. Zurayk. Edited by H. Nashabe. Washington, D.C.: Institute for Palestine Studies, 1989.

Studies on Palestine During the Ottoman Period. Edited by M. Maoz. Jerusalem: Magnes Press, 1975.

"Taking of Jerusalem." *Current History Magazine* 7 (1918): 92.

Thomas, L. J. *With Allenby in the Holy Land.* London: Cassell, 1938.

Thompson, E. *Crusader's Coast.* London: E. Benn, 1929.

Tibawi, A. L. *A Modern History of Syria, Including Lebanon and Palestine.* London: Macmillan, 1969.

Tolkowsky, S. *Achievements and Prospects in Palestine.* London: English Zionist Federation, 1917.

———. *The Gateway to Palestine: A History of Jaffa.* London: Routledge, 1924.

The Transformation of Palestine. Edited by I. Abu-Lughod. Evanston, Ill.: Northwestern University Press, 1971.

"Turkey's Disaster in Palestine." *Current History Magazine* 9 (1918): 269.

"Under the Sultan's Sway." *Chamber's Journal* 31 (1859): 362.

Vilnay, Z. *Legends of Palestine*. Philadelphia: Jewish Publication Society, 1932.

———. *The Sacred Land*. Philadelphia: Jewish Publication Society, 1973–78. Vol. 1, *Legends of Jerusalem*; Vol. 2, *Legends of Judea and Samaria*; Vol. 3, *Legends of Galilee, Jordan, and Sinai*.

———. *Toldot he-Arvim veha-Muslamim be-Erets Yisra'el*. Tel Aviv: A. Y. Shtibel, 1931.

Vision and Conflict in the Holy Land. Edited by R. I. Cohen. New York: St. Martin's Press, 1985.

Vital, D. *The Origins of Zionism*. Oxford: Clarendon Press, 1975.

Wad-el-Ward, G. *Palestine Through the Eyes of a Native*. New York: Revell, 1907.

"War's Desolation in Palestine." *Literary Digest* 49 (1914): 958.

Wavell, A. *The Palestine Campaigns*. 1931. Reprint. Freeport, N.Y.: Books for Libraries Press, 1972.

Weldon, L. F. *Hard Living: Eastern Mediterranean, 1914–1919*. London: Jenkins, 1926.

Whitehair, C. W. "An Old Jewel in the Proper Setting: An Eyewitness Account of the Reconquest of the Holy Land by Twentieth-Century Crusaders." *National Geographic Magazine* 34 (1918): 325.

Wilken, R. L. "Byzantine Palestine: A Christian Holy Land." *Biblical Archaeologist* 51 (1988): 214.

———. "From Time Immemorial? Dwellers in the Holy Land." *Christian Century* 103 (1986): 678.

"William II and Palestine." *Fortnightly Review* 70 (1898): 548.

Wittlin, A. S. *Abdul-Hamid: The Shadow of God*. London: J. Lane, 1940.

Yaari, A. *The Goodly Heritage*. Jerusalem: Youth and Hechalutz Department of the Zionist Organization, 1958.

Yapp, M. E. *The Making of the Modern Near East, 1792–1923*. London: Longman, 1987.

Zahavi, Y. *Eretz Israel in Rabbinic Lore*. Jerusalem: Tehilla Institute, 1962.

Zionism and Arabism in Palestine and Israel. Edited by E. Kedourie and S. G. Haim. Totowa, N.J.: F. Cass, 1982.

Travel, Tourism, and Pilgrimage

Adams, L. L. *A Ride on Horseback Through the Holy Land, Written for Children*. Boston: H. Hoyt, 1874.

Adams, P. G. *Travelers and Travel Liars, 1660–1800*. New York: Dover, 1980.

Adeney, W. F. "Palestine in 1884." *Congregationalist* 13 (1884): 657.

Alder, L. D. *The Holy Land*. Salt Lake City, Utah: Deseret News, 1912.

Allen, M. S. *From West to East; or, The Old World as I Saw It*. Chicago: Free Methodist Pub. House, 1898.

"Americans Abroad." *Annals of the American Academy of Political and Social Science* 368 (1966): 1.

Appel, T. *Letters to Boys and Girls About the Holy Land*. Reading, Pa.: D. Miller, 1886.

Appleton, T. G. *Syrian Sunshine*. Boston: Roberts Brothers, 1877.

Arnold, F. S. *The Land That Illumines the Book.* Portsmouth, Ohio: Blade Printing, 1904.

Ascham, J. B. *A Syrian Pilgrimage.* New York: Abingdon Press, 1914.

Babcock, M. D. *Letters from Egypt and Palestine.* New York: Scribner, 1902.

Baedeker, K. *Palestine and Syria: Handbook for Travelers.* Leipzig: K. Baedeker, 1898.

"Baedeker's Palestine and Syria." *Nation* 83 (1906): 333.

Bailey, A. E. "Samaritan Passover." *Biblical World* 34 (1909): 8.

Baldwin, E. F. "German Royal Visit to Jerusalem." *Harper's Weekly* 42 (1898): 983.

————. "Jerusalem of Today." *Outlook* 49 (1894): 486.

Barr, R. *The Unchanging East.* Boston: L.C. Page, 1900.

Bartlett, S. C. *From Egypt to Palestine Through Sinai, the Wilderness, and the South Country.* New York: Harper, 1879.

Barton, W. E. *The Old World in the New Century.* Boston: Pilgrim Press, 1902.

Bausman, B. *Sinai and Zion.* Philadelphia: Lindsay & Blakiston, 1861.

Beckman, N. S. *Backsheesh: A Woman's Wanderings.* San Francisco: Whitaker & Ray, 1900.

Bell, A. *The Spell of the Holy Land.* Boston: Page, 1915.

Bellows, H. W. *The Old World in Its New Face.* New York: Harper, 1868–69.

Benziger, M. A. *Off to Jerusalem.* New York: Benziger Brothers, 1906.

Bevis, R. W. *Bibliotheca Cisorientalia: An Annotated Checklist of Early English Travel Books on the Near and Middle East.* Boston: G. K. Hall, 1973.

The Blessings of Pilgrimage. Edited by R. Ousterhout. Urbana, Ill.: University of Illinois Press, 1990.

Boddy, A. A. *Days in Galilee and Scenes in Judea, Together with Some Account of a Solitary Cycling in Southern Palestine.* London: Gay & Bird, 1900.

Boll, J. A. *Letters of Travel in Europe, Egypt, and Palestine: Written for the Gettysburg Compiler.* Baltimore: Kreuzer Brothers, 1883.

Boswell, J. I. *Palestine.* New York: Walden & Stowe, 1883.

Bradford, S. S. "Holy Land Today." *Travel* 13 (1907): 113.

Bredeson, R. C. "Landscape Description in Nineteenth-Century American Travel Literature." *American Quarterly* 20 (1968): 86.

Brettel, C. B. "Nineteenth-Century Travelers' Accounts of the Mediterranean Peasant." *Ethnohistory* 33 (1986): 159.

Briggs, W. "Modes of Travel in Palestine." *Treasury* 14 (1896): 773.

Brown, H. A. "Jaffa to Jerusalem." *Lippincott's Monthly Magazine* 4 (1869): 546.

Browne, J. R. *John Ross Browne: His Letters, Journals, and Writings.* Edited by L. F. Browne. Albuquerque: University of New Mexico Press, 1969.

————. *Yusef; or, The Journey of the Frangi: A Crusade in the East.* New York: Harper, 1853.

Bryan, W. J. *The Old World and Its Ways.* St. Louis: Thompson, 1907.

Bryant, J. "Citizens of a World to Come: Melville and the Millennial Cosmopolite." *American Literature* 59 (1987): 20.

Bryant, S. *Old and New Joppa.* Lynn, Mass.: L. C. Parker, 1895.

Bryant, W. C. *Letters from the East.* New York: Putnam, 1869.

Bryce, J. "Impressions of Palestine." *National Geographic Magazine* 27 (1915): 293.

Budd, L. J. *Our Mark Twain: The Making of His Public Personality*. Philadelphia: University of Pennsylvania Press, 1983.

Bulkey, J. E. "Women in Palestine." *Biblical World* 11 (1898): 69.

Burt, N. C. *The Land and Its Story*. New York: D. Appleton, 1869.

Bush, E. C. *My Pilgrimage to Eastern Shrines*. London: Hurst & Blackett, 1867.

Carradine, B. *A Journey to Palestine*. St. Louis: C. B. Woodward, 1891.

Champney, E. W. *Three Vassar Girls in the Holy Land*. Boston: Estes & Lauriat, 1892.

Chandler, L. H. "A Naval Officer's Trip to Jerusalem." *Granite Monthly* 22 (1897): 201.

Clark, F. E. *In Christ's Own Country*. New York: Christian Herald, 1914.

Clemens, S. L. *The Complete Travel Books of Mark Twain*. Edited by C. Nieder. Garden City, N.Y.: Doubleday, 1966–67.

―――. *The Innocents Abroad; or, The New Pilgrims' Progress*. With an introduction by A. Kazin. New York: Bantam Books, 1964.

―――. *Mark Twain on the Damned Human Race*. Edited by J. Smith. New York: Hill & Wang, 1962.

―――. *Mark Twain's Notebook*. Edited by A. B. Paine. New York: Harper, 1935.

―――. *Traveling with the Innocents Abroad: Mark Twain's Original Reports from Europe and the Holy Land*. Edited by D. M. McKeithan. Norman, Okla.: University of Oklahoma Press, 1958.

―――. *The Travels of Mark Twain*. Edited by C. Nieder. New York: Coward-McCann, 1961.

Cleveland, H. *The Overseas Americans*. New York: McGraw-Hill, 1960.

Colvile, H. E. *The Accursed Land*. London: S. Low, 1884.

Conry, J. P. "Some Old Biblical Customs in Modern Palestine." *Ecclesiastical Review* 39 (1908): 169.

Conwell, R. H. "The New Palestine." *Sunday School Times* 40 (1898): 315.

Cook, C. F. "Jewish Colonization in Palestine." *Popular Science Magazine* 83 (1913): 428.

Cook, J. "From Bethlehem to Beersheba." *Travel* 16 (1910): 82.

Cook, T., and sons. *Cook's Tourist Handbook for Egypt, the Nile, and the Desert*. London: T. Cook, 1876.

―――. *Cook's Tourist Handbook for Palestine and Syria*. London: T. Cook, 1876.

―――. *Cook's Tours to the Orient: Including the Mediterranean, Egypt, Palestine, the Levant, and the Nile*. London: T. Cook, 1907.

―――. *Over the Seven Seas: A Story of World Tours with Cook and Son*. New York: G. B. Clarkson, 1914.

Correspondence of Palestine Tourists: Comprising a Series of Letters by George A. Smith (and others). 1875. Reprint. New York: Arno Press, 1977.

Cox, S. S. *A Buckeye Abroad; or, Wanderings in Europe and in the Orient*. New York: Putnam, 1852.

―――. *Orient Sunbeams*. 1882. Reprint. New York: Arno Press, 1977.

Crane, J. "The Rewards of Travel." *Focus* 36 (1986): 1.

Cudahy, P. *Experiences of Mr. and Mrs. Patrick Cudahy on a Journey to a Portion of the Oldest Historical Parts of the Old World During the First Four Months of 1906*. Milwaukee, Wis.: Author, 1907.

Cummings, J. *A Tour to the Holy Land and Six Weeks in Jerusalem in the Interest of the Nation of Israel.* Cambridgeport, Mass.: Harvard Pub. Company, 1890.

Curtis, W. E. *To-day in Syria and Palestine.* Chicago: Revell, 1903.

Dana, C. A. *Eastern Journeys: Some Notes of Travel in Russia, in the Caucasus, and to Jerusalem.* New York: D. Appleton, 1898.

———. "Jerusalem of Today." *Review of Reviews* 9 (1894): 98.

———. "Recent Visit to Jerusalem." *McClure's Magazine* 2 (1893): 86.

Davis, R. B. *George Sandys: Poet-adventurer.* London: Bodley Head, 1955.

Devins, J. B. "Americanization of the Holy Land." *Woman's Home Companion* 32 (1905): 18.

———. "International Sunday School Invasion of the Holy Land." *Woman's Home Companion* 32 (1905): 3.

Dicey, E. *The Morning Land.* London: Macmillan, 1870.

Dickinson, L. T. "Mark Twain's *Innocents Abroad*: Its Origins, Composition, and Popularity." Ph.D. diss., University of Chicago, 1945.

———. "Mark Twain's Revisions in Writing the *Innocents Abroad.*" *American Literature* 19 (1947): 139.

———. "Marketing a Best Seller: Mark Twain's *Innocents Abroad.*" *Papers of the Bibliographical Society of America* 41 (1947): 107.

Dilly, R. S. "Tourist Brochures and Tourist Images." *Canadian Geographer* 30 (1986): 59.

Dorr, D. *A Colored Man Round the World.* Cleveland, Ohio: Author, 1858.

Dowsett, E. "Camp Life in Palestine." *Sunday Magazine* 34 (1905): 641.

Dulles, F. R. *Americans Abroad: Two Centuries of European Travel.* Ann Arbor: University of Michigan Press, 1964.

Dulles, J. W. *The Ride Through Palestine.* Philadelphia: Presbyterian Board of Publication, 1881.

Dumont, J.-P. "A Matter of Touristic 'Indifference'." *American Ethnologist* 11 (1984): 139.

Duncan, N. *Going Down from Jerusalem: The Narrative of a Sentimental Traveler.* New York: Harper, 1909.

Dunn, L. A. *Footprints of the Redeemer in the Holy Land.* Des Moines, Iowa: Mills, 1880.

Durwood, J. T. *Holy Land and Holy Writ.* Baraboo, Wis.: Pilgrim, 1913.

Early Travels in Palestine. Edited by T. Wright. London: H. G. Bohn, 1948.

Elliott, C. W. *Remarkable Characters and Places of the Holy Land.* Hartford, Conn.: J. B. Burr, 1867.

Elmendorf, D. L. *A Camera Crusade Through the Holy Land.* New York: Scribner, 1912.

Elsey, C. W. *Journeying with Jesus: As the Days Go by in That Dormant Land Where Rest the Ashes of Patriarchs, Prophets, and Kings of Whom the World Was Not Worthy.* Boston: R. G. Badger, 1913.

Ensor, A. *Mark Twain and the Bible.* Lexington: University of Kentucky Press, 1969.

Fairbanks, M. M. "The Cruise of the *Quaker City* with Chance Recollections of Mark Twain." *Chautauqua* 14 (1892): 430.

Farrar, F. W. *Places That Our Lord Loved.* Boston: L. Prang, 1891.

Field, H. M. *Among the Holy Hills.* New York: Scribner, 1884.

Fields, A. A. *Charles Dudley Warner.* 1904. Reprint. Freeport, N.Y.: Books for Libraries Press, 1972.

Firestone, C. B. *The Coasts of Illusion: A Study of Travel Tales.* New York: Harper, 1924.

Foner, P. S. *Mark Twain: Social Critic.* New York: International Publishers, 1958.

Ford, A. H. "Around the Holy Land." *Travel* 15 (1909): 123.

Franck, H. A. "Tramping in Palestine." *Century Magazine* 79 (1910): 434.

Freer, A. C. "Jottings About Jerusalem." *Eclectic Magazine* 141 (1903): 476.

Freese, J. R. *The Old World.* Philadelphia: Lippincott, 1869.

———. *Travels in the Holy Land.* Philadelphia: Crombarger, 1882.

"From Jaffa to Jerusalem." *Once a Week* 15 (1866): 399.

Fullerton, A. F. *A Lady's Ride Through Palestine and Syria.* London: S. W. Partridge, 1872.

Fulton, J. *The Beautiful Land: Palestine as It Was and as It Now Is.* Chicago: Standard Columbian, 1891.

Gage, W. L. *The Land of Sacred Mystery; or, The Bible Read in the Light of Its Own Scenery.* Hartford, Conn.: Worthington, Dustin, 1871.

———. *Palestine, Historical and Descriptive.* Boston: Estes & Lauriat, 1883.

———. *Studies in Bible Lands.* Boston: American Tract Society, 1869.

Ganzel, D. *Mark Twain Abroad: The Cruise of the "Quaker City."* Chicago: University of Chicago Press, 1968.

Godbey, W. B. *Footprints of Jesus in the Holy Land.* Cincinnati: M. W. Knapp, 1900.

Goodspeed, F. L. *Palestine: A "Fifth Gospel."* Springfield, Mass.: F. A. Bassette, 1901.

Gould, J. H. *Grand Winter Excursion to the Mediterranean, the Orient, and the Holy Land.* New York: Compagnie Generale Transatlantique, 1895.

Graham, S. "On the Banks of the Jordan." *Harper's Monthly Magazine* 127 (1913): 409.

———. "On the Pilgrim Boat." *Harper's Monthly Magazine* 127 (1913): 204.

———. *With the Russian Pilgrims to Jerusalem.* London: Macmillan, 1914.

Grant, J. D. *The Personal Memoirs of Julia Dent Grant.* New York: Putnam, 1975.

Gray, A. Z. *The Land and the Life: Sketches and Studies in Palestine.* New York: A.D.F. Randolph, 1876.

Green, L. *A Girl's Journey Through Europe, Egypt, and the Holy Land.* Nashville, Tenn.: Pub. House of the Methodist Episcopal Church South, 1889.

Gribben, A. "The Importance of Mark Twain." *American Quarterly* 37 (1985): 30.

Grindon, H. M. "Traces of the Middle Ages in Palestine." *Chamber's Journal* 75 (1897): 647.

Griswild, L. M. *A Woman's Pilgrimage to the Holy Land; or, Pleasant Days Abroad.* Hartford, Conn.: J. B. Burr, 1871.

Hacket, H. B. *Illustrations of Scripture, Suggested by a Tour Through the Holy Land.* New York: Sheldon, 1860.

Hale, E. E. *A Family Flight over Egypt and Syria.* Boston: D. Lothrop, 1882.

———. "The Holy Land." *Unitarian Review* 13 (1880): 97.

———. "A Visit to Jerusalem." *Atlantic Monthly* 49 (1882): 368.

Hale, H. G. "Observation and Imagination in French Seventeenth-Century Travel Literature." *Journal of European Studies* 14 (1984): 117.

Hale, L. P. "Our Pilgrimage." *Old and New* 3 (1871): 438.

———. "Visit to Jerusalem." *Old and New* 5 (1872): 687.

Hallock, G. B. *Journeying in the Land Where Jesus Lived.* New York: American Tract Society, 1903.

Hardy, E. J. *The Unvarying East.* New York: Scribner, 1912.

Harman, H. M. *A Journey to Egypt and the Holy Land, in 1869–1870.* Philadelphia: J. B. Lippincott, 1873.

Harris, C. D. *Through Palestine with Tent and Donkey.* Baltimore: Southern Methodist Pub. Company, 1913.

Hartzell, R. S. *In the Early Footsteps of the Nazarene.* Philadelphia: A. J. Holman, 1898.

Haynes, J. *The Humanist as Traveler: George Sandys's "Relation of a Journey Begun An. Dom. 1610."* Rutherford, N.J.: Fairleigh Dickinson University Press, 1986.

Hazard, C. *A Brief Pilgrimage in the Holy Land Recounted in a Series of Addresses Delivered in Wellesley College Chapel.* Boston: Houghton, Mifflin, 1909.

Headley, J. T. *The Life and Travels of General Grant.* Philadelphia: Hubbard Brothers, 1879.

———. *Sacred Mountains, Characters, and Scenes in the Holy Land.* New York: Scribner, 1875.

Herbuck, E. *Under Eastern Skies.* Dayton, Ohio: Press Reformed, 1889.

Heusser, A. H. *The Land of the Prophets.* New York: T. Y. Crowell, 1916.

Hichens, R. S. *The Holy Land.* New York: Century, 1910.

———. "Holy Week in Jerusalem." *Century Magazine* 80 (1910): 854.

———. "Jerusalem." *Century Magazine* 80 (1910): 558.

Hicks, W. H. *General Grant's Tour Around the World.* Chicago: Rand McNally, 1879.

Hodder, E. *On Holy Ground.* New York: Nelson & Phillips, 1874.

Holland, F. W. "Jerusalem." *Lippincott's Magazine* 8 (1871): 631.

Holman Company. *A Pictorial Pilgrimage Through Bible Lands.* Philadelphia: Holman, 1898.

Honeyman, A. *From America to the Orient.* Plainfield, N.J.: Honeyman, 1899.

Hoskins, F. E. *From the Nile to Nebo.* Philadelphia: Sunday School Times Company, 1912.

Howard, D. R. *Writers and Pilgrims: Medieval Pilgrimage Narratives and Their Posterity.* Berkeley and Los Angeles: University of California Press, 1980.

Howard, P. E. *The Story of Five World's Conventions.* Philadelphia: Executive Committee of the World's Sunday School Association, 1910.

Hunter, D. "Jerusalem as It Is Today." *Cosmopolitan* 36 (1903): 81.

Hurlbut, J. L. *Traveling in the Holy Land Through the Stereoscope.* New York: Underwood & Underwood, 1900.

Hutton, E. V. "A Little Visit to Jerusalem." *Christian Union* 47 (1893): 1,250.

Hutton, L. *Literary Landmarks of Jerusalem.* New York: Harper, 1895.

Hyde, O. *A Voice from Jerusalem.* Boston: A. Morgan, 1842.

Iden, T. M. *Upper Room Letters from Bible Lands.* Chicago: Revell, 1904.

Ish-Shalom, M. *Mas'e Notsrim le-Erets Yisra'el.* Tel Aviv: Am Oved, 1965.

Israel, J., and H. Lundt. *Journal of a Cruise in the U.S. Ship "Delaware."* 1835. Reprint. New York: Arno Press, 1977.

Jacobson, E. H. "Sojourn Research: A Definition of the Field." *Journal of Social Issues* 19 (1976): 123.

"Jerusalem Delivered to Improvement." *Literary Digest* 48 (1914): 906.

Keating, J. M. *With General Grant in the East.* Philadelphia: J. B. Lippincott, 1879.

Kellman, S. G. "Mark Twain in the Middle East." *Texas Quarterly* 20 (1977): 35.

Kelman, J. "Picturesque Life of the Holy Land." *Current Literature* 35 (1903): 649.

Kenny, V. *Herman Melville's "Clarel": A Spiritual Autobiography.* Hamden, Conn.: Archon Books, 1973.

Kent, C. F. *Description of One Hundred and Forty Places in Bible Lands.* New York: Underwood & Underwood, 1911.

Kerr, R. P. *The Holy Land of Holy Light.* Richmond, Va.: Presbyterian Committee of Publication, 1891.

Khuri, M. "The Straddlers: A Critical Study of British Political-Literary Middle East Travel Writers, 1900–1950." Ph.D. diss., Florida State University, 1961.

Kirby, R. K. "Melville's Attitude Toward the Historicity and Interpretation of the Bible." Ph.D. diss., Indiana University, 1983.

Klatzker, D. "American Catholic Travelers to the Holy Land, 1861–1929." *Catholic Historical Review* 74 (1988): 55.

———. "American Christian Travelers to the Holy Land, 1821–1939." Ph.D. diss., Temple University, 1987.

Knox, T. W. *Backsheesh.* Hartford, Conn.: A. D. Worthington, 1875.

Kollek, T., and M. Pearlman. *Pilgrims to the Holy Land.* London: Weidenfeld & Nicolson, 1970.

Konvitz, M. "Herman Melville in the Holy Land." *Midstream* 25 (1979): 50.

Krimsky, J. *Pilgrimage and Service.* New York: Arno Press, 1977.

Leary, L. G. *The Real Palestine of To-day.* New York: McBride, Nast, 1911.

———. "Tiny Palestine." *Travel* 16 (1911): 216.

Leech, H. H. *Letters of a Sentimental Idler, from Greece, Turkey, Egypt, Nubia, and the Holy Land.* New York: D. Appleton, 1869.

Lees, G. R. "The Poor of Jerusalem." *Sunday Magazine* 24 (1894): 469.

———. "Scenes in the Marketplace of Jerusalem." *Sunday Magazine* 31 (1902): 936.

———. *Village Life in Palestine.* New York: Longmans, Green, 1905.

Lent, W. B. *Holy Land from Landau, Saddle, and Palanquin.* New York: Bonnell, Silver, 1899.

Letters from the East in the Spring of 1882. Liverpool: A. Holden, 1882.

Levy, C. H. "Palestine-Americanized." *Independent* 74 (1913): 622.

Lincoln, M. T. *Mary Todd Lincoln: Her Life and Letters.* Edited by J. Turner. New York: Knopf, 1972.

Linsor, C. H. "Sunset New Jerusalem." *Century Magazine* 50 (1906): 165.

Lothrop, T. K. *William Henry Seward.* 1899. Reprint. New York: AMS Press, 1972.

Loysor, E. J. *To Jerusalem Through the Lands of Islam.* Chicago: Open Court, 1905.

McCabe, J. D. *A Tour Around the World by General Grant.* Philadelphia: National, 1879.

MacCannell, D. *The Tourist: A New Theory of the Leisure Class.* New York: Schocken Books, 1976.

McCullough, D. *Mornings on Horseback*. New York: Simon & Schuster, 1981.

Macdonald, A. *The Gospel in Its Native Land*. Chicago: Gospel Press, 1909.

McFeely, W. S. *Grant*. New York: Norton, 1981.

McGarvey, J. W. *Lands of the Bible*. Philadelphia: J. B. Lippincott, 1881.

McKenzie, A. "Of the Holy Land." *Andover Review* 1 (1884): 244.

McLean, A. *A Circuit of the Globe*. St. Louis: Christian Pub. Company, 1897.

Macmillan & Company. *Guide to Palestine and Egypt*. London: Macmillan, 1901.

MacMinn, E. *Amal: A Prince of the Amalakites*. Philadelphia: American Baptist Publication Society, 1886.

MacPhie, J. P. *The Homeland of the Bible*. Chicago: Revell, 1903.

Mathews, S. "A Reading Journey Through Palestine." *Chautauquan* 43 (1906): 493.

Maundrell, H. *A Journey from Aleppo to Jerusalem at Easter, 1697*. Oxford: G. Delaune, 1703.

Maus, A. P. *Our Lord's Birthday and Birthplace*. Governor's Island, N.Y: Author, 1913.

Maxwell, E. H. *Griffin Ahoy: A Yacht Cruise to the Levant and Wanderings in Egypt, Syria, the Holy Land, Greece, and Italy in 1881*. London: Hurst & Blackett, 1882.

Melville, H. *Clarel: A Poem and Pilgrimage in the Holy Land*. Edited by W. E. Bezanson. New York: Hendricks House, 1960.

———. *Journal of a Visit to Europe and the Levant, October 11, 1856–May 6, 1857*. Edited by H. C. Horsford. Princeton: Princeton University Press, 1955.

———. *The Melville Log*. Edited by J. Leyda. New York: Harcourt, Brace, 1951.

Mendenhall, J. W. *Echoes from Palestine*. Cincinnati: Walden & Stowe, 1883.

Metwalli, A. M. "The Lure of the Levant." Ph.D. diss., State University of New York at Albany, 1971.

Michelson, B. "Mark Twain the Tourist: The Form of the *Innocents Abroad*." *American Literature* 49 (1977): 385.

Miller, E. E. *Alone Through Syria*. London: K. Paul, Trench, Trubner, 1891.

Mitchell, L. C. "Verbally Roughing It: The West of Words." *Nineteenth-Century Literature* 44 (1989): 67.

Mitford, J. "The Travail of-Travel." *New Statesman* 108 (1984): 42.

Mulvey, C. *Anglo-American Landscapes: A Study of Nineteenth-Century Anglo-American Travel Literature*. New York: Cambridge University Press, 1983.

Munro, E. *On Glory Roads: A Pilgrim's Book About Pilgrimage*. New York: Thames & Hudson, 1987.

Murphy, A. A. "Homiletic Advantages of a Trip to the Holy Land." *Homiletic Review* 21 (1891): 86.

Muslim Travellers: Pilgrimage, Migration, and the Religious Imagination. Edited by D. F. Eickelman and J. Piscatori. Berkeley and Los Angeles: University of California Press, 1990.

Nadel, I. B. "G. W. Cooke and Laurence Oliphant: Victorian Travelers to the Orient." *Journal of the American Oriental Society* 94 (1974): 120.

Neil, J. *Everyday Life in the Holy Land*. London: Cassell, 1913.

———. *Palestine Explored*. London: J. Nisbet, 1881.

————. *Pictured Palestine.* London: J. Nisbet, 1904.

Neil's Photographs of the Holy Land. Philadelphia: H. Neil, 1893.

Nelson, W. S. *Habeeb, the Beloved.* Philadelphia: Westminster Press, 1913.

Neville, G. K. *Kinship and Pilgrimage: Rituals of Reunion in American Protestant Culture.* New York: Oxford University Press, 1987.

New York Public Library. *Literature as a Mode of Travel.* New York: New York Public Library, 1963.

Newman, J. P. *From Dan to Beersheba.* New York: Hunt & Eaton, 1892.

Newton, R. *Illustrated Rambles in Bible Lands.* Philadelphia: American Sunday School Union, 1875.

Nichols, J. T. *Lands of Sacred Story.* Des Moines, Iowa: Christian Union Press, 1910.

Obeidat, M. "Lured to the Exotic Levant: The Muslim East to the American Traveler of the Nineteenth Century." *Islamic Quarterly* 31 (1987): 167.

Odenheimer, W. H. *Jerusalem and Its Vicinity.* 1854. Reprint. New York: Arno Press, 1977.

Oehler, J. C. *Cruise to the Orient.* Richmond, Va.: Presbyterian Committee of Publication, 1906.

Olin, S. *Travels in Egypt, Arabia Petrea, and the Holy Land.* New York: Harper, 1843.

Oliphant, L. *The Land of Gilead.* New York: D. Appleton, 1881.

Oliphant, M. *Jerusalem: The Holy City.* New York: Macmillan, 1892.

Oliphant, R. D. *My Perilous Life in Palestine.* London: G. Allen, 1928.

Oliver, G. F. *A Trip Through Bible Lands and Europe.* Champaign, Ill.: Louden & Flaningam, 1913.

Osborn, H. S. *Palestine: Past and Present.* Philadelphia: J. Challen, 1859.

Otts, J. M. *The Fifth Gospel: The Land Where Jesus Lived.* New York: Revell, 1892.

Packard, J. F. *Grant's Tour Around the World.* Philadelphia: W. Flint, 1880.

"Palestine, the Same Yesterday and Today: Pictures." *Independent* 77 (1914): 198.

Palmer, L. T. *General Grant's Tour Around the World.* Chicago: J. Fairbanks, 1880.

Park, E. A. Correspondence, 1833–1879, Boston Public Library.

Parker, A. K. "Jerusalem and Thereabouts." *Biblical World* 7 (1896): 342.

Parkman, M. R. Diary, March 5–April 23, 1871. New York Public Library.

Pococke, R. *A Description of the East, and Some Other Countries.* London: Author, 1743–45.

Porter, J. L. *The Giant Cities of Bashan.* New York: T. Nelson, 1866.

Prime, W. C. *Tent Life in the Holy Land.* New York: Harper, 1857.

Raidabaugh, P. W. *The Pilgrims; or, Uncle Joseph and Rollin Through the Orient.* Cleveland: Evangelical Association, 1887.

Read, E. G. *A Domine in the Bible Lands.* Somerville, N.J.: Unionist-Gazette Association, 1894.

Rendall, M. J. *Sinai in Spring.* New York: E. P. Dutton, 1911.

Ridgaway, H. B. *The Lord's Land.* New York: Nelson & Phillips, 1876.

Rix, H. *Tent and Testament: A Camping Tour in Palestine.* New York: Scribner, 1907.

Robinson, F. G. "Patterns of Consciousness in the *Innocents Abroad*." *American Literature* 58 (1986): 46.
Robinson, G. L. "Beersheba Revisited." *Biblical World* 31 (1908): 327.
———. "Modern Palestine and Syria from Port Said to Beirut." *Chautauquan* 32 (1901): 409.
Rogers, M. E. "Domestic Architecture in Palestine and Syria." *Art Journal* 32 (1880): 49.
———. *Domestic Life in Palestine*. London: Bell & Daldy, 1862.
"Romance of Jerusalem." *Outlook* 117 (1917): 677.
Roosevelt, H. *Odyssey of an American Family: An Account of the Roosevelts and Their Kin as Travelers, from 1613 to 1938*. New York: Harper, 1939.
Roosevelt, T. *Diaries of Boyhood and Youth*. New York: Scribner, 1928.
———. *The Roosevelt Album*. Boston: A. Q. Cole, 1907.
Rowland, J. M. *A Pilgrimage to Palestine*. Richmond, Va.: Acme Printing, 1915.
Ryder, W. H. "Palestine." *Universalist Quarterly Review* 8 (1851): 137.
St. Clair, G. *Buried Cities and Bible Countries*. London: K. Paul, Trench, Trubner, 1891.
Sandys, G. *A Relation of a Journey Begun An. Dom. 1610*. 1615. Reprint. New York: Da Capo Press, 1973.
Schaff, P. *Through Bible Lands*. New York: American Tract Society, 1878.
Scharnhorst, G. "Mark Twain and the Millerites: Notes on *A Connecticut Yankee in King Arthur's Court*." *American Transcendental Quarterly* 3 (1989): 297.
Scheuerman, K. B. *The Holy Land as Seen Through Bible Eyes*. Seattle, Wash.: Metropolitan Press, 1910.
Schilling, G. "Life at the Holy Sepulchre." *North American Review* 159 (1894): 77.
Schoch, J. F. *From the Hudson to the Jordan*. Decatur, Ill.: Decatur Printing, 1887.
Schur, N. *Jerusalem in Pilgrims' and Travellers' Accounts: A Thematic Bibliography of Western Christian Itineraries, 1300–1917*. Jerusalem: Ariel, 1980.
Scott, J. *A Pilgrimage to Canaan*. Sioux City, Iowa: Perkins Brothers, 1908.
Seaton, D. P. *The Land of Promise*. Philadelphia: Pub. House of the A.M.E. Church, 1895.
Severance, E. A. *Journal Letters of Emily A. Severance, Quaker City, 1867*. Cleveland: Gates Press, 1938.
Seward, W. H. *William H. Seward's Travels Around the World*. Edited by O. R. Seward. New York: D. Appleton, 1873.
Shaw, J. B. "Recent Changes in the Holy Land." *Independent* 52 (1900): 2,083.
Shear, W. "Twain's Early Writing and Theories of Realism." *Midwest Quarterly* 30 (1988): 93.
Siddall, W. R. "Transportation and the Experience of Travel." *Geographical Review* 77 (1987): 309.
Sinclair, W. "Pilgrimage to Palestine." *Sunday Magazine* 33 (1904): 380.
Sivan, H. "Holy Land Pilgrimage and Western Audiences: Some Reflections on Egeria and Her Circle." *Classical Quarterly* 38 (1988): 528.
Smith, J. J. *The Wonders of the East*. New York: E. Goodenough, 1873.

Sommer, D. A. *Meditations in Bible Lands*. Indianapolis: Octographic Review, 1910.

Stebbing, H. *The Christian in Palestine*. London: G. Virtue, 1847.

Steinbrink, J. "How Mark Twain Survived Sam Clemens' Reformation." *American Literature* 55 (1983): 299.

———. "Why the Innocents Went Abroad: Mark Twain and American Tourism in the Late Nineteenth Century." *American Literary Realism* 16 (1983): 278.

Stephens, J. L. *Incidents of Travel in Egypt, Arabia Petrea, and the Holy Land*. Norman, Okla.: University of Oklahoma Press, 1970.

Stewart, M. *From Nile to Nile: Rambles of a Kansan in Europe, Palestine, and Africa*. Wichita, Kans.: Eagle Printing, 1888.

Stewart, R. L. *Memorable Places Among the Holy Hills*. New York: Revell, 1902.

Stine, M. H. *A Winter Jaunt Through Historic Lands*. Philadelphia: Lutheran Publication Society, 1890.

Studley, E. F. *A Trip to the Holy Land*. Providence, R.I.: Snow & Farnum, 1904.

Sutton, W. A. "Travel and Understanding: Notes on the Social Structure of Touring." *International Journal of Comparative Sociology* 8 (1967): 218.

Swift, J. F. *Going to Jericho*. New York: A. Roman, 1868.

Talmage, T. D. *Talmage on Palestine*. 1890. Reprint. New York: Arno Press, 1977.

Taylor, B. *The Lands of the Saracen; or, Pictures of Palestine, Asia Minor, Sicily, and Spain*. New York: Putnam, 1855.

Taylor, J. I. *A Gyre Thro' the Orient*. Princeton, Ill.: Republican Book and Job Printing Office, 1869.

Temple, C. R. *American Abroad*. New York: Bold Face Books, 1961.

Terhune, A. P. *Syria from the Saddle*. New York: Silver, Burdett, 1896.

Terhune, M. V. *Home of the Bible: What I Saw and Heard in Palestine*. New York: Christian Herald, 1896.

Theilmann, J. M. "Medieval Pilgrims and the Origins of Tourism." *Journal of Popular Culture* 20 (1987): 93.

"Thirsty Jerusalem." *Harper's Weekly* 54 (1910): 26.

Thompson, D. D. "American Artists in North Africa and the Middle East, 1797–1914." *Antiques* 126 (1984): 303.

Tiffany, F. *This Goodly Frame the Earth*. Boston: Houghton, Mifflin, 1895.

Tissot, J. J. "Round About Jerusalem." *Century Magazine* 35 (1898): 859.

Tompkins, E. S. *Through David's Realm*. Troy, N.Y.: Nims & Knight, 1889.

Train, G. F. *An American Merchant in Europe, Asia, and Australia*. New York: Putnam, 1857.

"Travel Literature, Ethnography, and Ethnohistory." *Ethnohistory* 33 (1986): 127.

Travel Literature Through the Ages: An Anthology. Edited by P. G. Adams. New York: Garland, 1988.

Trumbull, C. G. *Kadesh-Barnea*. New York: Scribner, 1884.

———. *A Pilgrimage to Jerusalem*. Philadelphia: Sunday School Times Company, 1905.

———. *Studies in Oriental Social Life and Gleanings from the East on the Sacred Page*. Philadelphia: J. D. Wattles, 1894.

Turner, L. *The Golden Hordes: International Tourism and the Pleasure Periphery.* London: Constable, 1975.

Turner, V., and E. Turner. *Image and Pilgrimage in Christian Culture: Anthropological Perspectives.* New York: Columbia University Press, 1978.

Turner, W. M. *El-Kuds the Holy.* Philadelphia: J. Challen, 1861.

"Two Months in Palestine." *Leisure Hour* 18 (1869): 492.

Vance, W. L. *America's Rome.* New Haven: Yale University Press, 1989.

———. "The Sidelong Glance: Victorian Americans and Baroque Rome." *New England Quarterly* 58 (1985): 501.

vandeBilt, E. F. "Proximity and Distance: American Travelers to the Middle East, 1819–1918." Ph.D. diss., Cornell University, 1985.

Van Deusen, G. G. *William Henry Seward.* New York: Oxford University Press, 1967.

Van Dyke, H. "Journey to Jerash." *Scribner's Monthly* 44 (1908): 405.

———. *Out-of-Doors in the Holy Land.* 1908. Reprint. New York: Arno Press, 1977.

Van Horne, D. *Tent and Saddle Life in the Holy Land.* Philadelphia: American Sunday School Union, 1885.

Van Schoick, R. W. *The Book and the Land.* New York: Eaton, 1904.

Vetromile, E. *Travels in Europe, Egypt, Arabia Petrea, Palestine, and Syria.* New York: D. & J. Sadlier, 1871.

Vincent, J. H. *Early Footsteps of the Man of Galilee.* New York: Thompson, 1893.

"A Visit to Jerusalem." *All the Year Round* 24 (1870): 588.

Walker, D. A. "Summer Touring in the Holy Land." *Old and New Testament Student* 12 (1891): 97.

Walker, F. D. *Irreverent Pilgrims: Melville, Browne, and Mark Twain in the Holy Land.* Seattle, Wash.: University of Washington Press, 1974.

"Wanderings in Palestine." *Lippincott's Magazine* 10 (1872): 261.

Warner, C. D. *In the Levant.* Cambridge, Mass.: Riverside Press, 1893.

———. "Jerusalem." *Atlantic Monthly* 38 (1876): 143.

———. "Palestine." *Atlantic Monthly* 38 (1876): 1.

Warner, D. S. *Glimpses of Palestine and Egypt.* Chicago: W. B. Rose, 1914.

Warren, I. P. *Jerusalem: Ancient and Modern.* Boston: Elliot, Blakeslee & Noyes, 1873.

Warren, W. W. *Life on the Nile in a Dahabeeh and Excursions on Shore Between Cairo and Assouan; Also a Tour in Syria and Palestine in 1866–1867.* New York: C. T. Dillingham, 1883.

"Wasting Eternity." *Atlantic Monthly* 113 (1914): 711.

Waters, C. E. *A Simple Story of What One of Your Lady Friends Saw in the East.* Boston: Avery & Frye, 1869.

Wells, J. "A Day in Palestine." *Sunday Magazine* 25 (1896): 261.

———. "The Favorite Wall in Palestine." *Sunday Magazine* 24 (1894): 751.

———. "Palestine, Cradle of Christianity." *Sunday Magazine* 25 (1896): 599.

———. *Travel Pictures from Palestine.* London: Isbinter, 1896.

Wheeler, V. "Travelers' Tales: Observations on the Travel Book and Ethnography." *Anthropological Quarterly* 59 (1986): 52.

Whiting, J. D. "Jerusalem's Locust Plague." *National Geographic Magazine* 28 (1915): 511.

———. "Village Life in the Holy Land." *National Geographic Magazine* 25 (1914): 249.

Whittle, W. A. *A Baptist Abroad.* New York: J. A. Hill, 1890.

Wilett, H. L. "Jerusalem, Past and Present." *Biblical World* 26 (1905): 325.

Wilhelm, K. *Roads to Zion: Four Centuries of Travelers' Reports.* New York: Schocken Books, 1948.

Williams, W. "Fire-Balls of Jerusalem." *Radical: A Monthly Magazine* 8 (1871): 201.

Willis, J. E. *My Experiences in the Holy Land.* Washington, D.C.: Author, 1914.

Wilson, E. L. *In Scripture Lands: New Views of Sacred Places.* New York: Scribner, 1895.

———. "Round About Jerusalem." *Century Magazine* 16 (1889): 42.

———. "Some Wayside Places in Palestine." *Century Magazine* 17 (1890): 737.

Wilson, E. S. *An Oriental Outing.* Cincinnati: Cranston & Curtis, 1894.

Wilson, T. W. *A Knight Templar's Pilgrimage to the Holy Land.* San Francisco: H. S. Crocker, 1908.

Wood, C. "Roughing It in Palestine." *Lippincott's Magazine* 36 (1885): 387.

Wood, G. W. "Jerusalem and Bethlehem." *Sunday Magazine* 21 (1892): 408.

Woodward, A. "Nineteenth-Century Delawareans and the Grand Tour." *Delaware History* 22 (1987): 125.

World's Sunday School Convention (Jerusalem, 1904). *Glimpses of Bible Lands.* Boston: WSSC Central Committee, 1905.

Wright, N. *Melville's Use of the Bible.* 1949. Reprint. New York: Octagon Books, 1969.

Young, J. R. *Around the World with General Grant.* New York: American News, 1879.

Zurbonsen, A. *Rambles Through Europe, the Holy Land, and Egypt.* St. Louis: B. Herder, 1903.

Missionaries

Abu-Ghazaleh, A. "American Missions in Syria: A Study of American Missionary Contribution to Arab Nationalism in Nineteenth-Century Syria." *Journal for Arab and Islamic Studies* 3 (1982): 5.

Adams, W. *Christianity Designed for the World, and the World Designed for Christianity.* Boston: Press of T.R. Marvin, 1854.

Addison, J. T. *The Christian Approach to the Moslem.* 1942. Reprint. New York: AMS Press, 1966.

After Fifty Years: A Record of God's Working Through the Christian and Missionary Alliance. Harrisburg, Pa.: Christian Publications, 1939.

Anderson, G. H. "American Protestants in Pursuit of Mission, 1886–1986." *International Bulletin of Missionary Research* 12 (1988): 98.

Anderson, R. *History of the Missions of the American Board of Commissioners for Foreign Missions to the Oriental Churches.* Boston: Congregational Pub. Society, 1873.

———. *Memorial Volume of the First Fifty Years of the American Board of Commissioners for Foreign Missions.* Boston: The American Board of Commissioners for Foreign Missions, 1861.

Andrew, J. A. *Rebuilding the Christian Commonwealth: New England Congregationalists and Foreign Missions, 1800–1830.* Lexington: University Press of Kentucky, 1976.

"The Attitude of Missionaries Toward the Historical Criticism of the Bible." *Biblical World* 42 (1913): 47.

Baldwin, M. B. "Missionary Work in Palestine." *Spirit of Missions* 40 (1874): 57.

Barclay, J. *The City of the Great King.* Philadelphia: J. Challen, 1858.

Baron, Mrs. D. "The Sacred Land of Palestine." *Missionary Review of the World* 14 (1891): 898.

Bartlett, S. C. *Historical Sketches of the Missions of the American Board.* 1876. Reprint. New York: Arno Press, 1972.

Barton, J. "The Turkish Government: Analysis of Its Inherent Evils." *Inquiry Document 43*, n.d. U.S. National Archives.

Beahm, W. M. *Factors in the Development of the Student Volunteer Movement for Foreign Missions.* Chicago: University of Chicago Libraries, 1941.

Beaver, R. P. "Pioneer Single Women Missionaries." *Occasional Bulletin of the Missionary Research Library* 4 (1953).

Ben-Obiel, A. "Jerusalem's Crying Wants." *Missionary Review of the World* 14 (1891): 924.

Bird, I. *Bible Word in Bible Lands.* Philadelphia: Presbyterian Board of Publications, 1872.

Bliss, D. *The Reminiscences of Daniel Bliss.* New York: Revell, 1920.

Bliss, E. M. *The Missionary Enterprise: A Concise History of Its Objects, Methods, and Extension.* New York: Revell, 1908.

Blyth, E. *When We Lived in Jerusalem.* London: J. Murray, 1927.

Bond, A. *Memoir of the Reverend Pliny Fisk, A.M.: Late Missionary to Palestine.* Boston: Crocker & Brewster, 1828.

Booth, A. R. "Imperialism, Economic Development, and the Christian World Mission." *Ecumenical Review* 21 (1969): 216.

"The Boys School at Jaffa." *Spirit of Missions* 43 (1878): 30.

Bridgeman, C. *The Episcopal Church and the Middle East.* New York: Morehouse-Gorham, 1958.

Brown, A. J. "Moslem Attitudes Toward Christian Missions in the Holy Land." *Missionary Review of the World* 25 (1902): 891.

————. *One Hundred Years: A History of the Foreign Missionary Work of the Presbyterian Church in the U.S.A.* New York: Revell, 1936.

Burnet, D. S. *The Jerusalem Mission: Under the Direction of the American Christian Missionary Society.* Cincinnati: American Christian Publication Society, 1853.

Cauthen, B. J. *Advance: A History of Southern Baptist Foreign Missions.* Nashville, Tenn.: Broadman Press, 1970.

Chaney, C. L. *The Birth of Missions in America.* South Pasadena, Calif.: William Carey Library, 1976.

Chester, S. H. *Behind the Scenes: An Administrative History of the Foreign Work of the Presbyterian Church in the United States.* Austin, Tex.: Press of Von Boeckmann–Jones, 1928.

Christlieb, T. *Protestant Foreign Missions: Their Present State.* Boston: Congregational Pub. Society, 1880.

Codman, J. *The Duty of American Christians to Send the Gospel to the Heathen.* Boston: Crocker & Brewster, 1836.

Collins, G. W. *Missionaries and Muslims.* Wichita, Kans.: Wichita State University, 1975.

Cumming, J. E. "Christian Missions in the Holy Land." *Missionary Review of the World* 21 (1898): 903.

Dafesh, A. "Mary Jane Lovell: Mother of the Blind in Bible Lands." *Moslem World* 23 (1933): 56.

Daniel, R. L. *American Philanthropy in the Near East, 1820–1960.* Athens, Ohio: Ohio University Press, 1970.

Dodge, B. "American Educational Missionary Effort in the Nineteenth and Early Twentieth Centuries." *Annals of the American Academy of Political and Social Science* 401 (1972): 15.

Earle, E. M. "American Missions in the Near East." *Foreign Affairs* 7 (1929): 398.

Eddy, D. B. *What Next in Turkey: Glimpses of the American Board's Work in the Near East.* Boston: The American Board of Commissioners for Foreign Missions, 1913.

Elbert, S. "'Anywhere with Jesus, Everywhere with Jesus': American Women's Foreign Mission." *American Quarterly* 37 (1985): 755.

Ellis, W. T. "American and Turk in Holy War." *Century Magazine* 85 (1913): 456.

Emery, J. C. *A Century of Endeavor, 1821–1921: A Record of the First Hundred Years of the Domestic and Foreign Missionary Society of the Protestant Episcopal Church in the United States of America.* New York: Department of Missions, 1921.

Ewing, W. *Arab and Druze at Home.* London: T. C. Jack, 1907.

———. "Palestine and Revelation." *Biblical World* 24 (1904): 86.

———. *Paterson of Hebron, "the Hakim": Missionary Life in the Mountain of Judah.* London: J. Clark, 1930.

———. "Taxes and Tax Gatherers in Galilee." *Sunday School Times* 40 (1898): 67.

Fisher, S. *God's Purpose in Planting the American Church.* Boston: Press of T. R. Marvin, 1860.

Fisk, P. *The Holy Land: An Interesting Field of Missionary Enterprise.* Boston: S. T. Armstrong, 1819.

Ford, G. A. "Evangelical Missions in Syria." *Missionary Review of the World* 16 (1893): 906.

Forder, A. *With Arabs in Tent and Town.* London: Marshall Brothers, 1902.

Foreign Missions Conference of North America. *Report of the Meeting of the Conference of Foreign Mission Boards in Canada and the United States.* New York: Foreign Missions Conference of North America, 1893–1950.

Garrison, W. E. *The Disciples of Christ: A History.* St. Louis: Christian Board of Publications, 1948.

Goodell, W. *Forty Years in the Turkish Empire.* New York: R. Carter, 1883.

Goodsell, F. F. *They Lived Their Faith.* Boston: The American Board of Commissioners for Foreign Missions, 1961.

Grabill, J. L. "Protestant Diplomacy and Arab Nationalism, 1914–1948." *American Presbyterians* 64 (1986): 113.

————. *Protestant Diplomacy and the Near East: Missionary Influence on American Policy, 1810–1927*. Minneapolis: University of Minnesota Press, 1971.

Gracey, A. R. *Eminent Missionary Women*. New York: Eaton & Mains, 1898.

Green, A. *Presbyterian Missions*. New York: A.D.F. Randolph, 1893.

Greene, J. K. *Leavening the Levant*. Boston: Pilgrim Press, 1916.

Hall, W. H. *The Near East: Crossroads of the World*. New York: Interchurch Press, 1920.

Hamilton, J. T. "The Leper Hospital of the Moravian Church at Jerusalem." *Missionary Review of the World* 15 (1892): 132.

Hanauer, J. *Tales Told in Palestine*. Cincinnati: Jennings & Graham, 1904.

————. *Walks in and Around Jerusalem*. London: London Society for Promoting Christianity Among the Jews, 1926.

Hanselmann, S. *Deutsche Evangelische Palästinamission*. Erlangen: Verlag der Ev. Luth. Mission, 1971.

Harding, H. G. "Present Situation in Palestine." *Missionary Review of the World* 33 (1910): 692.

Heim, D. "Evangelicals Reconsider the Meaning of Missions." *Christian Century* 103 (1986): 636.

Hill, P. R. *The World Their Household: The American Woman's Foreign Mission Movement and Cultural Transformation, 1870–1920*. Ann Arbor: University of Michigan Press, 1985.

Hood, E. P. *The Villages of the Bible*. Philadelphia: Lippincott, 1874.

Hooper, W. "Mission Work in Palestine." *Missionary Review of the World* 29 (1906): 932.

Hopkins, C. H. *John R. Mott, 1865–1955: A Biography*. Grand Rapids, Mich.: Eerdmans, 1979.

Horstmann, J. H. "Syrian Orphans' Home." *Missionary Review of the World* 32 (1909): 92.

Hunter, J. *The Gospel of Gentility: American Women Missionaries in Turn of the Century China*. New Haven: Yale University Press, 1984.

Hutchison, W. R. *Errand to the World: American Protestant Thought and Foreign Missions*. Chicago: University of Chicago Press, 1987.

Jessup, H. H. "Are the Jews Returning to Palestine?" *Review of Reviews* 13 (1896): 89.

————. *Fifty-Three Years in Syria*. New York: Revell, 1910.

————. "The Jews in Palestine and Syria." *Missionary Review of the World* 18 (1895): 887.

————. *The Setting of the Crescent and the Rising of the Cross*. Philadelphia: Westminster Press, 1898.

————. "Syria and Missions." *Missionary Review of the World* 26 (1903): 605.

————. *Syrian Home Life*. New York: Dodd & Mead, 1874.

————. *The Women of the Arabs*. New York: Dodd & Mead, 1873.

————. "A Word from Syria." *Missionary Review of the World* 26 (1903): 605.

"A Jewish Conversion Epidemic." *Missionary Review of the World* 37 (1914): 881.

Johnson, S. B. *Hadji in Syria*. Philadelphia: J. Challen, 1858.

Joint Committee on the Survey of Christian Literature for Moslems. *Christian Literature in Moslem Lands*. New York: Doran, 1923.

Jones, C. *The Untempered Wind: Forty Years in Palestine.* London: Longman, 1975.

Jong, J. A. de. *As the Waters Cover the Sea: Millennial Expectations in the Rise of Anglo-American Missions, 1640–1810.* Kampen: J. H. Kok, 1970.

"Joppa Mission School." *Spirit of Missions* 40 (1875): 316.

Kelsey, A. E. "The Conquest of the Holy Land." *Missionary Review of the World* 37 (1914): 895.

Kinney, B. *Kingdom Preparedness: America's Opportunity to Serve the World.* New York: Revell, 1916.

Lane, O. M. *Missions in Magazines: An Analysis of the Treatment of Protestant Foreign Missions in American Magazines Since 1810.* Tientsin: Tientsin Press, 1935.

Latourette, K. S. *Christianity in a Revolutionary Age.* New York: Harper, 1958–62.

———. *A History of the Expansion of Christianity.* Grand Rapids, Mich.: Zondervan, 1970.

———. *Missions and the American Mind.* Indianapolis: National Foundation Press, 1949.

———. *World Service: A History of the Foreign Work and World Service of the Young Men's Christian Associations of the United States and Canada.* New York: Association Press, 1957.

Laymen's Foreign Missions Inquiry. Commission of Appraisal. *Rethinking Missions.* New York: Harper, 1932.

Lee, R. E. *The Story of the Ram Allah Mission.* Manchester, N.H.: Nutfield Press, 1912.

Lindsay, R. H. *Nineteenth-Century American Schools in the Levant.* Ann Arbor: University of Michigan, School of Education, 1965.

Livingstone, W. P. *A Galilee Doctor: Being a Sketch of the Career of Dr. D. W. Torrance of Tiberias.* New York: Doran, 1923.

MacInnes, A. C. *The Episcopal Church and the Middle East.* New York: Morehouse-Gorham, 1958.

McLean, A. *The History of the Foreign Christian Missionary Society.* New York: Revell, 1921.

Madden, R. R. *The Turkish Empire in Its Relation with Christianity and Civilization.* London: T. C. Newby, 1862.

Maddry, C. E. *Mightily Grew the Word of God in Europe and Palestine.* Richmond, Va.: Foreign Mission Board, Southern Baptist Convention, 1935.

Masterman. E.W.G. "Medical Mission Hospitals of Palestine." *Missionary Review of the World* 30 (1907): 901.

May, H. F. "Missionaries and Their Doubts." *Reviews in American History* 16 (1988): 55.

Meadowcroft, L. V. *Two Studies in Christian Missions* Philadelphia: Eastern Baptist Theological Seminary, 1939.

Meyer, L. "Encouragements in Missionary Work Among the Jews." *Missionary Review of the World* 26 (1903): 899.

———. "One Hundred Years of Missionary Work Among the Jews." *Missionary Review of the World* 32 (1909): 92.

———. "Outlook of Jewish Missions." *Missionary Review of the World* 31 (1908): 901.

————. "Protestant Missions to the Jews." *Missionary Review of the World* 25 (1902): 901.

Miller, E. C. *Eastern Sketches.* 1871. Reprint. New York: Arno Press, 1977.

Miller, R. M. *Harry Emerson Fosdick: Preacher, Pastor, Prophet.* New York: Oxford University Press, 1985.

"Mission School at Joppa." *Spirit of Missions* 39 (1874): 111.

"Mission to the Motherland of Missions." *Survey* 40 (1918): 261.

Missionary Conference on Behalf of the Mohammedan World, First, Cairo, 1906. *Methods of Mission Work Among Moslems.* New York: Revell, 1906.

"Missions in Palestine and Syria." *Missionary Review of the World* 25 (1903): 710.

Montgomery, H. B. *The Bible and Missions.* West Medford, Mass.: Central Committee of the United Study of Foreign Missions, 1920.

————. *Following the Sunrise: A Century of Baptist Missions, 1813–1913.* Philadelphia: American Baptist Publication Society, 1913.

————. *From Jerusalem to Jerusalem.* North Cambridge, Mass.: Central Committee of the United Study of Foreign Missions, 1929.

————. *The Preaching Value of Missions.* Philadelphia: Judson Press, 1931.

————. *Western Women in Eastern Lands.* New York: Macmillan, 1910.

Morgan, C. H. "The Status of Field Work in the Protestant Theological Seminaries of the United States." Ph.D. diss., University of Pennsylvania, 1942.

Morton, D. O. *Memoir of Reverend Levi Parsons.* 1824. Reprint. New York: Arno Press, 1977.

Mott, J. R. *The Vision of the Student Missionary Pioneers Realized by Students of the Present Generation.* New York: Student Volunteer Movement for Foreign Missions, 1911.

Ostling, R. N. "Protestantism's Foreign Legion." *Time* 129 (16 February 1987): 62.

"Palestine." *Spirit of Missions* 42 (1877): 522.

"Palestine and the Jews." *Missionary Review of the World* 41 (1918): 5.

Palmer, H. P. *Joseph Wolff: His Romantic Life and Travels.* London: Heath, Cranton, 1935.

Pardington, G. P. *Twenty-Five Wonderful Years, 1889–1914: A Popular Sketch of the Christian and Missionary Alliance.* New York: Christian Alliance, 1914.

Parsons, L. *The Dereliction and Restoration of the Jews.* Boston: S. T. Armstrong, 1819.

Payne, A. W. "Missions in Palestine." *Missionary Review of the World* 16 (1893): 899.

Phillips, C. J. *Protestant America and the Pagan World: The First Half Century of the American Board of Commissioners for Foreign Missions, 1810–1860.* Cambridge, Mass.: Harvard University, East Asian Research Center, 1969.

Pierard, R. V. "John R. Mott and the Rift in the Ecumenical Movement During World War I." *Journal of Ecumenical Studies* 23 (1986): 601.

Pierson, A. T. "Modern Biblical Criticism and Missions." *Missionary Review of the World* 29 (1906): 812.

Pitman, E. *Mission Life in Greece and Palestine: Memorials of Mary Briscoe Baldwin, Missionary to Athens and Joppa.* London: Cassell, Pelter, Galpin, 1881.

Porter, A. N. "'Commerce and Christianity': The Rise and Fall of a Nineteenth-Century Slogan." *The Historical Journal* 28 (1985): 597.

Ramsey, D. G. "College Evangelists and Foreign Missions: The Student Volunteer Movement, 1886–1920." Ph.D. diss., University of California at Davis, 1988.

Reed, J. E. "American Foreign Policy, the Politics of Missions, and Josiah Strong, 1890–1900." *Church History* 41 (1972): 230.

Richter, J. *A History of Protestant Missions in the Near East.* 1910. Reprint. New York: AMS Press, 1970.

Rohold, S. B. "Are Missions to Jews a Failure?" *Missionary Review of the World* 37 (1914): 887.

Sarna, J. D. "American Christian Opposition to Missions to the Jews, 1816–1900." *Journal of Ecumenical Studies* 23 (1986): 225.

Scott, F. E. *Dare and Persevere: The Story of One Hundred Years of Evangelism in Syria and Lebanon, from 1860 to 1960.* London: Lebanon Evangelical Mission, 1960.

Scult, M. "English Missions to the Jews—Conversion in the Age of Emancipation." *Jewish Social Studies* 35 (1973): 3.

Shaw, P. E. *American Contacts with the Eastern Churches, 1820–1870.* Chicago: American Society of Church History, 1937.

Simpson, A. B. *Larger Outlooks on Missionary Lands.* New York: Christian Alliance, 1893.

Smith, E. *The Missionary Character.* New Haven: B.L. Hamlen, 1840.

Smith, F. G. *Missionary Journeys Through Bible Lands.* Anderson, Ind.: Gospel Trumpet, 1915.

Strong, W. E. *The Story of the American Board: An Account of the First Hundred Years of the American Board of Commissioners for Foreign Missions.* Boston: Pilgrim Press, 1910.

Student Volunteer Movement for Foreign Missions. International Convention, Fourth, Ontario, 1902. *Evangelization: The Urgent Business of the Church.* New York: Student Volunteer Movement for Foreign Missions, 1902.

Taylor, A. R. "The American Protestant Mission and the Awakening of Modern Syria, 1820–1870." Ph.D. diss., Georgetown University, 1958.

Thompson, A. E. *A Century of Jewish Missions.* Chicago: Revell, 1902.

———. *The Life of A. B. Simpson.* New York: Christian Alliance, 1920.

———. "Message from Palestine." *Missionary Review of the World* 38 (1915): 881.

Tibawi, A. L. *American Interests in Syria, 1800–1901.* Oxford: Clarendon Press, 1966.

———. *British Interests in Palestine, 1800–1901.* London: Oxford University Press, 1961.

"Time to Favor Zion." *Missionary Review of the World* 37 (1914): 561.

Torbet, R. G. *Venture of Faith: The Story of the American Baptist Foreign Mission Society and the Women's American Baptist Foreign Mission Society, 1814–1954.* Philadelphia: Judson Press, 1955.

Tracy, J. *History of the American Board of Commissioners for Foreign Missions.* Worcester, Mass.: Spooner & Howland, 1840.

Tucker, W. E. *Journey in Faith: A History of the Christian Church Disciples of Christ.* St. Louis: Bethany Press, 1975.

Tupper, H. A. *Uncle Allen's Party in Palestine.* Philadelphia: American Baptist Pub. Society, 1898.

Turtle, H. J. *Quaker Service in the Middle East.* London: Friends Service Council, 1975.

Van Ess, D. *Pioneers in the Arab World.* Grand Rapids, Mich.: Eerdmans, 1974.

Van Lennep, H. J. *Bible Lands.* New York: Harper, 1903.

———. *The Oriental Album.* New York: A.D.F. Randolph, 1862.

———. *Travels in Little-Known Parts of Asia.* New York: A. O. Van Lennep, 1870.

Welter, B. "She Hath Done What She Could: Protestant Women's Missionary Careers in Nineteenth-Century America." *American Quarterly* 30 (1978): 624.

White, A. "Counting the Cost of Faith: America's Early Female Missionaries." *Church History* 57 (1988): 19.

Wilder, R. P. *The Great Commission: The Missionary Response of the Student Volunteer Movements in North America and Europe.* London: Oliphants, 1937.

Williams, H. F. *In Four Continents: A Sketch of the Foreign Missions of the Presbyterian Church, U.S.A.* Richmond, Va.: Presbyterian Committee of Publication, 1910.

Wilson, E. G. "The Christian and Missionary Alliance: Development and Modification of Its Original Objectives." Ph.D. diss., New York University, 1984.

Wilson, J. K. "The Uncanonical Missionary in Palestine." *Missionary Review of the World* (1892): 267.

Wolff, J. *Missionary Journal and Memoir of the Reverend Joseph Wolff: Missionary to the Jews.* London: J. Duncan, 1824.

Wright, J. *Christianity and Commerce: The Natural Results of the Geographical Progression of Railways.* London: Dolman, 1854.

Young Men's Christian Association, Jerusalem. *The Jerusalem YMCA.* Jerusalem: Young Men's Christian Association, 1933.

Zwemer, S. M. *The Golden Milestone: Reminiscences of Pioneer Days Fifty Years Ago in Arabia.* New York: Revell, 1938.

———. *The Impending Struggle in Western Asia.* New York: Student Volunteer Movement, 1910.

———. *The Moslem World.* New York: Young People's Missionary Movement of the United States, 1908.

Settlers and Colonists

Amann, P. "Prophet in Zion: The Saga of George J. Adams." *New England Quarterly* 37 (1964): 477.

———. "U.S. Colonists in the Holy Land." *American History Illustrated* 5 (1971): 28.

Berendsohn, W. A. *Selma Lagerlof: Her Life and Work.* 1931. Reprint. Port Washington, N.Y.: Kennikat Press, 1968.

Boettner, L. *The Millennium.* Philadelphia: Presbyterian and Reformed Pub. Co., 1958.

Carmel, A. *Christen als Pioniere im Heiligen Land.* Basel: F. Reinhardt, 1981.

———. *Der Orientmaler Gustav Bauernfeind, 1848–1904.* Stuttgart: E. Hauswedell, 1990.

———. *Die Siedlungen der Würtembergischen Templer in Palästina, 1868–1918.* Stuttgart: W. Kohlhammer, 1973.

Case, S. J. *The Millennial Hope: A Phase of War-Time Thinking.* Chicago: University of Chicago Press, 1918.

Chamberlain, G. W. "A New England Crusade." *New England Magazine* 36 (1907): 195.

Christian Protagonists for Jewish Restoration. New York: Arno Press, 1977.

Cohn, N. R. *The Pursuit of the Millennium.* New York: Oxford University Press, 1970.

Davis, H. "The Jaffa Colonists from Downeast." *American Quarterly* 3 (1951): 344.

Eidelberg, S. "The Adams Colony in Jaffa, 1866–1868." *Midstream* 3 (1957): 52.

Elman, P. "The American Swedish Kibbutz." *Swedish Pioneer Historical Quarterly* 32 (1981): 205.

Feinberg, C. L. *Millennialism: The Two Major Views.* Chicago: Moody Press, 1980.

———. *Premillennialism or Amillennialism.* Wheaton, Ill.: Van Kampen Press, 1954.

Ford, A. H. "Our American Colony at Jerusalem." *Appleton's Magazine* 8 (1906): 643.

Friends of Jerusalem in the United States. *Memorial to the Executive and the Congress of the United States of America.* Schenectady, N.Y.: Friends of Jerusalem, 1868.

Gelber, N. M. "A Pre-Zionist Plan for Colonizing Palestine." *Historia Judaica* 1 (1939): 81.

Hanauer, J. E. "Notes on the History of Modern Colonization of Palestine." *Palestine Exploration Fund Quarterly Statement* (1900): 124.

Haslip, J. *Lady Hester Stanhope.* London: Heron Books, 1970.

Henderson, P. *The Life of Laurence Oliphant: Traveller, Diplomat, and Mystic.* London: R. Hale, 1956.

Hobart, G. S. "The Matson Collection: A Half Century of Photographing in the Middle East." *Quarterly Journal of the Library of Congress* 30 (1973): 19.

Hoffmann, C. *Missives, Treating of the Temple and the Sacraments.* Buffalo, N.Y.: P. Paulus, 1905.

Holmes, R. M. *The Forerunners.* Independence, Mo.: Herald, 1981.

———. "G. J. Adams and the Forerunners." *Maine Historical Society Quarterly* 21 (1981): 19.

Johnson, J. A. "The Colonization of Palestine." *Century* 2 (1882): 293.

Kautsch, E. "Work of the German Society for Palestine." *Andover Review* 5 (1886): 262.

Kraus, C. N. *Dispensationalism in America*. Richmond, Va.: John Knox Press, 1958.
Lagerlof, S. *The Diary of Selma Lagerlof*. 1936. Reprint. Millwood, N.Y.: Kraus Reprint Company, 1975.
———. *The Holy City: Jerusalem*. New York: Doubleday, Page, 1918.
———. *Jerusalem*. 1903. Reprint. Westport, Conn.: Greenwood Press, 1970.
Lagerroth, E. *Selma Lagerlof's Jerusalem*. Lund: Gleerup, 1966.
Larsen, H. A. *Selma Lagerlof*. 1936. Reprint. Millwood, N.Y.: Kraus Reprint Company, 1975.
McEwen, R. W. "Factors in the Modern Survival of Millennialism." Ph.D. diss., University of Chicago, 1933.
Matson, G. E. *The Middle East in Pictures*. New York: Arno Press, 1979.
Matson, O. G. *A Guide-Book to Jerusalem and Environs*. Jerusalem: F. Vester, 1920.
Minor, C. *Meshullam; or, Tidings from Jerusalem*. Philadelphia: Author, 1850.
Moorhead, J. H. *American Apocalypse: Yankee Protestants and the Civil War, 1860–1869*. New Haven: Yale University Press, 1978.
Oliphant, L. *Haifa; or, Life in the Holy Land, 1882–1885*. 1887. Reprint. Jerusalem: Canaan Pub. House, 1976.
Parker, J. M. "A Fanatic and Her Mission." *The Churchman* 74 (1896): 448.
The Rise of Adventism: Religion and Society in Mid-Nineteenth-Century America. Edited by E. S. Gaustad. New York: Harper & Row, 1974.
Smith, T. L. "Righteousness and Hope: Christian Holiness and the Millennial Vision." *American Quarterly* 31 (1979): 21.
Thrupp, S. L. *Millennial Dreams in Action*. New York: Schocken, 1970.
Toon, P. *Puritans, the Millennium, and the Future of Israel*. Cambridge, Mass.: James Clarke, 1970.
Vester, B. S. "Jerusalem: My Home." *National Geographic Magazine* 126 (1964): 826.———. *Our Jerusalem*. Garden City, N.Y.: Doubleday, 1950.

Consuls, Diplomacy, and Commercial Interests

Adler, C. *With Firmness in the Right: American Diplomatic Action Affecting Jews, 1840–1945*. 1946. Reprint. New York: Arno Press, 1977.
Almond, G. A. *The American People and Foreign Policy*. 1950. Reprint. Westport, Conn.: Greenwood Press, 1977.
Angell, J. B. "The Turkish Capitulations." *Annual Report of the American Historical Association* 1 (1901): 511.
Bailey, T. A. *A Diplomatic History of the American People*. Englewood Cliffs, N.J.: Prentice-Hall, 1980.
Bartour, R. "Early Christian Lovers of Zion: A Vignette of Edwin Wallace." *Perception* 1 (1978): 5.
Beard, C. A. *The Idea of National Interest*. Chicago: Quadrangle Books, 1966.
Bryson, T. A. *American Diplomatic Relations with the Middle East, 1784–1975: A Survey*. Metuchen, N.J.: Scarecrow Press, 1977.
Bullard, R. W. *Large and Loving Privileges: The Capitulations in the Middle East and North Africa*. Glasgow: Jackson, 1960.

"Concrete in Palestine." *Scientific American Supplement* 69 (1910): 267.

Consular Evils and Their Remedy. New York: Dry Goods Economist, 1893.

Cox, S. S. *Diversions of a Diplomat in Turkey.* New York: C.L. Webster, 1887.

———. *Liberalities of Trade—Consular and Diplomatic Relations.* Washington, D.C.: U.S. Government Printing Office, 1880.

Cresson, W. *Jerusalem: The Centre and Joy of the Whole Earth; and the Jew: The Recipient of the Glory of God.* Philadelphia: J. Harding, 1844.

———. *The Key of David.* Philadelphia: Author, 1852.

DeHass, F. S. *Buried Cities Recovered; or, Explorations in Bible Lands.* 1882. Reprint. New York: Arno Press, 1977.

———. *Recent Travels and Explorations in Bible Lands.* New York: Phillips & Hunt, 1880.

Farah, C. E. "Protestantism and British Diplomacy in Syria." *International Journal of Middle East Studies* 7 (1976): 321.

Field, J. A. "Trade, Skills, and Sympathy: The First Century and a Half of Commerce Between the United States and Turkey." *Annals of the American Academy of Political and Social Science* 401 (1972): 1.

Finn, E. A. *A Home in the Holy Land.* New York: T.Y. Crowell, 1882.

———. *Reminiscences of Mrs. Finn.* London: Marshall, Korgan, & Scott, 1929.

Finn, J. *Stirring Times.* London: C.K. Paul, 1878.

———. *A View from Jerusalem, 1849–1858: The Consular Diary of James and Elizabeth Anne Finn.* Edited by A. Blumberg. Rutherford, N.J.: Fairleigh Dickinson University Press, 1980.

Fisher, G. S. *A Condensed Narrative of the Persecution of an American Consul by Some American Missionaries at Beirut, Syria.* Washington, D.C.: L.G. Stephens, 1879.

Foster, H. S. *American Public Opinion and U.S. Foreign Policy.* Washington, D.C.: U.S. Department of State, 1960.

Frankel, C. "Culture, Information, and Foreign Policy." *Public Administration Review* 29 (1969): 593.

Friedman, I. "Lord Palmerston and the Protection of Jews in Palestine, 1839–1851." *Jewish Social Studies* 30 (1968): 23.

Gillman, H. "On the Site of the Holy Sepulchre." *Quarterly Statement of the Palestine Exploration Fund* (1891): 93.

———. "Pool of Bethesda." *Scientific American* 63 (1890): 37.

Gordon, L. J. *American Relations with Turkey, 1830–1930: An Economic Interpretation.* Philadelphia: University of Pennsylvania Press, 1932.

Greenfield, H. *The Policymakers: The Foreign Policy Role of Americans Abroad.* New York: Exposition Press, 1965.

Heald, M. *Culture and Diplomacy: The American Experience.* Westport, Conn.: Greenwood Press, 1977.

Hyamson, A. M. *The British Consulate in Jerusalem in Relation to the Jews of Palestine, 1838–1914.* 1939–41. Reprint. New York: AMS Press, 1975.

Jones, C. L. *The Consular Service of the United States: Its History and Activities.* Philadelphia: University of Pennsylvania, 1906.

Karp, A. "The Zionism of Warder Cresson." In *Early History of Zionism in America,* edited by I. Meyer. 1958. Reprint. New York: Arno Press, 1977.

Klineberg, O. *The Human Dimension in International Relations*. New York: Holt, Rinehart & Winston, 1964.

Livermore, S. W. "Desiring Democrats: The Foreign Service Under Woodrow Wilson." *South Atlantic Quarterly* 69 (1970): 144.

McKee, I. *"Ben-Hur" Wallace: The Life of General Lew Wallace*. Berkeley and Los Angeles: University of California Press, 1947.

Manual, F. E. *The Realities of America-Palestine Relations*. 1949. Reprint. Westport, Conn.: Greenwood Press, 1975.

Merrill, S. *Ancient Jerusalem*. 1908. Reprint. New York: Arno Press, 1977.

——. "An Archaeological Visit to Jerusalem." *Biblical World* 14 (1899): 267.

——. "Assyrian and Babylonian Monuments in America." *Bibliotheca Sacra* 30 (1875): 320.

——. "Birds and Animals New to Palestine." *Quarterly Statement of the Palestine Exploration Fund, 1890*, p. 40.

——. "Charities in Jerusalem." *Sunday School Times* 38 (1896): 520.

——. "Discoveries in Jerusalem." *Presbyterian and Reformed Review* 3 (1892): 630.

——. *East of the Jordan*. New York: Scribner, 1881.

——. "Food and Habits of Eating in the East." *Sunday School Times* 36 (1894): 818.

——. *Galilee in the Time of Christ*. Boston: Congregational Pub. Society, 1881.

——. "Jaffa and Jerusalem Railway." *Scribner's Magazine* 13 (1893): 289.

——. "Labor in Asia: Palestine." In U.S. Department of State, *Labor in America, Asia, Africa, Australia, and Polynesia*. Washington, D.C.: U.S. Government Printing Office, 1885.

——. "Modern Researches in Palestine." *American Geographical Society Journal* (1877): 109.

——. "Pilgrim Caravans in the East." *International Review* 5 (1878): 639.

——. "Recent Explorations in Palestine." *Magazine of Christian Literature* 3 (1890): 385.

——. "The Site of Calvary." *Andover Review* 4 (1885): 483.

——. "Underground Treasures and Monuments." *Sunday School Times* 37 (1895): 178–179.

——. "Wagon Roads in Palestine." *Scientific American Supplement* 52 (1901): 21,533.

——. "Walled Cities in Palestine." *Atheneum* 2 (1882): 635.

——. "Within Thy Gates, O Jerusalem." *Biblical World* 12 (1898): 293.

Paullin, C. *Diplomatic Negotiations of American Naval Officers, 1778–1883*. 1912. Reprint. Gloucester, Mass.: P. Smith, 1967.

Plesur, M. *America's Outward Thrust: Approaches to Foreign Affairs, 1865–1890*. DeKalb, Ill.: Northern Illinois University Press, 1971.

Plischke, E. *Conduct of American Diplomacy*. 1961. Reprint. Princeton: Van Nostrand, 1964.

The Puritan Ethic in United States Foreign Policy. Edited by D. L. Larson. Princeton: Van Nostrand, 1966.

Ravndal, G. B. *American Trade Relations with the Near East*. Chicago: Stromberg & Allen, 1912.

————. *The Origin of the Capitulations and of the Consular Institution.* Washington, D.C.: U.S. Government Printing Office, 1921.

Rhodes, A. *Jerusalem as It Is.* London: J. Maxwell, 1865.

————. "Our Consul at Jerusalem." *Galaxy* 14 (1872): 437.

Rosen, F. *Oriental Memories of a German Diplomatist.* London: Methuen, 1930.

Schuyler, E. *American Diplomacy and the Furtherance of Commerce.* New York: Scribner, 1886.

Smylie, J. E. "Protestant Clergymen and American Destiny: Prelude to Imperialism, 1865–1900." *Harvard Theological Review* 56 (1963): 297.

Statham, W. M. "Industries of Palestine." *Sunday Magazine* 21 (1892): 21.

Susa, N. *The Capitulatory Regime of Turkey.* Baltimore: Johns Hopkins University Press, 1933.

Thomson, C. A., and W. H. Laves. *Cultural Relations and U.S. Foreign Policy.* Bloomington: Indiana University Press, 1963.

Tsakonas, A. *American Trade with the Levant and Its Possibilities.* Philadelphia: Wick-Gapp Co., 1906.

Twiss, T. *On Consular Jurisdiction in the Levant and the Status of Foreigners in the Ottoman Law Courts.* London: W. Clowes, 1880.

United States. *Commerce Reports.* Washington, D.C.: U.S. Government Printing Office, 1910–40.

————. *Commercial Relations of the United States with Foreign Countries.* Washington, D.C.: U.S. Government Printing Office, 1855–1912.

————. Consular Records for Jerusalem, Jaffa, and Haifa. U.S. National Archives.

————. *Daily Consular and Trade Reports.* Washington, D.C.: U.S. Government Printing Office, 1898–1910.

————. *Monthly Consular and Trade Reports.* Washington, D.C.: U.S. Government Printing Office, 1880–1910.

————. *Special Consular Reports.* Washington, D.C.: U.S. Government Printing Office, 1890–1923.

United States Department of Commerce and Labor. *Report on Trade Conditions in Asiatic Turkey.* Washington, D.C.: U.S. Government Printing Office, 1907.

United States Department of State. *Message from the President of the United States, Transmitting, . . . A Report of the Secretary of State, Touching the Capitulations of the Ottoman Empire.* Washington, D.C.: U.S. Government Printing Office, 1882.

————. *Message from the President of the United States, Transmitting, in Response to the Resolution of the Senate. . . .* Washington, D.C.: U.S. Government Printing Office, 1881.

————. *Report on the Commercial Relations of the United States with All Foreign Nations.* Washington, D.C.: A.O.P. Nicholson, Printer, 1856–57.

Verete, M. "Why Was a British Consulate Established in Jerusalem?" *English Historical Review* 85 (1970): 316.

Wallace, E. S. "American Lumber in Foreign Markets: Palestine." In *American Lumber in Foreign Markets*, United States Department of State. Washington, D.C.: U.S. Government Printing Office, 1896.

————. "Homes and Home Life in Jerusalem." *Independent* 49 (1897): 1,683.

————. *Jerusalem: The Holy.* New York: Revell, 1898.

————. "The Jews in Jerusalem." *Cosmopolitan* 26 (1898): 317.

Wallace, L. *Lew Wallace: An Autobiography*. New York: Harper, 1906.
Wallace, S. A. *The City of the King: What the Child Jesus Saw and Heard*. Indianapolis: Bobbs-Merrill, 1903.
———. "Jerusalem as It Is Today." *Ladies Home Journal* 18 (1900): 10.
Wright, L. C. *United States Policy Toward Egypt, 1830–1914*. New York: Exposition Press, 1969.
Young, R. *Recent American Policy Concerning the Capitulations in the States of the Middle East*. Lancaster, Pa.: n.p., 1948.

Archaeologists, Explorers, and Scholars

Abbot, L. "Recovery of Jerusalem." *Harper's Magazine* 43 (1871): 195.
Adler, C., and I. M. Casanowics. *Biblical Antiquities*. Washington, D.C.: U.S. Government Printing Office, 1898.
Aharoni, Y. *The Land of the Bible: A Historical Geography*. Philadelphia: Westminster Press, 1979.
Albright, W. F. "Archaeology Confronts Biblical Criticism." *American Scholar* 7 (1938): 176.
———. *The Archaeology of Palestine*. London: Penguin Books, 1954.
———. *The Archaeology of Palestine and the Bible*. New York: Revell, 1935.
———. *History, Archaeology, and Christian Humanism*. New York: McGraw-Hill, 1964.
———. "How Well Can We Know the Ancient Near East?" *American Oriental Society Journal* 56 (1936): 121.
Allegro, J. *The Shapira Affair*. Garden City, N.Y.: Doubleday, 1965.
Alpert, C. "Two American Naval Expeditions to Palestine, 1848 and 1854." *Publications of the American Jewish Historical Society* 40 (1951): 281.
American Palestine Exploration Society (also known as "Palestine Exploration Society, New York"). *Catalogue of Photographs Taken Expressly for the American Exploration Society, During a Reconnaissance East of the Jordan in the Autumn of 1875*. Beirut: American Palestine Exploration Society, 1876.
———. Collection of Photographs, Union Theological Seminary Museum, New York.
———. *Statement*, 1871–77.
American School of Oriental Research in Jerusalem. *Annual Report of the Managing Committee of the American School*. Norwood, Mass.: American Schools of Oriental Research, 1902–22.
The Answers Lie Below: Essays in Honor of Lawrence Edmund Toombs. Edited by H. O. Thompson. Lanham, Md.: University Press of America, 1984.
The Archaeological Encyclopedia of the Holy Land. Edited by A. Negev. New York: Prentice Hall Press, 1990.
"Archaeological Exploration at Jerusalem." *American Architect and Building News* 49 (1895): 123.
Archaeology and Biblical Interpretation: Essays in Memory of D. Glenn Rose. Edited by Leo G. Perdue et al. Atlanta, Ga.: John Knox Press, 1987.
"Archaeology and Old Testament Critics." *Methodist Review* 56 (1896): 136.

Avi-Yonah, M. *Masot u-Mehkarim bi-Yedi'at ha-Arets*. Tel Aviv: M. Neuman, 1964.

Bacon, B. W. "Institute of Archaeology in Jerusalem." *Yale Divinity Quarterly* 2 (1905): 124.

Baikie, J. *The Glamour of Near East Excavation*. London: Seeley & Service, 1927.

Baily, W. M. "William Robertson Smith and American Biblical Studies." *Journal of Presbyterian History* 51 (1973): 285.

Balmer, E. R. "When the U.S. Navy Sailed the Dead Sea." *Foreign Service Journal* 35 (1958): 22.

Barton, G. A. *Archaeology and the Bible*. Philadelphia: American Sunday School Union, 1937.

———. "Jerusalem of David and Solomon." *Biblical World* 22 (1903): 8.

———. *A Year's Wandering in Bible Lands*. Philadelphia: Ferris & Leach, 1904.

Ben-Arieh, Y. "Nineteenth-Century Historical Geographies of the Holy Land." *Journal of Historical Geography* 15 (1989): 69.

———. *The Rediscovery of the Holy Land in the Nineteenth Century*. Jerusalem: Magnes Press, 1979.

———. "William F. Lynch's Expedition to the Dead Sea, 1847–1848." *Prologue* 5 (1973): 15.

Bennett, W. H. "Archaeology and Criticism." *Contemporary Review* 89 (1906): 518.

Bentwich, N. "Romance of Biblical Archaeology." *Contemporary Review* 189 (1956): 270.

Besant, W. *Autobiography of Sir Walter Besant*. New York: Dodd, Mead, 1902.

———. "Survey of Palestine." *International Review* 2 (1875): 488.

———. *Thirty Years' Work in the Holy Land*. London: A. P. Watt, 1895.

Biblical Archaeology Today: Proceedings of the International Congress on Biblical Archaeology, Jerusalem, April 1984. Jerusalem: Israel Exploration Society, 1984.

"Biblical Researches in Palestine." *Current Literature* 41 (1906): 78.

Biran, A. "An American Scholar." *Biblical Archaeologist* 50 (1987): 14.

Bissell, E. C. *Biblical Antiquities: A Handbook*. Philadelphia: American Sunday School Union, 1888.

Blaikie, W. G. "The Witness of Palestine to the Bible." *Living Papers* 2 (1892): 2.

Bliss, F. J. *The Development of Palestine Exploration*. New York: Scribner, 1906.

———. *Excavations at Jerusalem, 1894–1897*. London: Palestine Exploration Fund, 1898.

———. *Excavations in Palestine During the Years 1898–1900*. London: Palestine Exploration Fund, 1902.

———. *A Mound of Many Cities: Tell el Hesy Excavated*. London: Palestine Exploration Fund, 1898.

———. "The Mounds of Palestine." *Sunday School Times* 37 (1895): 82.

———. "The Recent Pilgrimage to Jerusalem." *Quarterly Statement of the Palestine Exploration Fund, 1894*, p. 101.

———. *The Religions of Modern Syria and Palestine*. New York: Scribner, 1912.

———. "Summer in Palestine." *Biblical World* 20 (1902): 89.

The Book and the Spade: A Guide to Biblical Archaeology. Edited by M. Mansoor. Madison, Wis.: Biblical Archaeological Exhibition / University of Wisconsin at Madison, 1975.

Breasted, C. *Pioneer to the Past: The Story of James Henry Breasted.* New York: Scribner, 1943.

Breasted, J. H. *The Battle of Kadesh.* Chicago: University of Chicago Press, 1903.

———. "The Eastern Mediterranean and Early Civilization in Europe." *Annual Report of the American Historical Association, 1914,* p. 103.

Brown, J. W. *The Rise of Biblical Criticism in America, 1800–1870.* Middleton, Conn.: Wesleyan University Press, 1969.

Browne, G. F. "Archaeological Frauds in Palestine." *National Review* 5 (1885): 190.

Burrage, H. S. "Ordnance Survey of Jerusalem." *Baptist Quarterly* 2 (1868): 156.

Burrows, M. *What Mean These Stones?* New Haven: American Schools of Oriental Research, 1941.

Butlin, R. "George Adam Smith and the Historical Geography of the Holy Land: Contents, Contexts, and Connections." *Journal of Historical Geography* 14 (1988): 381.

"Charles Foster Kent." *Journal of Biblical Literature* 45 (1926): v.

Clay, A. T. "Archaeological Research in Palestine." *Art and Archaeology* 7 (1918): 160.

Clermont-Ganneau, C. S. "The Arabs in Palestine." *Macmillan's Magazine* 32 (1875): 361.

———. *Archaeological Researches in Palestine During the Years 1873–1874.* London: Palestine Exploration Fund, 1899.

———. *L'authenticité du Saint-Sepulcre et le Tombeau de Joseph d'Arimathie.* Paris: E. Leroux, 1877.

———. *Les Fraudes Archeologiques en Palestine.* Paris: E. Leroux, 1885.

Coburn, C. M. *Recent Explorations in the Holy Land and Kadesh Barnea.* Meadville, Pa.: Published for the World's Bible Conference by the Tribune Pub. Company, 1914.

Coleman, L. "Palestine." *Bibliotheca Sacra* 21 (1864): 752.

Conder, C. R. "Ancient Palestine and Modern Exploration." *Contemporary Review* 46 (1884): 856.

———. *Palestine.* London: G. Philip, 1891.

———. "Palestine Exploration." *Homiletic Review* 38 (1899): 291.

———. *The Survey of Eastern Palestine.* London: Palestine Exploration Fund, 1889.

———. *The Survey of Western Palestine.* London: Palestine Exploration Fund, 1881–83.

———. *Tent Work in Palestine.* London: R. Bentley, 1878.

Crosby, H. *The Bible View of the Jewish Church.* New York: Funk & Wagnalls, 1888.

———. "Exploration in Palestine." *American Presbyterian Review* 20 (1871): 638.

———. *The Land of the Moslem: A Narrative of Oriental Travel.* New York: R. Carter, 1851.

Crosby, M. *Memorial Papers and Reminiscences of Howard Crosby.* New York: W. Knowles, 1892.

Curtiss, S. I. "The German Occupation of Jerusalem." *Independent* 50 (1898): 1,739.
———. *The Name Machabee Historically and Philologically Examined.* Leipzig: Ackermann & Glaser, 1876.
———. *Primitive Semitic Religion Today.* Chicago: Revell, 1902. Translation of his *Ursemitische religion im volksleben des heutigen Orients.*
Daiches, S. *Lord Kitchener and His Work in Palestine.* London: Luzac, 1915.
Daly, C. P. "Palestine Exploration." *American Geographical Society Journal* 5 (1874): 166.
Daly, R. A. "Palestine as Illustrating Geological and Geographical Controls." *American Geographical Society Bulletin* 31 (1899): 444.
Daniel, G. E. *A Hundred and Fifty Years of Archaeology.* London: Duckworth, 1975.
———. *The Origins and Growth of Archaeology.* New York: Galahad Books, 1967.
Davis, T. W. "A History of Biblical Archaeology." Ph.D. diss., University of Arizona, 1987.
Dawson, J. W. *Modern Science in Bible Lands.* New York: Harper, 1889.
Dever, W. G. *Archaeology and Biblical Studies.* Evanston, Ill.: Seabury-Western Theological Seminary, 1974.
———. *Recent Archaeological Discoveries and Biblical Research.* Seattle, Wash.: University of Washington Press, 1990.
Dinsmoor, W. B. "Early American Studies of Mediterranean Archaeology." *Proceedings of the American Philosophical Society* 87 (1943): 70.
Duncan, C. S. "Archaeology and the Old Testament." *Biblical World* 22 (1903): 116.
Dupre, A. H. *Science in the Federal Government: A History of Policies and Activities to 1940.* Cambridge, Mass.: Harvard University Press, Belknap Press, 1957.
"Excavations at Jerusalem." *Methodist Review* 76 (1894): 964.
"Excavations in Palestine." *New Church Review* 1 (1894): 461.
"Exploration of Palestine." *Journal of Science* 19 (1882): 346.
"Explorations in Palestine." *Art Journal* 20 (1868): 14.
"Explorations in Palestine." *Littell's Living Age* 117 (1873): 3.
Fairchild, D. "American Research Institution in Palestine: The Jewish Agricultural Experiment Station at Haifa." *Science* 31 (1910): 376.
Fargo, V. M. "Sir Flinders-Petrie." *Biblical Archaeologist* 47 (1984): 220.
Ffrench, Y. *Transatlantic Exchanges: Cross-Currents of Anglo-American Opinion in the Nineteenth Century.* New York: Library Publishers, 1952.
Frank, H. T. *Bible, Archaeology, and Faith.* Nashville, Tenn.: Abingdon Press, 1971.
Glock, A. E. "Tradition and Change in Two Archaeologies." *American Antiquity* 50 (1985): 464.
Goodspeed, T. W. *William Rainey Harper.* Chicago: University of Chicago Press, 1928.
Graham, W. C. *Culture and Conscience: An Archaeological Study of the New Religious Past in Ancient Palestine.* Chicago: University of Chicago Press, 1936.
Grant, E. "A New Era in Palestine Exploration." *Annual Report of the Smithsonian Institution* (1921): 541.
———. *Palestine Our Holy Land.* Baltimore: J. H. Furst, 1940.

———. *Palestine Today*. Baltimore: J. H. Furst, 1938.

———. *The Peasantry of Palestine*. Boston: Pilgrim Press, 1907.

———. Review of *Palestine and Its Transformation*, by E. Huntington. *Yale Review* 1 (1912): 504.

Hackett, H. B. "Exploration Palestine." *Blbliotheca Sacra* 27 (1870): 570.

Harper, A. "Archaeology and Biblical Criticism." *Christian Literature* 12 (1894): 89.

Harry, M. *The Little Daughter of Jerusalem*. London: J. M. Dent, 1918.

The Haverford Symposium on Archaeology and the Bible. New Haven: American Schools of Oriental Research, 1938.

Heindel, R. H. *The American Impact on Great Britain, 1898–1914*. 1940. Reprint. New York: Octagon Books, 1968.

Herbst, J. *The German Historical School in American Scholarship*. Ithaca, N.Y.: Cornell University Press, 1965.

Hilprecht, H. V. *A New Gallery of Illustrations Portraying Recent Archaeological Excavations and Discoveries in Babylonia, Egypt, Arabia, Syria, and Asia Minor*. Philadelphia: A. J. Holman, 1897.

———. *Recent Research in Bible Lands*. Philadelphia: J. D. Wattles, 1896.

Hitchcock, R. D. *The Life, Writings, and Character of Edward Robinson*. 1863. Reprint. New York: Arno Press, 1977.

———. "Palestine Exploration Beyond the Jordan." *American Geographical Society Journal* 8 (1876): 204.

Hodder, I. "Writing Archaeology: Site Reports in Context." *Antiquity* 63 (1989): 268.

Hogarth, D. G. *Authority and Archaeology, Sacred and Profane*. 1899. Reprint. Freeport, N.Y.: Books for Libraries Press, 1971.

Holland, F. W. "Explorations in Jerusalem." *Old and New* 4 (1871): 88.

Hovenkamp, H. *Science and Religion in America, 1800–1860*. Philadelphia: University of Pennsylvania Press, 1978.

Howard Crosby Butler, 1872–1922. Princeton: Princeton University Press, 1923.

Huntington, E. "Across the Thor to the Land of Og." *Harper's Monthly Magazine* 120 (1910): 667.

———. "Arabian Desert and Human Character." *Journal of Geography* 10 (1912): 169.

———. "Canvas Boat on the Dead Sea." *Harper's Monthly Magazine* 120 (1910): 186.

———. *Palestine and Its Transformation*. Boston: Houghton Mifflin, 1911.

———. *The Pulse of Progress*. New York: Scribner, 1926.

"James Turner Barclay: Explorer of Nineteenth-Century Jerusalem." *Biblical Archaeology* 51 (1988): 163.

Kennedy, G. *Evolution and Religion: The Conflict Between Science and Theology in Modern America*. Boston: Heath, 1957.

Kent, C. F. "The Present and Possibilities of Excavation in Palestine." *Biblical World* 2 (1893): 220.

Kenyon, K. M. *Jerusalem: Excavating 3,000 Years of History*. New York: McGraw-Hill, 1967.

King, P. J. "American Archaeological Heritage in the Near East." *Bulletin of the American Schools of Oriental Research* 217 (1975): 55.

———. *American Archaeology in the Mideast*. Philadelphia: American Schools of Oriental Research, 1983.

———. "ASOR at 85." *Biblical Archaeologist* 47 (1984): 197.

Klein, S. *Toldot Hakirat Erets Yisra'el*. Jerusalem: Mosad Bialik, 1937.

Kyle, M. G. *The Deciding Voice of the Monuments in Biblical Criticism*. Oberlin, Ohio: Bibliotheca Sacra, 1912.

———. "Recent Testimony of Archaeology to the Scripture." *Bibliotheca Sacra* 67 (1910): 373.

Lapp, P. W. *Biblical Archaeology and History*. New York: World Pub. Company, 1969.

Lewin, T. "Site of the Temple at Jerusalem." *Archaeologia* 44 (1873): 17.

Long, R. C. "Walls of Jericho: The Story of the Disinternment of the Famous Stronghold." *World To-day* 16 (1909): 370.

Lynch, W. F. *Commerce and the Holy Land*. Philadelphia: King & Baird, 1860.

———. *Narrative of the United States' Expedition to the River Jordan and the Dead Sea*. Philadelphia: Lea & Blanchard, 1849.

———. *Naval Life; or, Observations Afloat and on Shore*. New York: C. Scribner, 1851.

———. *Official Report of the United States Expedition to Explore the Dead Sea and the River Jordan*. Baltimore: J. Murphy, 1852.

Macalister, A. "Uncovering a Buried City: Tel-El-Je-Zair." *Harper's Magazine* 107 (1903): 83.

Macalister, R. A. *Bible Side-Lights from the Mound of Gezer*. New York: Scribner, 1906.

———. *A Century of Excavation in Palestine*. Chicago: Revell, 1925. Reprint. New York: Arno Press, 1977.

MacCoun, T. *The Holy Land in Geography and in History*. New York: T. MacCoun, 1897.

McCown, C. C. *The Ladder of Progress in Palestine: A Story of Archaeological Adventure*. New York: Harper, 1943.

Madeira, P. C. *Men in Search of Man: The First Seventy Years of the University Museum of the University of Pennsylvania*. Philadelphia: University of Pennsylvania Press, 1964.

Marek, K. W. *Gods, Graves, and Scholars: The Story of Archaeology*. New York: Knopf, 1967.

Martin, G. J. *Ellsworth Huntington: His Life and Thought*. Hamden, Conn.: Archon Books, 1973.

Masterman, E.W.G. "Agricultural Life in Palestine." *Biblical World* 15 (1900): 185.

———. "Jews in Modern Palestine." *Biblical World* 21 (1903): 17.

———. "Occupations of the Jews in Palestine." *Biblical World* 22 (1903): 88.

———. "Social Customs in Palestine." *Biblical World* 15 (1900): 262.

Matthews, V. H., and J. C. Moyer. "The Use and Abuse of Archaeology in Current One-Volume Bible Commentaries." *Biblical Archaeologist* 53 (1990): 104.

Mazar, B. *The Mountain of the Lord*. Garden City, N.Y.: Doubleday, 1975.

———. *Toldot ha-Mehkar ha-Arkhi'ologi be-Erets Yisra'el*. Jerusalem: Mosad Bialik, 1936.

Melhorn, G. I. "America's Contribution to Palestinian Archaeology." Master's thesis, Lutheran Theological Seminary, Gettysburg, Pa., 1936.

Meyers, E. M. "The Bible and Archaeology." *Biblical Archaeologist* 47 (March 1984): 36.

Miles, J. A. "Understanding Albright: A Revolutionary Étude." *Harvard Theological Review* 69 (1976): 151.

Mitchell, T. C. *The Bible in the British Museum: Interpreting the Evidence.* London: British Museum Publications, 1988.

"Modern Science in Bible Lands." *Westminster Review* (London), 131 (1889): 474.

"Modern Walls of Jerusalem." *Scientific American Supplement* 53 (1902): 21,945.

Montague, E. P. *Narrative of the Late Expedition to the Dead Sea: From a Diary by One of the Party.* Philadelphia: Carey & Hart, 1849.

Montgomery, J. A. "The Opportunity for American Archaeological Research in Palestine." *Annual Report of the Smithsonian Institution, 1919,* p. 431.

———. "The Story of the School in Jerusalem." *Annual of the American Schools of Oriental Research* 6 (1924): 1.

Moulton, W. J. "The American Palestine Exploration Society." *Annual of the American Schools of Oriental Research* 8 (1926): 55.

Murphy-O'Connor, J. *The Holy Land: An Archaeological Guide from the Earliest Times to 1700.* New York: Oxford University Press, 1986.

Near Eastern Archaeology in the Twentieth Century: Essays in Honor of Nelson Glueck. Edited by J. A. Sanders. Garden City, N.Y.: Doubleday, 1970.

Palestine Exploration Fund. *Annual.* 1911–18.

———. *Our Work in Palestine.* London: Bentley, 1875.

———. *Quarterly Statement.* 1869–1936.

———. *The Survey of Western Palestine.* London: Palestine Exploration Fund, 1881.

"The Palestine Exploration Fund." *Biblical World* 2 (1893): 391.

"Palestine Today." Review of *Palestine and Its Transformation,* by E. Huntington. *Nation* 93 (1911): 627.

Paton, L. B. "Archaeology and the Book of Genesis." *Biblical World* 45 (1915): 10.

———. *The Early History of Syria and Palestine.* New York: Scribner, 1901.

———. *Jerusalem in Bible Times.* 1908. Reprint. New York: Arno Press, 1977.

———. "Report on the Geography, History, Ethnology, Religions, Economics, Domestic Life, and Government of the Land of Palestine, April 15, 1918." *Inquiry Document 459.* U.S. National Archives.

———. "Results of Recent Archaeology for the History of Palestine." *Hartford Seminary Record* 15 (1904): 175.

———. *Spiritism and the Cult of the Dead in Antiquity.* New York: Macmillan, 1921.

———. "Survivals of Primitive Religion in Modern Palestine." *Annual of the American Schools of Oriental Research* 1 (1919): 53.

Paul, C. K. "Wilson's Recovery of Jerusalem." *Theological Review* 8 (1871): 407.

Peladan, S. "Sacred Archaeology: True Place of the Holy Sepulchre." *Fortnightly Review* 82 (1904): 1,073.

Peters, J. P. *Bible and Spade.* New York: Scribner, 1922.

———. "Exploration in Palestine." *American Antiquarian* 25 (1903): 314.

———. "Hilprecht's *Explorations in Bible Lands.*" *Nation* 77 (1903): 137.

———. "Jerusalem Redeemed." *Review of Reviews* 57 (1918): 47.

———. "Notes on Eastern Travel." *American Journal of Archaeology* 8 (1893): 325.

———. "Some Ruins Beyond the Jordan." *Nation* 53 (1891): 404.

Petrie, H. U. *Side Notes on the Bible: From Flinders Petrie's Discoveries.* London: Search Pub. Company, 1933.

Petrie, W.M.F. "Archaeology in the Past Century." *Scientific American Supplement* 51 (1901): 20,960.

———. *Eastern Exploration: Past and Future.* London: Constable, 1918.

Professor George A. Barton: An Appreciation. Baltimore: Privately published, 1919.

Put Your Future in Ruins: Essays in Honor of Robert Jehu Bull. Edited by H. O. Thompson. Bristol, Ind.: Wyndham Hall Press, 1985.

Ramsey, G. W. *The Quest for the Historical Israel.* Atlanta, Ga.: John Knox Press, 1981.

Rawson, A. L. "Palestine." *American Geographical Society Journal* 7 (1875): 101.

———. *Recent Explorations in Bible Lands.* Philadelphia: A. J. Holman, 1875.

"Recent Researches in Palestine—1867." *Eclectic Magazine* 69 (1867): 641.

Reinach, S. "Archaeology and Turkish Officials." *Nation* 39 (1884): 30.

Reisner, G. A. *Harvard Excavations at Samaria, 1908–1910.* Cambridge, Mass.: Harvard University Press, 1924.

"Researches of the American School in Palestine." *Journal of Biblical Literature* 22 (1903): 164.

Rice, E. W. *Orientalisms in Bible Lands.* Philadelphia: American Sunday School Union, 1910.

Richardson, G. H. "Abuse of Biblical Archaeology." *Biblical World* 46 (1915): 98.

———. "Value of Archaeological Study for the Biblical Student." *Open Court* 28 (1914): 197.

Robinson, E. *Biblical Researches in Palestine, Mount Sinai, and Arabia Petrea.* Boston: Crocker & Brewster, 1841.

———. *Later Biblical Research in Palestine and in the Adjacent Regions.* 1856. Reprint. New York: Arno Press, 1977.

———. *Outlines of a Journey in Palestine in 1852.* London: W. Clowes, 1852.

———. *Researches in Palestine.* Edinburgh: T. Clark, 1843.

Sarton, G. "James Henry Breasted: Father of American Egyptology." *Isis* 34 (1943): 288.

Saulcy, L. F. *Narrative of a Journey Round the Dead Sea, and in the Bible Lands in 1850 and 1851.* London: R. Bentley, 1854.

Sayce, A. H. "Biblical Criticism on the Warpath." *Contemporary Review* 70 (1896): 728.

———. "Oriental Archaeology: The Vindicator of the Old Testament." *Outlook* 54 (1896): 469.

———. "The White Race of Palestine." *Nature* 38 (1888): 321.

Schaff, P. "Disputed Scripture Localities." *Princeton Review* 1 (1878): 851.

Schumacher, G. *Across the Jordan.* New York: Scribner, 1886.

Silberman, N. *Digging for God and Country.* New York: Knopf, 1982.

"Site of Mt. Sion and the Temple of Jerusalem." *Christian Remembrancer* 43 (1862): 422.

Smith, G. A. *The Historical Geography of the Holy Land*. London: Collins, 1966.
Society of Biblical Literature. Annual Meeting, 1964. *The Bible in Modern Scholarship*. Edited by J. P. Hyatt. Nashville, Tenn.: Abingdon Press, 1965.
Stanley, A. P. "Palestine Exploration." *Good Words* 9 (1868): 173.
Stearns, M. B. "Biblical Archaeology and Higher Criticism." *Bibliotheca Sacra* 96 (1939): 307.
"The Study of Scriptural Geography." *Biblical World* 11 (1898): 65.
"Subterranean Jerusalem." *Popular Science Monthly Supplement* 1 (1877): 379.
Tappan, D. *Lectures on Jewish Antiquities*. Cambridge, Mass.: W. Hilliard & E. Lincoln, 1807.
Taylor, W. E. *Vestiges of Divine Vengeance*. London: Wertheim & Macintosh, 1854.
Thompson, H. O. *Biblical Archaeology: The World, the Mediterranean, the Bible*. New York: Paragon House, 1987.
Thompson, J. P. "The Exploration of Palestine." *North American Review* 113 (1871): 154.
———. "Palestine: A Perpetual Witness for the Bible." *New Englander* 17 (1859): 192.
Towards a History of Archaeology: Being the Papers Read at the First Conference on the History of Archaeology in Aarhus [Denmark], 29 August–2 September 1978. New York: Thames & Hudson, 1981.
"Treasure Hunters at Jerusalem." *Independent* 70 (1911): 1,017.
Tristam, H. B. *The Land of Moab: Travels and Discoveries on the East Side of the Dead Sea and the Jordan*. London: J. Murray, 1873.
———. *The Survey of Western Palestine*. London: Palestine Exploration Fund, 1884.
"Unhappy Antiquities of Palestine." *Scientific American Supplement* 51 (1901): 21,125.
U.S. Department of the Navy. *Report of the Secretary of the Navy with a Report Made by Lieutenant W. F. Lynch of an Examination of the Dead Sea*. Washington, D.C.: United States Senate, 1849.
Vos, H. F. *An Introduction to Bible Archaeology*. Chicago: Moody Press, 1983.
Wachsmann, S., and K. Raveh. "In the Footsteps of Napoleon at Tantura, Israel." *Archaeology* 37 (1984): 58.
Ward, W. H. "The Latest Palestinian Discoveries." *Homiletic Review* 24 (1892): 403.
Warren, C. *The Survey of Western Palestine: Jerusalem*. London: Palestine Exploration Fund, 1884.
———. *The Temple or the Tomb*. London: R. Bentley, 1880.
———. *Underground Jerusalem*. London: R. Bentley, 1876.
Waterman, H. B. *The Holy Land in the Light of Recent Surveys and Explorations*. Chicago: C. F. Rassweiler, 1895.
Waterman, L. "Half-Century of Biblical and Semitic Investigation." *American Journal of Semitic Languages* 32 (1916): 219.
Webster, G. "Baroness Angela Georgina Burdett-Coutts." *Biblical Archaeologist* 48 (1985): 186.
———. "Elizabeth Ann Finn." *Biblical Archaeologist* 48 (1985): 181.
Weigall, A. E. "Morality of Excavation." *Nineteenth Century* 72 (1912): 382.

White, E. A. *Science and Religion in American Thought*. 1952. Reprint. New York: AMS Press, 1968.

Williams, G. *The Holy City: Historical, Topographical, and Antiquarian Notices of Jerusalem*. London: J. W. Parker, 1849.

Wilson, C. A. *Rocks, Relics, and Biblical Reliability*. Grand Rapids, Mich.: Zondervan, 1977.

Wilson, C. W. *Ordnance Survey of Jerusalem*. London: H. M. Stationary Office, 1865.

———. *Picturesque Palestine, Sinai, and Egypt*. New York: D. Appleton, 1881–84.

———. *The Recovery of Jerusalem*. London: R. Bentley, 1871.

Wilson, J. A. *Biographical Memoir of James Henry Breasted, 1865–1935*. Washington, D.C.: National Academy of Sciences, 1937.

Wright, G. E. "Archaeological Method in Palestine—an American Interpretation." *Eretz Israel* 9 (1959): 120.

———. *Biblical Archaeology*. Philadelphia: Westminster Press, 1962.

Wright, G. F. "Great Jordan Fault." *Nation* 72 (1901): 250.

———. "Possible Population of Palestine." *Bibliotheca Sacra* 58 (1901): 740.

Wright, G.R.H. *As on the First Day: Essays in Religious Constants*. New York: E. J. Brill, 1987.

Wright, J. K. *Geography in the Making: The American Geographical Society, 1851–1951*. New York: The American Geographical Society, 1952.

Yahuda, A. S. "The Story of a Forgery and the Mesa Inscription." *Jewish Quarterly Review* 35 (1944): 139.

Past Places and Sacred Spaces

Abed, S. *Israeli Arabism: The Latest Incarnation of Orientalism*. Kingston, Ont.: Near East Cultural and Educational Foundation of Canada, 1986.

Acquaviva, S. S. *The Decline of the Sacred in Industrial Society*. New York: Harper & Row, 1979.

Alkjaer, E. *Images and Realities in Transportation, Tourism, and Regional Economy*. Copenhagen: Samfunslitteratur, 1978.

Allen, J. L. "Geographical Knowledge and American Images of the Louisiana Territory." *Western Historical Quarterly* 2 (1971): 151.

———. *Passage Through the Garden: Lewis and Clark and the Image of the American Northwest*. Urbana, Ill.: University of Illinois Press, 1975.

"America to Watch Over Israel." *Literary Digest* 54 (1917): 710.

American Image: Past and Present. Edited by G. D. Lillibridge. Lexington, Mass.: Heath, 1968.

Ausband, S. C. *Myth and Meaning, Myth and Order*. Macon, Ga.: Mercer University Press, 1983.

Aziz, B. N. "Personal Dimensions of the Sacred Journey: What Pilgrims Say." *Religious Studies* 23 (1987): 247.

Baker, A.R.H. "On Geographical Literature as Popular Culture in Rural France, 1860–1900." *Geography Journal* 156 (1990): 39.

Bar-Gal, Y. "The Subjective Significance of the Landscape of Tsfat." *Folklore* 95 (1984): 245.

Baritz, L. *City on a Hill: A History of Ideas and Myths in America.* New York: Wiley, 1964.

Baudet, H. *Paradise on Earth: Some Thoughts on European Images of Non-European Man.* New Haven: Yale University Press, 1965.

Bermingham, A. *Landscape and Ideology: The English Rustic Tradition, 1740–1860.* Berkeley and Los Angeles: University of California Press, 1986.

Bernstein, B. "Some Sociological Determinants of Perception: An Inquiry into Sub-Cultural Differences." *British Journal of Sociology* 9 (1958): 159.

Birenbaum, A. *People in Places: The Sociology of the Familiar.* New York: Praeger, 1973.

Bishop, P. *The Myth of Shangri-la: Tibet, Travel Writing, and the Western Creation of Sacred Landscape.* Berkeley and Los Angeles: University of California Press, 1989.

Bokser, B. M. "Approaching Sacred Space." *Harvard Theological Review* 78 (1985): 279.

Boorstin, D. J. *America and the Image of Europe.* New York: Meridian Books, 1960.

————. *The Image: A Guide to Pseudo-Events in America.* New York: Atheneum, 1987.

Boulding, K. E. *The Image: Knowledge in Life and Society.* Ann Arbor: University of Michigan Press, 1956.

Bowden, M. J. "The Great American Desert in the American Mind, 1890–1972." *Proceedings of the Association of American Geographers* 4 (1973): 167.

————. "The Perception of the Western Interior of the United States." *Proceedings of the Association of American Geographers* 1 (1969): 16.

Bowen, B. M. *The Folklore of Palestine.* Grand Rapids, Mich.: Eerdmans, 1940.

Brown, J. *The Everywhere Landscape.* London: Wildwood House, 1982.

Brueggemann, W. *The Land: Place as Gift, Promise, and Challenge in Biblical Faith.* Philadelphia: Fortress Press, 1977.

Bultmann, R. K. *Jesus Christ and Mythology.* New York: Scribner, 1958.

Carpenter, F. I. "American Myth: Paradise (to be) Regained." *Publications of the Modern Language Association* 74 (1959): 599.

Chapple, J. A. *Documentary and Imaginary Literature, 1880–1920.* London: Blanford Press, 1970.

Clifford, C. M. *The Palestine Question in American History.* New York: Arno Press, 1978.

"Columbus and Cathay, and the Meaning of America to the Orientalist." *American Oriental Society Journal* 51 (1931): 87.

Conceptual Revolution in Geography. Edited by W.K.D. Davies. London: University of London Press, 1972.

Cooper, R. "The Unifying Structure of the Experience of the Holy." *Philosophy Today* 32 (1988): 54.

Cords, N. *Myth and the American Experience.* New York: Glencoe Press, 1973.

Correa, C. "The Public, the Private, and the Sacred." *Daedalus* 118 (1989): 93.

Cosgrove, D. E. *Social Formation and Symbolic Landscape.* London: Croom Helm, 1984.

Cox, D. *History and Myth.* London: Darton, Longman & Todd, 1961.

Curtiss, R. H. *A Changing Image: American Perceptions of the Arab-Israeli Dispute.* Washington, D.C.: American Educational Trust, 1982.

Cutten, G. B. *Instincts and Religion.* New York: Harper, 1940.

Dansereau, P. M. *Inscape and Landscape: The Human Perception of the Environment.* 1973. Reprint. New York: Columbia University Press, 1975.

Davis, J. "Frederick Church's 'Sacred Geography'." *Smithsonian Studies in American Art* 1 (1987): 79.

Day, J. A., et al. *Dimensions of the Environmental Crisis.* New York: Wiley, 1971.

De Rivera, J. *The Psychological Dimension of Foreign Policy.* Columbus, Ohio: Merrill, 1968.

Discovery of Europe. Edited by P. Rahv. Garden City, N.Y.: Doubleday, 1960.

Downs, R. M. *Maps in Minds.* New York: Harper & Row, 1977.

Dudden, A. P. "Nostalgia and the American." *Journal of the History of Ideas* 22 (1961): 515.

Duggan, W. J. *Myth and Christian Belief.* Notre Dame, Ind.: Fides, 1971.

Eaton, G. "Knowledge and the Sacred." *Studies in Comparative Religion* 15 (1983): 210.

Ecology and Religion in History. Edited by D. Spring. New York: Harper & Row, 1974.

Eddy, G. S. *The Kingdom of God and the American Dream.* New York: Harper, 1941.

Eliade, M. *A History of Religious Ideas.* Chicago: University of Chicago Press, 1978–85.

———. *Images and Symbols: Studies in Religious Symbolism.* London: Harvill Press, 1961.

———. *The Myth of the Eternal Return; or, Cosmos and History.* 1959. Reprint. New York: Garland Press, 1985.

———. *Myths, Dreams, and Mysteries: The Encounter Between Contemporary Faiths and Archaic Realities.* New York: Harper, 1961.

———. *Patterns in Comparative Religion.* New York: Sheed & Ward, 1958.

———. *The Sacred and the Profane.* New York: Harcourt, Brace, 1959.

———. *Symbolism, the Sacred, and the Arts.* New York: Crossroads, 1985.

———. *The Two and the One.* 1965. Reprint. Chicago: University of Chicago Press, 1979.

Elizur, J. N. "The Image of Israel in Protestant Eyes." Ph.D. diss., Harvard University, 1972.

Encountering the Environment. Edited by A. Meyer. New York: Van Nostrand Reinhold, 1971.

Entrikin, J. N. *The Betweenness of Place: Towards a Geography of Modernity.* Baltimore: Johns Hopkins University Press, 1991.

Environment and Americans: The Problem of Priorities. Edited by R. Nash. New York: Holt, Rinehart & Winston, 1972.

Environmental Perception and Behavior. Edited by D. Lowenthal. Chicago: University of Chicago, Department of Geography, 1967.

Firestone, C. B. *The Coasts of Illusion: A Study of Travel Tales.* New York: Harper, 1924.

Firey, W. "Sentiment and Symbolism as Ecological Variables." *American Sociological Review* 10 (1945): 140.

Foster, S. W. *The Past Is Another Country: Representation, Historical Consciousness, and Resistance in the Blue Ridge.* Berkeley and Los Angeles: University of California Press, 1988.

Frankel, C. "Culture, Information, Foreign Policy." *Public Administration Review* 29 (1969): 593.

Freedberg, D. *The Power of Images: Studies in the History and Theory of Response.* Chicago: University of Chicago Press, 1989.

Frimmer, S. *Neverland: Fabled Places and Fabulous Voyages of History and Legend.* New York: Viking Press, 1976.

Geographies of the Mind: Essays in Historical Geosophy in Honor of John Kirtland Wright. Edited by D. Lowenthal. 1975. Reprint. New York: Oxford University Press, 1976.

Gerard, H. B., and G. S. Roller. "Time Perception, Consistency of Attitudes, and Social Influence." *Journal of Abnormal and Social Psychology* 62 (1961): 565.

Germaner, S. *Orientalism and Turkey.* Istanbul: Turkish Cultural Service Foundation, 1989.

Glacken, C. J. *Traces on the Rhodian Shore: Nature and Culture in Western Thought from Ancient Times to the End of the Eighteenth Century.* Berkeley and Los Angeles: University of California Press, 1967.

Gogarten, F. *Demythologizing and History.* London: SCM Press, 1955.

Gombrich, E. H.; J. Hochberg; and M. Black. *Art, Perception, and Reality.* Baltimore: Johns Hopkins University Press, 1972.

Goodey, B. *Images of Place.* Birmingham, Eng.: University of Birmingham, Centre for Urban and Regional Studies, 1974.

Graber, L. H. *Wilderness as Sacred Space.* Washington, D.C.: Association of American Geographers, 1976.

Graves, P. *Palestine: The Land of Three Faiths.* 1923. Reprint. Westport, Conn.: Hyperion Press, 1976.

Greenbie, B. B. *Spaces: Dimensions of the Human Landscape.* New Haven: Yale University Press, 1981.

Gulick, J. "Images of the Arab City." *American Institute of Planners Journal* 29 (1963): 179.

Haddon, J. "A View of Foreign Lands." *Geography* 45 (1960): 286.

Hanauer, J. E. *Folklore of the Holy Land: Moslem, Christian, and Jewish.* 1935. Reprint. Folcroft, Pa.: Folcroft Library Editions, 1977.

Harrington, S.P.M. "Sacred Places." *Archaeology* 43 (1990): 42.

Helm, B. P. *Time and Reality in American Philosophy.* Amherst, Mass.: University of Massachusetts Press, 1985.

Heschel, A. J. *Israel: An Echo of Eternity.* New York: Farrar, Straus, & Giroux, 1969.

Hill, R. "Will the War End in the Holy Land?" *Travel* 26 (1915): 33.

Hiss, T. *The Experience of Place.* New York: Knopf, 1990.

Hodgkins, T. "Palestinian Utopia." *Magazine of Christian Literature* 2 (1890): 199.

Hong, C. C. *To Whom the Land of Palestine Belongs.* Hicksville, N.Y.: Exposition Press, 1979.

Hopkins, I. W. "Nineteenth-Century Maps of Palestine: Dual Purpose of Historical Evidence." *Imago Mundi* 22 (1968): 30.

Howard, P. "Painters' Preferred Places." *Journal of Historical Geography* 11 (1985): 138.

Hunter, J. M. *Land into Landscape.* New York: Godwin, 1985.

"Idyls of Palestine." *All the Year* 13 (1865): 541.

Image and Reality in World Politics. Edited by J. C. Farrell. New York: Columbia University Press, 1968.

Imagery: Current Cognitive Approaches. Edited by S. J. Segal. New York: Academic Press, 1971.

Interpretation of Ordinary Landscapes: Geographical Essays. Edited by D. W. Meinig. New York: Oxford University Press, 1979.

Isaac, E. "Mythological Geography." *Geographical Review* 57 (1967): 123.

Jackson, J. B. *Discovering the Vernacular Landscape.* New Haven, Conn.: Yale University Press, 1984.

———. *Landscapes: Selected Writings of J. B. Jackson.* Edited by E. H. Zube. Amherst, Mass.: University of Massachusetts Press, 1970.

———. *The Necessity for Ruins, and Other Topics.* Amherst, Mass.: University of Massachusetts Press, 1980.

Jakle, J. A. *The Visual Elements of Landscape.* Amherst, Mass.: University of Massachusetts Press, 1987.

Jenkins, H. D. "Palestine: Land of Ecstasy and Sorrow." *Asia* 18 (1918): 134.

Jerusalem Colloquium on Religion, Peoplehood, Nation, and Land, 1970. *The Jerusalem Colloquium on Religion, Peoplehood, Nation, and Land, October 30–November 8, 1970: Proceedings.* Jerusalem: H. S. Truman Research Institute of the Hebrew University, 1972.

"Jews Look Askance at Restored Palestine." *Literary Digest* 55 (1917): 38.

Kabbani, R. *Europe's Myths of Orient.* Bloomington: Indiana University Press, 1986.

Kelsey, M. T. *Myth, History, and Faith: The Remythologizing of Christianity.* New York: Paulist Press, 1974.

Kern, S. *The Culture of Time and Space, 1880–1918.* Cambridge, Mass.: Harvard University Press, 1983.

Kleitz, D. R. "Orientalism and the American Romantic Imagination: The Middle East in the Work of Irving, Poe, Emerson, and Melville." Ph.D. diss., University of New Hampshire, 1988.

Kollerstrom, O. *The Actual and the Real.* London: Turnstone Books, 1974.

Kosslyn, S. M. *Image and Mind.* Cambridge, Mass.: Harvard University Press, 1980.

Kushner, L. "Ladder Standing on Earth: The Psycho-Spiritual Evolution of Holy Places." *Studies in Formative Spirituality* 8 (1987): 55.

Landa, M. J. "Restoration of Palestine." *Hibbert Journal* 16 (1918): 223.

Landscape and Culture: Geographical and Archaeological Perspectives. Edited by J. M. Wagstaff. Oxford: B. Blackwell, 1987.

Landscape Assessment: Values, Perceptions, and Resources. Edited by E. H. Zube et al. Stroudsburg, Pa.: Dowden, Hutchinson & Ross, 1975.

Landscape Meanings and Values. Edited by E. C. Penning-Rowsell and D. Lowenthal. Boston: Allen & Unwin, 1986.

Lane, B. C. "Fierce Landscapes and the Indifference of God." *Christian Century* 106 (1989): 907.

Lang, A. *Myth, Ritual, and Religion.* New York: AMS Press, 1968.

Lazarus-Yafeh, H. "The Sanctity of Jerusalem." *Century Magazine* 18 (November/December 1985): 58.

Lee, J. W. *The Romance of Palestine.* St. Louis: N. Thompson, 1897.

Let the Earth Bless the Lord: A Christian Perspective on Land Use. Edited by C. A. Cesaretti. New York: Seabury Press, 1981.

Levenson, J. D. "The Temple and the World." *Journal of Religion* 64 (1984): 275.

Loughney, P. G. "The First American Film Spectacular." *Quarterly Journal of the Library of Congress* 40 (1983): 57.

Lowenthal, D. "The American View of Nature as Virtue." *Landscape* 9 (1959): 24.

———. *Environmental Assessment* (various individual cities). Several separate studies, not listed separately here.

———. *Environmental Structures: Semantic and Experiential Components.* New York: American Geographical Society, 1972.

———. "Geography, Experience, and Imagination." *Association of American Geographers Annals* 51 (1961): 241.

———. *Milieu and Observer Differences in Environmental Associations.* New York: American Geographical Society, 1972.

———. "The Nature of Perceived and Imagined Environments." *Environment and Behavior* 4 (1972): 189.

———. *The Past Is a Foreign Country.* New York: Cambridge University Press, 1985.

———. "Past Time, Present Place: Landscape and Memory." *Geographical Review* 65 (1975): 1.

———. "The Place of the Past in the American Landscape." *Proceedings of the Association of American Geographers* 4 (1973): 208.

———. *Structures of Environmental Associations.* New York: American Geographical Society, 1972.

———. "The Timeless Past: Some Anglo-American Historical Preconceptions." *Journal of American History* 75 (1989): 1,263.

Lucas, F. L. *The Decline and Fall of the Romantic Ideal.* New York: Macmillan, 1936.

Lurie, E. *Nature and the American Mind.* New York: Science History Publications, 1974.

Lynch, K. *What Time Is This Place?* Cambridge, Mass.: MIT Press, 1972.

McDougall, W. *The Group Mind.* 1920. Reprint. New York: Arno Press, 1973.

Making Sense of Time. Edited by T. Carlstein et al. London: E. Arnold, 1978.

Mann, T. W. "Israel and the Land: A Note from the Christian Perspective." *Theology Today* 35 (1979): 421.

Marks, B. "The Concept of Myth in *Virgin Land.*" *American Quarterly* 5 (1953): 71.

Marsh, G. P. *Man and Nature.* Edited by D. Lowenthal. Cambridge, Mass.: Harvard University Press, Belknap Press, 1965.

Marx, L. *The Machine in the Garden: Technology and the Pastoral Ideal in America.* New York: Oxford University Press, 1964.

Moore-Gilbert, B. J. *Kipling and "Orientalism."* New York: St. Martin's Press, 1986.

Morris, W. *Earthly Delights, Unearthly Adornments: American Writers as Image-Makers.* New York: Harper & Row, 1978.

Musallam, B. *Power and Knowledge: A Review of Said's Orientalism.* Washington, D.C.: Middle East Research & Information Project, 1979.
Myths, Dreams, and Religion. Edited by J. Campbell. New York: Dutton, 1970.
Nash, R. *Wilderness and the American Mind.* New Haven: Yale University Press, 1973.
Neff, K. L. *Foreign Images and American Policy.* Washington, D.C.: World Affairs Bookshop, 1955.
Neil, J. *Palestine Re-Peopled.* London: J. Nisbet, 1883.
Nir, Y. *The Bible and the Image: The History of Photography in the Holy Land, 1839–1899.* Philadelphia: University of Pennsylvania Press, 1985.
———. "Cultural Predisposition in Early Photography: The Case of the Holy Land." *Journal of Communication* 35 (1985): 32.
Orientalism and History. Edited by D. Sinor. Bloomington: Indiana University Press, 1970.
Orientalism, Islam, and Islamists. Edited by A. Hussain et al. Brattleboro, Vt.: Amana Books, 1984.
Osgood, C. E., and P. H. Tannenbaum. "The Principle of Congruity in the Prediction of Attitude Change." *Psychological Review* 62 (1955): 42.
Osmen, S. A. *Sacred Places.* New York: St. Martin's Press, 1990.
Otto, R. *The Idea of the Holy.* New York: Oxford University Press, 1970.
Our Past Before Us: Why Do We Save It? Edited by D. Lowenthal and M. Binney. London: T. Smith, 1981.
Owens, G. *Golden Day, Silver Night: Perceptions of Nature in American Art, 1850–1910.* Ithaca, N.Y.: H. F. Johnson Museum of Art, 1982.
Paige, H. W. "Sacred Places." *America* 106 (1989): 34.
"Palestine Redeemed." *New Republic* 16 (1918): 274.
"Palestine—the Same Yesterday and Today." *Independent* 77 (1914): 198.
Parfit, M. "Mapmaker Who Charts Our Hidden Mental Demons." *Smithsonian Magazine* 15 (May 1984): 122.
Parrington, V. L. *American Dreams: A Study of American Utopias.* New York: Russell & Russell, 1964.
"Pastor Russell's Forecast of the Jews Returning to Jerusalem." *Overland* 71 (1918): 170.
Patai, R. *Myth and Modern Man.* Englewood Cliffs, N.J.: Prentice-Hall, 1972.
Pocock, D. C. *The Nature of Environmental Perception.* Durham, Eng.: University of Durham, Department of Geography, 1974.
Postman, L. "Personal Values as Selective Factors in Perception." *Journal of Abnormal and Social Psychology* 43 (1948): 142.
"The Potency of Myth." *Courier* 40 (1987): 8.
Pred, A. "Place as Historically Contingent Process." *Annals of the Association of American Geographers* 74 (1984): 279.
Price, C. *Landscape Economics.* London: Macmillan, 1978.
Prior, K. P. *The Way of Holiness: The Christian Doctrine of Sanctification.* Chicago: Intervarsity Press, 1967.
"Progress of the Jewish Hope in Palestine." *Current Opinion* 65 (1918): 318.
Rappoport, A. S. *Myth and Legend in Ancient Israel.* New York: Ktav, 1966.
"Rebuilding Zion." *World Outlook* 2 (1916): 8.
Reik, T. *Dogma and Compulsion: Psychoanalytic Studies of Religion and Myths.* New York: International Universities Press, 1951.

Relph, E. C. *Rational Landscapes and Humanistic Geography.* London: Croom Helm, 1981.

Robertson, J. O. *American Myth, American Realities.* New York: Hill & Wang, 1980.

Robinson, G. L. *The Biblical Doctrine of Holiness.* Chicago: Winona, 1903.

Robinson, J. P. "Perceptual Maps of the World." *Public Opinion Quarterly* 32 (1968): 273.

Said, E. W. *Orientalism.* New York: Vintage Books, 1979.

Sandmel, S. *The Several Israels.* New York: Ktav, 1971.

Sauer, C. O. *Land and Life: A Selection from the Writings of Carl Ortwin Sauer.* Edited by J. Leighly. Berkeley and Los Angeles: University of California Press, 1963.

Scheltema, J. F. "Jerusalem and the Holy Land." *North American Review* 207 (1918): 842.

Schmitt, P. J. *Back to Nature: The Arcadian Myth in Urban America.* New York: Oxford University Press, 1969.

Sears, J. F. *Sacred Places: American Tourist Attractions in the Nineteenth Century.* New York: Oxford University Press, 1989.

Segall, M. H. *The Influence of Culture on Visual Perception.* Indianapolis: Bobbs-Merrill, 1966.

Serpell, R. "How Perception Differs Among Cultures." *New Society* 20 (1972): 620.

Sheehan, P. W. *The Function and Nature of Imagery.* New York: Academic Press, 1972.

Smith, H. N. *Virgin Land: The American West as Symbol and Myth.* Cambridge, Mass.: Harvard University Press, 1950.

———. "The West as an Image of the American Past." *University of Kansas City Review* 18 (1951): 29.

Smith, J. Z. *To Take Place: Toward Theory in Ritual.* Chicago: University of Chicago Press, 1987.

Smith, Q. "An Analysis of Holiness." *Religious Studies* 24 (1988): 511.

Snyder, G. "Good, Wild, Sacred." *Coevolution Quarterly* 38 (1983): 8.

"Spiritual Meaning of Jerusalem's Deliverance." *Literary Digest* 56 (1918): 30.

Sprout, H. H. *Man-Milieu Relationship Hypotheses in the Context of International Politics.* Princeton: Princeton University, Center of International Studies, 1956.

Stein, H. F. *Developmental Time, Cultural Space: Studies in Psychogeography.* Norman, Okla.: University of Oklahoma Press, 1987.

Strout, C. *The Image of the Old World.* New York: Harper & Row, 1963.

Studies in Landscape Perception. Edited by E. H. Zube. Amherst, Mass.: University of Massachusetts, Institute for Man and Environment, 1976.

Thomas, T. *Hollywood and the American Image.* Westport, Conn.: Arlington House, 1981.

Thompson, K. "Insolubrious California: Perception and Reality." *Association of American Geographers Annals* 59 (1969): 50.

Toumey, C. P. "Religious Values and Spatial Behavior in Jerusalem." *Ekistics* 53 (1986): 137.

Tuan, Y-f. *The Hydrologic Cycle and the Wisdom of God: A Theme in Geoteleology.* Toronto: University of Toronto Press, 1968.

———. *Landscapes of Fear.* New York: Pantheon Books, 1979.

————. *Man and Nature*. Washington, D.C.: Association of American Geographers, 1971.

————. *Segmented Worlds and Self: Group Life and Individual Consciousness.* Minneapolis: University of Minnesota Press, 1982.

————. *Space and Place: The Perspective of Experience*. Minneapolis: University of Minnesota Press, 1977.

————. *Topophilia: A Study of Environmental Perception, Attitudes, and Values.* Englewood Cliffs, N.J.: Prentice-Hall, 1974.

Valued Environments. Edited by J. R. Gold and J. Burgess. Boston: G. Allen & Unwin, 1982.

Vauzelles-Barbier, D. *The Perception of the Environment: Why and How to Study It.* Paris: UNESCO, 1977.

Vesey, L. R. "Myth and Reality in Approaching American Regionalism." *American Quarterly* 12 (1960): 31.

Warr, P. B. *The Perception of People and Events*. London: Wiley, 1968.

Warren, A. G. *The Ever Magnetic Eastern Question: Jerusalem, the Centre of the Land.* Welden, N.C.: Harrell's Printing House, 1897.

"Wasting Eternity." *Atlantic* 113 (1914): 711.

Watson, J. W. "Image Geography: The Myth of America in the American Scene." *Advancement of Science* 26 (1970): 71.

————. *Mental Images and Geographical Reality in the Settlement of North America.* Nottingham, Eng.: University of Nottingham, 1968.

Wilbers, S. "Lake Wobegon: Mythical Place and the American Imagination." *American Studies* 30 (1989): 5.

Wilken, R. L. "Early Christian Chiliasm, Jewish Messianism, and the Idea of the Holy Land." *Harvard Theological Review* 79 (1986): 298.

Woodward, D. "Reality, Symbolism, Time, and Space in Medieval World Maps." *Annals of Association of American Geographers* 75 (1985): 510.

Worcester, W. L. "The Holy Land a Type of Heaven." *New Church Review* 5 (1898): 543.

Wright, J. K. *The Geographical Lore of the Time of the Crusades*. New York: Dover Publications, 1965.

————. *Human Nature in Geography*. Cambridge, Mass.: Harvard University Press, 1968.

————. "Terrae Incognitae: The Place of the Imagination in Geography." *Association of American Geographers Annals* 37 (1947): 1.

Index